PRAISE FOR

The Chief

"Joan Biskupic has written the definitive account of the consummate lawyer and deft politician at the helm of our nation's judiciary. Avoiding legal jargon while steering clear of slogans and stereotypes, Biskupic paints a highly readable and deeply informative three-dimensional portrait of the man whom fate has placed front and center in an unfolding drama bound to shape American life for decades to come."

—LAURENCE TRIBE, professor of Constitutional Law,
Harvard University

"Joan Biskupic draws on meticulous reporting and deep knowledge of the Supreme Court to bring us a fascinating real-time portrait of Chief Justice John Roberts, one of the country's most powerful but least known individuals, a man now in a unique position to shape the law in the age of Trump."

—LINDA GREENHOUSE, lecturer at Yale Law School and
former *New York Times* Supreme Court correspondent

THE
CHIEF

ALSO BY JOAN BISKUPIC

*Breaking In: The Rise of Sonia Sotomayor
and the Politics of Justice*

*American Original: The Life and Constitution
of Supreme Court Justice Antonin Scalia*

*Sandra Day O'Connor: How the First Woman on
the Supreme Court Became Its Most Influential Justice*

THE
CHIEF

The Life and Turbulent Times
of Chief Justice John Roberts

Joan Biskupic

BASIC BOOKS
NEW YORK

Basic Books
Hachette Book Group
1290 Avenue of the Americas, New York, NY 10104
www.basicbooks.com

Printed in the United States of America
First Edition: March 2019

Published by Basic Books, an imprint of Perseus Books, LLC, a subsidiary of Hachette Book Group, Inc. The Basic Books name and logo is a trademark of the Hachette Book Group.

The Hachette Speakers Bureau provides a wide range of authors for speaking events. To find out more, go to www.hachettespeakersbureau.com or call (866) 376-6591.

The publisher is not responsible for websites (or their content) that are not owned by the publisher.

Print book interior design by Linda Mark.

Library of Congress Cataloging-in-Publication Data
Names: Roberts, John G., 1955– author. | Biskupic, Joan, author.
Title: The Chief : the life and turbulent times of Chief Justice John Roberts /
  John Roberts, Joan Biskupic.
Description: New York : Basic Books, [2019] | Includes bibliographical references
  and index.
Identifiers: LCCN 2018039502 (print) | LCCN 2018039671 (ebook) |
  ISBN 9780465093281 (ebook) | ISBN 9780465093274 (hardcover : alk. paper)
Subjects: LCSH: Roberts, John G., 1955– | Judges—United States—Biography. |
  United States. Supreme Court—Officials and employees—Biography. | United
  States. Supreme Court—History.
Classification: LCC KF8745.R6 (ebook) | LCC KF8745.R6 A3 2019 (print) |
  DDC 347.73/2634 [B] —dc23
LC record available at https://lccn.loc.gov/2018039502

LSC-C

10 9 8 7 6 5 4 3 2 1

For Clay and Elizabeth

Contents

PROLOGUE

ON A STICKY EIGHTY-DEGREE JUNE MORNING, THE US SUPREME Court ascended the bench at 10:00 for the last sitting of the 2017–2018 session. Chief Justice John Roberts knew what would happen later that morning. Most of the other justices did not. For the second time in two years, a dramatic change among the nine would test the man who was presiding over America's highest court.

At sixty-three, Roberts still had a fit, compact physique that recalled his days as a high school wrestler. His neatly trimmed brown hair was graying. He exuded a pleasant, regular-guy earnestness, and he often referred to his Indiana childhood. Yet he was no average midwestern boy. Roberts appeared to have been hardwired from birth for success. The son of a steel company executive, he had attended an elite boarding school, earned a Harvard bachelor's degree in three years, and then attended Harvard Law School. He had become a sterling oral advocate, arguing his first case before the Supreme Court at the age of thirty-four. By then he had spent several years clerking, serving in the Reagan administration, and working in a Washington, DC, law firm. He was known for his powers of persuasion and tireless preparation. He was also known for an austere law firm office notably lacking in photos and personal mementos.

By dint of drive and intellect—and the political connections he had forged—Roberts had become chief justice of the United States in 2005. Then just fifty years old, he was the youngest new chief in more than two centuries. President George W. Bush had initially nominated him as an associate justice to replace Sandra Day O'Connor after she announced that summer she intended to retire. But before Roberts's Senate hearings could be held, Chief Justice William Rehnquist died. At the time, the Bush administration was besieged by criticism over its handling of the collapse of civil order in New Orleans during Hurricane Katrina, one of the country's deadliest natural catastrophes. Within hours of Rehnquist's death, Bush decided to elevate Roberts, brushing away advisers who suggested he choose an older, more experienced nominee.[1]

When he appeared before the Senate Judiciary Committee, Roberts was composed, confident. "Watching Roberts on television was like watching one of the radiantly wholesome heroes that Jimmy Stewart and Henry Fonda played," Janet Malcolm commented in *The New Yorker*. "It was out of the question that such a man be denied a place on the Supreme Court."[2]

ON JUNE 27, 2018, AS HE WAS FINISHING HIS THIRTEENTH YEAR AS chief justice, the first order of business was the announcement of decisions in the last cases from the session that had begun back in October. The term had been difficult, and the Court had delivered more fractious 5–4 rulings than usual. The ideological conflicts among them had spilled out with greater spite. The day's most awaited dispute, concerning whether states could allow unions to collect fees from non-union members to support collective bargaining activities, reinforced that pattern. By another 5–4 vote, with conservatives prevailing over liberals, the justices ruled against America's already struggling labor unions and declared the fees a violation of First Amendment free-speech rights. The decision overturned a 1977 ruling that had let states require "fair share" fees of non-members to finance unions' efforts on behalf of employee pay and benefits but not political activities.

In the courtroom seats reserved for the justices' guests were, as was customary on the last day of the term, spouses of the justices. Among them was Mary Kennedy, the wife of Justice Anthony Kennedy, the Court's pivotal central-conservative justice, who had steadied the Court for decades. He was about to turn eighty-two. He was weary and weathering several health problems. So was Mary, whom he had known since their childhood in Sacramento. Justice Kennedy had been less engaged at oral arguments over the past session. Even with hearing aids tucked behind his ears under his gray, thinning hair, he had trouble following some conversations. His six-foot-three frame hunched a bit more as he walked.

But most of his colleagues believed Kennedy was not ready to retire. His influence on the law in America could not be overstated. He had held the key vote in so many cases that the Roberts Court was sometimes known among lawyers and the news media as the Kennedy Court. Yet, unlike at the end of most annual sessions, Kennedy's voice was not heard at all this day, either with one of the final big rulings or a retirement announcement from the bench. Justices Samuel Alito and Elena Kagan provided the rhetorical drama with their dueling opinions in the labor union case. Speaking on behalf of the conservative majority, Alito declared that unions had gotten an undeserved "windfall" for four decades. For the dissenting liberals, Kagan argued that the majority was "weaponizing the First Amendment" and throwing out a precedent not on principle but for the sole reason that the justices on the right did not like it. There was no denying the political overtones in a case involving labor. "Big loss for the coffers of the Democrats!" President Donald Trump responded immediately on Twitter.[3]

After the justices descended the bench, Chief Justice Roberts, Justice Kennedy, and the others met in a private conference room to resolve some lingering cases. Here in the oak-paneled room off the chambers of the chief justice, they were alone, absent clerks or secretaries. Roberts directed the discussion as the justices dispatched their final business together. Then he gestured to Kennedy and watched the response of the others when they learned the news that Kennedy was retiring. Kennedy asked them to keep his retirement quiet until after their lunch together, when he would ride over to the White House to tell President Trump personally.

The justices were shocked. When their final sitting had come and gone that morning, it seemed he was settling in for another term. Yet no one at the conference table—even the liberal justices, who counted on his vote in important social policy cases—asked him to reconsider. As he spoke, sometimes wandering off his point, it was clear that Kennedy was ready to move on. They hugged him and shook his hand. The justices then retreated to a dining room to have lunch together. Kennedy left the gathering early, to get to the White House shortly after 1:00 p.m. Chief Justice Roberts stayed behind, but his top assistant, counselor Jeffrey Minear, went with Kennedy. President Trump, less than two years in office, would now have a chance to name a second new justice.

Kennedy's retirement would change the Court and give Roberts more control. Since 2005, Roberts had had to work around Kennedy, restrain his own conservatism, try to persuade Kennedy, appease Kennedy, to get his vote. Roberts moderated his views in some cases and inevitably lost in others. When Roberts and Kennedy could not come together, and Kennedy joined the four liberals, it was usually in a blockbuster social policy dispute, such as the 2015 case that led to a constitutional right to same-sex marriage.

The Court was now Roberts's in name and reality. The turn of events represented a dramatic reversal from what had appeared to be Roberts's fate only two years earlier after a separate startling occurence. At that point, Roberts could have assumed that he and the other conservatives would be in the minority on the Court for the foreseeable future.

That news had come during a February recess in 2016 and reverberated for many months. It was the Saturday of a long President's Day weekend, and Roberts had been playing golf and relaxing with a friend in Miami.

Away from the winter chill of Washington, DC, and the frenzied chatter of the 2016 presidential primaries then under way, he was vacationing with his wife, Jane, and his daughter, Josie, at the home of Dean Colson, a friend since 1980 when they had met as fellow law clerks to then associate justice Rehnquist.[4]

Other justices were also seeking some diversion on that Saturday. Ruth Bader Ginsburg, the senior liberal who tangled the most with Roberts on the law, was in her Watergate apartment overlooking the Potomac River. She was getting ready to attend an opera at the nearby Kennedy Center that evening. Justice Elena Kagan, a fellow liberal, was planning to join Ginsburg, but first she went to her office at the Supreme Court Building to work on cases. Justice Clarence Thomas was at his suburban Virginia home, reading through legal briefs.

Antonin Scalia, at that point the longest serving of the nine justices, had been hunting at an exclusive West Texas resort. The excursion was Scalia's second trip of the February recess. The first had been a long journey to a legal conference in Singapore. Scalia was nearing his eightieth birthday, as was Kennedy at the time, and the two men had just talked about how hard it was getting to be to travel at their age. Scalia told him, "Tony, this is my last long trip."[5]

Roberts received the call in Miami midafternoon. Scalia had been found dead in his room at the ranch. Roberts could scarcely believe that the man who had occupied the chair next to him, a conservative ally and a person he had regarded as a friend, was dead. "It was stunning," recalled Dean Colson. "Everything came to a stop. He was in shock. It was unbelievable."[6]

Most important, for the nation, Democratic president Barack Obama would name Scalia's successor. Not only would liberals suddenly be able to claim a majority on the bench, but it would also be the first time in decades that a chief justice who was in the minority ideologically would preside over the Court. Immediately, Roberts's friends wondered, once he no longer held a majority, how the man so accustomed to control would recalibrate expectations.

Conservatives had controlled the Court for the previous half century. When Chief Justice Earl Warren, a liberal icon, had retired in 1969,

Republican president Richard Nixon had replaced him with Warren Burger, a law-and-order jurist who believed the Court had been wrongly meddling in social controversies that were properly the responsibility of the state legislatures. Nixon and a succession of Republican presidents had appointed most of the new justices over the following years as vacancies opened up through justices' retirements and deaths. Of the sixteen appointments made since 1969, twelve were Republicans, four Democrats.[7]

That meant that from January 1972, when President Nixon's third and fourth appointees were sworn in, until February 13, 2016, when Scalia died, at least five and sometimes as many as eight justices on the nine-member Court had been selected by Republican presidents. Even though a number of Republican appointees, such as Harry Blackmun and David Souter, had moved to the center or had become reliable liberal votes, lawyers of Roberts's generation had known nothing but a conservative Court.

SENATE REPUBLICAN LEADER MITCH MCCONNELL OF KENTUCKY changed what could have been the course of history. A Scalia family friend had alerted McConnell before news of his death was public. So by the time Roberts announced he had died, in a statement that Saturday evening, McConnell was ready with his own immediate statement. "This vacancy should not be filled until we have a new President," McConnell said, referring to the upcoming November election and January 20 inauguration. President Obama had nearly a full year left in office. McConnell's announcement was audacious, coming as soon as it did after Scalia's death. Even some Republicans derided it as inappropriate.[8]

That same evening, Republicans vying for their party's presidential nomination appeared in a nationally televised debate. From a winnowed field of more than a dozen Republican contenders, six men, including Donald Trump, took the stage. Scalia's death generated a round of questions for the candidates, who in turn spoke of the importance of a successor who would adhere to Scalia's views.[9]

To fill the vacancy, Obama nominated veteran US appeals court judge Merrick Garland, a sixty-three-year-old former prosecutor with a record of moderate rulings. Obama considered Garland a compromise candidate who would be acceptable to enough Republican senators that the chamber's leadership would hold hearings and put his name to a vote. But McConnell and fellow Republicans who constituted the majority took no action on Garland's nomination.

Roberts, always careful and strategic, was silent about this vacancy, and he remained so. He knew that the Court would be hobbled with just eight justices, and that 4–4 deadlocks could become common. He waited and watched.[10]

Hillary Clinton, who became the Democratic presidential nominee that summer, was expected to beat Republican candidate Trump, a political novice known for his incendiary statements and outrageous behavior. It was widely assumed in Washington—including by Roberts—that a Democratic appointee would eventually join the Court. Liberals on the bench and beyond were still planning for a new Court. "She is bound to have a few appointments," Justice Ginsburg said of Clinton, based on the advanced ages of some of the justices. Liberal advocates began strategizing about litigation to reverse conservative trends on various issues, such as campaign finance law.[11]

But, of course, that did not happen. On Tuesday, November 8, 2016, nine months after Scalia's death, Roberts was again with his family. This time they were at his Chevy Chase, Maryland, home. It was election night. National polls still favored Clinton. Commentators were predicting an early evening, with initial results in favor of the Democratic candidate. By 8:00 p.m. on the East Coast, the networks reported that Maryland was going, as predicted, for Clinton. But there seemed to be something unusual happening in Pennsylvania, where Roberts's ancestors had settled. Trump was overtaking Clinton in the state, and Michigan and Wisconsin appeared to be tipping in his direction, too. As did Florida. The notion that liberal justices would control the Supreme Court for the first time in four decades gave way to the reality that Chief Justice Roberts would get his conservative Court back. Trump declared victory just before 3:00 a.m.

Later that morning, when the justices gathered in a private robing room before taking the bench for oral arguments, Ginsburg, in subtle protest, was wearing a black collar with silver crystal accents over her robe. It was the collar she reserved for days when she would offer a dissenting opinion. Although it annoyed him, Roberts said nothing to her about the obvious gesture of political opposition. After he emerged from behind the red velvet drapes and took his chair, he announced the morning case, No. 15-1191, *Lynch v. Morales-Santana*, a dispute over citizenship rights. There was no sign that Roberts had stayed up late watching the returns. His voice was crisp.

Roberts has an uncanny ability to size up a situation and calibrate his responses. His longtime associates compare him to a master of three-dimensional chess who anticipates all the possible moves his opponents might make. "John Roberts has always seen everything with pristine clarity, and almost instantly," said J. Michael Luttig, whose career paralleled Roberts's from the Reagan administration to the federal appellate court level to the day in July 2005 that they were both interviewed by President George W. Bush as part of the nomination process for the Supreme Court.[12]

The chief justice is appointed for life, as are the eight associate justices. Like each of them, he is entitled to a single vote on cases. But the chief justice has special authority to oversee oral arguments and set the agenda for the justices' private sessions. He regularly decides who writes the opinions that become the law of the land. As such, the chief justice has been called "the first among equals." To appreciate the influence of a chief justice, one need only understand that while there have been forty-five presidents of the United States, there have been only seventeen chief justices.

The chief justice position is mentioned only once in the Constitution, and that mention is not in Article III, which establishes the judiciary. It is in Article I, covering Congress, and says the chief justice presides over the Senate during any impeachment trial of the president. The power of the position has grown over time and today the chief justice runs the Judicial Conference of the United States, a group that sets policy for federal courts nationwide. The chief justice also chooses the individual judges who sit on the Foreign Intelligence Surveillance Court and other select panels.[13]

Even from the beginning of his tenure, Roberts could count on four like-minded votes for most of his positions: those of Scalia, Kennedy, Thomas, and Alito. Of course, Kennedy split off on some social issues, most notably involving gay rights and abortion. But Roberts prevailed, with Kennedy's vote, to eliminate campaign finance regulations, erode the federal Voting Rights Act, and expand opportunities for the expression of religion in public places. Two decisions that defined the Roberts Court were the 2010 *Citizens United v. Federal Election Commission* and the 2013 *Shelby County v. Holder.* Respectively, these rulings made it easier for corporations and labor unions to influence the outcome of elections and sharply reduced the ability of African Americans and other minorities to block discriminatory electoral practices. *Shelby County* capped Roberts's decades-long effort (sometimes obvious, sometimes subtle) to limit the reach of the Voting Rights Act.[14]

Those and a series of other 5–4 rulings, including the decision that would transform labor union funding in June 2018, buttressed the perception that the Court majority was politically motivated and that Roberts was engaged in the partisanship he claimed to abhor. If the chief justice had a single message for the public, it was that the Court was above politicking. "We don't work as Democrats or Republicans," he told one audience in 2016.[15]

Roberts understood that public regard was crucial to the Supreme Court's stature in American life. He had studied the reputations of past chief justices and had worried, too, about what history would make of him. "You wonder if you're going to be John Marshall or you're going to be Roger Taney," he had said in an earlier appearance, referring to the revered forefather of judicial review and to the reviled author of the *Dred Scott* decision that said slaves were not citizens. "The answer is, of course, you are certainly not going to be John Marshall. But you want to avoid the danger of being Roger Taney."[16]

ROBERTS HAS ALMOST ALWAYS HAD PERFECT TIMING. WHEN HE CAME to Washington in 1980 and teamed up with Dean Colson in Rehnquist's chambers, conservatism was on the rise. He participated in the Reagan and George H.W. Bush administrations' efforts to select individuals for the federal bench who fit their agenda of less government regulation and less intervention on social issues to help the needy.

Indeed, behind Roberts's affable demeanor and his calibrated opinions is a judge with deep ideological roots. Like other conservatives, Roberts believes in a "color-blind" approach, and therefore favors an end to affirmative action and other racial remedies launched in the 1960s. "The way to stop discrimination on the basis of race is to stop discriminating on the basis of race," he wrote in an opinion soon after becoming chief justice. He likened the programs that *benefited* minorities to the segregation that was prohibited in the landmark 1954 decision in *Brown v. Board of Education*.[17]

Yet Roberts has at times set aside his ideological and political interests on behalf of his commitments to the Court's institutional reputation and his own public image. In 2012, when he voted to uphold the healthcare overhaul known as the Affordable Care Act, sponsored by President Obama, he outraged conservatives. He had, in fact, first voted behind closed doors with other conservative justices to invalidate the law. But then he changed his vote.

That episode, involving not just one but a series of switched votes, revealed in full for the first time, forms a central part of this book exploring the work and motivations of the most powerful judge in America. It is also an example of one of two possible paths now before Roberts: to hew even more to his conservative roots or to work for common ground.

At sixty-four, Roberts is grayer, although he still has the upright carriage that makes him look taller than his five feet and nine inches. He moves with tight discipline, arms close to his sides, shoulders squared. He favors white dress shirts, nondescript ties, and gold cuff links. When he addresses audiences outside the Court, his core message remains the same: the justices do not advance political positions.

"First, I want to point out one thing," he said in an appearance following the Senate's confirmation of Neil Gorsuch for the long-vacant Scalia seat in April 2017. "Throughout this whole process, the Supreme Court has been quietly going about its business of deciding the cases before it, according to the Constitution, in a completely nonpartisan way." Roberts imagines that the polarized confirmation process of Gorsuch and especially Brett Kavanaugh, who succeeded Kennedy, can lead people to believe that any justice who emerges from such a process must be similarly partisan. "That's very unfortunate," Roberts said, "because we in the judiciary do not do our business in a partisan, ideological manner."[18]

The celebrated former advocate, who seemed to be able to persuade anyone of anything, said that over and over again.

Now in his fourteenth year on the Court, Roberts could preside for another two decades. Where Roberts goes, on a bench no longer steadied by Justice Kennedy, in especially turbulent times, will likely be determined by where he has been. What follows is the story of Roberts's climb to the pinnacle of the judiciary, beginning with his youth in Indiana, his formative judicial clerkships, and his time in the Reagan and first Bush administrations. He now sits at the exact center, the determinative center, of the law in America.

December 22, 1968

Dear Mr. Moore,

The main reason I would like to attend La Lumiere School is to get a better education. I've always wanted to stay ahead of the crowd, and I feel that the competition at La Lumiere will force me to work as hard as I can. At an ordinary high school it would probably be easy to stay ahead. I realize that going to La Lumiere will be a lot of study and hard work, but I feel confident that these labors will pay off in large amounts when it comes time to apply for admission to college. I'm sure that by attending and doing my best at La Lumiere I will assure myself of a fine future. I won't be content to get a good job by getting a good education, I want to get the best job by getting the best education.

Sincerely yours,
John Roberts Jr.

When John Roberts was 13 years old, he applied to the elite La Lumiere boarding school in northern Indiana. His December 22, 1968, letter was addressed to the school's headmaster, James Moore. Roberts was admitted and went on to graduate first in his class. CREDIT: Photograph of letter courtesy of La Lumiere School.

CHAPTER I

FROM LANCASHIRE TO WONDER STREET

A T AGE THIRTEEN, JOHN GLOVER ROBERTS JR. ALREADY HAD a clear plan for his life. "I've always wanted to stay ahead of the crowd," he wrote as he applied to an exclusive boarding school. "I won't be content to get a good job by getting a good education, I want to get the best job by getting the best education."[1]

The son of a steel company executive living with his family in Long Beach, Indiana, Roberts was not going to follow the pattern of other eighth-graders at his Catholic grammar school and attend a parochial high school. Instead, he wanted to enroll in a new elite boarding school for boys in nearby La Porte. The school had been created by wealthy businessmen who bemoaned the lack of educational opportunities for their sons. They wanted an academy in the tradition of the elite boarding schools of the East Coast but with a lay Roman Catholic character. They had bought a five-hundred-acre tract of pine groves and spring lakes from the family of Edward Lalumier, an executive of a Chicago meat-packing company. The founders called the school La Lumiere, a French variation on the family name meaning "The Light."[2]

"I feel that the competition at La Lumiere will force me to work as hard as I can," Roberts wrote in neat longhand on unlined paper on December 22, 1968. "At an ordinary high school it would probably be easy to stay ahead. I realize that going to La Lumiere will be a lot of study and hard work, but I feel confident that these labors will pay off in large amounts when it comes time to apply for admission to college. I'm sure that by attending and doing my best at La Lumiere I will assure myself of a fine future."

THE PARENTS OF THE FUTURE CHIEF JUSTICE OF THE UNITED States, John Glover Roberts Sr. and the former Rosemary Podrasky, had arrived in northern Indiana by way of steel towns in Pennsylvania and New York. Both were born in Johnstown, Pennsylvania, but in different communities. The divide between English and Slovakian families ran deep in the city, which was known for coal mines, steel mills, and a devastating 1889 flood.

The Roberts ancestral line traced to the English mining village of Atherton, where the chief justice's great-great-grandfather, Richard Glover, was born in 1832. Coal was the economic lifeblood of this Lancashire region of northwestern England, and Richard became a miner. When he was twenty-one years old, he married Mary Linskey, an Irish woman, in the Bedford Catholic Chapel in the village of Leigh. They soon had three daughters, Margaret, Mary Ann, and Alice. Looking for a better life in America, the family obtained passage on the SS *Hecla* in the summer of 1863. They traveled in steerage with nearly five hundred other men, women, and children and docked in New York City on June 29, 1863.[3]

America hardly offered a peaceful refuge. The Civil War was raging: at the time of the Glovers' arrival, newspapers were chronicling the siege of Vicksburg, Mississippi. Two years of fierce fighting had left thousands of men dead or wounded. Desertions on both sides were common. Congress passed the Conscription Act, the nation's first draft, in March 1863. It was deeply unpopular in New York, which until the early 1800s had been a slave-trading center. The city was also inflamed by President Abraham Lincoln's Emancipation Proclamation, which had taken effect in January 1863.[4]

Less than two weeks after the Glover family arrived in America, the first draft lottery was held, on July 11, 1863, at a provost marshal's office on New York City's East Side. As names were being drawn, white residents began smashing windows and setting fires. In the days that followed, protesters torched government buildings and attacked patrolmen. Mobs roamed the city, descending on the homes of black families and white abolitionists. They burned the Colored Orphan Asylum on Fifth Avenue to the ground. A century and a half later, New York's Draft Riots remain one of America's deadliest protests.[5]

For John Roberts's forebears, the riots and Civil War cast a pall over their early life in America. The war continued to consume the country for nearly two years after their arrival. By 1865, Richard Glover and his family were living in western Pennsylvania, a state known for its coal-rich lands and winding valleys, reminiscent of Lancashire. His daughter Mary Ann married George Roberts, and one of their sons, also named George, became the ambitious driver of the twentieth-century Roberts clan and grandfather to the chief justice. The younger George and his wife, Rebecca, settled in Johnstown.[6]

John Roberts's maternal line—the Podraczkys and Gmuczas, as the names were originally spelled—also put down roots in the Johnstown region, which had become a center of iron and steel production. They had left their home country in the 1880s along with a tide of other Eastern European immigrants. Like the English and Irish who had come a generation earlier, they were fleeing famine and political turmoil. But unlike the earlier arrivals, many of the immigrants from Eastern Europe had been landless peasants and had limited skills. Most spoke no English and struggled in their new country. Irrespective of their particular place of origin, they were all called Hungarians—or by the slur "Hunkie." The old and new Europeans were wary of each other. The Eastern Europeans took the more dangerous jobs in the mines, and those caste-like divisions were mirrored in company housing and the social and political life of Johnstown.[7]

Still, newcomers felt a sense of opportunity. "Life in Johnstown meant a great deal of hard work for just about everybody," historian David McCullough wrote. "Not only because that was how life was then, but because people had the feeling they were getting somewhere. The country seemed hell-bent for a glorious new age, and Johnstown, clearly, was right up there booming along with the best of them. Pittsburgh and Chicago were a whole lot bigger, to be sure, and taking a far bigger part of the business. But that was all right. For Johnstown these were the best years ever."[8]

Then catastrophe struck.

In May 1889, an unprecedented rainstorm soaked the valley, breaking an earthen dam that had been built fourteen miles upstream of the city. The dam had created a lake for an exclusive sports club frequented by the region's wealthy industrialists. When it broke, Johnstown was crushed by a wall of water with a force as powerful as the Mississippi River. As water swept down into the city, mines and rail lines were washed out. Buildings, people, animals, and freight cars were carried through the valley in a massive wave. An estimated 2,200 people died. Scores of bodies were never recovered.[9] The 1889 Johnstown flood remains one of the most catastrophic events in American history. No direct ancestors of John Roberts were among the dead, however, according to public lists and family information.

The city rebuilt, the men returned to the mines, and by 1900, Johnstown was the third-largest steel producer in the country. George Roberts (grandfather to the chief justice) became a mine inspector. In Johnstown, he and his wife, Rebecca, built a home high on a hill in the desirable Southmont neighborhood, situated on a new lane called Wonder Street.[10]

In 1928, when George was forty-three and Rebecca was forty-one, their tenth child was born. It had been two decades since the birth of their first. They named the baby John Glover Roberts. The man who would become father to the chief justice would go by "Jack." In high school, he played football, joined the band, and enlisted in a civic leadership club. He wrote in the yearbook that he wanted to become mayor. Instead, he traveled the family path into the steel industry. At the University of Pittsburgh, he studied electrical engineering, setting his sights on a management job at Bethlehem Steel, where his older brothers already worked.[11]

ROSEMARY PODRASKY (AS THE NAME BECAME AMERICANIZED) WAS born in Johnstown in 1929. The Slovakian side of the future chief justice's family settled into crowded neighborhoods in the valley amid boardinghouses and corner saloons. Rosemary's kin, who hailed from Szepes, Hungary, labored in the mines but also found whatever work they could in the hotels, taverns, and pool halls. Their homes were smaller and on narrower streets than that of the Roberts family, which was on high ground. The people in the valley stuck with their own, worshiping at St. Stephen's Catholic Church, which had been named after a martyred Hungarian king. The Podrasky family rented their house for about $20 a month, according to the 1930 census, whereas Jack Roberts lived on Wonder Street in a home valued at $7,000.[12]

When Rosemary graduated from Johnstown Central Catholic High School in 1947, her ambition was to travel abroad. But her family did not have the money for her to go anywhere, including college. A year later, in 1948, Rosemary's father died at the age of fifty-four, leaving her mother on her own to care for three children—two more had grown up and moved out. That ended any opportunity Rosemary might have had to go to college.[13]

No one is quite sure how Rosemary, who worked for the local telephone company as a young woman, first crossed paths with Jack. On their dates, her family sometimes asked her to bring along her younger brother Richard, ostensibly as a baby-sitting chore for Rosemary, but really as a watchful chaperone for his older sister. The courtship continued as Jack went to the University of Pittsburgh and then secured a job with Bethlehem Steel at the company's Lackawanna, New York, plant near Buffalo.[14]

Bethlehem Steel had risen to prominence as a shipbuilder during World War II, and when Jack joined the company ranks in 1951 its steel production capacity was contributing to the postwar expansion of cities, bridges, and roads across the country.

Jack and Rosemary married on October 11, 1952. He was twenty-four, and she was twenty-three. They exchanged vows in the grand baroque setting of St. Stephen's, a church distinguished by its two five-story bell towers. Officiating at the marble altar was Rosemary's uncle, the Right Reverend Stanislaus Gmucza, an abbot in the Order of St. Benedict.[15]

After the ceremony, the couple settled into a home near the Bethlehem Steel plant on Lake Erie in Lackawanna. Jack was on the executive track. Rosemary still spoke of going to college and the possibilities that more education could bring. But that was not to be, as she grew busy with their family and his work. They would move from one Bethlehem plant to another for Jack's career.

For some relatives and family friends, Rosemary came to be regarded as the more ambitious member of the couple. She pushed her husband to strive for advancement at Bethlehem Steel, clipping news stories that would keep him informed on industry developments and encouraging him to improve his golf game. She wanted him to impress his bosses and rise in the company hierarchy.[16]

Then, as her son John grew up and excelled at school, Rosemary excitedly awaited the academic honors he brought home. The tradition-steeped steel industry was not unlike the judiciary that her son would eventually join. Both prized hierarchy, seniority, and custom. Institutional interests reigned.

JACK AND ROSEMARY ROBERTS'S FIRST CHILD, KATHY, WAS BORN IN October 1953, one year after they had married and settled near the Lackawanna steel mill just south of Buffalo. Then came their only son, on January 27, 1955. They gave him a name that evoked the family's English roots: John Glover Roberts Jr.

At the time, Dwight Eisenhower was president and Earl Warren was chief justice of the United States. It was an era of widespread prosperity. Housing construction and automobile production were soaring. Bethlehem Steel's profits were up. The GI Bill made college affordable for a generation of veterans, including some of young John's uncles. Suddenly it seemed every living room had a TV set and every kitchen an electric mixer. Roast beef was served at Sunday dinner, along with Jell-O and green bean casserole made with Campbell's soup, in homes across America, including the Robertses'.

While the Roberts household and much of the rest of white America enjoyed the boom, large swaths of the country had been left behind. Many Americans struggled in poverty and suffered under discriminatory laws and practices. Eight months before John's birth, the Supreme Court addressed a fundamental gap in white and black educational opportunities in the landmark decision *Brown v. Board of Education*. This defining opinion of Chief Justice Warren's tenure was issued on May 17, 1954. *Brown v. Board of Education II* followed a year later. The rulings struck down the principle of "separate but equal" schools and called for desegregation "with all deliberate speed." That was the ideal. It was not the reality.[17]

"Segregation of white and colored children in public schools," Warren wrote in his opinion in *Brown I*, "has a detrimental effect upon the colored children." Furthermore, he added, "The impact is greater when it has the sanction of the law, for the policy of separating the races is usually interpreted as denoting the inferiority of the negro group. A sense of inferiority affects the motivation of a child to learn."[18]

If anyone understood the reverse phenomenon—that is, the potential for education to inspire and lift up children—it was parents like Jack and Rosemary Roberts, who found better schools and better opportunities for their children than they had ever had themselves.

Chief Justice Warren, the son of Scandinavian immigrants, had been a prosecutor and three-term governor of California before becoming chief justice. President Eisenhower had appointed him to the Court in 1953, and he would go on to serve until 1969. *Brown* was only one of several milestone decisions buttressing individual and civil rights that the Court heard during his tenure. Warren led by the force of his ideas and with the strategic assistance of Associate Justice William Brennan, a former New

Jersey state judge whom Eisenhower had appointed in 1956. The rulings affected most areas of American life and social policy, and many were undergirded by a commitment to constitutional equality and inclusion.[19]

The Warren Court's groundbreaking opinions dealing with race and the rights of criminal defendants provoked resistance. That pushback was seen most vividly in the South, where school boards fought integration, and where "Impeach Earl Warren" signs appeared along roadsides. Less obvious at the time was the emerging backlash against the judiciary. Soon enough, Republican presidents Richard Nixon and Ronald Reagan would argue that elected lawmakers should have more control than judges over the social dilemmas throughout the country, including those emerging in the schools and prisons. They would appoint judges who would launch a counterrevolution to try to limit the Warren Court's expansive readings of individual rights and the federal government's authority to protect those rights, and John Roberts would join this movement.

Much of America's social turbulence centered on race. The Ku Klux Klan, which had roots in the Reconstruction era in the late nineteenth century, remained a violent force in the South. In 1963, Klansmen bombed the Sixteenth Street Baptist Church in Birmingham, Alabama, killing four young girls. That same year, in his January Inaugural Address, Alabama governor George Wallace declared, "In the name of the greatest people that have ever trod this earth, I draw the line in the dust and toss the gauntlet before the feet of tyranny, and I say segregation now, segregation tomorrow, segregation forever."[20]

The North had its share of racial tensions and rioting, particularly in cities like Chicago, which was not far from the Indiana home where Roberts spent his youth. Chicago was the scene of bloody clashes between Vietnam War protesters and city police at the August 1968 Democratic National Convention. When the young Roberts sat down to write his letter of application to La Lumiere School in December 1968, Chicago, just sixty miles away, was still recovering from the convention protests, as well as the rioting and deaths triggered by the assassination of Martin Luther King Jr. that spring. Richard Nixon was elected president in November

1968. The decade culminated with the "Days of Rage" in October 1969, when an antiwar group that came to be known as the Weather Underground carried out three days of pipe-wielding vandalism and violence in Chicago. Roberts was then a boy of fourteen.

HE WAS INSULATED FROM THE UNREST THROUGHOUT HIS CHILDhood. Roberts spent his earliest years in a newly built development of Hamburg, New York, a town of forty thousand people south of the grittier Lackawanna. Situated on the western edge of Lake Erie, Lackawanna was a working-class town of smokestacks and steeples. As in Johnstown, Pennsylvania, where Jack and Rosemary Roberts had grown up, the immigrants in Lackawanna had built churches for themselves. Generation after generation of men cast steel for a living, and their lives revolved around the mill.

After John was born, Jack and Rosemary had two more daughters, Margaret and Barbara. One of Jack's older brothers, Dick, and his wife, Bernice, lived nearby. Dick and Bernice had a son named Paul who was the same age as young John, and the families were close. At Bethlehem Steel's Lackawanna plant, Jack was an electrical engineer, and Dick a mechanical engineer. Both men had served in the army, but Dick was nine years older and had seen combat in World War II. He had been in the infantry at the Battle of the Bulge, the great final Allied battle with the Germans in 1944. He was awarded a Bronze Star.[21]

Jack and Rosemary regularly dined and danced at the Bethlehem Management Club. Bernice, who joined them with Dick, remembered Jack and Rosemary as well matched: smart, attractive, and always wearing clothes from the high-end stores. "Jack was a heck of a swell guy, and she always looked just perfect," Bernice recalled. On the dance floor, they were a handsome couple. Jack was effusive about "Rosie," as he called her. "It was always, 'Rosie thinks this' and 'Rosie thinks that,'" their daughter-in-law Jane Roberts said years later. "He was really lovely to his wife."[22]

Young John, nicknamed "Jackie" in these years, impressed relatives with his intelligence and earnestness. "We used to call him sober puss because he was always so serious," Bernice Roberts said fondly about the bookish boy. "Other kids would be playing with trucks or cars. I don't remember Jackie doing that at all." She remembered one episode in particular that had taken place when Bernice and Dick had arrived at the Roberts home for dinner.[23]

"Uncle Dick, Jackie had all A's on his report card," Rosemary had announced when they'd arrived.

"That calls for a dollar bill," Dick responded, opening his wallet. A dollar was a big deal for a boy in the early 1960s.

THE FORTUNES OF BOTH ROBERTS FAMILIES TRACKED THOSE OF the steel industry. After World War II, steel consumption rose, and Bethlehem Steel emerged as one of the largest industrial companies in the world. The Lackawanna plant produced the cold-rolled steel sheets used in manufacturing automobiles, building exteriors, and appliances. Its workforce grew to twenty-one thousand in the early 1960s.[24]

Jack Roberts had been admitted to the exclusive Bethlehem Loop Course, a career track designed for young managers who had been identified for their leadership potential. The course included an orientation at the home office in Bethlehem, Pennsylvania, and rotations to various plants, where the trainees learned about the company's larger operations. Jack was well prepared for his promotion when it came, and he was assigned to the Burns Harbor plant in northern Indiana.

The plant was formally inaugurated the year John Roberts turned ten years old. The September 1965 opening festivities were extravagant, with a week of tours, dinners, and performances. The nation's number-two steelmaker had chosen the location adjacent to Chicago on Lake Michigan to challenge U.S. Steel. The leading steelmaker already operated plants in nearby Gary and South Chicago that were supplying the booming industries of the region. For the Burns Harbor plant's opening,

Bethlehem Steel's public relations team brought in newspaper reporters from across the country. The company invited titans of the steel industry and elected officials as well, and at the end of that inaugural week, the company's executives held a gala dinner at a mill warehouse that had been converted into a banquet hall for the event. They dined on sirloin steaks and lobster, and entertainment was provided by the sultry night-club singer Julie London and the jazz great Woody Herman. The events reflected the high expectations the company had for the fully integrated plant. There, Jack Roberts would rise from the assistant head of the electrical engineering department to head of the department, and ultimately to assistant plant manager.[25]

Edmund Martin, the project manager for the Burns Harbor plant and later Bethlehem Steel's CEO, said the opening constituted the kind of extravaganza that would have made the company's founders, Charles Schwab and Eugene Grace, proud. In addition, it offered an example of the corporate high life, reflecting a company aspiration that would continue to shape its culture. Executive titles came with generous bonuses and country club memberships. As Martin boasted in his memoir, Bethlehem Steel always made sure there was a golf course near its plants. If none existed before the arrival of Bethlehem Steel, the company built one.[26]

When Jack was promoted, he and Rosemary moved their family to an enclave on Lake Michigan known as Long Beach, an idyllic setting twenty miles north of the Burns Harbor plant. It had been developed in the early 1900s as a vacationland for nearby Chicagoans escaping the summer heat and congestion. An early promotional brochure described Long Beach as "America's finest country home community and playground." Offering "20 reasons why better people live in Long Beach," the brochure referred to the glistening blue waters, the safe sandy beaches, and a fashionable golf course. It also touted the "good moral character" of the residents, noting that "Long Beach is a highly restricted home community. All residents are Caucasian Gentiles."[27]

By the time the Roberts family arrived, housing covenants—as these racial restrictions were known—could no longer be enforced, as a result of the Supreme Court's 1948 decision in *Shelley v. Kraemer*. The justices had ruled unanimously that although private parties could enter into such contracts, the Fourteenth Amendment's guarantee of equal protection prohibited government enforcement of racial real estate covenants. Nevertheless, Long Beach, and the suburbs of Chicago and northern Indiana in general, remained segregated. Wealth inequities, mortgage loan policies, and covert discrimination kept industrial Gary, for example, predominantly black, while the Long Beach environs stayed white. A contemporary visitor to the region could not help but be struck by the contrast between the smokestacks of the city and the manicured green lawns of Long Beach. The region was one of the most segregated areas of the nation.[28]

The Robertses built a four-bedroom yellow split-level home adorned with brown mock-Tudor styling. It was set back from the street, Roslyn Trail, with an expansive front lawn. The town, overwhelmingly Roman Catholic, like much of neighboring Chicago, sent legions of boys in navy blue pants and girls in plaid skirts marching off each morning to Notre Dame Catholic elementary school. On weekends or after school in Long Beach, children raced around on bikes and regularly visited Ronnie's, a neighborhood store known for its candy counter filled with licorice, chocolate bits, and Mary Jane taffy-like candies. When the weather warmed, they swam in the lake. The Roberts family owned a boat, and the children learned to water ski.

This was the era of memorable if improbable TV sitcoms: *The Addams Family*, *Gilligan's Island*, *I Dream of Jeannie*. The young Roberts and his siblings watched these shows, but only after they had done their homework. They were good students, and they were college bound. Their mother, Rosemary, assumed the traditional role of homemaker. She helped her husband keep up on the news, clipping the *Chicago Tribune*, and she was always ready for golf or a party at the country club. But mainly she cared for the children and cooked the meals. On occasion, she would help the nuns at the elementary school, where her son had a reputation for acing every test, winning every spelling bee, and serving as a dutiful altar boy.

John, as he now wanted to be called, had thick brown hair and wore glasses. Teachers said that if he ever failed to understand a lesson, it meant no one in the class had understood it. He took trumpet lessons and played football in grade school, and he did well enough at both, but his strength was in his studies. If a teacher offered the option of reading one of three books, he sometimes read all three.

From many accounts, the Roberts family lived in a warm, traditional household that was conventional for its time and place. Jack's job did not prevent him from attending his son's football games. He served as a model for a boy who always signed his name with "Jr." after it.

When the Roberts family moved to Long Beach, a group of businessmen was in the process of establishing the La Lumiere School on an estate in nearby La Porte. The large garage and chauffeur's quarters were turned into classrooms in what was to be a Catholic boarding school. The first students enrolled in 1964. Andrew McKenna, one of the school's founders, lived in the same Long Beach neighborhood as the Roberts family and remembered John as the rare boy who would shake his hand. "Sometimes it's a little hard for kids to engage," McKenna said. Not so with John. "I remember he said, 'Mr. McKenna, great to meet you.'" He said young John also expressed gratitude for the new school when it accepted him.[29]

La Lumiere mandated student attendance at daily chapel and Sunday Mass. The daily chapel talks were intended for character-building more than anything else. The school was staffed by lay faculty with academic training that generally surpassed that of most teachers at schools sponsored by religious orders. The curriculum was rigorous, including a Latin requirement for all four years along with calculus and other college-level coursework. Tuition stood at about $6,000 when John entered, and it would climb annually. Most of the students therefore came from affluent families. Each class (freshman to senior) enrolled roughly twenty students.[30]

A jacket and tie were required for classes and the dining hall. John Roberts thrived in the formality, becoming a proctor who enforced the dress code. When he was a junior, he wrote an editorial for the school newspaper objecting to any change to the boys-only admissions policy. "I tend to think that the presence of the opposite sex in the classroom will be confining rather than catholicizing," he wrote. "I would prefer to discuss Shakespeare's double entendre and the latus rectum of conic sections without a Blonde giggling and blushing behind me." "Game times should be interesting too," Roberts added. "Imagine the five cheerleaders on the sidelines, with block 'L's' on their chests, screaming, 'Give me a "L"!' Give me a break!"[31]

The dormitory setting fostered male camaraderie. The students watched movies on weekends, including, in Roberts's years, *The Great Race*, *The Caine Mutiny*, and *The Bridge on the River Kwai*. They also played ice hockey and went tobogganing. For dances and the choir, they enlisted girls from St. Mary's Academy, a high school in nearby South Bend, Indiana. The boys had nicknames for each other, for the teachers, and even for the nightly entrees in the dining hall.[32]

Most of La Lumiere's students came from homes much like Roberts's, but there were some troublemakers. Some of the boys from Chicago had been kicked out of local Catholic high schools for drugs or alcohol. "There were those who needed to be kept out of trouble," said Chris Balawender, a former history teacher and football coach at La Lumiere. But according to Balawender, Roberts never appeared to be tempted to join those groups. "He saw kids doing all sorts of stuff. He decided that traditional, conservative, was the way to go," Balawender said. Although boys sometimes snuck out to drink or to take the school car for joy rides, Roberts followed the straight and narrow, devoting himself to his studies.[33]

Balawender cultivated the young Roberts's interest in history. His students staged a mock trial of Joan of Arc and reenacted other historical events. For one assignment, they were tasked with writing a book report on their choice of seven texts that covered human history from ancient Greece to the Enlightenment. Balawender said Roberts consumed all seven and produced a report that he delivered orally while wearing a bedsheet and pretending to be a toga-clad Socrates. Roberts also arranged to have his classmates pound on the doors as "barbarians at the gate."

"Focus. It's the first word you'd say about him," recalled Dave Kirkby, a former assistant head of school, history teacher, and wrestling coach. "At 8 at night John would be studying," classmate Allen "Chris" Filipic recalled. And "at 8 in the morning John would be studying." Roberts's roommate, Robert MacLeverty, said Roberts "would be physically exhausted at the end of each evening from studying." He even sought out more difficult Latin lessons. "He was hardwired from day one to be a judge," MacLeverty said. "He was never going to be a stand-up comic. He wasn't the goofball."[34]

On Sundays after Mass, Roberts would often visit his parents and sisters at home, about thirteen miles away, for midday dinner, occasionally bringing MacLeverty or another friend along. John had a special place in the family as the only boy. His three sisters doted on him, Jane Roberts later said, "and if he brought another nice boy home, all the better."[35]

Sports were a core part of the curriculum at La Lumiere, and Roberts threw himself into athletics. He had the most success with wrestling. No one remembers a time when he had trouble making his weight class, or remembers him salivating as other wrestlers did when bowls of mashed potatoes and gravy went by at dinner. Filipic, Roberts's practice partner, said he was tenacious on the mat and skilled at leveraging his opponents. "If you don't have a sense of leverage, you're not going to move anybody," Filipic said, describing shoulder and leg moves against an opponent.[36]

At a larger high school, John Roberts might not have had the opportunity to play varsity football, let alone to become a linebacker and co-captain of the team as he was. Coach Kirkby, who was defensive coordinator, said Roberts could compensate for his smaller size: "You could have a bigger guy who would make a harder, tougher tackle, but maybe 40 percent of the time he hadn't run to the right place. Or you could have John, who is feisty and sort of ferocious, sort of like a mean little dog, always at the right place."[37]

Roberts assisted with religious services, joined student government, and wrote for the school paper. He sang in the choir, served as a chapel assistant, and acted in school plays, including taking on the role of Peppermint Patty in *You're a Good Man, Charlie Brown*. His classmates were later hard pressed to think of any true setback he may have experienced. He did lose the election for student government president, which some classmates chalked up to lingering resentment that he was first in nearly everything else.

Roberts developed a self-deprecating sense of humor, perhaps to ward off resentment, as he honed skills that would define him into adulthood. He was academically brilliant, and that shrewd eye for leverage on the mat would eventually be transferred to the courtroom.

By his senior year, the boys all had draft cards from the Selective Service. Roberts had registered at the Indiana Local Board No. 46 in La Porte. But like all new registrants of his age in 1973, when the Vietnam War was ending, Roberts was 1-H, not subject to processing for induction. Classmates recalled that the talk among the boys was more about which colleges they would attend than about what they would do if they were drafted.[38]

La Lumiere, like Long Beach, was nearly all white. The boys followed the urban unrest and antiwar demonstrations from afar, sometimes watching the news on a television set in the La Lumiere rec room. "The Vietnam War protests were still there," Filipic later said. "I can tell you, even back then, John was very conservative. He would have been a supporter of the government," though "not blindly."[39]

When Roberts attended La Lumiere, two of the students recruited for diversity were Paris and Neil Barclay, who had grown up in a southern suburb of Chicago. "No one ever called me the N-word," Paris Barclay, who became a Hollywood director, told an interviewer for the *Los Angeles Times* in 1999. "They were a little too sophisticated for that." Paris Barclay, who was a grade below Roberts, added, "I felt I was not as good as these kids with their big families and big houses. It may have been responsible for my excessive overachieving. The best I could do was study my ass off and work at football."[40]

When he graduated in 1973, Roberts was first in his class, and he was La Lumiere's first Harvard-bound graduate. He later said he learned the value of persistence in the face of disappointment at La Lumiere. "No quality is more essential to achieving your hopes for the future," he told a group of graduates in 2013. "And unlike many other keys to success—intellect, talent, physical ability, health, looks, where you were born, into what sort of family, luck—persistence is entirely, *entirely* within your control." Roberts, who emphasized perseverance and certainly showed it, was fortunate to have started with those other advantages too.

Perhaps it was this idea, that so much was within one's own control, that took him to the heights of the judiciary. Once he became a lawyer and a judge, it might also have made it difficult for him to champion people who remained at the bottom rungs of society. "The slogan 'press on' has solved and will always solve the problems of the human race," Roberts insisted.[41]

As Roberts was finishing his last months of prep school, the federal government was turning its attention to the civil rights records of major companies, including in the steel industry, where Jack Roberts worked. After passage of the Civil Rights Act of 1964, federal contractors had to recruit, hire, and promote more minorities. "Freedom is not enough," President Lyndon Johnson asserted in a June 1965 speech at Howard University, three months before he signed a historic executive order, no. 11246, implementing affirmative action. "You do not wipe away the scars of centuries by saying: Now you are free to go where you want, and do as you desire, and choose the leaders you please. You do not take a person who, for years, has been hobbled by chains, and liberate him, bring him up to the starting line of a race and then say, 'you are free to compete with all the others,' and still justly believe that you have been completely fair." Johnson said "the gates of opportunity" had to be opened and that all citizens "must have the ability to walk through those gates."[42]

The US Department of Justice, using Title VII of the Civil Rights Act, began investigating the steel industry's seniority systems for patterns of race discrimination. It then launched a series of cases on behalf of black steelworkers. Steel companies and their unions had long-standing seniority rules that kept blacks in unskilled jobs and denied them admission to apprenticeships for skilled craft work. Blacks were assigned to the most dangerous and lowest-paying steel jobs. In addition, at many steel plants, whites could carry their seniority from division to division, but if a black worker transferred to another division, his tenure started anew, with no credit for the prior years. The practice locked blacks into segregated, dead-end labor classifications, while whites got the higher-paying, cleaner jobs with paths to the upper echelons of skilled classifications.[43]

A lawsuit begun by Attorney General Ramsey Clark in 1968 alleging discrimination at Bethlehem Steel's Lackawanna plant yielded a milestone decision, *United States v. Bethlehem Steel Corp.*, in 1970, when US District Court Judge John Henderson declared that Bethlehem Steel and its union had violated Title VII by using assignment practices relegating blacks to less desirable jobs. Judge Henderson found that employment officers had "falsely raised aptitude test scores of white applicants," had given "preferences to white over black workers," and had "perpetuated the idea that Negroes could stand heat better than whites."[44]

Since at least 1961, Henderson wrote, the Lackawanna plant had "followed a practice of generally assigning Negroes to the hotter, dirtier and less desirable jobs and departments." That included work in the hot coke ovens department. Henderson described the Lackawanna plant as "a microcosm of classic job discrimination in the North, making clear why Congress enacted Title VII of the Civil Rights Act of 1964." When the US Court of Appeals for the Second Circuit upheld Henderson's finding of Title VII violations at Lackawanna, it referred to the "sorry picture" of bias drawn and a history of "long-seated and utterly indefensible racial discrimination against various employees."[45]

In 1973, during John Roberts's final year at La Lumiere, the US Department of Labor ordered Bethlehem Steel to compensate black workers for the long-standing discrimination at its Sparrows Point, Maryland, facility. The following year, the US Equal Employment Opportunity Commission brokered an agreement with Bethlehem Steel and other major producers. The consent decree, as it was known, provided $31 million in back pay to minority and women employees and set timetables for the hiring and promotion of African Americans, Hispanics, and other racial minorities as well as women. That pact settled several hundred claims of bias and offered new opportunities to workers in predominantly black divisions, but it did not end discrimination in the industry. More lawsuits followed, some initiated by white workers alleging reverse bias.[46]

Cycles of unfair discrimination, government intervention, and white backlash continued. But greater challenges for the industry were coming. John Roberts's successful years at Harvard, in fact, coincided with the decline of Big Steel. The energy crisis of the mid-1970s resulted in a push for smaller, more fuel-efficient automobiles. The use of lighter materials meant less need for steel. At the same time, Europe and Japan claimed more and more of the US steel market. Bethlehem Steel, like other American steel companies, nevertheless moved ahead with unchanged manufacturing methods and management attitudes.

"Bethlehem Steel remained inward looking," wrote historian Kenneth Warren, "preserving much of the parochialism that had ruled during Eugene Grace's long leadership. The traditional close-knit character and very comfortable life-style of its top officers and staff continued. A headquarters lunch remained a 'four-star dining experience.'" Warren and other historians of the steel industry have documented that American companies largely ignored the economic warning signs. Bethlehem Steel continued to expand. It opened its opulent Martin tower at the Bethlehem, Pennsylvania, headquarters in 1972, on the eve of the energy crisis.[47]

Jack Roberts, for his part, tried to learn from foreign competition and bridge the gap between management and labor. His children remembered their father's trip to Japan in the 1970s to determine why Japanese companies were gaining an advantage on American ones. He studied the Japanese language for months ahead of the scheduled visit, and upon his return he tried to find ways to adapt Japanese methods to US factories.[48]

Yet, by late 1982, about half the nation's 450,000 steelworkers had been laid off, and production had fallen to under 50 percent of capacity. Steel shipments were expected to reach only 62 million tons, compared with 87 million tons just a year earlier. One by one, the places that Jack Roberts had helped to manage were shuttered.[49]

In 1983, Jack became general manager at Bethlehem Steel's Sparrows Point plant. For two years, he was caught in cycles of employee layoffs and recalls as the plant attempted to modernize. "It's pretty simple," he told the *Washington Post* in 1983, shortly after he arrived. "The guys with the lowest costs and the best quality are the ones who are going to stay in operation."[50]

Bethlehem Steel's problems eclipsed any remedies Jack Roberts could propose. In 1985, as layoffs continued to decimate once vibrant plants and steelmakers bled billions of dollars in losses, he retired from the company. He was only fifty-seven years old.[51]

CHAPTER II

THE EDUCATION OF JOHN ROBERTS

A S JOHN ROBERTS PREPARED TO LEAVE HIS NORTHERN INDI-
ana home for Harvard College in 1973, President Richard Nixon
was fighting for his political life. The Senate Watergate Committee was
investigating the president's role in the break-in at the Democratic National Committee headquarters, and the country was seized by the televised Watergate hearings. The burglary in the Watergate office building
had occurred a year earlier, during the presidential contest between Nixon,
the Republican incumbent, and George McGovern, a Democratic senator
from South Dakota. Senators on the Watergate Committee tried to determine whether Nixon or anyone else in his administration had obstructed
justice or engaged in illegal behavior. "What did the president know and
when did he know it?" Republican senator Howard Baker of Tennessee
had famously asked, coining a phrase that would be repeated in subsequent political investigations. Former White House counsel John Dean
testified that Nixon had authorized up to $1 million to buy the silence
of the Watergate burglars. Presidential aide Alexander Butterfield then
shocked senators and the national audience by revealing the existence of

an Oval Office tape-recording system that would have captured Nixon's conversations about the Watergate affair.[1]

Roberts's undergraduate and law school education—including his time clerking for two prominent jurists, Henry Friendly and William Rehnquist—occurred during a period that witnessed Nixon's downfall, the election of Democrat Jimmy Carter, and the resurgence of the Republican Party under Ronald Reagan. Watergate and the Vietnam War captured most of the headlines of the times, but major developments occurred in the nation's courts, too. In January 1973, the Supreme Court declared that women had a constitutional right to end a pregnancy. *Roe v. Wade* had been brought by a Texas carnival worker, Norma McCorvey, who claimed she'd been raped. The Court majority sided with McCorvey, grounding her right to an abortion in the Fourteenth Amendment's due process guarantee of personal liberty. For Roman Catholics like the Roberts family, the *Roe* decision violated the belief that life began at conception. During Mass, priests likened abortion to murder. The *Roe* ruling fueled the right-to-life movement as well as the pro-choice countermovement. Catholic opposition to abortion had begun shaping American politics even before *Roe*, however. Pressured by the church, the New York legislature had repealed a liberal abortion law in 1972 that it had passed just two years earlier.[2]

The Supreme Court ruling in *Roe* also galvanized women's rights activists, who in 1973 were still trying to win ratification of an Equal Rights Amendment. A year earlier, the American Civil Liberties Union had launched its Women's Rights Project, selecting law professor Ruth Bader Ginsburg to serve as its coordinator. Ginsburg challenged sexually discriminatory practices based on the Constitution's guarantee of equal protection, taking several cases to the Supreme Court.[3]

The racial conflicts of the 1960s persisted into the 1970s as federal judges continued to attempt to alleviate the effects of discrimination. The Supreme Court had ruled in 1971, in *Swann v. Charlotte-Mecklenburg Board of Education*, that judges could order busing of schoolchildren to integrated schools to offset the vestiges of segregation. Roberts's new home of Cambridge, Massachusetts, was just outside of Boston, a city riven by battles over school segregation and busing. A 1974 court-ordered plan in Boston that arose from *Morgan v. Hennigan* to bus black children into white neighborhoods, and whites into black neighborhoods, provoked sit-ins, mass demonstrations, and deadly violence.[4]

A few miles away, at Harvard, Roberts avoided direct involvement in the issues of the day. Which is not to say he was apolitical. On the contrary, he experienced a kind of culture shock and reacted against the liberalism dominant in his new surroundings. "Harvard was a lot different than Indiana and I didn't certainly view myself as conservative or really politically conscious or involved in any way, until I went there and kind of reacted against the orthodoxy that was established there," Roberts said in a 2006 appearance at the University of Miami. He said he had been "taken aback" by the student protests: "I remember there were some demonstrations, really quite sympathetic to the Viet Cong, and I remember thinking that wasn't right, and whatever the merits of the dispute and whether we should be there or not, I didn't understand celebrations in favor of our enemies."[5]

In a decade known for shag haircuts and shag carpets, wild plaids and wide collars, there was nothing faddish about Roberts. He dressed the part of the prep school student that he was, favoring crew-neck sweaters. He retained the boyish looks of his high school years, with his dark brown hair swept neatly across his forehead. Roberts, who had come from a small cohort of students at La Lumiere, became one of nearly five thousand college undergraduates on the storied campus of the country's oldest institution of higher education. While his horizons expanded in some ways, in other ways they did not. He kept to a small circle of friends, re-creating the tiny, trusted worlds of Long Beach and La Lumiere at Harvard. The sprawling new home was as unsettling to him as the student activism of the day.

Disinclined at first to debate current events, Roberts immersed himself in history, his undergraduate major, with a focus on modern European history. He demonstrated an interest in politics, too, taking classes that covered the eighteenth-century American experience, Marxism and the Russian Revolution, and early twentieth-century British liberalism.

Roberts approached his coursework with his customary discipline. He had gained sufficient college-level credit at La Lumiere to enter Harvard as a sophomore, and to stay on track to finish in three years, he skipped the extracurricular activities that had consumed so much of his time in high school. He played some intramural football and soccer, and occasionally joined his old La Lumiere pal Bob MacLeverty, a student at nearby Boston University, for a game of squash. Roberts attended Catholic Mass every Sunday at St. Paul Church in Harvard Square. He later advised new college students to follow this example, saying, "Give your faith a chance. . . . At a time in your life when so much is new, and when how you respond to new choices can affect so much of your future, you may find that it is good to be in a place where things are not new, but familiar and permanent."[6]

Even as the Nixon administration spiraled downward and social inequities dominated front-page news, Roberts was not shaken from the conservatism he had expressed at La Lumiere. Republicans were in the minority at Harvard in the mid-1970s, but at least Roberts was not alone. Upperclassmen in the Harvard Young Republican Club assumed that because of Watergate few freshmen would join. But the opposite happened in 1973. Some 250 students expressed interest, about a fifth of the incoming class. "At first we were surprised that so many people came to sign up," the president of the club told the campus newspaper, the *Crimson*, in September. A spokeswoman for the leftist Students for a Democratic Society was quoted as saying she worried Harvard was admitting too many conservative students, or, as she put it, students "from a preppy background."[7]

Still, Republican numbers at Harvard were small compared to Democrats. A year earlier, during the presidential election, the vast majority of Harvard students had supported the liberal candidate, McGovern, over Nixon. McGovern lost decisively. Before the Paris Peace Accords, the university had been the scene of recurring student protests over Vietnam, including the headline-making 1969 strike and takeover of the imposing white granite building on campus known as University Hall. Even as the era of sit-ins and marches faded, few at Harvard would have predicted the ascendance of right-wing politics.

One student from that era, Eric Rofes, looking back on his time at the university decades later, told the *New York Times* that "conservatives were like the queers on campus." Rofes, who had been a gay organizer, added that "people made fun of [conservatives]. They mocked them as jokers or losers. I don't think in the moment many people realized this was the start of an ascending movement. People felt it was like the last cry of the 1950's."[8]

Soon enough, Roberts would play a role in proving that conservatism was not the last cry of the 1950s, but the first stirrings of the 1980s.

As Roberts settled into his dormitory room in Harvard Yard, his fellow students clamored for Nixon's resignation. The *Crimson* chronicled the downfall of Vice President Spiro T. Agnew, who had taken kickbacks from public works projects when he was governor of Maryland (and even while vice president), as well as Nixon's wrath toward special Watergate prosecutor Archibald Cox. A graduate of Harvard Law, Cox served on the faculty between his stints in government. He had been named special prosecutor in May, about a year after the June 1972 break-in. Now, as Roberts's college classes began, Cox was pursuing the Oval Office tapes that could implicate the president in the cover-up. Nixon contended that executive privilege shielded him from any legal requirement to turn over the tapes.

When the White House tried to cut a deal with the Senate Watergate Committee and Cox, the special prosecutor rejected any compromise that would restrict his access to evidence, and Nixon grew angrier. On October 20, after Cox announced at a news conference that he would not relent on the tapes, Nixon ordered Attorney General Elliot Richardson to fire him. Richardson refused and resigned. Deputy Attorney General William Ruckelshaus then also refused to carry out the order and resigned. The deed fell to Robert Bork, who was then the US solicitor general and the number-three official at the Justice Department, who assumed the role of acting attorney general. Bork fired Cox in the culminating episode of what became known as the "Saturday Night Massacre." "Whether ours shall continue to be a government of laws and not men," Cox responded in a statement, "is now for Congress and ultimately the American people."[9]

Cox and Richardson became heroes on campus just as Roberts was beginning his first semester. Richardson had graduated from Harvard College and Harvard Law School, where he had been president of the *Harvard Law Review*. Harvard seniors invited Richardson to be the Class Day speaker at Commencement that year. Cox was replaced as special prosecutor by Leon Jaworski, and the Watergate investigation continued.[10]

ON A BIG CAMPUS, AMONG WELL-CONNECTED LEGACY STUDENTS and such obvious talents as the young cellist Yo-Yo Ma, Roberts sometimes felt as if he were invisible.[11] But if in some respects he blended into the background, in others he stood out, especially with his professors. Roberts earned top grades and won prizes for his writing. After his first year, he merited the Edwards Whitaker Scholarship for his outstanding scholastic ability and intellectual promise. His essay "Marxism and Bolshevism: Theory and Practice" won the William Scott Ferguson Prize, given annually to recognize an outstanding essay by a sophomore history major. He aspired to be a history professor and expected to one day earn a PhD.[12]

Roberts demonstrated an orderly, sequential way of thinking. In his dorm room in Harvard Yard and then when he moved into Leverett House, the largest of the Harvard residences, he routinely stayed up past midnight, studying or writing papers until he was physically drained. He used antacids to relieve his stomach distress. As his roommate Bob Bush later told the *Crimson*, "he was a great consumer of Pepto Bismol and always had a bottle or two on hand." Through the years, friends would recount Roberts's episodes of nausea before he had to make a presentation or argue a case.[13]

One of Roberts's most lauded papers was titled "The Utopian Conservative: A Study of Continuity and Change in the Thought of Daniel

Webster," a subject that suggested Roberts's early interest in Supreme Court oral advocacy. The New Hampshire–born Webster had dominated American politics in the early nineteenth century. He had become a United States senator and secretary of state, but he was also regarded as the greatest advocate of his day before the Supreme Court. Roberts's essay focused on Webster's conception of property rights as a fundamental component of America's founding, beginning with the Pilgrims at Plymouth. He was intrigued by Webster's idea of the symbiotic relationship between business and government, taking note of "government helping business which helped the country which helped the government."[14]

In the essay, Roberts used one of Webster's arguments in front of the Supreme Court as an example of Webster's nationalistic interest in property. In an 1819 case, *Dartmouth College v. Woodward*, Webster had protested a law that would have put Dartmouth, a privately chartered college, under New Hampshire state control. Webster, a Dartmouth alumnus, implored Chief Justice John Marshall and the Court to uphold private property rights, famously saying, "It is, Sir, as I have said, a small college. And yet there are those who love it!"[15]

Webster insisted that the Constitution protected contractual obligations for private property, and Roberts said this argument "struck a responsive chord in Chief Justice Marshall, whose decision closely followed the lawyer's reasoning. Bench and bar cooperated." More broadly, though, Roberts concluded that Webster had been blind to the changing times. "Webster . . . based his thought on the harmony he wanted to see rather than the conflict which existed, conflict which presented itself to any eyes not clouded by affinities to wealth or high ambition," Roberts wrote. "For Webster needed an idealistic society in which class and sectional conflict did not exist. The America of the 1850s was no such society; neither is the America of the 1970s." The essay earned Roberts Harvard's esteemed Bowdoin Prize in 1976 for the best undergraduate essay.

While Roberts was in the second semester of his first year, Nixon was forced to release transcripts of the Watergate tapes but not yet the actual tapes. The transcripts revealed the president's vindictiveness and frequent use of profanity, along with his racist attitudes. The *Chicago Tribune*, read daily in the Roberts home, published the entire transcript and an editorial that began: "We saw the public man in his first administration, and we were impressed. Now in about 300,000 words we have seen the private man, and we are appalled." The Republican-run newspaper called on Nixon to resign, an indication of the erosion of Nixon's support.[16]

Then, on July 24, 1974, the Supreme Court ruled that Nixon was required to comply with a subpoena for the White House tapes themselves. Picking up where Cox left off, Jaworski had continued to pursue evidence of Nixon's alleged obstruction of justice after the Watergate burglary. To obtain the tapes, Jaworski had appealed directly to the justices, who ruled that Nixon could not claim executive privilege in this instance because it involved a pending criminal trial. The decision in *United States v. Nixon* was 8–0, with Associate Justice Rehnquist recusing himself from the case (he had worked in the Justice Department with several figures indicted in the Watergate scandal). The decision, requiring Nixon to produce the tapes, spelled the end of his presidency. He resigned on August 9, 1974.[17]

Vice President Gerald Ford then became president. The former Michigan congressman, whom Nixon had chosen to succeed Agnew, faced a national economic crisis and the ongoing Vietnam War. But Ford's short tenure offered him a significant opportunity for legacy-building through the Supreme Court. A vacancy on the bench occurred just as Roberts was contemplating whether he wanted to continue to pursue a PhD in history or study law.

In January 1975, Justice William O. Douglas suffered a paralytic stroke, and he never fully recovered. By the time the seventy-seven-year-old retired that November, he had served on the Court for thirty-six years and seven months. (He remains the nation's longest-serving justice.) President Franklin D. Roosevelt had appointed him in 1939, when Douglas was just forty years old. At the time, Douglas had been chairman of the Securities and Exchange Commission, and once on the bench he became a reliable vote for Roosevelt's Depression-era initiatives to regulate the national economy. Later he also became a robust voice for civil liberties and individual rights. Douglas in fact wrote the 1965 decision in *Griswold v. Connecticut*, which had led to the *Roe v. Wade* ruling legalizing abortion. In *Griswold*, the Court had struck down as unconstitutional a Connecticut law prohibiting the sale or use of contraceptives. Douglas wrote that an implicit right to privacy prevented states from interfering with a married couple's choices on contraception.[18]

In 1975, Attorney General Edward Levi, who led the search for possible candidates to succeed Douglas, favored John Paul Stevens, a self-effacing scion of a family in the luxury hotel business. Stevens, a fellow Chicagoan (Levi was a former president of the University of Chicago), had earned a Bronze Star in World War II for his work monitoring secret Japanese transmissions. After college at the University of Chicago and law school at Northwestern, he had clerked for Supreme Court Justice Wiley Rutledge. Stevens had specialized in antitrust law before his appointment by Nixon in 1970 to the Chicago-based US Court of Appeals for the Seventh Circuit.

Stevens's confirmation hearings in late 1975 for elevation to the Supreme Court were brief. Senate Judiciary Committee members never asked Stevens his views on *Roe v. Wade*, a sign that the decision had not yet been politicized. The Senate confirmed Stevens by a 98–0 vote on December 17, 1975.

That same December, Roberts was in the middle of his second year at Harvard, and former Georgia governor Jimmy Carter visited the campus as part of his campaign for president. He drew an overflow crowd of five hundred students and faculty. A fifty-one-year-old Democrat, Carter projected a down-home image that appealed to a country seeking to get past the Watergate scandal and find a new approach to inflation and unemployment.

Carter aimed to become the face of the New South, an antidote to former Alabama governor and segregationist George Wallace, who was also making a bid for the 1976 Democratic nomination. In his campus campaign visit, Carter touted the Civil Rights Act of 1964 and the Voting Rights Act of 1965, emphasizing their value particularly to people in the South.[19]

The debate over civil rights was central to the presidential campaign and a burning issue in higher education. At Harvard, the primary question concerned what should be done to offset the years of discrimination in the United States and bring more blacks, Latinos, and other minorities to campus. The question roiled university officials as well as faculty and students. During Roberts's time as an undergraduate, Harvard's president, Derek Bok, working with the college's chief affirmative action coordinator, Walter J. Leonard, developed what later became the national model for universities taking race and ethnicity into account for student admissions.

The term "affirmative action" had originated with President John F. Kennedy, who required government contractors to ensure they did not discriminate on the basis of race, creed, color, or national origin. After passage of the Civil Rights Act of 1964, Lyndon B. Johnson mandated that federal contractors recruit, hire, and promote more minorities. Such requirements were extended to universities and other employers in the 1970s as a condition of federal funding. With the government pressuring schools to hire more women and minority faculty members, millions of dollars were at stake in Cambridge.

When Roberts arrived at Harvard in 1973, women represented just 2 percent of the tenured faculty, and blacks represented 1.4 percent. Women students were formally admitted to Harvard for the first time in 1972, although undergraduate classes had been co-ed for decades, with Radcliffe College students attending. Even with the tiny percentages of women and minority faculty, however, male professors and administrators complained that the university's efforts to draw a more diverse faculty might dilute standards. Countering such complaints, Walter Leonard pointed to the intransigence of department heads, saying, "It is difficult to explain or believe that the Department of History or the Department of English cannot find a black man or woman in the entire country with the qualifications to hold a tenured position in their august departments."[20]

One conspicuous racial incident involving law school recruitment occurred while Roberts was on campus. An African American student in her third year at Harvard Law School said that a law-firm recruiter told her she was a risky hire, because she could be quickly lured away by a big corporation. "They have to keep the quotas, too," she said he had told her.

According to her account, the recruiter had remarked that "the last black to leave [the firm] went to Clorox. . . . Isn't that funny, a black man going to work for a bleach company?" The Harvard student's tale of humiliation was similar to what (future justice) Sonia Sotomayor experienced at Yale. As Sotomayor entered her third and final year of law school in 1978, a law-firm recruiter asked her, "Do you believe in affirmative action? Would you have been admitted to Yale if you were not Puerto Rican?"[21]

On the flip side of the racial debate, the "reverse discrimination" case of Allan Bakke, a thirty-five-year-old white man rejected for admission to the University of California at Davis, was moving toward Supreme Court review. Bakke, a Minnesota native who had served as a naval officer in Vietnam and an engineer at NASA, had tried to enroll in UC Davis's medical school. A university admissions officer told him his scores were nearly high enough, but he had missed the cut because of the state university's preference for minorities. California officials said they allocated a certain number of seats for minorities to offset past discrimination and to create a diverse mix of students to enhance the academic experience on campus. Bakke asserted that whatever their purpose, the university's racial classifications violated the Fourteenth Amendment's equal protection guarantee.

In a split ruling in *Regents of the University of California v. Bakke*, the Supreme Court forbade the use of racial quotas in admissions practices but allowed universities to take race into account as one of several factors based on a compelling interest in assembling a diverse student body. In his opinion, Justice Lewis F. Powell Jr., who cast the key vote, relied on the Harvard College admissions model, which used race as a "plus" among other factors in an applicant's file.[22]

Roberts, in present-day interviews, has declined to discuss what he recalls of the 1970s debate over race and college admissions or how his opposition to racial remedies developed. But he chafed at the kinds of discussions that Justice Sotomayor went on to provoke in the professional legal world. Sotomayor drew attention to "the slights, the snickers" that minorities continued to face decades after she and Roberts had left their respective Ivy League enclaves and begun to serve together on the

Supreme Court. Roberts believed the country would get beyond racial discrimination only if it stopped focusing on race.[23]

Before graduating from Harvard, Roberts wrote an honors thesis on early twentieth-century British politics. For many students, the ordeal of notecards, late nights in the library, and multiple drafts pecked out on a typewriter could be a joyless enterprise. But Roberts was exhilarated in his exploration of David Lloyd George, Winston Churchill, and the failures of British liberalism. He was intrigued by the fall of the British Liberal Party, which had dominated in the 1910s and early 1920s, and attributed its success at the time partly to the mystique of personality around Prime Minister David Lloyd George, who was a prominent member of the party and became prime minister during World War I.

"Student was written all over him," said Wayne Strasbaugh, who was then a PhD student and tutor in the History Department working with Roberts on his paper. Strasbaugh and Roberts met regularly in the basement of the department's Robinson Hall as Roberts worked on the paper, which he titled "Old and New Liberalism: The British Liberal Party's Approach to the Social Problem, 1906–1914." Strasbaugh recalled Roberts as a careful writer who responded positively to his research suggestions and comments for organization and clarity.[24]

Like Roberts, Strasbaugh had aspired to earn a PhD and become a history professor. But Strasbaugh ended up turning to law school, as did Roberts. "I may have shared my frustration in finding an academic job," Strasbaugh said, musing about Roberts's shift in career plans. "I would have affirmed that decision and said the job market is very tight." Their switch proved smart. The decade produced a glut of history PhDs.[25]

Roberts graduated summa cum laude in 1976 with a bachelor's degree in history. He was in the top 5 percent of his class and headed to Harvard Law School, yet he still believed he would be a professor rather than a litigator. As he crossed campus in his first year of law school, he would have recognized many of his peers. Of the 550 newly enrolled law students in the fall of 1976, 80 came with a Harvard undergraduate degree. About a quarter of the class, 138 students, were women. Overall, minority enrollment—which was regularly tracked in student publications—was down in Roberts's first year, from a total of 78 minority students admitted the previous year to 64 in 1976. Of those, 45 were black, 12 Chicano, 3 Puerto Rican, and 3 Asian American.[26]

Roberts's transition to law school went smoothly. Although he would wring his hands about how he was performing, his mastery of the material was evident to his classmates—and likely to Roberts as well. "After an exam our first year, I remember standing in Shaw Hall, and he was going on and on about how he failed this exam," recalled his friend Richard Lazarus, who lived in the same residence hall as Roberts. "I said I will bet you twenty bucks you got at least an A minus. He wouldn't take the bet. That was unbelievable. He wouldn't take the bet. He was bemoaning, but he thought he did pretty well."[27]

Based on his first-year grades at the law school, Roberts won a coveted place on the *Harvard Law Review*. The following year, classmate David Leebron, who had also gone through Harvard College in three years, was elected president of the law review. Leebron, who was looking for talent, diligence, and integrity in his managing editor, chose Roberts for the position. "John seemed to me to hit all three of those at the highest level," Leebron said. But the men were not in agreement politically. "He struck me as very conservative," Leebron recalled. "There were probably some folks who held that against John. But I didn't."[28]

As managing editor, Roberts coordinated assignments and editing deadlines. He often spent the night at the *Review*'s office in Gannett House. Leebron said Roberts "was a quiet, thoughtful guy, somewhat reserved. I would describe John as an introvert who has learned to present a public persona which is not so introverted." Leebron was struck by the habits Roberts developed as he worked with him on issues of the *Review*. Every day they went to a nearby Baskin-Robbins ice cream store on a break from their work on the law review, and Roberts always ordered the same thing: a sundae with chocolate chip ice cream, topped with marshmallow.[29]

At the end of his third year, in the spring of 1979, Roberts began to feel ill. Exhausted, he checked himself into the local hospital. Nevertheless, he graduated in June, magna cum laude.[30]

The episode captured his Cambridge experience. Roberts was a stellar law student, always at the top of his class, just as he had been as an undergraduate. But he won that academic record at the expense of other pursuits, and perhaps at the expense of his physical health. Boston was just a short subway trip away, but he later said, with regret, that he went into the city only a couple of times.[31]

IF LA LUMIERE SCHOOL OFFERED THE BEST POSSIBLE EDUCATION for Roberts in Indiana, and Harvard College and Harvard Law School represented the pinnacle of academia, his next steps—two judicial clerkships—were no different. Clerkships offer young lawyers a highly confidential inside view of how legal rulings are crafted as well as prestige in the profession. Clerks frequently identify themselves by the judges they serve, and former law clerks of the same judge often band together in an enduring informal guild. When he became a judge, Roberts would go out of his way to quote his two judicial mentors.

Roberts's first clerkship was in New York City with US Appeals Court Judge Henry Friendly, one of the most respected jurists of the century. The second was with Supreme Court Justice William Rehnquist, an influential conservative who was on his way to becoming chief justice (an event that would take place in 1986), and who would be Roberts's immediate predecessor on the high court when Roberts joined in 2005.

The two men offered Roberts two distinct paths forward: Friendly was a model of intellectualism known for his modest judicial approach and respect for precedent. Rehnquist was brilliant but ideologically driven to reinterpret court precedents in accordance with his conservative views. While Friendly spent years in private practice handling corporate matters, Rehnquist was a political insider whose service in the Nixon White House helped shape his hard-right outlook. He exuded a lack of pretension and could be a prankster, while Friendly was always serious, a beacon of elitism.

Law clerks researched cases, helped to prepare judges for oral arguments, and assisted in the writing of opinions. They were admonished to keep their work secret. But just as Roberts set out on the clerkship track, the journalists Bob Woodward and Scott Armstrong published *The Brethren*, a juicy inside look at the Supreme Court demonstrating that scores of former law clerks, and a few Supreme Court justices themselves, could not keep the Court's secrets. Woodward and Armstrong revealed behind-the-scenes negotiations in several important cases that had taken place between 1969 and 1975. Although some of the substantive details of those cases did draw attention from the news media following the book's publication, the real public sensation was the window *The Brethren* provided into the bickering black-robed men of the Court. Woodward and Armstrong portrayed Chief Justice Warren Burger, for example, as an imperious and manipulative leader.

"Take any nine guys, lock them up in a room for life, and some silly things happen," syndicated columnist Richard Reeves wrote as he commented on the book soon after it debuted. "Some stupid things, some mean things, some human things, some decent things, some wise things. That is the message of 'The Brethren.' We all could have guessed that justices of the United States Supreme Court were probably just about like everybody else."[32]

Burger, who was appointed in 1969 as successor to Chief Justice Earl Warren, sometimes tried to control opinions by withholding his vote in the justices' private sessions until the other eight had all revealed their positions in a case. He would then cast his vote with the majority so he could determine who would write the opinion. (The chief justice, as the most senior member of the Court, assigns opinions unless he is in the minority; in such situations, the most senior associate justice in the majority determines who writes the opinion.)

The Brethren rattled the federal judiciary. It so troubled Judge Friendly, for whom Roberts was then working as a law clerk, that Friendly joined a letter with four associates defending Burger: "The individual judges are depicted as men of petty jealousy, connivers, crass, cynical talkers, backbiters, possessed of little virtue and few saving qualities," they said in the letter, which was drafted to *New York Times* executive editor Abe Rosenthal. "This picture is simply unrecognizable, both in spirit and in fact, to at least these authors [of the letter]. . . . The principal object of the attack is the Chief Justice whom one judge allegedly considers a 'blustering braggart' and to whom a second allegedly refers to as 'Dummy.' No reference is made at all to the almost monumental contributions of the Chief Justice to judicial administration."[33]

As it turned out, Roberts's second judicial boss, Rehnquist, had been one of Woodward's sources. For at least two years prior to publication of *The Brethren*, the justices who were talking to the journalists were also discussing the matter among themselves. Justice Lewis Powell kept notes on his conversations with Rehnquist and with Justice Potter Stewart about their participation in the research the authors were conducting. Powell grew worried about his involvement when he realized that Woodward and Armstrong had obtained private memos and draft opinions on cases from law clerks. Burger himself suggested in a personal note to Powell, referring to Woodward and Armstrong, that the law clerks were naïve children "in the hands of these sharpies."[34]

Roberts was not involved in this palace intrigue. He was working at the time as a law clerk to Judge Friendly at the Manhattan-based US Court of Appeals for the Second Circuit. When Roberts joined Friendly's Foley Square chambers in 1979, the judge was seventy-five years old and on "senior" status, which allowed him a reduced caseload. Yet he also was handling railroad cases as one of three judges on a panel established by the Regional Rail Reorganization Act of 1973. Friendly remained a vigorous interlocutor even as he experienced heart problems, eye ailments, and other age-related health difficulties. He was in regular correspondence with Supreme Court justices, leading law professors, and former government lawyers.

Friendly, an only child in a German Jewish family, had grown up in Elmira, New York. Like Roberts, he was a Harvard history major and a graduate of Harvard Law School. Friendly had then worked for Supreme Court Justice Louis Brandeis. That clerkship had left a deep impression on Friendly. On numerous occasions he invoked Brandeis's admonition, from his dissenting opinion in the 1928 case of *Olmstead v. United States*, that "the greatest dangers to liberty lurk in insidious encroachment by men of zeal, well-meaning but without understanding." Before Friendly's 1959 appointment to the federal appeals court, he had helped found the law firm of Cleary, Gottlieb, Friendly and Hamilton, and he had served as general counsel to Pan American World Airways.

As an appeals court judge, Friendly followed precedents set down by the Supreme Court. Ideologically, he leaned right, but not far. "If pressed to affix a label," Judge Friendly's biographer David Dorsen wrote, "one would say he was most of all a conservative in the traditional mold, judicially restrained and reserved, but not always agreeing with either the judicial or political right. . . . In today's parlance he would be a moderate or centrist on most constitutional issues, identified with John Marshall Harlan, Lewis Powell, Sandra Day O'Connor, and Anthony Kennedy rather than William Rehnquist, John G. Roberts Jr., Antonin Scalia, and Clarence Thomas." The nature of the New York–based circuit meant Friendly's cases centered on contractual disputes, financial crimes, and drug trafficking rather than the kinds of ideological flashpoints that defined the Supreme Court.[35]

Dorsen noted that Roberts was one of Friendly's more renowned law clerks, yet, along with the others, he had been intimidated by the judge, whose reputation was the exact opposite of his name. By many accounts, Friendly could be moody and indifferent. In one incident, Friendly asked Roberts into his office and complained that it seemed unusually dark. Roberts said he could not bring himself to tell the judge he was still wearing his clip-on sunglasses. He instead alerted Friendly's secretary and let her tell the judge about the clip-ons.[36]

Roberts was impressed by Friendly's deep engagement with the law and his connections to other jurists and academics. During Roberts's clerkship in the summer of 1979, Columbia law professor Jack Weinstein dropped Friendly a laudatory note about his opinion in a criminal procedure case. "Dear Jack," Friendly wrote back, "I was simply delighted to receive your letter. . . . [Supreme Court Justice Felix] Frankfurter used to say that he wrote his dissents for the cognoscenti, and when I was working on the concurring opinion . . . I thought many times that I was really writing it for you and hoping that you would agree, as I believed you would."[37]

Around the same time, Friendly corresponded with Supreme Court Justice Powell and former US solicitor general Erwin Griswold about the Court's earlier decision in *Regents of the University of California v. Bakke*, the 1978 affirmative action case. In a handwritten note, Friendly praised Powell for the "great service" he had "rendered the nation" with his "statesmanlike" controlling opinion. Friendly told Powell he believed the racial dispute had the potential to be "another Dred Scott," leaving the Court with a "self-inflicted wound." Learning of the reassuring comments to Powell, Griswold told Friendly, "I am glad that you wrote to Lewis Powell. I know that it must have meant much to him. It seems to me that he saved the day, because a clear decision either way would have been a disaster. Thanks to him, we are free, to some extent at least, to try to work things out, through admissions committees, employment practices, and other forms of private action, within reasonable limits, without rigid barriers, and with opportunity to use wisdom, compassion and common sense."[38]

While he was working for Friendly, Roberts lived in a high-rise at Waterside Plaza on the East River with another law clerk. Along with some of the others working at the courthouse, they occasionally picked up half-price tickets to Broadway shows. A group of them were together at the Waterside apartment on February 22, 1980, to watch the US Olympic hockey team's upset of the Soviet team at Lake Placid, New York, on television. That dramatic victory was a bright spot amid a weak economy and the ongoing Iranian hostage crisis, which began in November 1979 when the US embassy in Tehran was seized by followers of Ayatollah Khomeini.

The recession of the late 1970s altered public opinion about the role of the federal government. Faith in big government and in President Lyndon Johnson's Great Society initiatives was giving way to free-market and anti-regulation attitudes. The disillusionment with President Ford had morphed into disenchantment with President Carter. By the time Roberts had arrived in New York, the city had staved off bankruptcy, but the financial problems ran deep. A subway strike in the spring of 1980 forced Roberts, his fellow law clerks, and nearly everyone else in the city to find some other means of transportation for a week, and many people were riding bikes or hoofing it to work.

The Supreme Court was the ultimate destination for young lawyers on the clerkship path. It represented the brass ring of constitutional law and often led to academic positions or specialized work as an appellate litigator. Many clerks aspired themselves to be judges. While he was in the early months of his time with Judge Friendly, Roberts received word via telegram that Justice Rehnquist had chosen him for a Supreme Court clerkship in the upcoming term. Rehnquist appreciated Friendly's recommendation of Roberts and later wrote to Friendly of his "excellent experience with John Roberts." Robert Knauss, who had gotten to know Roberts as he was also clerking on the Second Circuit (to Judge Walter Mansfield), had applied to work for Rehnquist too. "I do remember that [Roberts] got the acceptance, the telegram, from Justice Rehnquist's secretary before I did," Knauss recalled. Knauss, who had graduated from Harvard College and the University of Michigan Law School, learned of his own acceptance a few weeks later. He was glad he would be sharing the plum opportunity with someone he already knew.[39]

Knauss said he believed Rehnquist had been looking for clerks who would work well together and accept his conservative ideology. "I went in there [to the interview] thinking I would get grilled on constitutional doctrine," Knauss said. "We didn't talk much about that. He said, 'You know my approach. Are you comfortable working for me?' And I said yes."[40]

Perhaps as a reflection of his attachment to Judge Friendly, Roberts as he left for Washington could not bring himself to turn in the leather case he had been issued at the start of his clerkship in New York. Roberts used the satchel, inscribed as property of the US government, for years, until it was worn beyond repair.

When he became a judge himself, Roberts would identify in public statements with Judge Friendly's neutral legal approach even as his own opinions aligned more with Rehnquist's. He constantly told audiences that the justices were not creatures of politics, and he took pains to avoid any suggestion that he had taken his second judicial mentor as an ideological model.[41]

ROBERTS SERVED AS A LAW CLERK TO THEN ASSOCIATE JUSTICE Rehnquist during the 1980–1981 Supreme Court term. Roberts later said the clerks gave Rehnquist a Lone Ranger doll because he staked out so many conservative positions by himself. Yet Rehnquist knew how to lay the groundwork, one opinion at a time, in his attempt to move the Court rightward. "Justice Rehnquist is one of the few members of the Court who approaches the docket from a clearly conceived ideological perspective," Linda Greenhouse of the *New York Times* wrote at the time. "When most Justices seem to consider each opinion in terms of the case at hand, Justice Rehnquist sows the seeds of future opinions in cases that will embody similar issues. This approach gives a tactical advantage to one who would move the Court in a particular direction." Years later Roberts would demonstrate a similar, but subtler, incremental approach, building with each case to achieve broader conservative outcomes.[42]

The Supreme Court Building, at One First Street in the northeastern quadrant of DC, was designed by the architect Cass Gilbert in the Beaux-Arts tradition and completed in 1935. It is distinguished by a broad plaza, fluted Corinthian columns, and a frieze inscribed with "Equal Justice Under Law." The front plaza is flanked by two huge sculptures: *Contemplation of Justice*, depicted as a woman holding a book of law, and *Authority of Law*, shown as a man holding a tablet and a sword. Up the wide front steps, the Court's huge bronze doors provide entry to a world of cream marble, red velvet, and oak carvings. In the Lower Great Hall rests an oversized bronze statue of a seated John Marshall, the nation's foundational fourth chief justice, who wrote *Marbury v. Madison*. Portraits of past chief justices hang in elegant conference rooms one flight up. The justices' conference room, where votes are taken and cases decided, is off the main chambers of the chief justice. In the room, nine black leather chairs surround a rectangular table. Volumes of past cases, the *United States Reports*, line the wall, and a portrait of John Marshall hangs above the black marble fireplace.

As one of the eight associate justices, Rehnquist had a three-room chamber that he shared with his clerks. Rehnquist had once been a Supreme Court law clerk himself. After graduating first in his class at Stanford Law School, he had worked for Justice Robert Jackson in the 1952–1953 term.[43] Rehnquist had grown up in the Milwaukee suburb of Shorewood in Wisconsin; his father had been a paper salesman and his mother a translator who knew many languages. She had changed his middle name to "Hubbs" when he was a teenager after a numerologist had predicted her son would achieve greater success with a name that began with the letter *H.*

Rehnquist had settled in Phoenix, Arizona, after Stanford and the clerkship and had become friends with the Republican operative Richard Kleindienst during Barry Goldwater's 1964 presidential campaign. Goldwater had lost to Johnson in a landslide. Four years later, when Nixon defeated Hubert Humphrey, Rehnquist had joined Kleindienst as the latter moved to Washington to become deputy to Attorney General John Mitchell. Rehnquist took a job overseeing the Justice Department's Office of Legal Counsel, which provided constitutional advice to the attorney general and the president. In that position he crafted the legal arguments needed to support Nixon's wiretapping and antiwar protest initiatives. Like Nixon, Rehnquist believed the Warren Court had undermined law enforcement in its effort to protect defendants' rights. When Nixon nominated Rehnquist, who was then only forty-seven, to the Supreme Court, in 1971, Nixon told Chief Justice Burger (in a conversation picked up by the Oval Office taping system), "I think Rehnquist is just made to order on this. He isn't going to be moved by the Georgetown set."[44]

Nixon and Burger had an unusually cozy relationship for a president and a chief justice. They did not hesitate to pick up the phone and discuss nominations and other matters with each other. Nixon had chosen Burger, who was distinguished by a full white head of hair, as chief in 1969. A man of modest roots in St. Paul, Minnesota, Burger had attended law school by night while working as an accountant for a life insurance company by day. He was active in the state's Republican Party organization and during the 1952 presidential election had supported Eisenhower's nomination at the GOP convention. When Eisenhower won the presidency, he had helped Burger obtain an assistant attorney general job and then appointed him to the US Court of Appeals for the District of Columbia Circuit. Burger's reputation as a conservative judge who was tough on crime had attracted the attention of President Nixon as he looked for a successor to Chief Justice Earl Warren.

Rehnquist's law-and-order record was even stronger than Burger's, and along with his position on racial matters it provoked a well-organized Senate opposition to his Supreme Court nomination in the fall of 1971. As a lawyer in Phoenix, Rehnquist had fought antidiscrimination and school integration programs. He had also participated in organized efforts at polling places to challenge the eligibility of black Democratic voters. Under Senate Judiciary Committee questioning, Rehnquist denied harassing blacks at the polls. After those hearings, but before the Senate confirmation vote, *Newsweek* uncovered a Court memo that Rehnquist had written during his clerkship with Justice Jackson related to the *Brown v. Board of Education* school desegregation litigation. In the memo, Rehnquist defended the "separate but equal" doctrine in schools.[45]

Rehnquist responded by saying he was simply reiterating Justice Jackson's views for use during his deliberations with his fellow justices. Richard Kluger, who later explored the issue in his book on *Brown v. Board of Education*, wrote that "a far more plausible explanation" was that Rehnquist was revealing his own sentiment. (Jackson had died in October 1954, and his version of events was not available.) The Senate, controlled by Democrats at the time, approved Rehnquist's nomination on a vote of 68–26. Explaining the difficulty of drumming up opposition to Rehnquist among American Bar Association leaders, Joseph L. Rauh Jr., of the Leadership Conference on Civil Rights, said during the confirmation controversy, "They think that a reactionary A student is better than a reactionary C student and that it's O.K. for him to go on the bench." Such was the elitism at the top rungs of the legal profession.[46]

Rehnquist turned out to be exactly what Nixon expected, and civil rights advocates feared: a staunch defender of law enforcement and a consistent opponent of racial classifications. A few months before John Roberts joined Rehnquist's chambers in 1981, the justice penned a rousing dissent in an affirmative action case. It was the kind of opinion that attracted young conservatives like Roberts for its hard stand against any measures that could be deemed quotas.

The case, *United Steelworkers of America v. Weber*, originated in 1974 when the Office of Federal Contract Compliance had pressed Kaiser Aluminum to boost its minority employment. Kaiser had signed a collective bargaining agreement with the United Steelworkers of America to reserve 50 percent of openings in a training program for blacks until their numbers reflected the proportion of African Americans in the local labor force. Brian Weber, a white production worker at Kaiser's plant in Gramercy, Louisiana, applied for skilled-craft job training and was not selected. When he discovered that two successful black applicants had less seniority than he did, Weber helped launch a class-action lawsuit alleging that the 50 percent requirement violated the 1964 Civil Rights Act's prohibition on race discrimination.

The Supreme Court ruled against Weber, declaring that Title VII of the act, which forbade discrimination in employment, did not prevent employers from adopting programs that gave a leg up to minorities that had been underrepresented.[47] Justice William Brennan's opinion for the Court noted that Congress had sought in Title VII to increase opportunities for minorities, and that race-conscious affirmative action would help employers reach that goal. Voluntary affirmative action was permitted, Brennan wrote, "to eliminate conspicuous racial imbalance in traditionally segregated job categories."[48]

In a provocative dissenting statement, Rehnquist opened with reference to George Orwell's *1984*: "In a very real sense, the Court's opinion is ahead of its time," he wrote. "It could more appropriately have been handed down five years from now, in 1984, a year coinciding with the title of a book from which the Court's opinion borrows, perhaps subconsciously, at least one idea." Rehnquist described a scene from the book in which a government official denounces an enemy country but gets the name wrong. Slipped a piece of paper midway through his speech, the official doesn't miss a beat as he switches to the correct country name. "Today's decision represents an equally dramatic and equally unremarked switch in this Court's interpretation of Title VII," Rehnquist wrote. "Thus, by a tour de force reminiscent not of jurists such as Hale, Holmes, and Hughes, but of escape artists such as Houdini," he continued, "the Court eludes clear statutory language, uncontradicted legislative history, and uniform precedent in concluding that employers are, after all, permitted to consider race in making employment decisions."[49]

That unequivocal view, along with his literary flourishes, excited young lawyers who had felt like lone voices of conservatism in liberal bastions such as Cambridge. A few years later, Roberts, as a White House lawyer, would endorse Rehnquist's dissenting opinion in *Weber*. He echoed Rehnquist's notion that nothing is "more destructive to the notion of equality" than a quota, and he adopted Rehnquist's belief that "whether described as 'benign discrimination' or 'affirmative action,' the racial quota is nonetheless a creator of castes, a two-edged sword that must demean one in order to prefer another."[50]

On a personal level, Rehnquist offered an antidote to Burger's stuffiness. He was unvarnished and direct. "He wore scuffed Hush Puppy shoes," Roberts recalled. "That was my first lesson: Clothes do not make the man. The justice sported long side burns and Buddy Holly glasses long after they were fashionable. He wore loud ties that I am certain were never fashionable."[51]

Rehnquist's three law clerks that session, Roberts, Knauss, and Dean Colson, whose home Roberts was later visiting when he heard of Scalia's death, worked in a cramped room in Rehnquist's chambers. "Our first day of work," Colson later said of Roberts, "he's there forty-five minutes before me, and I got there at 8 a.m." Colson, who was three years older and nearly a head taller, recalled that Roberts looked very young. "But I knew he had graduated from Harvard in three years and been on the law review. He's one of the best-educated people I've met."[52]

In their early weeks at the Court, Roberts developed a severe pain in his abdomen and discovered he needed an emergency appendectomy. "The appendectomy was really just a minor inconvenience," Roberts wrote to Judge Friendly after the surgery, minimizing the health scare, "and mindful of the example you set last year during your stay in the hospital, I had briefs and cert petitions brought over and was able to continue working on them with only occasional interruptions by doctors and nurses."[53]

For most of the annual term, Roberts and his fellow law clerks split their duties into three tasks: screening the hundreds of petitions that came to the Court to determine which ones merited hearings; helping the justice prepare for oral arguments in the cases that were accepted for review; and researching and assisting in the writing of decisions. During Roberts's short tenure, five of the nine justices, including Rehnquist, had their clerks join forces to screen the petitions (or "petitions for certiorari," as they were called), to determine which ones should be accepted for oral argument and full review. Chief Justice Burger had initiated the "cert pool" as a way to ease the Court's workload. Critics of the practice included Justice Brennan, who believed the cert pool would create an unhealthy bureaucracy at the Court. He also feared it could be manipulated by a chief justice who was already trying to exercise inordinate control over the outcomes of cases.[54]

The justices imposed a high bar for cases they would accept. They looked for areas in which lower courts had issued conflicting rulings that had led to an uneven application of the law across the nation. They also wanted to take on important cases that tested the reach of federal power. In his memos reviewing petitions for the cert pool, Roberts employed a clean, clear style. Occasionally his wit flashed: "The petition should be denied; losing counsel is simply letting off some steam."[55]

Working seventy-hour weeks, the clerks found diversion in games of basketball on the Court's top-floor gym. They loved it not only for the exercise but for the competition. "All of us looked forward to the basketball games," Knauss later said. "Dean, John, and I were regulars. He was shorter than we were. But he was scrappy." They were all still in their twenties, but they were not as agile as they once might have been. "We had a lot of injuries that year," Knauss recalled, including blows to ankles and wrists. "We had a lot of people in casts."[56]

When he wanted to discuss cases, Justice Rehnquist would enlist a law clerk for a walk through the surrounding neighborhood of brick row houses. "He'd point to one of us and say, 'Let's go for a walk,'" recounted Knauss. "Sometimes he would go first and say, 'Here's what I'm thinking about.' He'd listen to what we'd have to say. So, we would walk and talk. It was intellectual engagement. It was fun." Rehnquist also involved his clerks in practical jokes, skits, Christmas party arrangements, and constant betting. He was up for a wager on football games, snowfall tallies, political elections, or the length of a president's State of the Union speech. "We would bet on anything," Colson said. "But for just 50 cents or $1."

Roberts kept Judge Friendly up to date on the experience of working for Rehnquist. "Nothing that I have witnessed suggests that there will be any lessening of the divisions on the Court this term," Roberts wrote in his early months. "But I was pleased to see that the rumors of personal animosity and pettiness circulating in the wake of *The Brethren* do not seem to have any substance. The Justice [Rehnquist] is at once amiable and challenging and very open with me and my two co-clerks."[57]

In one of the more attention-getting cases that session, *H.L. v. Matheson*, Rehnquist joined a majority opinion by Chief Justice Burger upholding a Utah law that required a physician to notify the parents of a pregnant girl under the age of eighteen before performing an abortion. The Burger majority declared that the law did not violate the girl's privacy rights.[58] Rehnquist continued to vote against death penalty appeals and, writing alone, penned an opinion urging his colleagues to act to speed up executions for the scores of men who were on state death rows. Rehnquist's opinion came in the April 1981 case of Wayne Coleman, who had been convicted of the murder of six people in a family in Georgia. Coleman had filed a series of appeals that had delayed his execution. In *Coleman v. Balkcom*, a majority of the Supreme Court rejected Coleman's latest petition but left him with other avenues of appeal. Rehnquist wanted the Court to use the case to staunch repetitive petitions. "It seems to me that we have thus reached a stalemate in the administration of federal constitutional law," he wrote. "Although this Court has determined that capital punishment statutes do not violate the Constitution . . . and although 30-odd States have enacted such statutes, apparently in the belief that they constitute sound social policy, the existence of the death penalty in this country is virtually an illusion." Rehnquist complained that hundreds of prisoners condemned to die were engaged in protracted appeals and few faced imminent execution.[59]

None of Rehnquist's colleagues joined his opinion. Justice Powell wrote a private note telling Rehnquist he believed he was misguided. Justice John Paul Stevens went public with his concern, saying in a statement that it was unrealistic to think that the Court could review all appeals and speed up the administration of the death penalty. "If we were to hear even a substantial percentage of these cases on the merits, they would consume over half of this Court's argument calendar," Stevens wrote in a concurring opinion in the *Coleman* case.[60]

Rehnquist wrote two of the more important opinions of the session during which Roberts was a law clerk. Both were delivered at the end of the term. In the first, *Rostker v. Goldberg*, a six-justice majority affirmed Congress's power to exclude women from the draft. The case traced to President Carter's resumption of draft registration, prompted by the Soviet Union's invasion of Afghanistan in 1980. When Congress had reactivated the Military Selective Service, it had declined to amend it to include the registration of women, as Carter had recommended. In the Court's ruling, rejecting a challenge by several men, Rehnquist wrote that the exclusion of women was permissible, because they were barred from combat and thus not "similarly situated" with men for purposes of constitutional analysis. "The purpose of registration was to prepare for a draft of combat troops," Rehnquist wrote. "Since women are excluded from combat Congress concluded that they would not be needed in the event of a draft, and therefore decided not to register them."[61]

Three justices dissented. Justice Byron White said the Rehnquist majority was in effect imagining a false mandate requiring all service members to be combat-only troops. "Common sense and experience in recent wars, where women volunteers were employed in substantial numbers, belie this view of reality," White wrote in his dissenting opinion.[62]

The second major Rehnquist ruling came to the Court on the kind of fast-track schedule that played to Rehnquist's strengths and excited Roberts. Even as an associate justice, Rehnquist was known for his efficiency and for wresting quick work out of others. The case, *Dames & Moore v. Regan*, arose from a deal President Carter had worked out to win release of the fifty-two American hostages held in Iran. The Court took it up in a special June hearing near the end of the justices' annual term. The United States was facing a July 19 deadline for the transfer of more than $2 billion of Iranian assets out of the United States that had been frozen when the Iranian radicals had seized the embassy in Tehran.

President Carter had used frozen Iranian assets as a "bargaining chip" when negotiating for the freedom of the American hostages. An engineering firm, Dames & Moore, which had earlier won a $3.8 million judgment against Iran, had sued the US government when that judgment was voided as part of the hostage deal's discharge of the Iranian assets.

The justices unanimously upheld President Carter's power in the hostage-release deal and ruled against Dames & Moore. Rehnquist wrote that the president had constitutional and statutory authority to settle financial claims against foreign governments. But he also stressed that the ruling in the urgent matter at hand was a narrow one. He referred to a statement by his former boss, Robert Jackson, who had said that justices "decide difficult cases presented to us by virtue of our commissions, not our competence." Rehnquist declared, of the present Dames & Moore dispute, that the justices were not attempting "to lay down . . . general 'guidelines' covering other situations not involved here."[63]

Afterward, Rehnquist's fellow justices sent him notes of appreciation for producing the opinion on such short notice.[64] But the rushed case was hardly the only problem that descended on Rehnquist in June 1981, when Roberts was finishing the clerkship with him. As Rehnquist was pulling together the decision with the help of his clerks, he kept a speaking engagement in Jackson Hole, Wyoming, and on the return trip to Washington he developed pneumonia and had to be hospitalized. At the same time he was also rushing to get up to his family vacation home in Vermont, where one of his daughters was about to be married.

Roberts was juggling obligations of his own, arranging for a new job and studying for the bar exam with a fellow law clerk, Michael McConnell, a University of Chicago Law School graduate who was working for Justice Brennan. McConnell and Roberts had been introduced by a mutual friend who thought the two would be compatible. "It was probably that we were both conservatives," McConnell recounted. "It was pretty unusual in those years." McConnell recalled that he "would hang out in the Rehnquist chambers" on breaks.[65]

As they studied together, Roberts and McConnell shared their enthusiasm about the emergence of Ronald Reagan in the 1980 presidential campaign. "People had huge faith in Ronald Reagan," McConnell said. "It was something new and principled, something you could feel really good about. It was like a Golden Age."

Roberts had been in touch with Judge Friendly as he considered his various career options after he left Rehnquist's chambers. "I will soon have to confront the question of what to do when this clerkship ends," Roberts had told him, "and will be seeking your advice at that time."[66] When he heard Reagan deliver his Inaugural Address, Roberts knew precisely what his next move would be.

CHAPTER III

HEARING THE CALL

IN 1980 JOHN ROBERTS WAS CAPTIVATED BY RONALD REAGAN'S presidential campaign. The Hollywood actor turned California governor put forward a bold economic and social agenda. Reagan vowed to reduce public spending, lower taxes, and lessen government involvement in social issues. Religion was central to his worldview and candidacy. Speaking to Christian leaders who had rallied a crowd of fifteen thousand in Dallas that August, Reagan declared, "I know you can't endorse me . . . but I want you to know that I endorse you and what you are doing." Reagan said that to solve the problems of modern life and become "that shining city upon a hill," America needed to trust again in the Bible and "that old-time religion." With the economy sputtering and concerns about the erosion of "traditional values" spreading, his message hit home. The Moral Majority and Right to Life movements endorsed Reagan. Race, too, was central to his appeal. For the federal bureaucracy and judiciary, he advocated a "color-blind" approach, contending that racial remedies had gone too far. Reagan ended up winning a lopsided share of the white vote, 56 percent, to Democratic candidate Jimmy Carter's 36 percent and the independent John Anderson's 8 percent.[1]

Examining Reagan's victory, the political analyst William Schneider wrote in *The Atlantic* that "the single most prominent characteristic of public opinion during the seventies was wide-spread disillusionment with government. . . . [T]he feeling grew that the federal government had become excessively wasteful and ineffective." Not only did Reagan win, but the Republicans took over the Senate after a net gain of twelve seats in the 1980 elections. It was the first time in more than a quarter century that Republicans had gained control of either the House or the Senate.[2]

Roberts wanted to be part of what came next. "I felt he was speaking directly to me," Roberts later said, recalling how he had felt listening to Reagan's January 1981 Inaugural Address. Roberts heard a "call to action" in Reagan's admonition that he did not "believe in fate that will fall on us no matter what we do," but rather "in a fate that will fall on us if we do nothing." Roberts said Reagan persuaded him of the cost of inaction; it was time for Roberts to join the ideological battle.[3]

For attorney general, the new president chose William French Smith, who was then a partner at the California-based law firm of Gibson, Dunn and Crutcher. Smith, in turn, selected Ken Starr, a thirty-five-year-old associate at the firm, to be his chief of staff. The son of a Texas minister, Starr had graduated from Duke University Law School and then clerked for Chief Justice Warren Burger.

Soon after he arrived in Washington, in early 1981, Starr received a telephone call from Associate Justice William Rehnquist. "He said he had a law clerk who wanted to work in government before going into private practice," Starr recalled of the first time he heard of John Roberts. Starr was intrigued by Rehnquist's report on Roberts, especially his Harvard and clerkship credentials. A recommendation from Rehnquist carried considerable weight. After all, the justice's opinions over the years had constructed the intellectual scaffolding for the new Reagan social and legal agenda.[4]

Roberts became special assistant to Attorney General Smith at an annual salary of $46,685. It was about twice what he had made as a law clerk to Rehnquist. More importantly for the twenty-six-year-old Roberts, the position offered him a chance to weigh in on the most important social dilemmas of the day. It also provided him with a key connection to the legal network in Washington. An ambitious lawyer, Starr was becoming an adept political operator. Roberts immediately impressed Starr. "I think his deeply Catholic upbringing and his going to an intellectually stimulating high school are at the roots of his character," Starr later said. "He was able at that high school [La Lumiere] to be Mr. Everything."[5]

The social issues that had caused debate and conflict during Roberts's time at Harvard and as a law clerk, such as abortion rights and affirmative action, were at the top of Reagan's legal agenda. Roberts would have a chance to sharpen his own arguments. The Reagan administration position also offered him valuable experience in navigating the nation's capital and a perch from which to observe the politics of judicial nominations. It may not have seemed like a predictable start for a future chief justice. Most justices in the past half century did not have executive branch experience, yet many did, and like Roberts, forged important political connections in that service.[6]

Roberts passed the District of Columbia bar exam and arrived at the Department of Justice in the middle of August in 1981, in time to help prepare pending Supreme Court nominee Sandra Day O'Connor for her confirmation hearings. Some twenty-four years later, when O'Connor announced her retirement, Roberts would be the president's first choice as her successor.

In nominating O'Connor, a fifty-one-year-old Arizona state appellate court judge with long-standing political connections, Reagan fulfilled a campaign pledge to name the first woman to the Supreme Court. The opening arose a few months into his presidency, when Justice Potter Stewart, an Eisenhower appointee who had been on the bench since 1958, announced his retirement.

The eldest child of a pioneering ranch family, and once a popular state senator, O'Connor was her own best advocate when Reagan administration officials began screening candidates to be Stewart's successor. She had gone to Stanford Law School and had been a classmate of Rehnquist's.

Living in Phoenix, she had become the first woman in the nation to serve as the majority leader of a state senate. She had then run for a state trial judgeship and won. Through a mutual friend who had arranged a fortuitously timed vacation on Lake Powell in Utah, O'Connor also had developed a friendship with Chief Justice Burger. The chief justice, eager to influence administration officials, had passed on O'Connor's name to the White House counsel, Fred Fielding. Attorney General Smith was on the lookout, too, for women lawyers who might be Court candidates for Reagan. Smith had been given her name but he could not recall from whom. O'Connor had cochaired Nixon's 1972 presidential campaign in Arizona and had the backing of Republican senator Barry Goldwater.[7]

In her interview with Reagan, O'Connor easily pivoted from legal issues to life on her family ranch. Reagan announced her nomination on July 7 in the White House briefing room. She may have been more moderate than the Reagan legal team realized, however. She had supported the Equal Rights Amendment at one point and, in 1970, before the Court decided *Roe v. Wade*, had even voted to legalize abortion. When leading antiabortion activists in Arizona, along with Jerry Falwell's Moral Majority, complained, Reagan's legal team defended the president's choice and insisted that O'Connor regarded abortion as "repugnant." Goldwater, whose conservatism was incontrovertible, leapt to her defense. He said he had known O'Connor for two decades and could vouch for her traditional beliefs in marriage and the family. When Falwell was quoted as saying, "All good Christians should oppose O'Connor," Goldwater had a rejoinder: "All good Christians should kick him in the ass."[8]

The controversy was fading by the time Roberts joined Starr's team. But Starr nevertheless tapped Roberts to help ensure that O'Connor was ready to handle questions about abortion at her Senate Judiciary Committee hearing. Roberts assisted in preparing responses for her and later wrote a memo to Starr with advice on how a nominee could deflect senators' questions while appearing to answer them. "The approach was to avoid giving specific responses to any direct questions on legal issues likely to come before the court," Roberts recounted, "but demonstrating in the response a firm command of the subject area and awareness of the relevant precedents and arguments." To help O'Connor, Roberts pored over the confirmation transcripts of past nominees, including Chief Justice Burger and Justices John Paul Stevens and Harry Blackmun. This was, in a sense, the beginning of Roberts's own preparation for the moment decades later when he would take the witness chair.[9]

On O'Connor's first day of questioning before the committee in September 1981, the subject of abortion came up. She said she had made a mistake when she had voted for the proposed 1970 legislation in Arizona that would have decriminalized abortion in the state. She stressed that she had been a legislator at the time and that judges have a more limited role in American life. She portrayed herself as a supporter of traditional family values, introducing her husband, John, and their three sons, who had accompanied her into the room at the outset of the Senate hearing. Seated before the senators, she had then read from a text that she had often used as a judge when performing marriage ceremonies: "Marriage is far more than an exchange of vows. It is the foundation of the family, mankind's basic unit of society, the hope of the world, and the strength of our country."[10]

O'Connor parried the senators' questions masterfully and drew overwhelming support on Capitol Hill and beyond. The Senate confirmed her 99–0 on September 21, and she took the oath of office five days later. She would go on to demonstrate formidable negotiating skills and to become a steadying force on an ideologically divided bench. Having trained in politics, she knew how to count votes, and she appreciated the importance of compromise. In the beginning, to the satisfaction of Reagan and his top aides, she aligned frequently with Rehnquist, her old law school classmate, and with Chief Justice Burger.

At the Justice Department, Roberts turned to other controversies: the landmark Voting Rights Act, which had been adopted after the bloody march on Selma in 1965; school prayer and other church-state disputes; and women's equality and abortion rights. Whether he now felt free to reveal his true beliefs on these issues, or his new colleagues changed him, the seemingly mild-mannered Roberts suddenly turned combative. In his memos to superiors, he made clear that he felt they should challenge not only the status quo, but also fellow Republican officials who were not, in his view, sufficiently committed to the Reagan agenda. Within his first two months on the job, Roberts was alerting Attorney General Smith to inconsistencies in agency practices related to affirmative action and other racial policies.[11]

It was in this period that Roberts solidified his view that remedies tied to an individual's race were as repellant as racial discrimination in the first instance. He would argue the same in the early 1990s when he worked for President George H.W. Bush, and into the 2000s as chief justice of the United States. "Racial balancing," as he termed practices that gave preference to blacks and Hispanics to offset past discrimination, was patently unconstitutional, he believed, even when carried out in the name of diversity.[12]

During his 2005 Senate confirmation hearings, Roberts would reject assertions that his Reagan-era memos reflected his own core views rather than the administration's established positions. Certainly, he was an enthusiastic lieutenant for the Reagan administration, ready to do battle with its congressional "adversaries," as Roberts termed them, and to expose any insurgents who compromised the mandate that Attorney General Smith believed the American people had granted the president. Yet the ideas that Roberts espoused reappeared in his decisions after he became a justice. A straight line can be drawn from his positions on voting rights, affirmative action, religion, and abortion rights in the 1980s to his expressed views from the center chair at the Supreme Court after his appointment in 2005.[13]

It is unclear whether Roberts expected his memos to someday become public. He seemed to express some trepidation about that possibility in discussions about the Presidential Records Act of 1978, which Congress passed in response to the Watergate scandal. The law allowed disclosures of executive branch material twelve years after a president left office, which, in Reagan's case, would end up being twelve years from 1989. Urging top officials to seek ways to prevent the wholesale opening of files, Roberts argued in a 1985 memo that by 2001, any member of the public "need only go to the Reagan Library to see *any* internal White House deliberative document they want to see—at least under the current, untested provisions of the Presidential Records Act." He tried, in vain, to call attention to the "pernicious effect of that statute."[14]

Roberts urged top White House lawyers to seek an amendment that would keep most executive branch memos permanently confidential. "Twelve years is a brief lifetime in public life," he wrote in a follow-up missive on the subject. "Many of the personalities candidly discussed in sensitive White House memoranda, and certainly many of the authors of the memoranda, will be active twelve years from now." How correct he was. Roberts likely anticipated, without knowing exactly how it would happen, that his own once-confidential writings could one day be revealed.[15]

IN THE REAGAN YEARS, ROBERTS WAS SURROUNDED FOR THE FIRST time by plenty of people who loathed the liberalism of the 1960s and 1970s. "Everyone felt a sense of mission," said Michael McConnell, who had befriended Roberts when the two were Supreme Court clerks.[16] "It was a wonderful, exciting time for conservatives, especially young conservatives," said Roger Clegg, a friend and Reagan administration colleague of Roberts. "There was a high degree of consensus that judicial activism was a bad thing, federalism was a good thing."[17]

Roberts shared his own enthusiasm about the new administration with Judge Friendly. "This is an exciting time to be at the Justice Department, when so much that has been taken for granted for so long is being seriously reconsidered," Roberts wrote. He pointed to the administration's efforts "to halt unwarranted interference" by federal judges in the activities of the legislative and executive branches.[18]

Roberts toiled at the Justice Department's massive limestone building from early morning well into the night. The structure, built in 1934, filled an entire city block between Pennsylvania and Constitution Avenues. Inside were more than sixty murals depicting workers and daily life, mosaic inlaid ceilings, and terra cotta floor tiles. Allegorical themes of justice were represented throughout, both in painted plaster panels and in cast-iron statues.

William French Smith cut a figure very different from that of Roberts's prior boss, William Rehnquist. A scion of an old New England family, Smith was impeccably attired in dark suits and conveyed an aristocratic air more matched to a law firm than to politics. He was deeply committed to Reagan's view that government and the judiciary were intruding in the affairs of the states, in business, and on issues affecting all manner of people's lives.

Roberts focused on the Voting Rights Act of 1965, the milestone law that had been passed by Congress only after the Bloody Sunday march in Selma, Alabama, early in his time as an assistant to Attorney General Smith. Discriminatory voting practices remained a problem, especially in the South, but Roberts thought the law excessively interfered with activities that the states should be able to regulate. The scope of two major provisions of the act was in dispute: One was known as Section 2 (for its place in the statute) and prohibited state and local governments from instituting election practices that discriminated directly against minority voters. The other was more controversial and became a greater target for Roberts and other Reagan lawyers. It was Section 5, requiring certain localities to obtain Department of Justice approval before changing their election procedures. The counties and states that fell under this provision had a history of race discrimination, and most of the covered jurisdictions were in the Old South. The preapproval provision was intended to stop potentially discriminatory practices from being implemented before they could harm minority voters. But because Congress understood that the preclearance mandate veered into the states' domain, Section 5 (unlike Section 2 and other parts of the act) required renewal at designated intervals to be certain that the federal oversight was still needed.

Attorney General Smith believed that all the states should be allowed to regulate their voting procedures without federal intervention under Section 5. As he insisted later, in his memoir, "We felt that the administrative and bureaucratic costs involved could be greatly reduced by eliminating approval requirements that no longer served any real purpose or could be handled by the states or localities." Preapproval was used mainly to prevent the formation of racially gerrymandered districts, or to block the use of strict voter-identification rules and other measures that hurt black representation. But Smith complained that the rule applied to "such changes as moving a voting booth from one location to another across the street."[19]

Congress was going in the opposite direction in 1981, seeking to bolster, not diminish, the reach of the Voting Rights Act. A bipartisan coalition of members was working on legislation that would renew Section 5 for twenty-five more years. In the same piece of legislation, members of Congress were also trying to restore the full force of Section 2's prohibition against discrimination by the states, which had been weakened by the 1980 Supreme Court decision in *City of Mobile v. Bolden*. In that case, the justices had ruled that the provision applied only when proof of intentional discrimination existed. The bipartisan group in Congress wanted to ensure that the Voting Rights Act covered any state action that had the *effect*, not just the proven *intention*, of diluting minority representation.[20]

The City of Mobile offered an example of what federal voting rights protections aimed to correct. In the 1970s, Mobile had been steeped in historical discrimination, with blacks underrepresented on all city boards, discriminated against in public hiring, and routinely subjected to police brutality. Cross burnings and mock lynchings were still common. No black person had ever won election to Mobile's city commission, even though African Americans made up one-third of the city's voters. Their lack of political power was rooted in its at-large election, which effectively allowed the white majority to choose all three commissioners. A group of black Mobile residents had challenged the existing "winner-take-all arrangement," contending they would not be able to elect their fair share of representatives until the city was divided into multiple single-member districts.

Citing the city's history of black disenfranchisement, a federal trial judge agreed with the challengers that the at-large election process unfairly diluted black electoral power. The US Court of Appeals for the Fifth Circuit affirmed, and the City of Mobile appealed. In the spring of 1980, the Supreme Court reversed the appeals court and sided with city officials. A majority of the justices, including Rehnquist, ruled that the black residents had failed to prove that the city's electoral arrangement intentionally discriminated against them. The Court declared that a government action could be deemed a violation of the right to vote "only if motivated by a discriminatory purpose." Thurgood Marshall, the nation's first black Supreme Court justice, was among the three dissenters. He said requiring proof of intentional discrimination would leave "the politically powerless with nothing more than the right to cast meaningless ballots."[21]

Most members of Congress had such concerns, and the bipartisan group of Senate and House members began drafting legislation that would let judges look beyond the question of whether an electoral practice reflected intentional bias to consider all the circumstances surrounding the practice and its effects on minority residents. Attorney General Smith's team, however, wanted the *Mobile* decision's narrowing of Section 2 to stand and opposed the proposed twenty-five-year extension of Section 5. Smith was aware that the civil rights community was vigorously working with Congress to shore up the Voting Rights Act. "It was raw politics at work," Smith later wrote, "and a classic example of special interests superseding the public interest." He added that "by the time the measure got to the House floor it had been packaged as a real 'motherhood' issue: protecting the right to vote."[22]

John Roberts understood the optics of fighting a "motherhood" issue. He tried to fortify Smith in a chain of memos he wrote to prepare the attorney general for dealing with other members of the administration and Congress who were not so opposed to a broad interpretation of the Voting Rights Act. "The President's position is politically saleable," Roberts insisted, "since the position is a positive one." Roberts urged Smith to be forceful about limits on the act: "This meeting presents an opportunity to solidify the Administration's position once and for all, to head off any retrenchment efforts, and to enlist the active support of the White House personnel for our position."[23]

In forceful terms, and with an eye to the administration's public message, Roberts reiterated that "the president's position is a very *positive* one and should be put in that light. He is for the Voting Rights Act and wants to see it extended. . . . What the President opposes is not the Voting Rights Act but rather efforts to introduce confusion and uncertainty by dramatically altering its terms." Roberts wanted it made clear that Reagan "opposes changing the law by introducing an effects test into Section 2 because this would throw into litigation existing electoral systems at every level of government nationwide when there is no evidence of voting abuses nationwide supporting the need for such change." Roberts also asserted that the "effects test" would create a right to a quota-like "proportional racial representation" on city councils and all forms of government.[24]

That contention was not true. Nor was it true that no evidence of voting rights abuse existed. Race discrimination in voting was still widely documented, particularly in southern states such as Alabama. Even so, Roberts urged an "aggressive stance" and suggested Smith tell people at the White House they should not be "fooled" by an overwhelming House vote on the bipartisan measure or a large number of Senate sponsors. He said "many members of the House" were not aware of the full scope of the legislation aimed at the two planks of the Voting Rights Act.

Roberts worked closely with William Bradford Reynolds, the assistant attorney general for the Civil Rights Division of the Department of Justice. Reynolds was attracting much of the criticism from observers who believed the administration was trying to undercut protections for racial minorities. But Roberts thought Reynolds was unnecessarily hedging on the administration's effort to build support for its opposition to the legislation on the Voting Rights Act. "Brad Reynolds has expressed some reservations about circulating *any* written statement on this [Section 2] question to the Hill, for fear that the statement would end up in the press and be subject to attack," Roberts wrote to Attorney General Smith. "My own view is that *something* must be done to educate the Senators on the seriousness of this problem, and that written statements should be avoided *only* if a thorough campaign of meetings is undertaken."[25]

A few weeks later, Roberts, who had just turned twenty-seven, took his concerns directly to Reynolds, who was thirteen years his senior, and implored, "I tend to think it is more important to get *something* out some-where soon than to fiddle much more with exactly what that something is going to be. The frequent writings in this area by our adversaries have gone unanswered for too long." Roberts demonstrated that he was keep-ing abreast of developments in the House and Senate as well as among administration figures and outside critics. He devoured the accounts in the news media and tried to plot out how Reagan administration aides could use the press to their best advantage.[26]

Reynolds and other Justice Department lawyers meanwhile were embroiled in a separate race-related battle. Soon after coming to of-fice, Reagan had tried to reverse an Internal Revenue Service policy that denied federal tax exemptions to racially discriminatory private schools. Bob Jones University, a Christian school based in Greenville, South Carolina, banned interracial dating and marriage. The IRS said the prohibition made the school ineligible for a federal tax exemption. Bob Jones University sued, and the Reagan administration urged the Supreme Court to side with the school, contending the IRS lacked au-thority to deny tax-exempt status unless Congress specifically ordered such a policy. The administration's move constituted a major rejection of long-standing IRS policy and contradicted its claims that it was neutral on racial issues.

In *Bob Jones University v. United States*, the Supreme Court ruled for the IRS by an 8–1 vote, with only Justice Rehnquist, Roberts's former boss, dissenting. Chief Justice Burger, who wrote for the majority, said the federal government should not encourage universities to continue discriminatory practices by giving them special tax status. "The Gov-ernment has a fundamental, overriding interest in eradicating racial dis-crimination in education—discrimination that prevailed, with official approval, for the first 165 years of this Nation's constitutional history. That governmental interest substantially outweighs whatever burden denial of tax benefits places on petitioners' exercise of their religious beliefs." In dissent, Rehnquist wrote, "I have no disagreement with the Court's finding that there is a strong national policy in this country op-posed to racial discrimination. I agree with the Court that Congress has the power to further this policy by denying [tax-exempt] status to organizations that practice racial discrimination. But as of yet, Congress has failed to do so. Whatever the reasons for the failure, this Court should not legislate for Congress."[27]

The nearly unanimous rejection, in an opinion by Nixon appointee Burger, of the Reagan position demonstrated how far to the right the administration was on race. When Attorney General Smith appeared before a Senate committee in January 1982 to lay out the administration's position on the renewal of the Voting Rights Act, the Supreme Court had not yet ruled in the *Bob Jones* case, but it was plain that Reagan was retrenching on government action against racial discrimination. Senator Ted Kennedy, a Democrat from Massachusetts, questioned Reagan's true commitment to minorities. When Smith answered, "The President doesn't have a discriminatory bone in his body," the audience erupted in laughter, according to a *New York Times* report reflecting the fractious atmosphere of the day. (Roberts had not participated in the Bob Jones litigation.)[28]

Roberts believed the Reagan administration's position on voting rights was being mischaracterized in the press. But the Reagan approach would have retreated on voter protections. Roberts was furious when Samuel Pierce, the secretary for the Department of Housing and Urban Development (HUD) and the only black Cabinet member, publicly criticized the proposals that Smith and his team had made. The *Washington Post* quoted Pierce as saying he favored the congressional measure: "The Smith alternative," Pierce explained, would "cut the very heart out of the Voting Rights Act." On a copy of the newspaper article, Roberts scrawled, "Is there anything we can do about Pierce's outrageous statement?" Roberts volunteered to draft a letter on behalf of Attorney General Smith to Pierce, and a letter soon went out to the HUD secretary questioning the basis for his statement criticizing the Reagan proposal to alter voting rights legislation.[29]

In the end, Congress passed a twenty-five-year extension of the Voting Rights Act's Section 5 and, separately, in response to the Supreme Court's *Mobile* decision, established that citizens challenging election rules as discriminatory need not prove that officials acted with intentional bias. The legislation allowed federal judges to consider the "totality" of the circumstances surrounding an election to determine whether minorities were denied an equal opportunity to participate.[30]

THE VOTING RIGHTS BATTLE WAS JUST ONE OF MANY RACIALLY charged fights that Roberts joined. With Carolyn Kuhl, another special assistant to the attorney general, Roberts expressed dismay when the Supreme Court ruled that the State of Texas could not deny immigrant children who were in the United States illegally a free public education, based on the Fourteenth Amendment's equality guarantee. Justice William Brennan had pulled out a narrow victory in the June 1982 case of *Plyler v. Doe*, with the fifth vote coming from Lewis Powell, to require Texas to accept children without proper documentation into its public schools.[31]

US Solicitor General Rex Lee, the federal government's top appellate lawyer and the person who argued for the government at the Supreme Court, had not intervened in the case. A Mormon who had been the founding dean of Brigham Young University Law School, Lee constantly struggled for independence from the politics within the Reagan administration. In *Plyler*, Roberts believed Lee should have supported the Texas position against the Latino families that had sued. "The briefs for the State of Texas were quite poor," he and Kuhl told Attorney General Smith in a memo. "It is our belief that a brief filed by the Solicitor General's Office supporting the State of Texas—and the values of judicial restraint—could well have moved Justice Powell into the Chief Justice's camp and altered the outcome of the case. In sum, this is a case in which our supposed litigation program to encourage judicial restraint did not get off the ground, and should have."[32]

Roberts did not leave it there. The next day, he sent a second, more accusatory note to Smith asserting that the solicitor general was "not sufficiently sensitive to the policy views" of the Department of Justice's Civil Rights Division. Roberts told Smith that Lee's office had been presenting arguments to the Supreme Court that "were totally inconsistent not only with general Administration policies but with specific and announced priorities of your own." Roberts recommended that Smith tell Lee to advise and coordinate his positions with the Civil Rights Division, where Reynolds was at the helm.[33]

Though Roberts wanted the administration's muscle in *Plyler v. Doe*, it is unlikely that it would have made a difference at the high court. Correspondence from Justice Powell's files shows that he was with Justice Brennan on the judgment against Texas from the start. The tricky part for Brennan in the case was a rationale for constitutional equality in education that would satisfy Justice Powell, a moderate conservative. "Public education is not a 'right' granted to individuals by the Constitution," Brennan's final opinion said. "But neither is it merely some government 'benefit' indistinguishable from other forms of social welfare legislation. Both the importance of education in maintaining our basic institutions, and the lasting impact of its deprivation on the life of the child, mark the distinction." As the Court had in *Brown* almost three decades earlier, the Brennan majority highlighted the importance of education for a child's future.[34]

Solicitor General Lee complained that the White House agenda was an "albatross" around his neck. When he resigned at the end of Reagan's first term, he declared, "There has been a notion that my job is to press the Administration's policies at every turn and announce true conservative principles through the pages of my briefs. It is not. I am the Solicitor General, not the Pamphleteer General."[35]

The Reagan administration eventually found a way to make sure the solicitor general tracked an administration's goals more closely. A "political deputy" position was created, and the individual filling that number-two slot was expected to help ensure that the administration's legal priorities were being executed.

J. Harvie Wilkinson III, who worked in the Civil Rights Division and later became a respected federal appeals court judge, recalled that the Reagan view on race especially challenged the established consensus and that there was constant internal debate. "If I had one discussion on this with the career attorneys, I had a hundred," he said. Wilkinson's views aligned with Roberts's in that they both believed that the Fourteenth Amendment's equal protection clause meant that race should not matter. "The wording of the Fourteenth Amendment is so crystal clear: an indivisible dignity that attaches to every citizen," Wilkinson said. "Government has to respect that individual dignity." Yet the prevailing view of the Fourteenth Amendment's guarantee of equal protection, upheld by the Supreme Court, distinguished between laws that used racial classifications to harm blacks, Latinos, and other minorities and those that used race to benefit minorities. The Court allowed government to give a boost to racial minorities to remedy past discrimination and achieve racial diversity in government contracting, in the workplace, and in education.[36]

Wilkinson remembered regular meetings with fellow political appointees in the Department of Justice and the Old Executive Office Building, where Roberts also worked. "We wanted to coordinate with each other and have working groups so the Justice Department was aware of what the White House was doing," Wilkinson said. "There was a feeling that the bureaucracy might not be sympathetic to what President Reagan wanted to accomplish, so the idea was that we would maintain our esprit by having meetings of eight or nine or ten of us to go over these things, to remind ourselves why we were there. And John was a very important part of those groups. He was thoughtful and he would contribute good ideas."[37]

Roberts was eleven years younger than Wilkinson yet regarded "as a peer" because of his experience, notably his time clerking for Justice Rehnquist. Ken Starr recalled Roberts, whose youthfulness could not be obscured by his dark-framed glasses, as a lawyer who performed "at top levels." He remembered asking Roberts to prepare arguments regarding the constitutionality of legislation that would prevent the Supreme Court from ruling on abortion, busing, and school prayer—areas that Reagan believed were best left to elected officials. The prevailing view inside the department at the time, however, deemed such "court stripping" unconstitutional. That assessment, to which Starr asked Roberts to respond, had been established by Assistant Attorney General Theodore Olson, who oversaw the Office of Legal Counsel and was in charge of constitutional review of administration positions. Roberts prepared a comprehensive set of arguments asserting that Congress could change the Supreme Court's authority over such issues as abortion. Of Roberts, Starr said, "That was a break-out time for him, for showing the senior leadership of the department what he could do, since it was such a pressing issue."[38]

Outside advocates worried that such "court stripping" would leave racial and religious minorities unprotected. The American Jewish Committee wanted to meet with Attorney General Smith to express opposition to simmering Department of Justice proposals to end federal court power to rule on questions of prayer in public schools. Roberts drafted a response for Smith and asked, "Is this draft response OK . . . i.e., does it succeed in saying nothing at all?"[39]

Roberts developed "talking points" for multiple issues. When Smith was about to meet with Coretta Scott King, the widow of Martin Luther King Jr., about funding for the King Center in Atlanta, Roberts advised Smith to indicate support, but if pressed for additional federal money, to say it was not available.[40]

The Justice Department's political squad tangled regularly with the department's career lawyers, the people who worked at the agency through Democratic and Republican administrations. But Roberts and the other political appointees also had to worry about mixed messages that the president himself was sending to the public—with regard to *United Steelworkers of America v. Weber*, for instance, in which the Supreme Court had rejected a challenge brought by white steelworker Brian Weber against a race-based plan adopted by Kaiser Aluminum and the United Steelworkers of America. At a Reagan news conference, a reporter referred to the *Weber* decision and asked the president whether he supported affirmative action in the steel industry. Reagan said he was not familiar with the *Weber* case, but that he believed programs that provided training and "more opportunities in . . . voluntary agreement" were permissible. "I can't see any fault with that. I'm for that." Reporters seized on that apparent contradiction: Reagan was accepting voluntary affirmative action plans, but his Justice Department opposed any such use of racial classifications.[41]

It fell to Roberts to prepare materials explaining how the president's statements were consistent with the DOJ position. "The Department does not," he wrote, "support quotas or any other type of preference based on race or sex for those who have not been proven to be victims of specific acts of illegal discrimination." Roberts insisted that Reagan "can stand by his press-conference response [by] noting that he was referring to the type of affirmative action which the Department accepts, i.e., increased recruitment efforts and the like. His interrogator withheld from the President the fact that a rigid racial quota was endorsed in *Weber* and thus the President did not address this dimension of the *Weber* decision." Roberts favorably quoted Justice Rehnquist's dissent regarding the "destructive" nature of quotas: "Whether described as 'benign discrimination' or 'affirmative action,' the racial quota is nonetheless a creator of castes, a two-edged sword that must demean one in order to prefer another."[42]

Roberts remained in the background of the Reagan administration's policies, while Attorney General Smith and the Civil Rights Division chief, Reynolds, found themselves on the front pages. Still, Roberts had a keen understanding of the news media. He also realized that some members of the administration were intimidated by public criticism from the American Bar Association and prominent members of the legal establishment. "Real courage would be to read the Constitution as it should be read," he wrote on a 1982 memo that crossed his desk, "and not kowtow to the Tribes, Lewises and Brinks." He was referring to the liberal Harvard law professor Laurence Tribe, the *New York Times* columnist Anthony Lewis, and the American Bar Association president David R. Brink. Years later, Roberts praised Reagan's persistence in the face of "a great deal of criticism and mockery in the media." "He was not going to cave in," Roberts said. "He was going to have the courage of his convictions."[43]

Central to the Reagan revolution was the selection of federal judges appointed to the bench for life who would be conservative. Roberts sometimes assisted in the vetting of candidates. "There was a great deal of attention paid to the selection of judges," recalled Wilkinson. "Number one, there was a very clear directive that younger people were to be chosen; number two, that academics were to be chosen. Reagan was pilloried for not being an intellectual. But he believed strongly in the power of ideas.

That's why you got [Richard] Posner, [Robert] Bork, [Antonin] Scalia . . . and many others." Wilkinson himself was appointed to a US appeals court during Reagan's second term in office.[44]

Roberts later observed that Reagan demonstrated his interest in judicial appointments by personally reaching out to nominees. "He instituted the practice," Roberts said, "of calling nominees to the federal bench. It hadn't been done before. He called every one of them" upon appointment. Reagan had run in 1980 on a platform that included the nomination of Supreme Court justices who would "respect traditional family values and the sanctity of innocent human life," that is, oppose abortion rights. Presidents George H.W. Bush, George W. Bush, and Donald Trump would follow Reagan's model on social issues and judicial choices.[45]

During his time in the Reagan administration, Roberts shared an apartment in a Capitol Hill row house at Sixth Street and North Carolina Avenue Southeast with his old law school classmate Richard Lazarus. "We gravitated toward each other because we were from the Midwest," recalled Lazarus, who grew up in the university town of Urbana, Illinois, where his father was a physics professor. "Neither one of us was the most social person in the whole world. We were workers. We were not party animals." They played squash when they had time, watched sports on TV, and picked up pizza at the end of a long day. Roberts's younger sisters Barb and Peg lived nearby in Maryland and would drop by to straighten up the apartment, Lazarus said. "They doted on their brother," he remarked. "There was no question about it." Lazarus chalked up Roberts's excitement for Reagan partly to his experience on the "fringe" during his Harvard student days.[46]

By late 1982, White House counsel Fred Fielding had noticed Roberts's work at the Department of Justice and wanted him on his team at the counsel's office. Fielding had been a deputy to the White House counsel John Dean in the Nixon years, and he was an astute operator. He had avoided any entanglement in Watergate and the other Nixon scandals, and he was now overseeing a group of about a dozen lawyers responsible for examining administration proposals and Reagan communications to ensure there were no conflicts of interest or legal complications.

It was easy for Roberts to say yes to Fielding, and Starr congratulated him on the move to the influential White House counsel section: "Hope you're having fun there on the fast track," Starr wrote in a letter that included a signed photo of William French Smith. "Your friends back here in the quiet of the Department miss you badly." Roberts understood that Fielding, and his deputy Richard Hauser, who was also an old hand from the Nixon administration, had brought together an elite team of hard-hitting lawyers. Some of them, including Roberts and J. Michael Luttig, who would become a close friend, and later a rival, were in their twenties. Others were more experienced, such as H. Lawrence Garrett III, a decorated Vietnam veteran.[47]

Beyond the intellectual stimulation and a sense of mission, Roberts's new colleagues offered him another clubby world of pranks, nicknames, golf outings, and Christmas revelry, all of which would last long after they all went their separate ways. The camaraderie was evident on Roberts's first day at work. He was sitting at his desk when the telephone rang and a White House operator asked if he could hold for President Reagan. "Well, yes, I could," Roberts recalled saying. Minutes went by and Roberts dutifully held the line. A coworker poked his head into Roberts's office, but Roberts waved him off, mouthing that he was waiting for the president. Roberts then heard laughter outside his door. He realized his new colleagues had made the prank call. In fact, they had placed bets on how long he would remain on hold. "Whoever had the 15 to 20 minute slot won the money," Roberts later said.[48]

Fueled by donuts and candy, Roberts and the other lawyers undertook assignments ranging from the humdrum (stopping commercial establishments from using the presidential seal) to the urgent (what to say after the *Challenger* space shuttle exploded). "Sometimes, I worked on some petty problems, such as people using the president's name to sell their jelly beans," Roberts recalled. "I guess it was a mix of the momentous and the ridiculous." Most days, the work fell somewhere in the middle.[49]

At one point, the White House counsel's group received a recommendation from the deputy chief of staff's office that Reagan call Justice O'Connor about an opinion she had written. Aides wanted Reagan to commend her for her "wisdom, compassion, and courage" when she dissented from a majority opinion striking down an Ohio abortion regulation. Fielding immediately responded that the staff must "urge in the strongest possible terms that no such telephone call be made."[50]

"As a strictly followed rule that is but one aspect of the fundamental Constitutional doctrine of Separation of Powers," Fielding wrote, "Presidents *never* discuss with sitting Supreme Court Justices or other members of the Federal Judiciary their decisions in individual cases. I can think of no circumstances that would justify an exception to this rule. Such a call would be widely and accurately portrayed as, at a minimum, unseemly and inappropriate." Fielding noted the dilemma it could create for the justice, observing, "It would also place Justice O'Connor in an untenable and uncomfortable position, and even compromise her ability to participate in future decisions in this area without questions being raised about the independence and integrity of her opinions. She would be justified in terminating the conversation once the subject matter became clear, and might well do so." Fielding further noted that close relations between justices and presidents had been criticized in the past, including those between Franklin Roosevelt and Felix Frankfurter, between Lyndon Johnson and Abe Fortas, and between Richard Nixon and Warren Burger.

Roberts worked seventy to eighty hours a week, earning an annual salary of $54,000. "He looked like a choir boy, but had a wicked sense of humor," said Fielding. He thought Roberts's ideological commitment had been shaped by his youth in Indiana, by his family, and by his Catholicism. "It wasn't something that he just picked up to be fashionable," Fielding said. "It's what he believed. He has been very consistent." Fielding directed to Roberts matters involving race or the limits of the courts' jurisdiction over social issues. "There was a comfort level when he was sending stuff to me. Everybody thought: no one will read these," Fielding said, adding of Robert's memos, "They always had a smart-assed twist to them." Fielding enjoyed Roberts's sly humor.[51]

Richard Hauser, Fielding's deputy, was skilled at fostering loyalty within the counsel's office. He often took the young lawyers out for burgers. They celebrated birthdays and other personal milestones, sometimes with Hauser documenting the event with his handheld video recorder. They golfed together. They all had nicknames. Roberts was "Owl," because of his dark-framed eyeglasses, Hauser said. He noted that Roberts's first draft of a letter that would go out from the office was typically as good as the last drafts of other lawyers. Referring to Roberts's steel-trap memory, he said, "I don't think John's ever forgotten a fact."[52]

Roberts became especially close to Luttig, who was just a few months older and had also served in the Department of Justice. Luttig had grown up in Tyler, Texas. The son of an oil executive, he had attended Washington and Lee and then the University of Virginia Law School. He had clerked for Judge Antonin Scalia, who was then on the DC Circuit, and later for Chief Justice Warren Burger. Luttig recalled long dinners with Roberts and plenty of verbal sparring. "When he comes to a conclusion on the law," Luttig said, "he has you nine ways to Sunday if you're going to take a different view."[53]

In how they presented themselves to the world, they were opposites. Luttig, with a Texas twang and outsized personality, was as brash as Roberts was reserved. Luttig was elbows-out, Roberts elbows-in. Yet Roberts had an edgier side that emerged in the private memoranda he wrote while in the counsel's office. When Bob Jones III, president of Bob Jones University, was pressing the Reagan lawyers to intervene on a minister's immigration application, and attributing the White House's reluctance to its insensitivity "to the interests of Fundamental Christians who put Mr. Reagan there," Roberts wrote to Fielding: "The audacity of Jones' reply is truly remarkable, given the political costs this Administration has incurred in promoting the interests of Fundamental Christians in general and Bob Jones University in particular. A restrained reply to his petulant paranoia is attached for your review, telling Jones, in essence, to go soak his head."[54]

Roberts's memos also revealed his sarcastic bent. He ridiculed a proposal by three women members of Congress for legislation that would have allowed equal pay for comparable work based on factors such as skills and responsibility. Writing to Fielding, Roberts said the women contended "that more is required because women still earn only $0.60 for every $1 earned by men, ignoring the factors that explain that apparent disparity, such as seniority, the fact that many women frequently leave the workforce for extended periods of time." Roberts then added, "I honestly find it troubling that three Republican representatives are so quick to embrace such a radical redistributive concept. Their slogan may as well be, 'From each according to his ability, to each according to her gender.'"[55]

Referring to Congressman Leo Ryan, a California Democrat who had been shot to death while visiting the "Peoples Temple" settlement in Jonestown, Guyana, Roberts wrote, regarding a bill to honor him, "I am not certain I would have voted to give a gold medal to Ryan. The distinction of his service in the House is certainly subject to debate, and his actions leading to his murder can be viewed as those of a publicity hound. Nonetheless, I see no legal objection to the President signing this bill." More than nine hundred people in the Guyana settlement, many of them from California, ended up drinking poison the day after the shooting. Relatives of some of the cult members had asked Ryan to investigate to determine whether their leader, Jim Jones, was keeping them against their will. The mass suicide was carried out with a flavored drink and gave rise to the expression "drinking the Kool-Aid."[56]

Roberts communicated regularly with Judge Friendly, sometimes revealing his cynicism about the ways of Washington. In one instance, he criticized Chief Justice Burger's proposal for a new inter-circuit federal panel to assist with the burgeoning federal appeals. "In confidence," Roberts wrote to Friendly, "our office is fighting the good fight against it, and has delayed Administration support for almost a year, but we cannot hold out much longer against the combined assault of the Chief, Congressional leaders, and—at Professor [Paul] Bator's urging—our own Justice Department. Our only hope is that Congress will continue to do what it does best—nothing." Congress never approved the proposal.[57]

Roberts continued in his correspondence with Friendly to reiterate his criticism of Burger's proposal to set up a new intermediate tribunal below the Supreme Court. Roberts had earlier mocked Supreme Court justices' complaints about their large caseload, which, with 150 rulings issued, was about twice what it is today. "While some of the tales of woe emanating from the Court are enough to bring tears to the eyes," Roberts wrote, "it is true that only Supreme Court Justices and school children are expected to and do take the entire summer off."[58]

Some of his friends were startled later by the rigid views revealed in the memos, as well as by the sarcastic tone, when the documents were released in 2005. But not Lazarus, who had known Roberts since 1976. "I was not surprised at how conservative the memos showed him to be," Lazarus said. The "seeds" of Roberts's ideology had been planted before Roberts's time with Reagan, he added, and yet he thought there was "no question that those years fertilized them."[59]

Defending his friend's missives, Lazarus attributed the tone to the culture within the White House. "I've seen these cultures develop in offices," he said, responding to a question about the snarky remarks. "John Roberts does not strike me as someone who instigates snark, but if that's the way they're all talking to each other, it would not surprise me that he would not push himself aside from it. But I doubt that he instigated it. And my guess is that he was pretty good at it."[60]

In April 1986, Fielding decided to return to private law practice, and Roberts chose to move on from his associate counsel position. "As a lawyer it was a source of great satisfaction to serve a President who appreciated the Framers' vision of a limited Federal government of laws, not men," Roberts wrote in his resignation letter to Reagan. "As an American it was a source of pride to serve a President who recognized America's historic mission of safeguarding and promoting the cause of freedom throughout the world. I know you receive many letters like this, and I recognize that over time they must come to seem fairly routine. Please understand, however, that my years in your service will always be very special to me. The inspiration you have given me will burn brightly in my heart long after I have left the lights of the White House behind."[61]

"Dear John," President Reagan responded five days later, "Your April 10 letter was a far cry from 'routine'; indeed, it was heartfelt and leaves me with both regret in losing your talents and pride in your service to my Administration. You have served with exceptional integrity and devotion in a capacity that calls individuals of the highest calibre. It is people like you whom I proudly refer to as 'members of the team.'"[62]

The five years that Roberts devoted to Reagan ignited a quiet passion in him and clarified his ideological views. Equally important, the experience offered Roberts soulmates. The men of the White House counsel's office continued to golf together. They held reunion dinners and shared Christmas celebrations. When Roberts, a longtime bachelor, finally got married, he asked Michael Luttig to be a groomsman.

Roberts would return to the White House with subsequent Republican administrations. As he rose in Washington, Starr and Fielding would remain allies. But his relationship with Luttig would take a different turn.

CHAPTER IV

"MAY IT PLEASE THE COURT"

WHEN JOHN ROBERTS ARGUED FOR THE FIRST TIME BEFORE the Supreme Court, on January 17, 1989, William Rehnquist occupied the center chair on the bench. Two and a half years earlier, President Ronald Reagan had elevated Rehnquist to chief justice. The president's legal team had been impressed by Rehnquist's doctrinaire conservatism and role in moving the Court to the right. As other Republican appointees had joined the bench, the onetime "Lone Ranger" was no longer alone. Now, in the 1988–1989 session, the Court was in the middle of a watershed term, rolling back liberal decisions that had expanded constitutional rights regarding such issues as access to abortion, job discrimination, affirmative action, and capital punishment. The justices were less than a week away from handing down a decision in *Richmond v. Croson*, rejecting a remedial program in Richmond, Virginia, that had set aside 30 percent of the city's construction contract funds for minority-owned companies. That and other rulings coming during this session would make it harder for minority workers to obtain preferences or prove job bias and easier for whites to challenge affirmative action.[1]

Reagan was leaving office. A few days after Roberts appeared before the Court, Vice President George H.W. Bush, who had won the November 1988 election, would be inaugurated as the nation's next president. On an unusually mild January morning, as Roberts headed to the Court for his first argument, preparations were under way for the ceremony at the Capitol Building across the street. Bush's victory over the Democratic candidate, Michael Dukakis, a former Massachusetts governor, ensured the continuation of Reagan's conservative agenda.

Roberts, just days from turning thirty-four, was in private practice at the law firm of Hogan and Hartson. With Bush's victory, he had a chance to return to the executive branch. At the moment, however, he was immersed in his case, and naturally he was nervous about how it would go. He had long aspired to appear before the nine justices. His connection to Rehnquist had brought him the opportunity to argue pro bono for a man who lacked a lawyer. In *United States v. Halper*, the chief justice had chosen Roberts to represent a New Yorker convicted of defrauding the government by seeking Medicare reimbursement for nursing care at a higher rate than was allowed.[2]

The defendant, Irwin Halper, a medical services provider, had been fined $5,000 and sentenced to two years in prison. On top of that, the government had levied a civil penalty of $130,000 to recoup the cost of its investigation and prosecution of Halper. Halper had challenged that award as a violation of the Constitution's guarantee against double jeopardy, arguing that the six-figure penalty constituted a second punishment. A district court judge had ruled for Halper after estimating that the government's investigation had cost only about $16,000. The question on appeal was whether the double jeopardy bar on successive punishments applied to civil penalties, like those imposed on Halper, as it did in criminal cases.[3]

"Mr. Roberts, we'll hear from you now," Rehnquist said, summoning the young lawyer to the lectern in a gravelly voice inflected by his Wisconsin roots and decades of cigarette smoking.[4]

Roberts's opening words, also suggesting his origins in the Upper Midwest but distinct and clear, were direct. "After punishing Mr. Halper with two years in prison and a $5,000 fine for his $585 in false claims," Roberts told the justices, "the government brought a second proceeding against him seeking $130,000 penalty for those same false claims."

Byron White was one of the first justices to interrupt Roberts and express skepticism for his argument that the government was not justified in trying to recoup $130,000 for the cost of investigation and prosecution. Appointed to the Supreme Court in 1962 by President John F. Kennedy, White was a terse, demanding jurist who dug into the facts of a case. He asked Roberts how much time the Department of Justice had put into Halper's prosecution, perhaps wondering if an extensive inquiry had led to the high civil penalty. He questioned why a judge would have put forth a $16,000 price tag.

"I can't imagine that it only cost the federal government $16,000 to prosecute the criminal case," White said.

"Well, this was actually a fairly easy case," Roberts said. "This is not a complicated fraud."

"I suppose it started in another department," White said. "Somebody turned it over to Justice, didn't they? . . . Wasn't it referred to Justice by somebody?"

"I'm not aware that it was," Roberts answered. "It could have been from a Medicare fraud unit or something."

"I suppose it would, wouldn't you?" White said.

"If it had been, I would suppose that would reduce even further the costs of investigation and prosecution," Roberts posited.

"I don't know," White said. "It might increase it."

White then asked about the progression of the original criminal case. "Did the government have to go before a judge during the grand jury proceeding for some rulings or not?"

"I'm not sure," Roberts said. "I don't believe so."

If Roberts was flustered, his voice did not reveal it. He rode out the questioning and focused on his core argument: that no matter what resources the government had required, the cost did not reach $130,000. The government may seek compensation, Roberts said, but the amount had to be tied to the costs.

Roberts remained composed throughout his allotted thirty minutes at the lectern and as a government lawyer made his counterarguments. Roberts later admitted that he often feared reading the transcripts from any of his arguments, lest he become absorbed in what went wrong. Even after he became a regular advocate before the justices, representing multiple clients, and with dozens of notches in his belt, Roberts would concentrate to subdue his shaking hands before he presented a case. Once on his feet, grasping the sides of the lectern, he could keep his nerves in check. He presented the picture of calm.[5]

"The case is submitted," Chief Justice Rehnquist said as he brought the hearing to an end with the traditional closing.

Four months later, the justices handed down their opinion in *United States v. Halper*. Roberts had won. The Supreme Court said the Constitution's double jeopardy clause prevented the government from seeking a civil penalty unrelated to the actual loss. Justice Harry A. Blackmun, who wrote the opinion for the Court, referred to Halper as "a prolific but small-gauge offender," noting that the penalty was "overwhelmingly disproportionate to the damages he has caused." The decision was unanimous. Roberts was proud of the win and told the *Legal Times*, a Washington, DC, newspaper, that the ruling would force prosecutors to alter their strategy when adding fines to defendants in civil actions.[6]

THREE YEARS EARLIER, AFTER DECIDING TO LEAVE THE WHITE House counsel's office, Roberts had begun building a specialized appellate practice. The move would lead to a lucrative professional career, distinguish him as a lawyer, and eventually offer him a way to stand out from other Supreme Court candidates. This kind of legal work, requiring the skillful use of paper records and court precedents, was more intellectual than dramatic. Unlike trial lawyers, who typically perform before twelve jurors selected from the community where the litigants reside, appellate lawyers argue before a panel of judges who review cases not so much for

their facts as for whether the Constitution or applicable statutes were followed at a prior trial.

Appellate lawyers needed to know relevant case precedents and be
ready to respond to hypothetical questions. The regional circuit courts of
appeals and the US Supreme Court strive for consistency among multiple cases and across geographic regions. Judges want to hear arguments
that are concise, yet comprehensive enough to inform standards for future
cases. In the 1980s, there was new demand within law firms for appellate specialists. Big litigation firms wanted to be full-service operations
that were ready to represent a client in-house if a lawsuit went up to the
Supreme Court, or even to the important second-tier appeals court level.
The prominence of an argument before the justices typically brought the
kind of news media attention to a lawyer that could generate publicity for
a firm, help with recruiting, and spur more business.

For their part, the justices appreciated appellate attorneys who could
lucidly present the law both in briefs and at the lectern; seasoned advocates helped them understand the legal issues at the core of a case. Roberts, with his deep, methodical research and direct, unadorned rhetoric,
was especially adept at this.[7]

Like Roberts, many of the lawyers drawn to this type of practice had
been judicial law clerks. E. Barrett Prettyman, for whom Roberts initially
worked at the firm of Hogan and Hartson after he left the White House
in 1986, had served as a law clerk to three Supreme Court justices. That
was thought to be a record. Prettyman was the son of a prominent federal
appeals court judge in Washington, DC, and had worked for Attorney
General Robert F. Kennedy in the early 1960s.[8]

Another leader in 1980s appellate advocacy was Rex Lee, the first US
solicitor general under Reagan, who had joined the firm of Sidley and
Austin and quickly racked up multiple corporate cases before the Supreme Court. Other attorneys from Reagan's solicitor general's office also
worked for major firms after Reagan left office, and they created a tight-
knit cadre of appellate lawyers who competed with each other but also
formed a guild of their own.

Serving in the solicitor general's office, which participated in dozens of Supreme Court cases each term, was the best way to enhance an appellate career. That's where Roberts, in fact, wanted to be in early 1989. A specialized division of the Justice Department, the "SG's office," as it was called, oversaw all government appeals to the Supreme Court. That meant that when the federal government lost a case in a lower appeals court, the SG's office decided whether it warranted a petition to the nine justices. The SG and his assistants considered what arguments might be most persuasive to get a petition accepted, and ultimately, for it to prevail on the merits.

The Supreme Court has nearly complete discretion over which cases it accepts for review, and the justices take up less than 1 percent of the petitions submitted. They mainly look for conflicting lower court rulings and disputes of truly national importance. In a sign of the Court's long-standing regard for the SG's office, the Court grants most of its petitions. The Court often requests the SG's views even in cases in which the federal government is not one of the main parties. As a result, the solicitor general position has sometimes been described as the "tenth justice," or "handmaiden to the Court."

In the late 1980s, the SG's office was composed mostly of men who donned gray morning coats and striped pants when they appeared before the justices. All but two of the lawyers in the office were career staff. The two political appointees who served for a president's four-year term were the solicitor general and his influential political deputy. The latter position had been created when Roberts worked in the Reagan White House. Administration lawyers were concerned that the president's litigation agenda was not being carried out across all departments, and Roberts was one of the lawyers who believed that then solicitor general Lee was insufficiently committed to the administration's conservative social mandate.[9]

Now Roberts wanted this political deputy job.

President George H.W. Bush had enticed Ken Starr, Roberts's first boss and ally in Reagan's Department of Justice, to take the top solicitor general post. At the time, Starr was serving on the US Court of Appeals for the DC Circuit, having been appointed to the bench by Reagan in

1983. Starr was initially reluctant to relinquish the life-tenured judgeship for the limited-term SG post. "I was just hitting my stride and finding it very satisfying," Starr recalled.[10]

But the SG position was attractive in other ways. The SG, aside from being able to stand before the Court on behalf of the federal government, was on the inside and often consulted regarding major administration policy. Starr would be close to the center of power should a seat on the Supreme Court open. A former clerk to Chief Justice Burger, Starr exuded a polished, quiet demeanor that at the time suggested he would avoid controversy and remain well positioned for a Supreme Court nomination. (Starr's involvement in the Whitewater and Monica Lewinsky investigations during the Clinton presidency in the 1990s would change his reputation. Even before that, interoffice rivalries would foreclose a Supreme Court possibility.)

Once Starr agreed to take the position, he needed a political deputy. In his application, Roberts responded to a question about why he wanted the job with just four words: "To serve my country." Roberts noted that he had contributed money and provided "opposition research," as he described it, for the executive campaign committee of Bush and running mate Dan Quayle, a native of Roberts's home state of Indiana.[11] Beyond the written application, Roberts had made clear to Starr, whom he had known since 1981, that he understood what the position required and could rise to the task.

Roberts was among the youngest, least experienced attorneys in the running. "The biggest factor weighing against him was his age," Starr said. But in his earlier time in the Reagan White House, Roberts had proven he could navigate the politics of the executive branch. "The Bush administration might have been kinder, gentler, but there were no policy breaks," Starr said. "I felt that his experience was good for the political deputy position. He was a steady hand, a wise hand. He came in as a person not of vast experience but of vast ability."[12]

When Starr hired Roberts, he immediately raised Roberts's visibility among powerful conservatives. As Roberts took the lead in staking out contentious positions, he also found a new set of liberal critics. His work on behalf of the Reagan administration had been held confidential. He had been a backstage player, feeding advice to William French Smith, William Bradford Reynolds, and Fred Fielding. With his appointment by Starr, he suddenly became a lead signature on filings and the public face at the Court's lectern and in the media.

His new annual salary was $132,000, not as much as he had made in private practice, but still notable in 1989. (In 2018 dollars, it was the equivalent of $260,000.) Just before he took the job, Roberts moved into a handsome brick colonial in Bethesda, Maryland, on Cromwell Street. He golfed regularly. He dated, but not seriously enough to consider marriage, and he still socialized with the old gang from Fielding's White House counsel's office. They vacationed in Miami, playing golf and meeting for steak dinners. Former deputy counsel Richard Hauser said Roberts could consume the largest prime rib a restaurant had to offer.[13]

As Roberts advanced in the new Bush administration, so did other colleagues from the Reagan years. Michael Luttig landed a spot in the Justice Department's Office of Legal Counsel, first as a deputy and then as its director. The office's lawyers assessed the constitutionality of executive branch orders as they were developed, and it rivaled the SG's office for prestige. William Rehnquist and Antonin Scalia had run the Office of Legal Counsel earlier in their careers.

The friendship between Roberts and Luttig deepened, and Roberts often joined Luttig and his wife, Elizabeth, for dinner. Luttig aspired to a federal judgeship. Roberts was beginning to think along those lines, too. Their former Department of Justice colleague J. Harvie Wilkinson, who was older than Roberts and Luttig by a decade, had already been named to the federal bench. Wilkinson was proving himself a serious conservative thinker. He was already on media "short lists" of possible appointees to the Supreme Court.

AS THE DEPUTY SOLICITOR GENERAL, ROBERTS WORKED ON MANY of the same issues that had engaged—and excited—him during his time in the Reagan administration. Almost immediately after getting the job, he developed arguments against government policies that gave a boost to blacks, Hispanics, and other minorities. He rejected group-based remedies and believed that individuals who faced bias should be able to sue only for specific instances of discrimination.

Roberts took charge of a case that allowed him to argue against Federal Communications Commission (FCC) policies intended to increase the minority ownership of broadcast licenses through racial preferences. His approach meant abandoning the FCC and rejecting prior arguments to diversify broadcast licenses, but it would fulfill one of Reagan's goals. In the mid-1980s, Reagan had wanted to dismantle the FCC's racial preferences, but Congress had blocked the effort by prohibiting the FCC from spending appropriated funds to reconsider its preference policies.

The policies traced to the 1970s and were intended to address a lack of diversity in television programming. The FCC decided that as it assessed bids for new broadcast licenses, it would factor in race and gender issues alongside standard considerations such as a station owner's participation in civic activities and his or her broadcast experience. The FCC granted a "plus factor" to women and to owners who were black, Hispanic, American Eskimo, or American Indian.

The Supreme Court dispute began after the FCC assigned a television channel in Orlando, Florida, to Rainbow Broadcasting, whose ownership was 90 percent Hispanic. White-owned broadcasting companies challenged the FCC's decision, arguing that any preference based on sex or race violated the constitutional guarantee of equal protection of the law. The US Court of Appeals for the DC Circuit upheld the FCC's policy and the selection of Rainbow Broadcasting, finding that minority status was but one factor considered by the commission and therefore did not violate the Constitution's guarantee of equal protection.

This case became known as *Metro Broadcasting, Inc., v. Federal Communications Commission* when it went to the Supreme Court for review. Ken Starr, who had just left his position on the DC Circuit, recused himself, and thus Roberts took the helm, arguing that the preferences were unconstitutional. His decision to break from the FCC marked a sharp departure from the usual SG practice of defending a government policy if any reasonable argument could be made for it. Traditionally, the SG helped maintain the federal government's unified front. It was extraordinary for the solicitor general's office, even a new one, to argue that a federal agency's policy was unconstitutional. Roberts's position stunned some career lawyers in the office and became a topic of enduring interest among civil rights advocates, legal analysts, and law professors, who debated whether the move overly politicized the office.

Roberts believed that the Supreme Court, having shifted to the right, would welcome his arguments. He anchored his *Metro Broadcasting* brief in the Supreme Court's January 1989 ruling in *Richmond v. Croson*, a decision handed down around the time of Roberts's first argument before the justices in *Halper*. In the *Richmond v. Croson* case, the Court had rejected a municipal set-aside program intended to enhance opportunities for black and other minority contractors. That decision imposed the strictest judicial test for policies based on race, essentially shutting down such city and county programs. Thurgood Marshall, in his dissent, chastised his colleagues in the majority for rejecting the set-aside program, which had been aimed at reducing the lingering race discrimination in the former capital of the Confederacy. Sandra Day O'Connor, who wrote the Court majority's decision, declared, "While there is no doubt that the sorry history of both private and public discrimination in this country has contributed to a lack of opportunities for black entrepreneurs, this observation, standing alone, cannot justify a rigid racial quota in the awarding of public contracts in Richmond, Virginia."[14]

Roberts's brief in *Metro Broadcasting* urged the Supreme Court to extend the reasoning of *Richmond v. Croson*, which involved a municipal program, to federal programs. "A racial classification adopted by the federal government, no less than a state or local government, should be subject to the same exacting standard of review," he wrote. Roberts insisted that classifications based on race, even to lift up people who had long been relegated to society's bottom rungs, were "in tension with the fundamental principle embodied in the guarantee of equal protection that skin color and ethnic origin are generally inappropriate bases" from which to draw lines between people.[15]

The FCC countered that Supreme Court precedent had given the federal government great latitude to seek diversity and enrich the experience of all audiences. The commission was backed by US Senate leaders who were angered by the sudden reversal of the solicitor general's office. The FCC's chairman, Alfred Sikes, pleaded with the Department of Justice to reconsider. "I am writing to reiterate the request that we have already made to the Solicitor's office that the Department of Justice defend the Commission," he wrote. Sikes's letter, which was addressed to Attorney General Dick Thornburgh and then relayed to Roberts, did not change the department's position.[16]

Within the SG's office, Roberts's stance was troubling. "The decision was made pretty quickly and pretty abruptly by John," recalled Thomas Merrill, a deputy SG who was concerned about the institutional implications of arguments against the minority set-asides. Merrill said he came to the case "from an institutional, SG office" perspective, seeking to avoid the prospect of two Federal government briefs with opposing positions. Merrill, who later became a Columbia University law professor, recalled Roberts as being more focused on what he deemed the merits of the case. Roberts's message was straightforward, Merrill said: "This affirmative action program violated the Constitution, and we should present that to the Supreme Court."[17]

Roberts had the last word in the SG's office on matters concerning the case, but ultimately his arguments failed to convince the Supreme Court. Roberts was in the courtroom on June 27, 1990, when Justice William Brennan announced the decision upholding the FCC policy. Roberts was astonished. Brennan had persuaded a slim majority that federal broadcasting preferences tied to race need not meet the demanding standard the Court had set for municipal racial programs a year earlier. They needed only to be substantially related to "important" governmental objectives as directed by Congress.

Justice White, who had joined the majority in the earlier Richmond case, was now the pivotal fifth vote on Brennan's side. At the time, William and Mary law professor Neal Devins observed that commentators attributed White's position to respect for the role of Congress and federal power.[18] White, who had served as deputy attorney general during the Kennedy administration, a time of heated civil rights battles, was persuaded that the federal government had sufficient interest in ensuring diversity on the airwaves to justify the set-aside program. In his opinion for the majority, Brennan highlighted congressional findings that "past inequities stemming from racial and ethnic discrimination have resulted in a severe underrepresentation of minorities" in the media. He noted that Congress had for two decades supported the FCC's attempts to promote programming diversity by increasing minority ownership.[19]

The decision was Brennan's last. Less than a month later he suffered a stroke and stepped down. Brennan's departure after thirty-four years on the Court closed a chapter in the institution's history. Unlike Rehnquist and Roberts, Brennan believed the judiciary should vigorously protect individual liberties rather than wait for legislative efforts, whether at the federal or the state level. Appointed to the Supreme Court in 1956, two years after *Brown v. Board of Education* in 1954, Brennan had crafted the subsequent ruling in *Cooper v. Aaron*, which had denounced efforts by Little Rock, Arkansas, school officials to delay desegregation. Brennan had contributed to the Warren Court's decisions promoting political equality through cases involving the principle of one person, one vote. And his *Fay v. Noia* opinion in 1963 laid out the modern-era rights of inmates to challenge their imprisonment through a federal writ of habeas corpus, which became the bane of Nixon-era (and later) conservatives.[20]

With Brennan's retirement, it might have been Ken Starr's moment. When Starr gave up the judgeship for the appointment as solicitor general, the speculation inside the Bush administration and among Court watchers was that he would be at the top of the list should a vacancy open.[21] But Starr's interactions with other Justice Department insiders ended up hurting his chances, allies and critics said at the time. Attorney General Thornburgh was persuaded that Starr was not sufficiently conservative, that he was "too malleable," according to one account. The journalist Jan

Crawford Greenburg wrote that Thornburgh was particularly influenced by Luttig, who clashed with Starr.[22]

For Brennan's seat, Bush turned instead to David Souter, a former New Hampshire state court judge who had recently begun serving on a US appeals court. New Hampshire senator Warren Rudman, a moderate Republican whose state had been important to Bush in 1988, had persuaded the president to name Souter on the US Court of Appeals for the First Circuit and was equally enthusiastic about his possible elevation to the Supreme Court. White House Chief of Staff John Sununu, also of New Hampshire, characterized Souter as "a home run" for conservatives.[23]

But Souter, a fifty-one-year-old bachelor with a literary sensibility and a modest demeanor, would turn out to be just the opposite. After being named to the Court, he went on to voice expansive views of the Constitution's equal protection and due process guarantees. He began to dissent as the conservative majority—which his nomination was intended to strengthen—sought to shift power away from Washington in favor of the states. He would develop a friendship with and reverence for Brennan, the man he succeeded, eventually delivering a deeply personal eulogy at Brennan's funeral.

Souter was chosen on faith, based on the word of New Hampshire politicians, rather than on serious scrutiny of the nominee's record or ideological views. Souter never presented himself as anything other than the moderate he was, even in his confirmation hearings. He professed deep regard for privacy, equality, and the separation of church and state. Within two years, he voted with a slim five-justice majority to uphold *Roe v. Wade*. Souter's vote by then was not a surprise.

ALTHOUGH HE HAD BEEN DEALT A SETBACK IN *METRO BROADCASTING*, Roberts continued to shape the Bush administration's legal agenda. He wrote briefs in high-profile school desegregation cases that helped persuade the Supreme Court to limit judicial oversight of previously segregated systems. As with other matters concerning race, Roberts has been consistent throughout his career in protesting against government remedies for the lingering effects of segregation, particularly when imposed by judges. He would go further in 2007, as chief justice, voting against school district efforts to prevent the resegregation of schools in Seattle and Louisville.

In 1991, Roberts helped write a brief on behalf of the federal government that persuaded the Court to lower the standard for previously segregated school districts trying to get out from under federal judicial control. The Bush administration was siding with Oklahoma City schools that wanted to end a desegregation order that school officials asserted was no longer needed. African American parents, who challenged the school district, argued that the local schools would be resegregated if a district court judge lifted his desegregation order. The solicitor general's brief countered that "once a school district is declared unitary [that is, desegregated], and the decree is lifted, future conduct by the school authorities is once again governed by traditional equal protection standards, which prohibit only intentional acts of discrimination." The Roberts position would give federal judges grounds to intervene only upon evidence of intentional discrimination.[24]

Adopting that view, Chief Justice Rehnquist, Roberts's former boss, wrote for the majority that school districts could escape the supervision of federal judges once they had taken all "practicable" steps to eliminate the "vestiges" of unlawful segregation. A school district also had to show that it had complied with a desegregation order for "a reasonable period of time."

The decision meant that a desegregation order would be lifted even if the resegregation of the city's schools was likely. Justice Thurgood Marshall was among the Court's three dissenters, warning that the new standard threatened a "reemergence of one-race schools." The justice who, as a lawyer, had been the architect of the legal strategy that had led to *Brown v. Board of Education* wrote in the new case, "I believe a desegregation decree cannot be lifted so long as conditions likely to inflict the stigmatic injury condemned in *Brown I* persist and there remain feasible methods of eliminating such conditions."[25]

The approach the Court adopted in that 1991 case, *Oklahoma City v. Dowell*, enhancing the ability of local officials to persuade federal judges to withdraw supervision, became further entrenched in its 1992 decision in *Freeman v. Pitts*, again with guidance from the SG's legal position. In a brief for the Bush administration, Roberts's team stressed that local districts, not federal courts, should control local desegregation problems. DeKalb County had long maintained dual school zones for black and white children, and parents alleged that without continued federal monitoring of desegregation efforts the county would revert to old practices. The Supreme Court sent the DeKalb County case back to lower courts for review, ruling that judges should examine whether school boards had made "good faith" efforts to end segregation.[26]

Controversy over abortion rights preoccupied Roberts in his new position, too. Roberts had argued against the Supreme Court's 1973 decision declaring that women had a right to end a pregnancy since at least his days in the Reagan administration. He abhorred the fact that *Roe v. Wade* allowed for the termination of fetal life. His policy and legal position arose from the belief that the justices had entered territory that belonged to government officials elected by the people. Once he became a justice, Roberts would vote to give the states significant leeway to restrict abortion; he never found that regulations had gone too far in burdening a woman's right to end a pregnancy, including the regulations that led to the closing of clinics across Texas.[27]

President George H.W. Bush had continued the anti-abortion emphasis of Reagan. On January 23, 1989, the sixteenth anniversary of *Roe v. Wade*, Bush spoke through an amplified telephone hookup to a crowd of antiabortion demonstrators on the Ellipse south of the White House. He vowed to work for the reversal of the milestone case that had made abortion legal nationwide.[28]

Roberts and other Bush administration lawyers followed through with briefs arguing that *Roe v. Wade* had been wrongly decided and should be overturned. He took the lead in one case, *Rust v. Sullivan*, involving abortion counseling at family planning clinics. The Reagan administration had issued regulations preventing recipients of federal funds from offering such services. *Rust* tested whether the government was impermissibly restricting the free speech of physicians, nurses, and other health-care providers.

In the administration's September 1990 filing in the case, Roberts wrote that abortion counseling and referrals conflicted with Title X's "limited" goal of providing pre-pregnancy family planning services. Going further, he added, "We continue to believe that *Roe* was wrongly decided and should be overruled. . . . [T]he Court's conclusions in *Roe* that there is a fundamental right to an abortion and that government has no compelling interest in protecting prenatal human life throughout pregnancy find no support in the text, structure, or history of the Constitution."

When "disrobed of their rhetoric," Roberts insisted, the challengers' arguments would have the government subsidize abortion-related services. "While under *Roe* the government may not prohibit a woman from choosing to have a first trimester abortion," he told the justices, "this Court has repeatedly held that the government is not obligated to provide the means to exercise any such right. Thus, the government need not finance the provision of information about abortion, whether the information is provided in the form of abortion counseling, referral, or advocacy."[29]

That position prevailed. By a 5–4 vote, the Supreme Court upheld the regulation barring funding for such services, which often served the poor. In his opinion, Chief Justice Rehnquist deferred to the Bush administration's view that "the broad language of Title X" allowed its interpretation requiring the ban. The Court did not address the constitutionality of *Roe v. Wade* itself, declining the Bush administration's invitation to overturn abortion rights.[30] That was not a surprise. The Supreme Court as a general rule did not sweep broader than necessary, and the constitutionality of abortion was not directly at issue in the Title X dispute.

Abortion opponents were frustrated by their lack of progress in persuading the Court majority to reverse *Roe*. Some of the extreme elements of the movement increasingly took to picketing and blocking clinic access. In the early 1990s, protests turned violent, and health-care workers and women who wanted to receive the clinics' services felt terrorized. Federal judges ended up in the middle, trying to protect access to clinics and a woman's constitutional right to an abortion without infringing on free-speech rights.

Operation Rescue, a militant antiabortion organization, generated constant legal battles by blocking women from entering clinics that performed abortions. The Bush administration backed Operation Rescue. In one of the most visible fights of the era, Roberts supported the organization in its challenge to a federal judge in Wichita, Kansas, who had ordered the group to stop demonstrating in front of the city's three main health clinics. US District Court Judge Patrick Kelly, who issued an order against Operation Rescue's activities, said the protesters were interfering with abortion rights. Kelly relied on a law rooted in the late 1800s concerning the violence of the Ku Klux Klan. The law prohibited conspiracies to deprive "any person or class of persons of the equal protection of the law, or of equal privileges and immunities under the law."

Operation Rescue's attorneys contended that the law could not be used to keep protesters away from clinics because the protesters were not targeting minorities or any other protected class of persons. Roberts took the administration's support for that position to the news media. Appearing on PBS television's *MacNeil/Lehrer NewsHour* in August 1991, he argued that Judge Kelly lacked authority to intervene in the antiabortion protest action. Roberts said the civil rights statute the judge had invoked was intended to address class-based discrimination, and that Operation Rescue was not specifically targeting women as a class. Roberts noted that the law was called the Ku Klux Klan Act of 1871, and "that conveys a pretty good idea about what the law was intended to do." Roberts added, "It was directed against people going out and trying to interfere with the constitutional rights of blacks."[31] Roberts asserted that state laws regarding protest activities, not federal civil rights law, governed the situation.

"Mr. Roberts is doing a pretty good job of making the government's position sound fairly reasonable," countered liberal Harvard law professor Laurence Tribe, another guest on the *NewsHour* program. "But I'm afraid Mr. Roberts is not being very candid." Tribe insisted that if federal judges were not allowed to keep antiabortion protesters away from the entrance to a clinic, "there is no doubt that there would be a physical shutdown of that clinic." Tribe warned that staff and clients would not be able to enter or exit the clinics and that lifting the court order would unleash "the law of the jungle."

As he demonstrated in this early TV appearance, Roberts does have a way of sounding eminently reasonable. He speaks with a steady voice and in clear, direct sentences. He argues with a thoughtful tone. His confidence is manifest, but never brazen. Roberts almost never looks flustered, and he never stammers. He prepares intensively for every public appearance he makes, working both on the substance of what he will say and on his presentation.

Judge Kelly reacted angrily to the Department of Justice's intervention. "I am disgusted by this move by the United States," he said, asserting that the federal government's involvement was politically motivated. According to the Associated Press, Kelly said that Attorney General Thornburgh should personally review videotapes of Operation Rescue's Wichita action so that he could see the "mayhem and distress" the group caused.[32]

The chaos in Wichita continued. The city's police were overwhelmed, and its citizens were polarized by the disruptions. "For nearly three weeks now," wrote Isabel Wilkerson in the *New York Times*, "this city has become the most vivid symbol of an emboldened anti-abortion movement as members of Operation Rescue focus on the city's three abortion clinics, flinging themselves under cars, sitting by the hundreds at clinic doorways and blocking women from entering as they read them Scripture." The police had carried out more than 1,600 arrests, and the three area abortion clinics were closed for more than a week. Wilkerson reported that the day after Judge Kelly prohibited protesters from blocking entry to a clinic, they returned to pray, sing, and implore women not to enter.[33]

In separate Operation Rescue demonstrations in Virginia, Roberts again voiced the Bush administration's support for the antiabortion group. The case of *Bray v. Alexandria Women's Health Clinic* had progressed to the Supreme Court after a lower court judge found that protesters had conspired against women by blocking access to several clinics in the Washington, DC, area. Roberts contended that the obstruction of clinics was not harming women as a class, "because of their gender," in violation of civil rights law. Joining Operation Rescue's lawyer Jay Alan Sekulow in defense of the protesters, Roberts rejected the notion that opposition to abortion could be deemed sex discrimination. Roberts stressed that Operation Rescue was not trying "to deny to some what they would permit to others. They seek to prohibit the practice of abortion altogether."[34]

During oral arguments, Justice Harry Blackmun, the author of the Court's decision in *Roe v. Wade*, was skeptical of Roberts's backing of the antiabortion demonstrators, and he asked if the government was seeking to overturn the landmark case from 1973.

"No, your honor, the issue doesn't even come up," Roberts responded.

"Well, that hasn't prevented the Solicitor General from taking that position in prior cases," Blackmun rejoined. "Three or four of them in a row."

It would have been unusual for the Bush Justice Department to have broadly attacked abortion rights in the antidemonstration case, but, as Blackmun had noted, the administration had been persistent in seeking to overturn *Roe v. Wade* even when it was not squarely before the high court.

When the justices voted in their private conference, Blackmun was in dissent along with Justices Stevens and O'Connor (who at the time was the only woman on the Court). The majority, siding with Operation Rescue and the Bush administration, determined that opposition to abortion did not arise from a gender-based motivation. "Trespassing upon private property is unlawful in the States, as is, in many States and localities, intentionally obstructing the entrance to private premises," Justice Scalia wrote for the majority. "These offenses may be prosecuted criminally under state law, and may also be the basis for state civil damages. They do not, however, give rise to a federal cause of action simply because their objective is to prevent the performance of abortions, any more than they do so (as we have held) when their objective is to stifle free speech."[35]

Aside from their work on specific cases and the administration's litigation agenda, President George H.W. Bush's top lawyers also spent time considering candidates for judicial openings. The Reagan administration had carefully vetted conservative judicial nominees, and Bush was continuing the practice. By the spring of 1991, he had appointed Samuel Alito to the Philadelphia-based US Court of Appeals for the Third Circuit and Emilio Garza to the New Orleans–based US Court of Appeals for the Fifth Circuit. Alito had worked in both the solicitor general's office and the Office of Legal Counsel before becoming a US attorney, and Garza had been a trial court judge in Texas. Both men were known for their staunch conservatism. They were among the judges positioned for possible elevation to the Supreme Court. President Bush also was trying to appoint Roberts's friend Michael Luttig to a judgeship. Luttig had been promoted to an assistant attorney general position overseeing the Office of Legal Counsel. He was slated for the Richmond-based US Court of Appeals for the Fourth Circuit, which covers five mid-Atlantic states.

John Roberts regularly joined the Department of Justice team that met with potential nominees, and it was during one of these sessions that he first crossed paths with Sonia Sotomayor. Then in private practice with a small firm specializing in patents and other intellectual property, Sotomayor previously had been a Manhattan prosecutor and had influential patrons. Democratic senator Daniel Patrick Moynihan of New York was recommending her for a federal district court judgeship in Manhattan.[36] Roberts and the other Department of Justice lawyers who interviewed Sotomayor had little interest in following up on a nominee suggested by a Democrat. They also held her youth against her, but she and Luttig were both thirty-six, and Luttig had been tapped for a higher-level appeals court.[37]

Moynihan would not relent on the candidacy of Sotomayor, who had grown up in Bronx public housing with her Puerto Rican parents, then gone to Princeton University and Yale Law School on scholarships. Knowing what she had already overcome, he believed she could go far. Justice Department lawyers brushed off Moynihan's staff, refusing to return calls, and the wily New York senator sought leverage. In June 1991, Moynihan asked a top aide to call the staff of then Senate Judiciary Committee chairman Joseph Biden, a fellow Democrat, to temporarily block Luttig's nomination. "The Luttig card may work for us," aide Joseph Gale reported back to Moynihan. "Jeff Peck advised me that . . . Attorney General Thornburgh called Senator Biden and made a personal appeal to move the Luttig nomination quickly. Biden's reply was, in essence, 'why should I expedite a Justice Department candidate when Justice has been sitting on . . . Moynihan's recommendations and won't even return his staff's phone calls?'" Gale added, "You may want to call Biden to thank him."[38]

That move gained Sotomayor a second round of interviews at the Justice Department. Moynihan kept the pressure on, and she won a Bush trial court nomination and eventual Senate confirmation. The nomination of Luttig, Roberts's friend, eventually moved through the Senate, too. He was confirmed to the US Court of Appeals for the Fourth Circuit later in the summer of 1991.

At the same time, a more public battle was under way for a successor to the first African American justice. Thurgood Marshall announced in June 1991, as the annual session was ending, that he was stepping down because of poor health. Bush chose Clarence Thomas, a forty-three-year-old former head of the Equal Employment Opportunity Commission (EEOC), who had a year earlier been appointed to the DC Circuit. Thomas had a compelling personal story of a rise from poverty. His father had abandoned the family, and his mother had had few resources to support her three children. After their home in the hamlet of Pin Point, Georgia, burned down, seven-year-old Clarence was sent to live with his grandfather in Savannah.[39]

Thomas's record was deeply conservative. He subscribed to a "natural law" theory holding that individuals were endowed with certain inherent rights that could not be restrained by written law. Like Roberts, he opposed policies that gave preferences to minorities, a position that was especially controversial in his case, because he was African American. "I believe in compensation for actual victims, not for people whose only claim to victimization is that they are members of a historically oppressed group," he had said. Critics argued that he was turning his back on his own people.[40]

During Thomas's hearings before the Senate Judiciary Committee, he separated himself from his controversial writings and earlier positions at the EEOC, saying that he would remain open-minded as a Supreme Court justice. Senators deadlocked in the committee, 7–7, over whether to approve his nomination, yet they sent his name to the Senate floor. As a vote by the full Senate approached, Anita Hill, one of Thomas's former employees at the EEOC and the Department of Education, came forward to accuse him of sexual harassment. Public pressure forced the Senate Judiciary Committee to hold a second round of hearings. In nationally televised testimony, Hill described Thomas's alleged sexual overtures and his references to pornographic images in excruciating detail. Thomas categorically denied Hill's claims. "This is a circus," he declared. "It's a national disgrace. And from my standpoint as a black American, as far as I am concerned, it's a high-tech lynching for uppity blacks who in any way deign to think for themselves."[41]

Thomas was confirmed, but by the closest Senate vote in more than a century, 52–48. His elevation to the Court created an open spot on the DC Circuit, a prestigious court that handles disputes over government regulation. It seemed the perfect moment for Roberts, who had been looking for the right opportunity on a federal bench. The DC Circuit was also a proven stepping-stone to the Supreme Court, and Roberts was not the only lawyer who wanted the job. Another contender was Peter Rusthoven, who, like Roberts, had worked in the White House counsel's office under Fred Fielding. Rusthoven, four years older than Roberts, had been with Reagan during his 1980 campaign as a speech writer and had more varied legal experience. Senator Dan Coats, an Indiana Republican, had reached out to President Bush on Rusthoven's behalf, and friends had contacted Andrew Card, who was Bush's deputy chief of staff, to recommend him. But Rusthoven had moved back to his home state of Indiana and could not compete with Roberts on the inside track.[42]

For the previous two years, since taking the deputy SG post, a political position, Roberts had been at the center of the Bush legal agenda. He had proven himself a committed soldier in some of the toughest, most polarizing litigation battles of the time. Outside competition also came from Hispanic activists who were pressing Bush to bypass Roberts and the other white contenders and appoint the first Latino to the influential US appeals court in Washington. Justice Department lawyers, all colleagues of Roberts, put together a White House "talking points" memo describing Roberts as "a superstar." They asserted that "the President does not need to nominate a Hispanic to this seat to demonstrate commitment to reaching out to Hispanics."[43]

On January 27, 1992, the day he celebrated his thirty-seventh birthday, Roberts was officially nominated. He was a proactive nominee, collaborating with Justice Department aides Barbara Drake and John Mackey in trying to move his nomination through the Senate. They understood that his past positions on civil rights cases could be sticking points. To help his bid for confirmation, Roberts compiled a list of briefs, categorizing them as "Pro-civil rights," "Pro-voting rights," and "Pro-labor."[44]

"What would also be helpful now," Mackey explained, "is to have you think through the briefs or arguments you were involved with, that might be used against you if opposition develops. . . . [A]ny particular sections in those briefs that someone could likely focus on in opposition research, or even taken out of context, should be marked for particular attention. . . . Finally, a question or two on each controversial brief should be developed that you might want to have asked of you by a friendly Senator (if opposition arises), that you could use to recoup, if needed."[45]

Senate Judiciary Committee Democrats were wary of Roberts. He may have kept largely out of the public eye, but Democratic staffers and liberal public interest groups had been aware of his work on civil rights and abortion cases. They urged Democratic senators to stall on his nomination. Solicitor General Starr tried to help his protégé and called Senate Judiciary Committee chairman Biden, urging him to schedule a hearing on Roberts's nomination. Starr thought he had succeeded. But liberal advocates were actively—and successfully—discouraging Biden from taking so much as a first step toward a Roberts appointment.[46]

Roberts tried to persuade administration officials to push harder on his behalf, but it was an election year, which complicated things. Many of his friends in the administration thought Bush was going to be reelected and that Roberts would simply be renominated. Spring turned to summer and then fall with no progress. "He was in limbo," recalled Roberts's old boss in the White House counsel's office, Fred Fielding. "It was difficult." The nomination lapsed after the election of the Democratic presidential candidate Bill Clinton in November 1992.[47]

"Here's why I think it was really hard: it was public," said Richard Lazarus, Roberts's friend from law school, a quarter century later. "You get nominated. Everyone in the entire world says you're the most unbelievable person. It's all very positive and it's all out there. When you don't get it then everyone's feeling sorry for you. That's not pleasant. John Roberts felt very successful. . . . He had had this incredible career. And you think it [the failed nomination] is going to define you."[48]

When Bush left office in January 1993, Roberts returned to Hogan and Hartson. His litigation practice flourished. He began appearing before the Supreme Court with regularity, and soon enough he was on his way to earning a reputation as a superior appellate advocate. "Roberts possessed an unusually clear and straightforward manner of presenting his arguments, even in cases that were highly technical or arcane," Justice Sandra Day O'Connor later wrote. She believed "no one presented better arguments on a more consistent basis."[49]

Roberts occasionally engaged in policy debates that had persisted since the Reagan and Bush years. He was in private practice, but was sought out because of his Department of Justice background. "The most effective way to reduce crime is to catch criminals, convict them, and then punish them swiftly and surely," Roberts told a special US House of Representatives Republican crime panel in August 1993. "That may seem obvious but there's a good deal of rhetoric these days to the effect that we cannot respond to the crime problem simply by locking up criminals. Maybe not, but it's a good place to start."[50]

He claimed that excessive attention was paid to the social deprivation suffered by "a criminal who sticks a gun in a victim's face," rather than to the "victim who may have had just as deprived a childhood as the gunman," but who had chosen to be a law-abiding citizen. Roberts argued that judges were interpreting the 1966 case of *Miranda v. Arizona* too broadly, and he recounted the saga of a Washington, DC, murder suspect who was freed because police failed to administer "the Miranda warning" that he had a right to remain silent, before he confessed. The federal government appealed to the Supreme Court. With evident sarcasm, Roberts asked whether the panel members could remember what had happened in this "landmark" legal case. "No, you don't," he said, answering his own question. "That's because [the defendant] was released to the streets of the District [of Columbia] while the case was pending, and he ended up getting himself shot and killed, learning first-hand what the crime problem is like in the District."[51]

In 1995, Roberts again appeared on the *MacNeil/Lehrer NewsHour*. This time, he was a private advocate defending a Supreme Court decision against racial remedies. The June 1995 ruling in *Adarand Constructors, Inc., v. Peña* reversed the decision from *Metro Broadcasting, Inc., v. Federal Communications Commission*, the case Roberts had worked on in his early days in the solicitor general's office. The different outcome in 1995 was the result of Clarence Thomas succeeding Thurgood Marshall. Thomas cast the fifth vote to rule that federal affirmative action programs should be subject to the strictest judicial scrutiny.[52]

Roberts had a stake in the *Adarand* case as a lawyer for a trade organization, Associated General Contractors, that opposed required set-asides for minority-owned businesses in government contracting. On television, Roberts praised the ruling, which he said required government to treat people as individuals, not as simply part of a racial group. "What the Supreme Court said today," Roberts continued, "is that you don't overcome racism by engaging in it yourself."[53]

A few months later, the *Los Angeles Daily Journal* published an extensive profile of Roberts. "To the usual 'personal' questions, Roberts replies tersely that he is 'still single,' lives in suburban Bethesda, Md., and enjoys golf and squash when not lawyering," the legal journal's correspondent David Pike wrote. "His office, awash with briefs and other legal papers, contains no family photos, mementos or items that reflect his personality." Pike quoted lawyer Barrett Prettyman, who said Roberts "play[ed] things close to the vest, especially his personal life, and that's unusual for litigators. Most are very open."[54]

Most of Roberts's friends and colleagues regarded him as reserved, and even as enigmatic. This is still true today. "The notion that John plays his cards close to his vest is a dramatic understatement," said lawyer Michael Carvin, who also worked in the Reagan and Bush administrations, in 2016.[55]

In a separate interview, Prettyman later said that although Roberts was personally guarded, his politics were clear. "I sat with John Roberts every day for lunch for years," said Prettyman, who recalled the scene in Hogan and Hartson's upscale cafeteria (nicknamed Chez Hogan) and the table where partners congregated daily. "During that time," Prettyman recalled in an April 2012 interview for the Robert H. Jackson Center, "I had heard him expound on virtually everything. And it was clear to me that he was exactly what the Republicans . . . believed and what they were interested in and what they would want to have at a higher position [in the judiciary]. He espoused every theory that they were espousing. It just seemed to me that if they were looking for an ideal person for a place on the Court, this would be the person. Because he was smarter than hell."[56]

ROBERTS'S SINGLE STATUS WOULD NOT LAST FOREVER: HE WOULD soon connect with Jane Sullivan. For all that John Roberts and Jane Sullivan had in common, they possessed starkly different personalities. Sullivan talked effusively about her life and freely expressed her views. She exuded energy and laced her conversations with references to her Irish heritage and Catholic faith. She would frequently punctuate her remarks with phrases such as "That's who I am," or "That's who we are." Meanwhile, Roberts took pains to avoid revealing much about himself or his family. Sullivan also was spontaneous and had an immense appetite for adventure, as Roberts carefully plotted out his steps in life and work.

Jane Sullivan's mother, who had been born in Ireland, immigrated to the United States after World War II. She had met her future husband in New York. The eldest of their four children, Jane was raised in the Bronx. She went to Holy Cross, soon after it had begun admitting women, and then to Brown University for a master's degree in mathematics, and then to Georgetown University Law School. She worked as a waitress and in other jobs to pay for her education. She threw parties, she traveled, and she pushed herself out into the world.[57]

Sullivan, a lawyer in a Washington, DC, firm, had been on the edges of Roberts's circle for several years, and they were part of a large group that shared a beach house in Delaware. Like Roberts, she was socially conservative. A strong opponent of abortion rights, she was on the board of Feminists for Life.

In an interview, Jane recalled the morning in 1991 when she had first met Roberts. They were in Dewey Beach, Delaware. "A few of us are sitting around having breakfast. He walks in the door. . . . He is wearing a pink polo shirt and white shorts. People had said I would like him. And I looked at him and thought, hmmmm." She sized him up and decided she liked what she saw. "I said, 'I'm going for a swim.' And he said, 'I'll go in for a swim, too.'" They talked about Johnstown, his family's home, and the famous flood that had nearly destroyed it.

Soon after, she took a trip to Australia with her parents and a few friends. While there, a friend encouraged her to find a lawyering job and stay for a while. "So I came home, tied things up, and went back and then stayed for about eighteen months," she recalled. "But I did give myself a going-away party and I invited [Roberts] to that. He spent most of the evening talking to my mother. He charmed her."

Jane returned to Washington, DC, in late 1993. She and Roberts reconnected and decided to take each other to their respective Christmas parties. "Fast forward many years: I said to him, 'Do you remember our first conversation?' 'Yes,' he said, 'in the water, about the Johnstown flood.' I asked whether he remembered what I was wearing. He said yes and he described what I was wearing: a lavender T-shirt and flowered shorts."

In early 1996 they became engaged. Both were into their forties. "I think a lot of it was a lot of shared values," Jane said, describing what had drawn her to him. "Integrity, knowing I could count on him to do the right thing, for life. There's the initial charm and wit and good looks. But for life, it's that we share the same faith. He made moral choices and I could count on that integrity for life." She believed his work had prevented him from thinking about marriage earlier in his life. "He was fired up by work," she said. "He had jobs that were in many ways all-consuming."

They married in July 1996 under the vaulted ceilings and colorful mosaics of the Cathedral of St. Matthew the Apostle in downtown Washington. Their reception was held at the Metropolitan Club, where Roberts was a member. At his side was his best man, Dean Colson, whom he had met during his clerkship with Rehnquist. Among the groomsmen were Richard Lazarus from Harvard and Michael Luttig from the Reagan-Bush years. The toasts centered on family and the children they would raise.

Jane later said that neither her family nor his had pressured them to marry earlier. Nor did either mother interfere with the wedding planning. "They were not going to do anything to derail this marriage," Jane said. "It was all systems go."[58]

With Jane, that seemed even more the mantra of John Roberts's life.

CHAPTER V

THE STANDOUT

I N 2000, AS PRESIDENT BILL CLINTON NEARED THE END OF HIS
second term, a new campaign for the Oval Office was heating up.
The contest was between Clinton's vice president, Al Gore, and George
W. Bush, a former Texas governor and the son of George H.W. Bush.
John Roberts had been on the executive committee of Lawyers for Bush-
Quayle in 1988 and had served in the first Bush administration's solicitor
general's office. He now contributed money to the new Bush campaign,
in which the younger Bush teamed up with Dick Cheney, his father's secretary of defense, as his vice-presidential running mate. Roberts, with his
record from the Reagan and first Bush administrations behind him and
his continued connections in place, knew he had a chance for a judicial
appointment if Bush won.

Journalists focused on possible short lists for the Supreme Court.
Speculation among Republicans centered on Michael Luttig, Roberts's
longtime friend and former colleague, and other sitting appeals court
judges, such as J. Harvie Wilkinson III. Luttig and Wilkinson—Reagan

administration alumni like Roberts—served on the Richmond, Virginia–based US Court of Appeals for the Fourth Circuit.

Luttig and Wilkinson offered a contrast in styles. Wilkinson, then age fifty-five, had a courtly manner that reflected his Richmond upbringing as well as the influence of his mentor, the Supreme Court justice Lewis Powell. He had been a newspaper editor and professor. A decade younger at forty-five, Luttig, a Texan, was razor sharp in his arguments and writing. His temperament was close to that of Justice Antonin Scalia, for whom he had worked early in his career. Wilkinson and Luttig sometimes dueled in Fourth Circuit cases. Luttig was further to the right and sometimes called the most conservative judge on the nation's most conservative appeals court.[1]

Luttig had experienced a searing personal tragedy when his father, John Luttig, an executive in the oil industry, had been shot and killed at his home in Tyler, Texas, on April 19, 1994. Three carjackers had attacked him as he was pulling his car into the garage with his wife in the passenger seat. The couple had been returning from a divinity class. Luttig's mother survived by crawling under the car and playing dead. "I loved him more than life," said Luttig, who moved his judicial chambers to Tyler while the murder trial was under way.[2]

During the 2000 presidential campaign, speculation was rife that white jurists like Luttig and Wilkinson could face competition for a Supreme Court vacancy from candidates of color. Commentators predicted that the newly elected president might make history by naming the nation's first Hispanic justice. In 1964, President Lyndon B. Johnson had broken the Court's color line by nominating the first African American, Thurgood Marshall. In 1981, Ronald Reagan had chosen Sandra Day O'Connor as the nation's first woman justice. But as of yet, there had been no Hispanics on the Court.

One possible nominee on the GOP side was Alberto Gonzales, who had served as secretary of state in Texas before then governor George W. Bush appointed him to the Texas Supreme Court. Gonzales had been born in San Antonio to Mexican immigrants and was a graduate of Rice University and Harvard Law School. A longtime Bush confidant, Gonzales appeared to be well positioned for a top job in the administration if Bush won the presidency.

Roberts had been out of government service during Bill Clinton's two terms in the White House. He did not appear on the nominee lists kept by Bush supporters, the news media, or special interest groups. Yet his experience and expertise kept him in high regard among GOP insiders and he was naturally in line for the appeals court seat that had eluded him during the senior Bush's term in the White House. The US Court of Appeals for the DC Circuit was considered a launching pad to the Supreme Court. Former chief justice Warren Burger and Justices Antonin Scalia, Clarence Thomas, and Ruth Bader Ginsburg had all served on the DC Circuit before they were nominated to the high court.

During Clinton's presidency, Roberts had frequently appeared before the Supreme Court as an advocate for corporate clients. His meticulous preparation and unflagging composure inspired confidence among his well-heeled clients. Roberts's legal arguments, often in favor of less government regulation, appealed to Chief Justice William Rehnquist and like-minded conservative justices. Roberts also earned the respect of liberals on the Court, including Justice John Paul Stevens, for his rhetorical skill and straightforward style.[3]

Roberts left nothing to chance in his preparation for an appearance before the Court. He engaged in as many as ten practice rounds, or "moot courts." He believed he had to be ready to answer a very large number of possible questions: "You might get eighty, you might get a hundred, but you've got to be prepared to answer more than a thousand," he told the legal writing analyst Bryan Garner in an interview. Unfamiliar names could be a problem for him, so if he had trouble with a pronunciation during a moot court, he figured out a way to avoid the name by describing the person by his or her title or job. "If I stumble over a word, I get another word," Roberts told this author in a separate, earlier interview. He dreaded that something in his arguments would not sound quite right, adding, "The transcripts are always painful for me to read."[4]

When arguing in appellate courts outside of Washington, Roberts would arrive a day early to get a sense of the courtroom and chat up the bailiff. "How do the judges like to be addressed? Do they like to be addressed as 'Your Honor'? Do they like to be addressed as 'Judge'?"[5] Roberts told Garner that he wanted to avoid any phrasing, practice, or ploy, no matter how minor, that could distract or offend a judge. Roberts's law firm partner Barrett Prettyman said, "I've never seen someone become so sure of his position. He psychs himself up and is really convinced of it, and he is able to get that feeling across to the judges so that they're almost embarrassed to question him. It's a unique ability for an advocate."[6]

Roberts strove for a conversational tone. He synthesized the facts of a case into easy-to-follow arguments that he made without referring to his notes. He wanted the themes to be clear and succinct and accessible to non-lawyers, and he often imagined his three sisters as the audience while crafting his approach to a case in order to make sure he met this standard. "Every lawsuit is a story," he told Garner. "I don't care if it's about a dry contract interpretation; you've got two people who want to accomplish something, and they're coming together—that's a story. And you've got to tell a good story." Roberts learned the power of the poignant detail while writing a petition to the Supreme Court about the Red Dog Mine in Alaska. "Well, I didn't know why it was called the Red Dog Mine, so you do some research," he recalled about a brief for state officials in *Alaska Department of Environmental Conservation v. EPA*, a 2004 case. "It's a fascinating story about a guy with his plane and his faithful red dog delivering emergency medicine in a blizzard, and the plane crashes, and the dog dies. You waste a couple of sentences in a brief, but you put that in there, and it's kind of interesting. Then everybody remembers that. . . . And they're kind of invested in it, and they want to see how the story ends up, and it gives a little texture to the brief."[7]

On the day of an argument, Roberts would be anxious as he entered the Court building. Colleagues said he would try to calm his nerves by thinking about strangers in the Capitol and congressional office buildings. He thought of how lucky they were to be free of the stress that weighed on him. For good luck, he would tap a foot of the large bronze John Marshall statue on the ground floor of the building. As prepared as he was, Roberts still wrote out the opening words with which every lawyer who appears in Court begins: "Mr. Chief Justice and may it please the Court." He wanted it on paper, and handy, in case he froze.[8]

Jane Roberts began attending all of his arguments soon after they were married. "I was never nervous on his behalf," she said with her usual confidence. "I knew my husband always had it covered."[9]

THE COUPLE WAS LIVING IN BETHESDA, MARYLAND, A DESIRABLE suburb on the edge of Washington, DC. Each was a partner at a major law firm: John, at Hogan and Hartson, where he had worked since leaving the George H.W. Bush administration in 1993; Jane, at Shaw Pittman. Together, they were worth more than $5 million. One of their cherished assets was a cottage in Limerick, Ireland, which they co-owned with Jane's relatives. They enjoyed evenings of theater, dancing, and entertaining, and they were planning a summer vacation that included canoeing in the Algonquin Provincial Park in Ontario, Canada.[10]

John and Jane were both forty-five years old by 2000, and they had hoped for a baby by this point in their lives. When it became clear they would not conceive a child, they had turned to adoption. Like others in their situation, they experienced both hope and frustration. In one instance, they had already packed their bags for a flight to accept a new baby when they learned that the birth mother had changed her mind. "We expected, yes, to adopt a particular baby, and we didn't learn that it was falling through until she checked into the hospital," recalled Jane of the mother. They were heartbroken but worked through it. "I thought this was really just God's plan," Jane said. "God has a plan, and for every reason this was the right thing to happen." In the spring of 2000, however, their hopes remained high. They were working with adoption agencies and had prepared photos and written materials to illustrate the kind of parents they could be and the home they could offer a child.[11]

By that summer, they had an agreement with a pregnant woman who was scheduled to deliver a baby in December in Florida. They decided to go through with the planned trip to Algonquin Provincial Park in

Ontario. It was late July, and they were celebrating their fourth wedding anniversary. They toasted their new life as parents. But then unexpected news came. This time it was not bad news.[12]

"We've left the park and we're driving to the Toronto airport, and there's a telephone booth," Jane recounted. "We didn't have cell phones in those days. We both check our messages. We each have a message that a baby would be born the next day in Florida and would we like that baby. . . . I thought, 'The next day?! Really?'"

A separate adoption agency had informed them that a baby girl was about to be born whose mother had chosen the Robertses. But Jane and John worried about the reaction of the agency that had arranged the adoption of a boy expected in December. They wondered if they could manage two new babies so close in age. By the time they reached the Toronto airport, Jane had decided that they should seize the opportunity.

"We check in and we sit down and I say, 'I think we should do it.' He said, 'What changed?' And I said, 'I just worked through all the details.'" They called each of the agencies, Jane recounted, and told them of the new circumstances. Each said the babies would still be available to them, and the Robertses chose to adopt both children.

Jane believed that just as an earlier birth mother had changed her mind, leaving them bereft, this new mother's last-minute decision to offer her baby daughter for adoption was meant to be. She calculated that the woman had made her decision right around their July 27 wedding anniversary. "So, we're toasting, and soon we will be parents to [the baby expected in December], and at the very same time, this woman picked us." Jane also attributed their good fortune to the "adoption book" they had prepared for prospective birth mothers. "We had some pictures of what her family would be, which included cousins, cousins from America, cousins from Ireland. And we have a cottage in Ireland, which at the time was a thatched-roof cottage. And for some reason a thatched-roof cottage really appealed to [the baby's birth mother]. We had been advised not to put pictures of Ireland in there. And we said, 'That's who we are.' . . . She [the mother] told me that for their own sentimental reasons that struck a chord." They named the baby Josephine, after John's grandmother, and would call her "Josie." Jane arranged to stay home in Josie's early months and handled work-related calls in the evening after John returned from work and could help with the child care.[13]

Even with a new baby in the house, Roberts maintained his discipline, preparing for two Supreme Court hearings scheduled for that October and November. In each case, he represented corporations that had lost in the lower courts. He had overcome long odds in persuading the Supreme Court justices to exercise their discretion and accept his clients' petitions. In the first, he represented Eastern Associated Coal Corporation against the United Mine Workers of America, District 17. The coal company wanted to prevent reinstatement of a worker who had tested positive for marijuana and had undergone rehabilitation. The worker and his union said he was entitled to his job under federal labor law.

Arguing before the justices, Roberts opened with the drama of the driver's conduct: "Twice the driver in this case tested positive for illegal drugs, and twice the company tried to fire him, and twice the company that employed him to drive its 25-ton vehicles in West Virginia tried to fire him. Each time an arbitrator ordered the driver reinstated. The second time the company went to court, arguing that the reinstatement award should not be enforced because it was contrary to public policy to put this driver back behind the wheel."[14]

The justices asked whether they should essentially usurp the terms of the labor contract. Justice Ruth Bader Ginsburg observed that the employer could have—but had not—bargained with the union for a rule that said if an employee tested positive for drugs twice, he lost his job. Roberts said the courts had the authority to decline to enforce contracts that violated "public policy," that is, when there was some harm that would outweigh enforcement of the contract. "The public policy in this case is . . . against the use of illegal drugs by those in safety sensitive positions," Roberts said. The Court's resolution of the case would not come for weeks.

In early November, the nation was thrown into political turmoil that would last more than a month, alter Roberts's usual routines, and ultimately change his future. Election Day was November 7. Late that night, it became clear that the outcome would be decided by Florida and its crucial twenty-five electoral votes. Television news programs, relying on exit polling, at first declared that Gore had won the state. But about an hour later, news anchors backtracked and said it looked like Bush had carried Florida and won the presidency. Gore telephoned Bush to concede and to congratulate him. But then, in another twist, it appeared that the race was too close to call. Gore retracted his concession.

Over the next thirty-six days, the nation was riveted by a close examination of the Florida vote. The day after the election, the Florida Division of Elections announced that Bush had received 2,909,135 votes to Gore's 2,907,351. The margin was a mere 1,784 votes, less than 0.05 percent of the votes cast, triggering an automatic recount under Florida law. During the recount, Bush's margin of victory narrowed to 663 votes. Vice President Gore asked for hand recounts in four counties, including Palm Beach County, where voters had complained about the so-called butterfly ballot, which listed candidates in two columns. The voting holes were located between the two columns, which were not clearly aligned. Some confused voters thought they were voting for Gore but had actually cast their ballots for the independent candidate Patrick Buchanan. "My guess is I probably got some votes down there that really did not belong to me," said Buchanan, a former Reagan adviser and conservative commentator, on NBC's *Today* show.[15]

Both sides called in lawyers, who arrived with armies of paralegals, researchers, and computer technicians—essentially, mobile law firms. Democratic lawyers went to court asking for additional recounts. Republican lawyers sought to stop the recounts and protect Bush's slim lead. They fought, in vain, to preserve a decision by Florida's secretary of state, Katherine Harris, refusing to waive a November 14 deadline for counties to turn in their ballot totals. Harris was a cochair of Bush's Florida campaign.

Many of the GOP lawyers who raced to Florida to protect Bush's tenuous victory had made names for themselves in the Reagan and George H.W. Bush administrations. Michael Carvin and Theodore Olson, two of the men who played the most prominent courtroom roles in the case, which began in Florida but ended in Washington at the Supreme Court as *Bush v. Gore*, had worked with Roberts in the Department of Justice in the early 1980s.

Bush campaign leaders, who wanted as many experienced GOP attorneys at the scene as possible, naturally turned to former Supreme Court law clerks with political experience. Roberts was among more than a dozen former clerks who were enlisted to help prepare the case. Leaving Jane and four-month-old Josie behind, and putting his preparation for another upcoming high court argument on a back burner, Roberts heeded the call, agreeing to help as long as he could. He flew to Tallahassee, the Florida state capital, where the fight would take place, but made clear that he would have to return to Washington for his November 29 argument in the *TrafFix Devices, Inc., v. Marketing Displays, Inc.*, a patent dispute. "He came down on very short notice," Carvin recalled, adding that he knew Roberts would stay only a few days so he could return to Washington to prepare for his case. Roberts helped Carvin with practice questions as he readied for his argument before the Florida Supreme Court.[16]

During this intense period, on Saturday, November 18, Tallahassee hosted the latest iteration of one of the biggest rivalries in college football, between the University of Florida and Florida State University. "It was utter chaos," Carvin recalled. "There are bands. There are fistfights. We're in a law office in Tallahassee. We're arguing it on Monday. I've had maybe an hour sleep." Once they submitted the written brief in the case, Carvin had to practice for the oral arguments. "John and these other guys are sitting around the table, shooting questions at me."[17]

On November 21, the day after the oral arguments at the Florida Supreme Court, the court ruled against Bush, rejecting the Republican attempt to lock in a deadline for election certification. The state court extended the deadline for recounts to November 26. Cable TV and front-page newspaper stories chronicled the recount bedlam. They showed video and still photographs of workers holding up ballots to the light and squinting to see whether a chad had been cleanly or mostly severed. Teams of lawyers and rabble rousers roamed the state. In Fort Lauderdale, swarms of placard-waving GOP partisans chanted "Sore Loserman" at a crowd of Gore supporters, while members of a county canvassing board tried to review hundreds of disputed ballots. On November 26, the Florida Elections Canvassing Commission certified a new result. Bush had won by 357 votes. His lead had shrunk again, and his legal team wanted to finalize the certification. Gore's lawyers, naturally, wanted the recounts to continue.

Back in Washington in late November for his oral arguments in the patent case, Roberts experienced the highs and lows of a Supreme Court litigator all within forty-eight hours. On November 28, the Court announced its decision in the case of *Eastern Associated Coal Corp. v. United Mine Workers of America*. The truck driver who had failed the drug test could be reinstated, based on the company's collective bargaining agreement with the union. The justices refused to carve out the exception Roberts had wanted. And it was unanimous. (A well-worn Roberts joke was that when a client asked in disbelief, "How could we lose 9–0?," he responded, "Because there are only nine justices.")

Then, on November 29, Roberts argued for his second case of the fall, in *TrafFix Devices, Inc., v. Marketing Displays, Inc.*, which went as planned. He was representing TrafFix in a patent claim by Marketing Displays over a dual-spring mechanism that kept temporary road and outdoor signs from being blown over by the wind. Roberts distilled the complicated case over an expired patent with the aim of trying to protect his client from infringement litigation. He emphasized a "right to copy from an expired patent" and the improved stand TrafFix had marketed. Roberts included in his argument a quote from Justice Louis Brandeis in a 1938 case between the cereal makers Nabisco and Kellogg that had allowed Kellogg to produce its own version of a square-shaped shredded wheat biscuit. "Sharing in the goodwill of an article unprotected by patent," he said, "is the exercise of a right possessed by all—and in the free exercise of which the consuming public is deeply interested."[18]

A few days later, on December 4, the US Supreme Court, to which Bush's lawyer had appealed for relief from the Florida Supreme Court, summarily returned the election case to state supreme court judges, telling them to clarify their rationale for extending the recount beyond Harris's November 14 deadline for certification.

In response, Vice President Gore launched another series of legal moves seeking court approval for manual recounts. The Florida court was dominated at the time by Democratic appointees, and in short order, it ruled, on December 8, that the recounts could continue. The Florida justices relied on a section of state law saying that no vote shall be ignored "if there is a clear indication of the intent of the voter." The court asserted that "every citizen's vote" had to be counted whenever possible. That meant election workers should continue to scrutinize ballots and hanging chads.

To the Bush team, the Florida Supreme Court's December 8 ruling had multiple flaws. Bush's lawyers argued that the decision improperly gave the canvassing commission the power to certify results, in violation of Florida law. The campaign team also contended that the Constitution's guarantee of equal protection and due process precluded vote-counting standards that varied from county to county. This second argument was designed to attract the attention, again, of the US Supreme Court.

The next day, Saturday, December 9, the US Supreme Court ordered all the Florida recounts to halt. It issued an order agreeing to hear the merits of Bush's claim the following Monday. In the order, the five conservatives on the Court, led by Chief Justice Rehnquist, were in the majority, and the four liberals dissented. That split held for the final result three days later. After the expedited oral arguments were held, the Supreme Court ruled for Bush by the same 5–4 vote. The justices did not even take the bench, issuing the unsigned per curiam (that is, "by the court") opinion at 10:00 p.m. on Tuesday, December 12. The majority declared that Florida's standard for counting ballots varied too widely to be fair. "The Florida Supreme Court has ordered that the intent of the voter be discerned from such ballots," the majority wrote, referring to the ballot cards distinguished by hanging chads or mere indentations. But the state court's standards failed to "satisfy the minimum requirement for non-arbitrary treatment of voters necessary to secure the fundamental right."[19]

The Supreme Court majority said it could not return the dispute to the Florida court for more precise, uniform standards because December 12 was the national deadline for establishing any state's presidential electors. The four liberal justices, led by John Paul Stevens, disputed the firmness of that deadline. "Although we may never know with complete certainty the identity of the winner of this year's Presidential election," Stevens wrote in his dissent, "the identity of the loser is perfectly clear. It is the Nation's confidence in the judge as an impartial guardian of the rule of law."

The Court took pains to make clear that its ruling was "limited to the present circumstances." The thirty-six-day ordeal was over. Yet the bitterness from the momentous decision along partisan lines lasted years, through at least the end of Rehnquist's tenure. Law school and other audiences asked visiting justices about the case. ("Get over it," Justice Scalia would say.) It would be a decade before another decision, *Citizens United v. Federal Election Commission*, came close to matching *Bush v. Gore* as a partisan flashpoint.[20]

As the US Supreme Court was dealing with the Florida election controversy, the infant boy whom John and Jane Roberts planned to adopt was born. They named him John Glover Roberts III and gave him the same nickname as John's father, Jack. Like his sister, Josie, who was just five months older, he had blond hair, and the two children would sometimes be mistaken for twins.[21]

Friends of the Robertses remarked on how open the couple was about the adoptions. Kevin Lipson, who had befriended Roberts at Hogan and Hartson and vacationed with the Roberts family in Maine, was among those who contrasted the Robertses' attitudes with attitudes about adoption in earlier times. "This was never a subject that was taboo or secret," Lipson said. "I think they've created a real sense of trust between John and Jane and the kids on that subject. They're very, very open about it. As a result, the kids are very stable and centered."[22]

"God makes families many different ways," Jane says today. "And this is one way. 'This is clearly God's plan that you [children] be with us.' We just tell them that. There is no secret. Again, it's God's plan. I just never wanted what would be a shock, an undermining shock of 'Who am I?' My children know right from the start who they are and that this is part of God's plan."

In time, Jane would leave Shaw Pittman and work for Major, Lindsey and Africa, a legal recruiting firm placing clients with high-caliber firms. In a commencement address at her alma mater, Holy Cross, in May 2011, she recounted the not-so-predictable trajectory of her life and the circumstances that had induced her to leave a large corporate law firm. "Four years after we were married, we were blessed with our two children," she said, adding immediately, "In 2005, my brother was killed in a terrible car accident, leaving a wife and three children behind. Going through that tragedy made me realize that life is short and that I should be doing what I love and do best."[23]

A SUCCESSFUL LAWYER AND HUSBAND, AND NOW A FATHER OF TWO, John Roberts would soon experience another major change in his life. The newly inaugurated president was ready to nominate him to the US Court of Appeals for the DC Circuit, the bench that he had been denied in 1992 when the Democratically controlled Senate had refused to act on his nomination. Other lawyers who had come up through GOP administrations and worked on *Bush v. Gore* were rewarded with plum jobs in the administration, too, including Theodore Olson, who was chosen to be the new US solicitor general.

Roberts's nomination to the DC Circuit was officially announced on May 9, 2001, along with the nominations of ten other lawyers whom Bush had selected for prestigious appeals court positions. The administration made the announcement a major media event in the East Room of the White House, with Attorney General John Ashcroft and Senate Judiciary Committee leaders Orrin Hatch, a Republican from Utah, and Patrick Leahy, a Democrat from Vermont, attending. Administration staff distributed three-ring binders for each of the eleven nominees containing their personal backgrounds and glowing reviews.

The nominees were introduced as they stood on risers: in the group of eight men and three women were eight whites, two blacks, and one Latino. Roberts, wearing a dark suit and a red striped tie, was positioned in the middle row. His parents, Jack and Rosemary Roberts, were in the audience, and Jane was there with babies Josie and Jack.

It was a celebratory time. But Roberts was, as always, watching closely how he was portrayed in the news media. It irked him that a *Washington Post* business reporter had described him in a column about his nomination as a member of the conservative Federalist Society. Roberts had been careful not to be closely associated with the society, which liberals loathed. But he had attended the organization's events and was ideologically aligned with the group. Although he had been listed in its 1997–1998 leadership directory, Roberts had insisted to the reporter that he had never officially joined its membership ranks. He did not want to be lumped in with the usual right-wing crowd, especially at this crucial confirmation time. He had learned from his 1992 ordeal, when Senate leaders, conferring with liberal advocates, had declined to act on his nomination.[24]

"Roberts has burnished his legal image carefully," the *Washington Post*'s Charles Lane observed in 2005 as he chronicled Roberts's effort to avoid being depicted as a member of the Federalist Society. "In conservative circles, membership in or association with the society has become a badge of ideological and political reliability. . . . But the society's alignment with conservative GOP politics and public policy makes Roberts's relationship with the organization a potentially sensitive point for his confirmation because many Democrats regard the organization with suspicion."[25]

In 2001, Lane noted, Roberts had asked for a correction, saying that he was not and never had been a member of the Federalist Society. As much as Roberts wanted to distance himself from the organization, however, he might not have been up for nomination in the first place if he had not won its imprimatur. Federalist Society leaders, including some who had worked with him in the Reagan and Bush years, had helped to screen and select the inaugural group of Bush nominees.

By this point in Roberts's career, he had argued more than thirty times before the Supreme Court. He had a first-rate reputation among top appellate attorneys from both sides of the aisle, and he understandably did not want to be viewed as a member of the hard right. Carvin, a colleague from the Reagan and first Bush administrations who, unlike Roberts, wore his conservatism boldly, remembered an exchange he had with Roberts about this issue. "This will give you a sense of John's sense of humor," he said in an interview. "When I asked if there was anything I could do, he said, 'Can you write an op-ed for the [*Washington*] *Post* condemning me as a squish? That would be very helpful.'" In the slang of the day, a "squish" was someone who could not be counted on to be true to conservative principles. While such a reputation might hurt one's chances of winning a Republican judicial nomination, it could help draw bipartisan support for confirmation.[26]

In 2001, unlike in 1992, Republicans held a majority in the Senate. Roberts's chances looked good. But at the end of May, less than three weeks after Bush had nominated Roberts, a US senator from Vermont, Jim Jeffords, who was a Republican, became an independent. Republicans lost their one-vote majority in the Senate and control over committee leadership positions, and Roberts's nomination stalled.

Four months later, on September 11, nearly three thousand people died when Al Qaeda operatives flew hijacked airplanes into New York City's World Trade Center towers, the Pentagon in suburban Virginia, and a field in Pennsylvania. One of the victims was Theodore Olson's wife, Barbara, a passenger on the plane that crashed into the Pentagon. Like many Americans, John and Jane Roberts remembered exactly where they were that day.

"I was in the kitchen," Jane recalled. "I had two babies at the time. They were in their high chairs. My mother called. She was retired at that point, so she was watching TV. . . . 'A plane has just hit the World Trade Center.' So I went and turned on the TV. I saw the second plane. I saw the towers come down." Jane was desperate to talk to John. "He was unreachable," she said. "He was in some meeting in a windowless conference room and he came out from the meeting later that morning and said, 'What's going on? The streets are empty.'"[27]

In response to the attacks, the United States invaded Afghanistan to destroy Osama bin Laden's Al Qaeda network. The government's ensuing actions generated a new slate of federal disputes involving the detention of suspected terrorists, military tribunals, and electronic surveillance. The Bush administration claimed that the president and the executive branch had sweeping power over these national security issues. President Bush ordered the Pentagon to establish special military commissions to hear cases against Al Qaeda suspects captured in Afghanistan, Pakistan, and elsewhere. Detainees were transported to the US naval base at Guantánamo Bay, Cuba.

As the nation struggled with the post-9/11 world of terrorism, attention slowly returned to Bush's judicial nominees. Democrats and liberal activists targeted Miguel Estrada, who had been slated for the DC Circuit alongside Roberts. Bush's liberal opponents knew they could not wage multiple battles effectively. They chose to focus on fighting the nomination of Estrada, a lawyer in the Washington office of Gibson, Dunn and Crutcher whose right-wing views were well known in Washington and who, if confirmed to the DC Circuit, could be positioned by the Bush administration as the first Hispanic nominee to the Supreme Court. (Estrada eventually withdrew.)

In the 2002 midterm elections, Republicans won enough seats in the Senate to reclaim a majority. Roberts received a Senate Judiciary Committee hearing in January 2003 after the new members of Congress were sworn in. Many of Roberts's family members attended his hearing. Jane was there, along with Josie and Jack, both three years old. Rosemary and Jack Roberts came as well, as did Roberts's three sisters, two brothers-in-law, and a handful of friends.

Roberts was protected from particularly probing questions because the Republican Senate Judiciary Committee chairman, Senator Orrin Hatch, had scheduled him to appear with two other judicial candidates: Jeffrey Sutton, an Ohio state solicitor general; and Deborah Cook, an Ohio Supreme Court justice. Both Sutton and Cook had been nominated for appointment to the Cincinnati-based US Court of Appeals for the Sixth Circuit. Sutton's nomination was the most contentious of the three because of his advocacy on behalf of states trying to minimize the reach of federal civil rights statutes. The Democratic senators devoted most of their time to questioning his record. They did object to the format that lumped the three nominees together, but in vain, as the Republican majority controlled the committee.

Turning to Roberts, Hatch opened with references to the esteem in which he was held by fellow appellate lawyers. Hatch cited a letter of support for Roberts that had been signed by more than 150 members of the District of Columbia Bar, including Lloyd Cutler, who had been White House counsel to the Democratic presidents Jimmy Carter and Bill Clinton; Boyden Gray, who had been the White House counsel for President George H.W. Bush; and Seth Waxman, who had been President Clinton's solicitor general. "Although as individuals we reflect a wide spectrum of political party affiliation and ideology," the letter said, "we are united in our belief that John Roberts will be an outstanding Federal Court of Appeals Judge and should be confirmed by the United States Senate." The signatories added, "He is one of the very best and most highly respected appellate lawyers in the Nation, with a deserved reputation as a brilliant writer and oral advocate. He is also a wonderful professional colleague, both because of his enormous skills and because of his unquestioned integrity and fair-mindedness." The letter demonstrated Roberts's ability to win influential supporters on the left as well as the right.

The questions posed by fellow Republicans were designed, of course, to help Roberts. Republican senator John Cornyn of Texas asked Roberts to expound on a lawyer's ethical obligations, a leading question designed to allow Roberts to defend his record for two Republican administrations. "I think the standard phrase is 'zealous advocacy' on behalf of a client," Roberts answered. "If it's an argument that has a reasonable basis in the law . . . the lawyer is ethically bound to present that argument on behalf of the client."

No senator asked about Roberts's decision not to defend the Federal Communications Commission policy of racial preferences for broadcasters when he was deputy solicitor general and handling *Metro Broadcasting, Inc., v. Federal Communications Commission*. At the time, his Democratic critics either did not know that he had reversed the government's position in the case or chose not to focus on it. Documents from his deputy solicitor general years were not publicly available.

To a Republican senator's stock question about the effect of politics on the law, Roberts responded as an advocate rather than as a judge. "If it all came down to just politics in the judicial branch," he said, "that would be very frustrating for lawyers who worked very hard to try to advocate their position and present the precedents and present the arguments." He said he knew judges could be frustrated when they were identified in the press by their party affiliation. "That," he said, "gives so little credit to the work that they put into the case. They work very hard and all of a sudden the report is, well, they just decided that way because of politics."[28]

Yet Roberts did not deny that judges could be political. "I know as an advocate, I never liked it when I had a political judge, when I was in front of a political judge, because, again, you put a lot of work into presenting the case, and you want to see that same work returned." His message was that he would not be political, even if others were.

Democratic senators later submitted written questions, which put Roberts on the record on important issues but did not allow for pointed follow-up queries. He minimized his role in the Reagan and George H.W. Bush administrations and claimed, again, that he had merely followed directions from his superiors. Asked about the constitutionality of the Freedom of Access to Clinic Entrances Act of 1994, which had been designed to allow women seeking abortions to enter clinics that were the sites of antiabortion protests, he wrote, implausibly, "I do not recall having any opinion." Of abortion rights, he said simply that *Roe v. Wade* was "the settled law of the land."[29]

In response to a question about the Reagan administration's racial policies, Roberts wrote, "I had no enforcement responsibilities." He added that he had had no formal role in implementing the Reagan administration's policy of "color blindness." "I do not think it would be appropriate for me to discuss my personal beliefs concerning the relative effectiveness of particular desegregation remedies," he wrote. Answering a separate question, Roberts said he did not remember writing a memo regarding the administration's response to the Supreme Court's 1980 decision in *City of Mobile v. Bolden*. That case had concerned an at-large election system that African American voters said made it impossible for them to elect their own representatives. He referred to "certain assignments" from Attorney General William French Smith, casting himself as more of a functionary than the fervent lawyer whose voice emerges in the memos of the day.

Perhaps it was a memory lapse. Perhaps he was trying to smooth over an episode with complex dimensions that he believed need not be aired. But it is hard to believe that Roberts would not remember the correspondence related to the *Bolden* case. In 1982, Roberts had gone to great lengths to shape the administration's position on voting rights and to fight congressional legislation to reverse the 1980 *Bolden* ruling. He had expressed strong opposition to legislation intended to let judges look at the discriminatory effects of an electoral practice, not merely whether the practice arose from provable intentional discrimination. In his 2003 response to senators, Roberts wrote, "The issues with which Attorney General Smith was concerned involved what form the legislative response to *Bolden* should take, not any effort to oppose congressional intent."[30]

The Senate Judiciary Committee approved Roberts by a vote of 16–3. Only the liberal Democrats Ted Kennedy of Massachusetts, Chuck Schumer of New York, and Richard Durbin of Illinois opposed his nomination. The full Senate confirmed Roberts on May 8, 2003, by a voice vote. Democratic senators agreed to bypass a roll-call vote. They were still unsure of what to make of Roberts, and many did not want their votes on the record.

ROBERTS'S NEW CHAMBERS WERE IN THE E. BARRETT PRETTYMAN Federal Courthouse, named for the father of his former law partner and located on Constitution Avenue, a mile from the US Supreme Court Building. The job involved some adjustment for the former advocate, but he enjoyed the intellectual challenge. The new hours, more standard than those of an advocate, suited his home life. He no longer had to travel to meet with clients or to argue before regional appeals courts.

During his tenure, which began in May 2003, Roberts kept a relatively low profile. Most of the disputes involved government regulations, and the subjects ranged from the rights of unions in collective bargaining to defendants' protections against unreasonable stops and the ability of foreign nations to use sovereign immunity when sued over terrorist acts. In the approximately fifty opinions he penned while on the DC Circuit Court, Roberts displayed his characteristically crisp, clear writing style. He employed vivid imagery and clever turns of phrase. In one dispute over the reach of an endangered-species regulation and the arroyo toad, he referred to "a hapless toad that, for reasons of its own, lives its entire life in California."[31] He used French expressions and quoted passages from literature, including works by Voltaire, Ralph Waldo Emerson, and Homer. Many judges borrow from classic works, and Roberts did the same, but with an edge. In one instance involving a complicated probate case, he wrote, "Even Dickens would have been impressed by the modern twist in this chapter of the Jung family's *Bleak House*: the Probate Division ordered the exhumation of Mother Jung's body for DNA testing to settle the heirship dispute."[32]

"As a stylist, Roberts already seems intent on finding ways to leaven his utilitarian prose with personalized elements of diction, metaphor, allusion, syntax, and tone," the legal scholar Laura Krugman Ray wrote of Roberts's work on the appellate court. She praised his apparent commitment to choosing the *mot juste*, and to crafting the perfect phrase. "It is these elements that convey to the reader a particular judicial persona, someone whose legal conclusions are formed not only by his mastery of the law but also by his reading, his interest in the expressive capacity of language and his perceptions of human behavior." She noted that Roberts displayed a "whimsical playfulness" in his use of colloquialisms, such as "crying wolf," "cutting off its nose to spite its face," and "not being able to have your cake and eat it too."[33]

In the hands of a less adroit writer and thinker, these kinds of flourishes might be described as trite. But Roberts enlivened clichés: "Sometimes a car being driven by an unlicensed driver, with no registration and stolen tags, really does belong to the driver's friend, and sometimes dogs do eat homework," Roberts wrote in a dissent in *United States v. Jackson* in 2005, about a convicted felon who claimed the car he was driving, with stolen tags in the trunk, belonged to his girlfriend.[34]

One of his sharpest opinions came in a case involving a dispute over a child who carried french fries onto the Washington, DC, Metro. The subway banned food, and juveniles disobeying the rule were to be arrested, while adults were merely issued citations. Tracey Hedgepeth had filed a lawsuit on behalf of her daughter, Ansche, claiming the girl's arrest had violated the Fourth and Fifth Amendments to the Constitution. "No one is very happy about the events that led to this litigation," Roberts wrote in *Hedgepeth v. Washington Metropolitan Area Transit Authority*: "A twelve-year-old girl was arrested, searched, and handcuffed. Her shoelaces were removed, and she was transported in the windowless rear compartment of a police vehicle to a juvenile processing center, where she was booked, fingerprinted, and detained until released to her mother some three hours later—all for eating a single french fry in a Metrorail station. The child was frightened, embarrassed, and crying throughout the ordeal." Roberts noted that the policies that had led to her arrest were revoked "after those responsible endured the sort of publicity reserved for adults who make young girls cry."[35]

But Roberts ruled against the girl, rejecting the arguments Hedgepeth's lawyers presented for heightened judicial scrutiny of the policy concerning how juveniles and adults were to be treated. He said the policy only needed to be rationally related to a legitimate goal, in this instance, promoting parental involvement with children who might commit delinquent acts. "We are rightly skeptical of paternalistic arguments when it comes to classifications addressing adults, but the concern that the state not treat adults like children surely does not prevent it from treating children like children," he wrote in the 2004 case.

Having advised judicial candidates, dating to the 1981 appointment of Sandra Day O'Connor, Roberts knew better than most aspirants for promotion to the high court that his judicial opinions could and would be used against him. He understood, too, that his opinions could also draw positive attention. He would not have been surprised to know that White House lawyers were watching his work, wondering if he would meet their expectations for conservatism.[36] Roberts was naturally careful, and he would have the advantage of a relatively short DC Circuit tenure, leaving no lengthy record that could be exploited by potential critics.

IN JULY 2004, MASSACHUSETTS SENATOR JOHN KERRY WON THE Democratic nomination for president and challenged Bush in his bid for a second term. In October, just weeks before Election Day, Chief Justice Rehnquist, who was eighty years old, revealed that he had thyroid cancer. The Rehnquist news added another important dimension to the presidential race. Whoever won the election would likely have the rare opportunity to appoint the next person to preside over America's highest court. Rehnquist was only the sixteenth chief justice in the nation's history.

Rehnquist's illness unsettled his colleagues. Despite his unyielding conservatism, gruff manner, and regular grimace (he suffered chronic back pain), the chief was beloved inside the Court. The associate justices considered him a fair-dealer behind the scenes. He was not cagey about his views and, unlike his predecessor, Warren Burger, did not have a reputation for manipulating the assignment of opinions. Rehnquist regularly walked the halls of the building, greeting employees. Early in her tenure, Ruth Bader Ginsburg, a liberal, sent him a letter telling him he was "a true mensch," and adding, with some playfulness, that it was "Yiddish for fine human."[37] At the other end of the ideological spectrum, Justice Clarence Thomas also felt grateful to Rehnquist, who had gone out of his way to buck him up when Thomas was criticized in news reports. "Dear Chief: Thank you so much for your call this morning," Thomas wrote in one note. "It meant a great deal to me."[38]

Rehnquist's warmest relationship was with his old Stanford classmate O'Connor. They had dated in law school, and after each had married and started families in Phoenix, they renewed the friendship. They shared dinners together, played charades, and vacationed together with their families. In the fall of 1971, when President Nixon had nominated Rehnquist to the associate justice seat, then Arizona state senator O'Connor worked hard to build support for his nomination among local officials. Fittingly, ten years later, when President Reagan nominated O'Connor, Rehnquist was one of her boosters. Asked about the 1981 nominee by a friend from Arizona, Rehnquist—who was from suburban Milwaukee, the nation's self-proclaimed bowling capital—wrote back that she was a "ten strike."[39]

When Rehnquist revealed his illness, Justices O'Connor and Ginsburg wrote to him immediately. They had both survived their own forms of cancer, and when Rehnquist began his chemotherapy, Ginsburg sent him a copy of her own chemo certificate of completion as a bit of inspiration and fellow-feeling. Justice Antonin Scalia, who had been a poker buddy of Rehnquist's for years, was worried about the chief, yet he could not help but ponder his chances for elevation to the chief justice position if Rehnquist died or retired. Rehnquist had been elevated from associate justice to chief in 1986, when he was sixty-one. Scalia was sixty-eight—perhaps too old, he thought, but it still seemed a possibility. There is no requirement that a chief justice have prior Court service. Of the sixteen who had been appointed chief by that point, five had earlier served as associate justices.[40]

Reporters raised the prospect of a Scalia elevation. Soon after Rehnquist's illness became public, Scalia seemed to be out and about more than ever. "Lately, I've been running into Nino everywhere," a Washington lawyer told *Time* magazine, referring to Scalia by his nickname. "He's showing that he actually can be charming and gregarious. It's a sign he's really interested in the job." The item ran under the headline "Justice Scalia: The Charm Offensive." The authors noted that "the tart-tongued Justice may not have the people skills to manage the court, build consensus among its nine members and represent the institution in public. That may explain why the famously dyspeptic Scalia has become a merry mainstay on the A-list Washington social circuit of late."[41]

Roberts, forty-nine, was just in his second year as a US appeals court judge. He was seen as a possibility for an associate justice position if Scalia or another sitting justice was elevated to the top spot. But that was still unlikely at this point. Other candidates, such as Wilkinson and Luttig, had been on the short list for years.

President Bush won reelection on November 2 without the drama of his first presidential election in 2000. Rehnquist was getting weaker and was staying away from the Court building. He was even too sick to arrange a betting pool for the election, a sure sign to his colleagues of his deteriorating condition. "One offsetting benefit from your absence is that we did not have any election bets," Justice John Paul Stevens wrote him, "which means that most of us saved the amounts that we would otherwise have probably added to your coffers."[42]

As the White House began planning for the second Bush inauguration, officials wondered whether Rehnquist would be able to attend and administer the oath of office on January 20, 2005. "He hadn't been seen in public for weeks," President Bush later wrote.[43]

But Rehnquist, shaky and barely able to speak, made it. When his moment on the platform came, some TV anchors observed that this would surely be Rehnquist's last reading of the presidential oath. As Bush raised his right hand, and his wife, Laura, held a Bible, Rehnquist read the thirty-five-word oath of office for Bush to repeat. Spectators could hear his labored breathing, which was amplified by the loudspeakers: "Repeat after me: I, George Walker Bush, do solemnly swear. . . ." The ceremony ended as Bush uttered the final phrase of the oath, "and will to the best of my ability, preserve, protect, and defend the Constitution of the United States."

Bush had gone his whole first four-year term without an opportunity to appoint anyone to the Supreme Court. But as seemed evident in the scene on the inaugural platform, he would soon have at least the chief justice's position to fill. The question for his conservative advisers, and for liberals anxious about what was next for the Court, was how much the successor would reflect Rehnquist's conservative image.

CHAPTER VI

THE RIGHT PLACE

ALBERTO GONZALES, THE ATTORNEY GENERAL OF THE UNITED States, invited John Roberts to a private meeting in his Department of Justice suite on April 1, 2005. It was early in President George W. Bush's second term, and Gonzales, the former White House counsel, had just been appointed to the position. From the beginning of his time with Bush, Gonzales had been interviewing prominent appeals court judges for possible elevation to the Supreme Court, and he was continuing the effort in his new post on the fifth floor of the Justice Department building. Nearly twenty-five years earlier, Roberts had taken a job in the same building of Art Deco archways and wide yellow-tile floors as an assistant to then attorney general William French Smith.[1]

President Bush's first term had passed without a vacancy on the high court. In fact, there had been no change on the bench since 1994, when Stephen Breyer had succeeded Harry Blackmun. Now, with Chief Justice William Rehnquist's illness, Bush and his legal team were poised not simply to choose a new justice but also to choose a new chief. They were pondering other vacancies, too, as three other justices had eclipsed retirement age for most professions: John Paul Stevens was about to turn eighty-five, Sandra Day O'Connor was seventy-five, and Ruth Bader Ginsburg was seventy-two.

Gonzales had begun meeting one-on-one with potential candidates, mainly lower court judges, after he moved to Washington at the start of Bush's first term. "I brought in Sam Alito quietly to the West Wing to meet with him," Gonzales recalled. "I went out to Mike Luttig's home in Virginia. I brought in Emilio Garza to meet with him." Gonzales also talked to J. Harvie Wilkinson. The administration's interest in conservative Republican-appointed US appeals court judges was not surprising. Wilkinson, Luttig, and Garza had been on nominee lists for more than a decade. During the George H.W. Bush administration, Judge Garza of the New Orleans–based Fifth Circuit had been interviewed for the 1991 vacancy after the retirement of Thurgood Marshall, although the president had ultimately chosen Clarence Thomas. Around the same time in 1991, the president had named Luttig to the Richmond-based Fourth Circuit, where Wilkinson already was sitting, having been appointed in 1984 by President Reagan.

Alito had also served Republican presidents, first as an assistant to the US solicitor general in the 1980s. President Reagan had appointed him as the US attorney in New Jersey, and President George H.W. Bush had made him a judge on the Philadelphia-based Third Circuit. Alito was sufficiently conservative to earn a nickname of Sc'Alito, a reference to Justice Scalia. Alito loathed the moniker, feeling that it was an ethnic slur. Yet the Scalia comparison distinguished him from the many other federal appeals court judges in the administration's sights.[2]

Roberts had not been a candidate for a Supreme Court nomination during George W. Bush's first term; he had only been appointed to the DC Circuit in 2003. But now that two years had gone by, he was a contender. Gonzales, preparing for his meeting with Roberts, knew that President Bush would eventually be asking him for a "gut check," as Gonzales termed it, and a sense of whether Roberts, or any other candidate, for that matter, would deliver the consistent conservative votes Bush sought. "For

President Bush, this was a big deal," Gonzales said. "He made it clear to me in the transition he did not want another [David] Souter. He wanted no surprises."[3]

As President Bush later elaborated in his memoir, "I knew how proud Dad was to have appointed Clarence Thomas, a wise, principled, humane man. I also knew he was disappointed that his other nominee, David Souter, had evolved into a different kind of judge than he expected." The first president Bush had appointed Souter, who was then a rookie federal appellate judge, in 1990 based on advice from the Republican senator Warren Rudman and the White House chief of staff John Sununu. Both men had known Souter in their home state of New Hampshire, where Souter had been a former state attorney general and state supreme court judge. Rudman, who was also a former state attorney general, had pushed the hardest for his protégé and was instrumental in getting Souter on the US Appeals Court for the First Circuit earlier in 1990.[4]

But on the US Supreme Court, Justice Souter gradually leaned to the left, endorsing abortion rights, race-based affirmative action, and a higher wall of separation between church and state. He also favored a robust interpretation of federal power, as when he joined liberal dissenters who sought to uphold a federal statute that would have prohibited guns near local schools. "No more Souters," became the rallying cry of hard-right Republicans as the second President Bush prepared to fill a possible vacancy on the Court.

Gonzales certainly wanted to make sure the younger President Bush did not leave such a legacy on the Court. Earlier, Gonzales himself had been on an informal White House short list for the Supreme Court, and perhaps if an opening had come soon after his arrival in Washington, he could have become the country's first Hispanic justice. But over time some advisers to Bush doubted the depth of Gonzales's commitment to conservative causes. Gonzales had spoken in favor of affirmative action, and he had voted for abortion rights when he was a Texas Supreme Court justice. By early 2005, Bush had told Gonzales that he wanted to keep him as attorney general. Gonzales was disappointed, but he felt strongly about helping to select a nominee who would fulfill Bush's goals. That was becoming a more urgent task. Rehnquist returned to the Court in March, but he appeared weak, and his resignation seemed imminent.

When Gonzales met with Roberts, a former law clerk of the ailing chief justice, on April 1, Roberts was just fifty years old. Other top contenders were older and had worn judicial robes far longer than two years. But Roberts was more than ready for the conversation. He had been in Gonzales's position as an interviewer of prospective judges in the Reagan and first Bush administrations.

"We spent about an hour together," Gonzales recalled. "I said give me your views on statutory construction. What are your views on the Constitution? What's the right approach to interpreting the Constitution? Precedent? The main thing I was asking about was precedent: When is it appropriate for a Supreme Court justice to ignore precedent? What does your oath of office allow you to do? What about societal norms? What about reliance on foreign law? It was a very good conversation. John was extremely candid, very forthcoming. I came away from that conversation knowing I would be comfortable recommending him for the Court."[5]

Gonzales also considered whether Roberts could move through Senate confirmation relatively unscathed. Around this time, Senate Democrats had filibustered several of Bush's lower court nominations, and Senate Majority Leader Bill Frist, a Republican, was contemplating a change in Senate rules to try to counteract those efforts. In the end, a bipartisan group of fourteen senators averted the proposed overhaul in Senate filibuster rules by fashioning a compromise that allowed votes on some of President Bush's controversial lower court nominees yet preserved the right to block arguably extreme nominees in "extraordinary circumstances."[6]

"One of the major advantages is that he had a limited paper trail in the judiciary," Gonzales said, referring to Roberts's two years on the bench. But the relative brevity of his record also meant that a question mark hung over Roberts. Bush administration officials, and possible critics, would have to go back decades, to Roberts's earlier writings, for signs of the kind of justice he would be.

Gonzales said that Roberts's reputation and DC Circuit record advanced him to the next phase of White House vetting. Yet even with the positive early signals, Roberts would not become overly confident. The sting from 1992, when his nomination by Bush's father stalled in the Senate, had not worn off. He had seen too many colleagues, including his former boss Ken Starr, appear positioned for the high court only to be passed over.[7]

THREE DAYS AFTER THE MEETING WITH GONZALES, JUDGE ROBERTS sat on the three-judge DC Circuit panel that heard arguments in a significant post-9/11 case testing the boundaries of President Bush's powers, *Hamdan v. Rumsfeld*. (Cases in US courts of appeals are typically heard by three-judge panels randomly selected for each case; on rare occasions, a case is heard "en banc," that is, with all the judges sitting.) It was a coincidence, yet a potential clash of interests, that Roberts faced such a crucial dispute at a time when he was interviewing for a Supreme Court position.

Salim Ahmed Hamdan, a former driver for Al Qaeda leader Osama bin Laden, was one of hundreds of men being held at the US naval base at Guantánamo Bay, Cuba. Hamdan and other detainees were arguing that the Bush administration had failed to honor prisoner-of-war provisions in the 1949 Geneva Conventions when it attempted to use military commissions—rather than regular US courts—to try them. The Bush administration countered that so-called enemy combatants, who targeted civilians and engaged in possible terrorism, were properly tried by military commissions.

Judge Roberts asked skeptical questions of Hamdan's lawyer during the public arguments on April 4, and then privately cast his vote in favor of the administration and the military commission setup. The 3–0 vote and panel decision would not become public for several weeks. Meanwhile, the administration's vetting process continued.[8]

Soon after Roberts had cast his vote in *Hamdan v. Rumsfeld*, he was interviewed for a possible Supreme Court position again, on May 3. The setting was far more intimidating than Gonzales's office at the Justice Department. The interview occurred at Vice President Dick Cheney's home at Observatory Hill. Roberts faced Cheney and Gonzales along with White House Chief of Staff Andy Card, White House Counsel Harriet Miers, and Deputy Chief of Staff Karl Rove, who served as the president's top political adviser. This "working group" had been put together by Bush in anticipation of a vacancy as the end of the Supreme Court term drew near. Justices traditionally have announced retirements close to the end of a session in June.

The group did not start out predisposed to Roberts. Cheney preferred Luttig. He was also open to the possibility of elevating Associate Justice Scalia to the chief justice position. Cheney and Scalia had worked together in the Ford administration in the mid-1970s, and they remained friends and hunting partners. A year earlier, the two men had been on a duck hunting trip that had garnered intense media attention because it had taken place just three weeks after the Court had agreed to hear a White House appeal in a case involving the private meetings of Vice President Cheney's energy task force. Critics had questioned Scalia's impartiality, and lawyers for the Sierra Club, a party to the case, had asked him to recuse himself from the Cheney matter. Scalia rejected the recusal request, laying out his position in a forceful twenty-one-page response.[9]

At the vice president's residence, the top Bush aides loosely divided possible candidates for the chief justice and associate justice positions. "We would not have thought of John [Roberts] in the beginning for chief, because he had limited judicial experience," Gonzales later said. "But . . . there was a discussion about elevating someone like Scalia into the chief slot and putting someone like Roberts into that seat." Yet President Bush and Attorney General Gonzales knew that promoting the sharp-tongued, hard-right Scalia to chief justice would require an exhausting battle. "It was clear over time that [Bush] did not want a titanic fight over a Supreme Court nominee," Gonzales said.[10]

Around the same time, top aides to Bush and Cheney were conferring with conservative advocates, including Leonard Leo of the Federalist Society, which through the decades has become more active in vetting

Republican judicial candidates. Prompted by one of Cheney's aides, Leo arranged a breakfast meeting with Roberts in a private suite at the Mayflower Hotel to talk to him about his constitutional views.

Bush officials were also discreetly trying to keep tabs on Rehnquist's health through his network of clerks and the other justices. They did not know Justice O'Connor's thinking as she dealt with the deteriorating health of her husband, John, who had Alzheimer's. She pondered the possibility of retiring so that she could devote more time to his care, but she also thought that Rehnquist's cancer put him in line to retire first. O'Connor and Rehnquist understood the politics of the confirmation process, and that two justices should not retire at the same time, for risk of complicating and delaying Senate consideration of a successor. She was managing her husband's dementia in her determined way. She brought him into work on many days to keep an eye on him. He would sit in her chambers, sometimes join a conversation, and sometimes nod off.

She continued to write the ailing Chief Justice Rehnquist optimistic notes, never referring to her own personal difficulties. "John and I are enjoying two weeks in Arizona," she had told him in early 2005. "There has been a fair amount of rain and the desert is like a green carpet. It is green even from our airplane window. More like Ireland than Arizona. The wildflowers should be magnificent. Some say the best in 50 or more years."[11]

On May 23, Roberts had another interview, this time with White House counsel Miers. Roberts needed to have his financial information in order, as did every other potential nominee. Roberts was making $171,800 a year as a federal appeals court judge, but his net worth was more than $6 million. He had become wealthy through his successful private practice. He owned more than $1.6 million in stock, with his largest holdings in technology and entertainment companies.[12]

The annual Supreme Court term came to a close on Monday, June 27. The final decisions involved two closely watched and related cases concerning public displays of the Ten Commandments on government property. By two different sets of 5–4 votes, the justices struck down the posting of the Ten Commandments in Kentucky courthouses because

the displays were blatantly religious, but allowed a granite Commandments monument on the grounds of the Texas Capitol, because it was
surrounded by other historical markers. Justice Stephen Breyer cast the
deciding vote in both cases. He explained in a concurring statement that,
in the Kentucky situation, *McCreary County v. American Civil Liberties
Union*, a reasonable observer would think the counties "meant to empha-
size and celebrate the Commandments' religious message," while in the
Texas situation, *Van Orden v. Perry*, the physical setting on the Capitol
grounds suggested "that the state itself intended the nonreligious aspects
of the tablet's message to predominate."[13]

Chief Justice Rehnquist wrote the majority opinion upholding the
constitutionality of the Ten Commandments on the Texas Capitol
grounds. As Rehnquist briefly outlined the Court's rationale from the
bench, he spoke in a scratchy, unfamiliar voice. He occasionally wiped
secretions from the tracheotomy tube that helped him breathe. He then
announced the names of the other justices who had filed separate opinions in the Texas case, a long list that demonstrated the divisive nature
of the religious liberty rationales: Scalia and Thomas had each written
a concurring opinion; Breyer had concurred only in the judgment; Stevens had written a dissenting opinion joined by Ginsburg; O'Connor had
written a separate dissenting opinion; Souter had written another separate
dissenting opinion, joined by Stevens and Ginsburg.

"I didn't know we had that many people on our Court," Rehnquist
remarked, as he made it to the end of the unusually lengthy list. It was
the very last day of the 2004–2005 session, and his quip prompted spontaneous, unusually loud laughter from the spectators. It was as if everyone
in the courtroom sighed with relief that the ailing chief had made it to
the end of the term.

Over the next hours and days, White House officials, news reporters,
legal analysts, and other close observers of the Supreme Court waited for
an announcement. Was the chief justice, who was so obviously ill, going
to step down?

Justice O'Connor was not prepared to stand back and wait. She went
to her old friend and asked about his plans. He told her he believed he

could make it through another term. Justice O'Connor wondered whether he would, given his apparently deteriorating condition. But his decision nonetheless created an opening for her.

As she had done so many times before in her pioneering life, O'Connor seized the moment. She believed it was best for her husband of five decades that she leave the bench. Once O'Connor made up her mind, she informed only close aides. She gave a short letter of resignation to the Court's marshal, Pamela Talkin, and told her to keep it safe until Talkin could personally deliver it to the White House at the end of the week, on Friday, July 1. O'Connor did not tell Talkin what was in the letter. Talkin could have guessed, but she kept O'Connor's confidence and delivered her letter to White House Counsel Miers on the morning of the appointed day.

"We all assumed it was from Chief Justice William Rehnquist," Bush recalled of hearing that a letter from the Court was to be delivered. He expressed surprise when Miers alerted him that it was from O'Connor. "I was fond of Sandra and called her immediately after I received her letter," he later wrote. "She told me it was time for her to go take care of her beloved husband, John, who was suffering from Alzheimer's."[14]

When Gonzales received Miers's call, it had been exactly two months since he had met privately with Roberts. "We have a retirement," she told him. "It's not who we expected."[15]

O'Connor's retirement had greater implications for the direction of the Court than Rehnquist's would have had. O'Connor's record was more moderate than Rehnquist's, because, although she was a conservative, she was not doctrinaire. Her votes and her ability to craft consensus put her at the center of the Court—and in control of so many cases that the Rehnquist Court was often known among lawyers as the O'Connor Court. Over her quarter-century tenure the first woman justice had become the most influential justice. She cast decisive votes and crafted the legal reasoning—which would influence future cases—to uphold abortion rights and affirmative action. She determined rules for the right to counsel and death penalty appeals. She developed the contemporary standards for separation of church and state. Her ability to manage her multiple roles as lawyer, wife, and mother was legendary. In October 1957, three days after she was sworn in to the Arizona bar, she delivered her first son. She and John eventually had two more sons. When she was rejected for positions at large law firms, she hung out her own shingle and then turned to public service as a government lawyer. She became an Arizona state senator and a skilled back-room negotiator, experience that served her well as a justice.

O'Connor fostered civility and good relations among her colleagues. Around the time of her retirement, Clarence Thomas recalled in an interview that she had lobbied him and their other colleagues to eat lunch together after the justices' daily oral arguments, rather than return to their individual chambers. Thomas said he resisted her entreaties when he joined the Court in 1991: "I was not inclined to do so. I was really tired. I wanted to get my work done. We had mail piled up. . . . But she kept insisting . . . 'Clarence, you should join us for lunch now.'" Thomas eventually did. After Ginsburg and Breyer were appointed in the early 1990s, O'Connor ensured that all nine began dining together.[16]

By midmorning on July 1, the day her letter was delivered, the president had gathered Cheney, Rove, Miers, and Gonzales in the Oval Office. Bush made it clear that he did not want to begin with a list with only men on it. Up to that point, the most promising candidates were four US appeals court judges: Luttig, Wilkinson, Alito, and Roberts. No women candidates had been seriously screened or interviewed. Now, with pressure from the president and first lady, the team added US Appeals Court Judges Priscilla Owen and Edith Brown Clement, both members of the New Orleans–based Fifth Circuit and both reliably conservative.

The next days were critical for the leading candidates and their surrogates as all jockeyed for position. Among the considerations on the table were the conservatism of a potential nominee; his or her temperament and collegiality; whether the judge would enhance the president's standing; and how much political capital a confirmation fight might require. Would it draw attention and resources away from the administration's other priorities? Because O'Connor was known as a moderate conservative, Bush's political advisers wanted to pitch the nominee to replace her as someone who would not radically change the direction of the Court.

Three contenders—Wilkinson, Luttig, and Roberts—had cut their teeth in the Reagan administration and had well-placed friends and former colleagues (including law clerks and law partners) in the current Bush White House.

Judge Wilkinson was sixty-one and the most senior of the group. His age was a potential problem. Justice Ginsburg had been appointed by Democratic president Bill Clinton when she was sixty, in 1993. But Republican presidents tended to seek younger nominees who would serve and impact the law for a longer period of time. (The last GOP high court appointee had been Thomas, who was just forty-three at the time of his appointment.) Another sticking point was that Wilkinson seemed more restrained ideologically than his Fourth Circuit colleague Luttig. Some Bush aides wondered whether he would be "squishy" on issues of importance to conservatives.

Indeed, Luttig, then fifty, was the favorite of the hard-right members of the group. Yet his record also meant he likely would face a difficult confirmation battle. He had criticized abortion rights as he voted to uphold a Virginia law requiring young women to notify their parents of their choice to get an abortion, and he had authored a controversial emergency opinion that had kept the state's late-term abortion ban in place.[17]

At the time, it was difficult for reporters and other outsiders to assess how the backers of each Fourth Circuit judge were faring. There was a sense that each side might be canceling the other out. Roberts, who, like Luttig, was fifty years old, did not have anyone staunchly opposed to his potential nomination. Yet the president's advisers wondered what was really beneath Roberts's perfect self-presentation. He had been on the DC Circuit for only two years, and, when pressed by Cheney about his conservatism in his interview at Observatory Hill, had answered haltingly. Files from Roberts's years in the Reagan administration were not yet fully available, so Bush's staff did not know how hard he had fought for socially conservative positions. Among those vouching for Roberts were Fred Fielding and Ken Starr, along with a younger colleague, David Leitch, who had worked with Roberts at Hogan and Hartson. Leitch had become an associate White House counsel.

The fifty-five-year-old Alito was the dark horse. Owing to his appointment to a Newark-based seat on the Third Circuit in 1990 by George H.W. Bush, he had been away from Washington for fifteen years. He was not as well connected as his competitors, but he had an advantage in terms of experience with the process. Gonzales said that when he first met Alito, Alito had seemed nervous, "not ready for prime time." But in the summer of 2005, Gonzales said, Alito "was so concise in his answers that he finished early. He was one of the leading candidates."[18]

AS ADMINISTRATION OFFICIALS WERE SCREENING FINALISTS, SEN-ate leaders, both Republican and Democratic, launched the first phase of their constitutional "advice and consent" role. Democrats were especially wary of anyone Bush might nominate and wanted to persuade him to avoid judges they considered objectionable.

A few months earlier, a group of moderates from each party had brokered the deal to end a stalemate over lower court judicial nominations. The compromise had allowed a handful of controversial Bush nominees to win confirmation to federal appeals courts, and at the same time preserved the option of a Democratic filibuster for Bush judicial nominees in "extraordinary circumstances." The last successful filibuster of a Supreme Court candidate had occurred in 1968, when President Johnson had tried to elevate Justice Abe Fortas to the chief justice position.[19]

Knowing that it would be difficult to block a nominee once the selection was made, top Senate Democrats wanted to influence the choice from the outset. Senate Minority Leader Harry Reid of Nevada and the ranking Democrat on the Senate Judiciary Committee, Patrick Leahy, were scheduled to meet with Bush on July 12. They gathered the day before to try to devise a strategy to influence him. They did not know who was on the president's short list, but, according to a memo to Reid from his top counsel, Ronald Weich, they anticipated several possible contenders. "While all are conservative," Weich wrote in the July 9 memo, "they are not uniformly extreme, and your goal in this meeting should be to persuade the President to nominate one of the more mainstream candidates."[20]

Democratic staffers had divided the possible nominees into three categories. Civil rights groups had pressured them to designate several of the potential choices as "Unacceptable," but Reid and Leahy wanted to keep the "Unacceptable" list short in order to make it effective when they read it to Bush. They designated another group "Probably Acceptable, But Would Face Tough Questioning." This group included Attorney General Gonzales and Larry Thompson, a former deputy attorney general who had become Pepsi's general counsel. Neither of these men were under consideration—no doubt because their mixed records were indeed more acceptable to Democrats.

The middle category, labeled "Not Favored, but Probably Would Not Provoke a Major Confrontation"—that is, a filibuster—included Alito, Clement, Roberts, and Wilkinson. "You should be very careful how you talk about candidates in this middle category," Weich, who is now dean of the University of Baltimore School of Law, told Reid. "It would be disastrous if the White House could say later that you gave these candidates a green light. Rather, you are giving them a blinking red light: proceed with extreme caution." Weich said later there was debate among Democratic staffers about whether Roberts should be in the middle category or the "Unacceptable" category. Roberts ended up in the middle category, in part because of his Democratic lawyer friends and colleagues from white-shoe firms. They knew him through his Hogan and Hartson appellate work. The Reagan memos had not yet been publicly released.

The final category, which got the full title of "Unacceptable, Would Provoke a MAJOR confrontation," included Luttig and Garza. "The most important mission you can accomplish in this meeting is to warn the President away from nominating anyone in this category," Weich wrote in his memo to Reid. "These candidates are really right-wing zealots with plenty of smoking guns in their opinions and writings. . . . Your basic point to the President is: *for the good of the country, don't go there.*"[21]

Reid and Leahy spent an hour with Bush early on July 12. Also in the meeting were the Republican Senate majority leader, Bill Frist, and the Senate Judiciary Committee chairman, Arlen Specter. Miers and Card, along with other top Bush aides, had been keeping Frist and Specter apprised of the selection progress. President Bush still had not personally interviewed any of the candidates, so no one knew what lay in store.

THE DECISIVE DAY WAS JULY 15. THAT MORNING, THE THREE-JUDGE panel of the DC Circuit that had heard the *Hamdan* military-tribunal dispute happened to issue its decision. The court, which included Roberts, ruled unanimously that the 1949 Geneva Conventions did not bar the use of military commissions or give Osama bin Laden's former driver or any other detainee the right to seek enforcement of the conventions in US courts. The DC Circuit said a joint resolution that Congress had passed in response to the September 11 attacks, which authorized the president "to use all necessary and appropriate force" against nations, organizations, or people who had any part in the attacks, covered the creation of the military commissions to try detainees such as Salim Ahmed Hamdan.[22]

Later that day at the White House, President Bush interviewed Luttig and Roberts. They had been on parallel tracks since 1981, when they had met during the Reagan administration. And now they were interviewing for the highest court on the same day.

Getting to the interview turned out to be logistically complicated for Roberts. He was in London in early July, fulfilling a teaching commitment. He had been waiting for word from the administration about an interview, and when it came, he had to quickly race back to Washington. Still, he did not leave his preparation to chance. He found time to talk at length to two confidants from his Harvard Law School days and rehearse what he wanted to tell the president.

Roberts approached the interview as he did oral arguments, imagining various lines of questioning and devising ways to convey his message. He had learned from the interview run by Vice President Cheney, when he felt he had not put his best case forward or succinctly articulated his brand of conservatism. He knew he had to be clearer. Roberts also understood the importance of a human touch. Just as he knew that within every legal case was a compelling story, he realized that every Supreme Court nomination had a personal story. Roberts wanted Bush to see him as a well-rounded jurist. He was also ready to invoke the baseball metaphor that would become his signature during his confirmation hearing. It was a calculated move. The metaphor would appeal to a man who was a former owner of the Texas Rangers baseball team.

With all the finalists he interviewed, Bush began with a tour of the White House residence. "I tried to put them at ease by giving them a tour of the living area," Bush recounted. "Then I took them to the family sitting room that overlooks the West Wing. I had read the summaries of their legal opinions; now I wanted to read the people. I was looking for someone who shared my judicial philosophy, and whose values wouldn't change over time. I went into the interviews hoping one person would stand apart."[23]

Luttig, who had been waiting for years for his shot at the high court, vividly remembered the day of his interview with Bush. The president did not ask questions on particular legal issues. "The president is briefed about how to ask questions," Luttig said, referring to the president's interest in avoiding direct questions about how a judge would rule on cases. "It's much more conversational and personal. John talked baseball. . . . The president and I are both from Texas so we talked about Texas."

Luttig and Roberts spoke later that day about the coincidence of two longtime friends finding themselves at the White House on the same day. "We went back to back," Luttig recalled. "John and I talked that night. . . . We're both funny people. We're cutting up about it. There was no tension."[24]

As it turned out, Bush favored Roberts. "Behind the sparkling resume was a genuine man with a gentle soul," Bush later wrote of his impressions of Roberts in that White House meeting. "He had a quick smile and spoke with a passion about the two young children he and his wife, Jane, had adopted. His command of the law was obvious, as was his character." Yet when he discussed his preference for Roberts with Cheney, Gonzales, Miers, Rove, and Card, the president realized they did not all share his view. "They liked Roberts, but he was not at the top of all lists," Bush recalled. "Dick and Al backed Luttig, who they felt was the most dedicated conservative jurist. Harriet supported Alito because he had the most established judicial record. Andy and Karl shared my inclination toward Roberts."[25]

The president turned to younger lawyers in the White House counsel's office for advice. "One was Brett Kavanaugh, whom I had nominated to the D.C. Circuit Court of Appeals," Bush recounted. "Brett told me that Luttig, Alito, and Roberts would all be solid justices. The tiebreaker question, he suggested, was which man would be the most effective leader on the Court—the most capable of convincing his colleagues through persuasion and strategic thinking."[26]

That way of looking at it sealed Bush's choice of Roberts.

"I believed Roberts would be a natural leader," Bush wrote. Addressing the "Souter" issue, he recalled: "I didn't worry about him drifting away from his principles over time. He described his philosophy of judicial modesty with a baseball analogy that stuck with me: 'A good judge is like an umpire—and no umpire thinks he is the most important person on the field.'"[27]

Luttig had come close. Despite opposition by Senate Democratic leaders and a temperament that some Bush aides had warned could alienate other justices, he was in contention until the end. He and the other runners-up received calls on the morning of July 19. "We're going in another direction," White House Counsel Miers told them. "That was it," recalled Luttig. "Almost verbatim." He was deeply disappointed, and referred in an interview years later to the public spotlight that had been on him during the process. "At that point, you'll find that I was being followed by the media."[28]

The media attention directed at Luttig reflected the expectations around his candidacy. Television cameras were outside his suburban Virginia home. The day of the ultimate announcement of Roberts, Ed

Gillespie, a GOP political operative who was tapped to guide the new nominee through the Senate process, fielded a call from CNN's John King, who said, "I'm hearing that Michael Luttig has just loaded his family into their car in their Sunday best and are leaving Richmond for Washington. Do you know if that's true?"[29]

Luttig had trouble moving on. Attorney General Gonzales said years later that he had been aware of Luttig's feelings, but that, to his knowledge, no one had been "out to get Mike Luttig." Instead, they were concerned about the Senate confirmation process and "what kind of fight" they were "willing to take on." Fred Fielding, who had been a confidant to several presidents, had followed the twists and turns of the selection process and respected both Luttig and Roberts, who had worked for him in the Reagan years. "I had two of my people, my friends, in the race. I know that people were not against Mike Luttig. Mike thought they were," he later said.[30]

The public learned of President Bush's choice to nominate Roberts as the nation's 109th Supreme Court justice during a prime-time, nationally televised address on the night of July 19. The president referred to Roberts's "superb credentials," his Ivy League education, his work in earlier presidential administrations, and the thirty-nine cases he had argued before the Supreme Court. He said he had consulted with more than seventy members of the Senate in making the choice.

On stage with the president and nominee were Jane Roberts; their daughter, Josie, who was about to turn five years old; and their son, Jack, who was a few months younger than Josie. Although the cameras did not capture it, Jack pulled away from Jane and began dancing around under the lights. President Bush desperately tried to ignore the distraction and kept speaking. John Roberts stood stone-faced. Jane tensed and did not move. Josie watched, appearing concerned and clinging to her mother's side. Barbara Bush, the former first lady and an experienced mother and grandmother, tried to lure Jack toward where she was sitting. He refused and continued his antics. White House aides were terrified that he would begin to scream or that someone trying to help out would inadvertently exacerbate the situation and cause the cameras to move from President Bush and Roberts to the child.[31]

"Everything went according to plan until, during my primetime televised speech, four-year-old Jack Roberts slipped out of his mother's grip and started dancing around the floor," Bush recalled in his memoir about that moment in the East Room. "We later learned he was imitating Spider-Man. I saw him out of the corner of my eye, and it took all my concentration to continue my remarks."[32]

When Roberts moved to his place in front of the microphone, he had to use all his sense of focus to stay on script, which of course he did. He expressed appreciation and humility. He referred to his many years as a Supreme Court advocate and said that when he entered the Supreme Court Building and went up to argue a case, he always got a lump in his throat. He thanked his parents and sisters, Jane, and the children. While he was speaking, Jane managed to grab Jack and hand him off to a presidential aide.

Watching the full tape of Jack dancing and his parents' reaction, one cannot help but be impressed by how they handled the situation. Roberts later said that when administration officials had requested that Jack and Josie be present at the event, Jane had warned that it might not be a good idea. John, though, had given his assent. "It was, in retrospect, endearing," Roberts said. "I assure you, only in retrospect."[33]

"Jack is dancing," Roberts remembered, " . . . and I'm looking at Jane and . . . wondering . . . Jane, why aren't you doing anything? And as she explained later . . . if she had tried to corral Jack at that time, he could easily have run to me, . . . untied the president's shoes, or whatever. . . . Having young children is great to keep things in perspective."[34]

Ed Gillespie, the public relations man the administration had hired to help promote the nominee to the news media, the general public, and the senators, later wrote, "It may sound cynical but I knew the little guy had just made it impossible for Democrats to cast Judge John G. Roberts as 'another Robert Bork.'" Gillespie said his goal was to "make it harder for the extreme liberal groups to demonize our nominee." Of his first meeting with Jane, Gillespie wrote, "I was happy to see that she was an outgoing, attractive Irish lass!"[35]

Roberts likely knew better than Gillespie how to present himself. But Gillespie correctly predicted the initial response to Roberts. Republicans were effusive and Democrats muted their complaints throughout their initial encounters with the nominee. The reaction was the opposite of the reaction to Bork in 1987, when his nomination had galvanized the left in one of the most bitter, bruising confirmation hearings in history. "If Bork's nomination in 1987 heralded a new, more highly public and hyper-ideological era of judicial nominations," wrote *New York* magazine's Kurt Andersen, who graduated in the same Harvard College class as Roberts, and lived in the same dorm, "Roberts's appointment represents the next stage of politicization—of the nominee chosen like a golden boy by the party bosses, nice-looking and pleasant-seeming, a prospective justice who, positions aside, seems like a *good guy*."[36]

As Roberts began meeting with senators, he remained steady and up-beat. Democrats said they were cautiously studying the nominee's record. No one even suggested a filibuster fight. Some senators who had no intention of voting for him could not help but act as if they would.

In late August, while Roberts prepared for his Senate Judiciary Committee hearings, Hurricane Katrina slammed into New Orleans. The Category 5 storm surge overwhelmed the city's levees and flooded many neighborhoods. More than a thousand people died, many of them from drowning, many of them black and poor. The Bush administration was delayed and incompetent in responding. The nation watched in horror as people who had lost their homes crowded into unsanitary and dangerous conditions in the Superdome stadium. Others holed up in their attics or escaped to their roofs to wait for rescuers who were slow to arrive.

President Bush awkwardly praised the federal response to the crisis. "Brownie, you're doing a heckuva job," he told Michael Brown, head of the Federal Emergency Management Agency. Amid the death and devastation, Bush's response, which immediately became a TV punchline, generated only more criticism for his administration. Hundreds of people were stranded, drowned bodies were left in the streets, and civil order appeared to be collapsing.

During the ongoing catastrophe, Bush received a late-night call on September 3. Rehnquist had died. Thyroid cancer had overcome the man who believed he could beat it. The next morning, Bush summoned his top advisers to the White House. He had no appetite for more controversy. Roberts had been impressing senators on his courtesy visits. Bush was ready to make him his nominee for chief justice; he would decide on a new nominee to replace O'Connor later. When Cheney walked into the meeting, Bush said, "Dick, I'm going with Roberts."

Roberts learned later that day, on September 4, that he was suddenly the president's choice to replace Rehnquist, his mentor. The stakes were as high as they could be now, and Roberts could not help but be worried about how his confirmation process would go.

For other possible candidates, including Justice Scalia, the announcement of Roberts's nomination to the chief spot was disappointing. "That would have been a great honor," Scalia said years later in an interview. "But it was so unrealistic. Age. Age, for one. It's ridiculous. I would have advised them against doing that." Scalia had quietly hoped for the opportunity, but he was a realist.[37]

Rehnquist's funeral delayed Roberts's confirmation hearings, which had originally been set for early September. Roberts joined seven other pallbearers on September 6 to carry Rehnquist's flag-draped casket up the marble steps of the Supreme Court Building. All but two of the justices were in attendance (Kennedy and Souter were traveling). O'Connor's face was streaked with tears. The next day at the funeral, which was held at St. Matthew's Cathedral, where Roberts had been married nearly a decade earlier, Justice O'Connor took the lead in the tributes to her former classmate. "The chief was a betting man, . . . " she told the overflowing crowd. "I think the chief bet he could live out another term despite his illness. He lost the bet, as did all of us, but he won all the prizes for a life well lived. We love you, Chief." Turning to the congregation, she then declared, "Now as the chief would say, Counsel, the red light is on. Your time is up."[38]

ROBERTS APPEARED BEFORE THE SENATE JUDICIARY COMMITTEE for four days of testimony beginning on September 12, and he performed nearly flawlessly. When speaking of his roots in Indiana, he referred to "the limitless fields punctuated only by a silo or barn." The description evoked middle America more than might have been justified by his life in the exclusive Long Beach community on Lake Michigan or his education at La Lumiere, a selective boarding school. Of course, during televised Senate Judiciary Committee hearings, Supreme Court nominees always present an edited image of themselves. He left behind the cuff links and portrayed himself as a plainspoken, modest midwesterner.

Better than most lawyers, Roberts understood the value of a pitch, a slogan. He knew that just the right phrase or word could define the moment and his candidacy. In perhaps the most memorable part of his opening, Roberts said, "Judges are like umpires. Umpires don't make the rules, they apply them. The role of an umpire and a judge is critical. They make sure everybody plays by the rules, but it is a limited role. Nobody ever went to a ball game to see the umpire."[39]

Roberts had successfully used the umpire metaphor in his July meeting with President Bush. When he returned to it at his confirmation hearing, he gave the media a headline and viewers an accessible shorthand for understanding him. Many senators embraced the metaphor, even though they recognized there was no strike zone in the law or set of easy formulas on which judges could always rely. The US Constitution is open ended in many ways, and the words of a statute can be ambiguous. Judges necessarily bring in their own views as they balance competing interests.

Over the course of his four days in the witness chair before the senators, Roberts deployed not just unforgettable metaphors but wry humor. When Senator Lindsey Graham, a Republican from South Carolina, asked what he would like future historians to say about him, Roberts quipped, "I'd like them to start by saying: He was confirmed." After the laughter in the room had subsided, the nominee said, "I would like them to say I was a good judge."

Roberts described himself as a "modest judge" and assured the senators of his commitment to the legal concept of *stare decisis*, "to stand by things decided," the principle of ensuring continuity in the law by following precedent. Yet he made clear that patterns in the law could also be broken. Roberts described how precedents could be dismantled, by justices chipping away at the cornerstones of rulings until revered legal concepts were so weakened that they must fall.

In an exchange with the committee chairman, Arlen Specter, a long-time senator from Pennsylvania, Roberts elaborated on his view of when precedents could be reversed. "The principles of *stare decisis* look at a number of factors," Roberts said, including "whether the doctrinal bases of a decision had been eroded by subsequent developments . . . like settled expectations, like the legitimacy of the court, like whether a particular precedent is workable or not."

Seeking to reassure the senators, Roberts stressed, "I do think that it is a jolt to the legal system when you overrule a precedent. Precedent plays an important role in promoting stability and evenhandedness. It is not enough . . . that you may think the prior decision was wrongly decided."

The questioning fell into an easy rhythm, and Roberts's responses appeared effortless. (Subsequent nominees were told to study his tapes. Ted Cruz, who was then the Texas solicitor general, sent a note to his staff telling them to watch the hearings on television for a master class on advocacy.) But tensions rose when Democrats questioned his record in the Reagan administration. Of particular note to Democrats were Roberts's newly public memos expressing arguments against Voting Rights Act provisions. "You will recall that in the 1960s," said Massachusetts senator Ted Kennedy, a Democrat, "millions of our fellow citizens were denied access to the voting booth because of race, and to remedy that injustice, Congress passed the Voting Rights Act of 1965 that outlawed discrimination in voting."

Senator Kennedy recounted the congressional efforts in 1981 and 1982 to adopt legislation clarifying that discriminatory voting practices could be deemed illegal even without proof of intentional government bias. He noted that Roberts had attacked that position. Wisconsin Democratic senator Russ Feingold added a related complaint: "While you were in the

Reagan Justice Department, you seemed to have done almost everything in your power to thwart that congressional effort."

Roberts responded with two claims, essentially: first, that he believed in protecting voting rights. "Without access to the ballot box," he told senators, "people are not in the position to protect any other rights that are important to them." And second, that he had merely been following the wishes of his superiors in the Reagan administration.

When Senator Feingold continued asking about the memos, Roberts said: "You keep referring to what I supported and what I wanted to do. I was a 26-year-old staff lawyer. It was my first job as a lawyer after my clerkships. I was not shaping administration policy. The administration policy was shaped by the Attorney General on whose staff I served. It was the policy of President Reagan. . . . It was my job to promote the Attorney General's view and the President's view. . . . " Roberts's answers were firm but amiable, and they were vague enough that senators and spectators heard what they wanted to hear. Most people were ready to accept his explanations.

Some Democrats continued to press Roberts on his views of fractious issues. Senator Kennedy asked him about the Supreme Court's narrow 2003 ruling in *Grutter v. Bollinger*, in which Justice O'Connor cast the deciding vote to uphold the University of Michigan's practice of considering race as one factor in its law school admissions decisions. Senator Kennedy observed that O'Connor's majority opinion had given considerable weight to a brief submitted by military leaders explaining that a racially diverse officer corps is essential to the military's ability to fulfill its mission of national security. Kennedy asked about that opinion and the importance of looking to "the real-world impact of affirmative policies in universities."

"Well, Senator," Roberts said, answering carefully, "I think I can answer the specific questions you asked because as you phrased the question, do you agree with her that it's important to look at the real-world significance and impact, and I can certainly say that I do think that that is the appropriate approach, without commenting on the outcome or the judgment in a particular case, that you do need to look at the real-world impact in this area, and I think in other areas, as well." While Roberts agreed that a judge should examine the real-world impact of a case, he did not say what that consideration might be worth. He did not promise what he was not prepared to deliver: he simply evaded the question.

In a testy exchange with Senator Biden over legal rules covering assisted suicide, Roberts declined to offer his personal views, but said he would prevent them from shaping his actions on the Supreme Court. "Just talk to me as a father," Biden implored. "Do not talk to me—just tell me, just philosophically, what do you think? Do you think—not what the Constitution says. What do you feel? Do you feel personally, if you are willing to share with us, that the decision of whether or not to remove a feeding tube after a family member is no longer capable of making a judgment, they are comatose, to prolong that life should be one that the legislators in Dover, Delaware should make or my mother should make?"

"No, I'm not going to consider issues like that in the context as a father or a husband or anything else," Roberts responded. "Putting aside any of those considerations, these issues are the most difficult we face as people, and they are profoundly affected by views of individuality and moral views, and deeply personal views. That's obviously true as a general matter. But at the same time, the position of a judge is not to incorporate his or her personal views in deciding issues of this sort."

Under scrutiny from Democratic senator Dianne Feinstein of California regarding his faith and adherence to the separation of church and state, Roberts emphasized that his Catholicism would not be a factor in his rulings. The nominee said he relied on "law books . . . not the Bible." He said he believed that the right to abortion was a settled precedent. He referred to the 1992 Supreme Court decision in *Planned Parenthood of Southeastern Pennsylvania v. Casey*, which had largely affirmed *Roe*, saying, "I think one way to look at it is that the *Casey* decision itself, which applied the principles of *stare decisis* to *Roe v. Wade*, is itself a precedent of the Court, entitled to respect under principles of *stare decisis*."

Democratic senator Chuck Schumer of New York complained that Roberts's answers failed to reveal anything at all. A visibly frustrated

Schumer confronted him: "Let me just say, sir, in all due respect—and I respect your intelligence and your career and your family—this process is getting a little more absurd the further we move. You agree we should be finding out your philosophy and method of legal reasoning, modesty, stability, but when we try to find out what that modesty and stability mean, what your philosophy means, we don't get any answers. It's as if I asked you: 'What kind of movies do you like? Tell me two or three good movies.' And you say, 'I like movies with good acting. I like movies with good directing. I like movies with good cinematography.' And I ask you, 'No, give me an example of a good movie.' You don't name one. I say, 'Give me an example of a bad movie.'" The committee chairman, Specter, began to cut off Schumer, when Roberts interrupted: "I'll be very succinct," Roberts told the committee. "First, 'Dr. Zhivago' and 'North by Northwest.'" Schumer cut him off: "Now, how about the more important subject . . . "

But Chairman Specter told Schumer, "You're out of time."

The irritation was mutual. Roberts later questioned the value of the hearings. "It's not a very edifying process," he said. "The formula is very well established. The senators ask questions about current hot topics that they want to lay out a position on. They know the nominee can't properly answer those questions. The nominee then says I can't answer the question. The senator scowls and asks the question again. . . . Then the senator's time runs out. . . . It is not useful in any way."[40]

Roberts declined to answer questions about his vote in the *Hamdan v. Rumsfeld* case, which had been heard at the DC Circuit at the same time that Bush administration officials were interviewing him for the Supreme Court. "While the case was still pending, before a decision was issued," Senator Feingold observed, "you had additional interviews in May with the Vice President, the White House Counsel, Mr. Karl Rove, and other top officials. . . . Did the possibility of recusal because you were under serious consideration for the Supreme Court occur to you, or was it raised with you at any point prior to the oral argument in the case?"

"It's a matter I can't talk about outside of the judicial process," Roberts responded, asserting that a motion was pending related to his decision not to recuse himself from the case. "My hands are tied. It's not something I can discuss under the canons of ethics."

Legal ethicists debated Roberts's decision not to recuse himself in the lawsuit. Several experts cited a federal law designed to instill public trust in the courts by requiring judges to step aside if their "impartiality might reasonably be questioned." In an essay, three law professors—Stephen Gillers of New York University, David Luban of Georgetown University, and Steven Lubet of Northwestern University—quoted Justice John Paul Stevens, who had written in a 1988 Supreme Court opinion that "the very purpose of [the law on recusal] is to promote confidence in the judiciary by avoiding even the appearance of impropriety whenever possible."[41]

In their view, the problem was not that Roberts may have cast his vote to improve his chances of being selected for the high court. "We believe he is a man of integrity who voted as he thought the law required," Gillers, Luban, and Lubet wrote. "The problem is that if one side that very much wants to win a certain case can secretly approach the judge about a dream job while the case is still under active consideration, and especially if the judge shows interest in the job, the public's trust in the judiciary (not to mention the opposing party's) suffers because the public can never know how the approach may have affected the judge's thinking."

After Roberts's turn before the Senate Judiciary Committee, his supporters and critics testified. Roberts had earned the American Bar Association's top rating, and witnesses from both sides of the aisle lined up to speak on his behalf. His critics came largely from the civil rights community. One of them, Georgetown University law professor Peter B. Edelman, like Roberts, had been a law clerk to Judge Henry Friendly. Edelman warned that Roberts's pattern on civil rights and liberties would mean "renewed vulnerability for literally millions of Americans who fought for decades and even centuries to be included in our constitutional promises." Another critic was US Representative John Lewis, a Georgia Democrat who as a young civil rights activist had been beaten on the Edmund Pettus Bridge in the 1965 march to Selma. Lewis told the committee that Roberts had been "on the wrong side of history" during his years in the Reagan and first Bush administrations. "We cannot afford to elevate an individual to such a powerful, lifetime position, whose record demonstrates such a strong desire to reverse the hard-won civil rights gains that so many sacrificed so much to achieve."

The Senate voted 78–22 to approve Roberts's nomination. Every Republican senator and half the Democratic ones supported him. He had split the Democratic leadership. Patrick Leahy, the ranking Senate Judiciary Committee Democrat, voted for Roberts in the stated belief that he would not take the country backward on civil rights. Senate Minority Leader Harry Reid made a different calculation. He was impressed by Roberts's credentials and his personal style, but his Democratic base was set against Roberts. Reid adopted its view in voting no.

When then Democratic senator Barack Obama of Illinois took the floor to cast his vote against Roberts, he explained his reasoning—and his ambivalence—to the chamber: "When I examined Judge Roberts' record and history of public service, it is my personal estimation that he has far more often used his formidable skills on behalf of the strong in opposition to the weak. In his work in the White House and the Solicitor General's Office, he seemed to have consistently sided with those who were dismissive of efforts to eradicate the remnants of racial discrimination in our political process."[42] Such assessments irked Roberts, but he had been immersed in Washington politics long enough to know that it was an accomplishment to win the support of half of the opposing party's senators. Subsequent nominees would not fare as well.

ROBERTS'S FORMAL INVESTITURE AND RECEPTION WERE SCHEDuled for October 3, 2005. His old friends from the Reagan White House counsel's office were invited to the festivities. The day began in the courtroom as Roberts was seated in the ceremonial John Marshall chair, and it ended with food and drink in a pair of ornate conference rooms.

Fielding attended with his former deputy, Richard Hauser. As they were en route, they heard the news that President Bush was ready to fill the O'Connor seat, the one Luttig and other runners-up still hoped for. Bush's new choice, made public on the day of Roberts's investiture, was White House counsel Miers, Bush's close friend from Texas and a key player in the nominee screening process. This decision came out of the blue. She had never been on any of the short lists. The sixty-year-old Miers was a graduate of Southern Methodist University Law School and had been successful in the Texas bar, but she had virtually no experience in constitutional law.

The collective response among conservatives was a sense of dread. Robert Bork, the outspoken former appeals court judge who had been rejected for the Supreme Court in 1987, called the nomination "a disaster on every level." It was not only that critics on the right believed her qualifications lacking; they also questioned her conservative commitment and ability to influence the direction of the law.[43]

Some aides warned Bush beforehand that he might be accused of cronyism. Yet he could not have imagined the resulting criticism from his own conservative supporters. "It seemed to me that there was another argument against Harriet," Bush later recounted in his memoir, "one that went largely unspoken: How could I name someone who did not run in elite legal circles? Harriet had not gone to an Ivy League law school. Her personal style compounded the doubts. She is not glib. She is not fancy. . . . All of these criticisms came from so-called friends."[44]

After weeks of controversy, Miers withdrew. Bush then tapped Samuel Alito, without giving Luttig another look.

The vagaries of the process, particularly relative to Roberts, were not lost on the president. "The moment showed what unlikely turns life can take," Bush wrote when it was all over. "John Roberts, who thirteen years earlier assumed that his chance to be a judge had passed [when he was rejected for the DC Circuit], was now chief justice of the United States."[45]

Luttig did not take these events well. The following year, he quit the federal bench altogether. In his letter of resignation, he thanked George

H.W. Bush for the appointment, but he did not refer to then president George W. Bush at all. "For three, four, five years, there had been this white-hot attention on every word I had written or spoken," he said later. "But I had known my whole life that it either happens or it doesn't. No one deserves to be on the Supreme Court."[46]

The friendship between Roberts and Luttig dissolved, and in time Luttig's became one more voice in the chorus of Roberts's conservative critics.

CHAPTER VII

BLACKS, WHITES, AND *BROWN*

I N HIS FIRST MONTHS AS CHIEF JUSTICE, JOHN ROBERTS AND HIS family came to realize how much his day-to-day life would change. "We went to a White House dinner with Prince Charles and Camilla. It was a magical evening," Jane Roberts said in one interview. "I spend a lot of time just pinching myself, wondering, 'Is this my life?'" The Roberts children observed the difference, too, in their own ways. "Daddy, do you get a sword?" Jack had asked after noticing that one of the great stone figures in front of the Court building was armed with one. When Josie was being chased around by a young friend's brother, she said, "Stop it, my Daddy is the Chief Justice." According to Jane, it "seem[ed] like she made a connection between her father and some authority." Roberts was the rare chief justice who was raising young children, and as he became accustomed to his new responsibilities at the helm of the federal judiciary he also dealt with familiar ordeals. Josie was learning to play "Twinkle, Twinkle, Little Star" on her new violin, he said, while Jack was trying to figure out how to use the instrument as a weapon.[1]

Managing his relationships with the other justices was more compli-cated. At age fifty, and with only about two years of appellate court expe-rience behind him, Roberts was younger and far less experienced than his eight colleagues. When he joined the Court in September 2005, before Alito's nomination, the other eight associate justices had been together for eleven years, and over that time they had developed patterns of trust among themselves. When William Rehnquist had become chief in 1986, he had had the benefit of fourteen years on the bench as an associate justice. "He had enough years on the Court to toughen his hide," Justice Antonin Scalia later said.[2]

For all Roberts's expertise and ambition, he was shy and lacked sig-nificant managerial experience. No one made much of the latter at the outset, perhaps because he appeared to navigate administrative matters so effortlessly. Yet as the justices became acquainted with their new chief, personal conflicts emerged. Within six months, for example, tensions spilled out in a dispute over whether police may search a home without a warrant when one of the occupants allows it but another refuses to grant consent. The majority, in an opinion by Justice David Souter in the case of *Georgia v. Randolph*, declared that police could not carry out a search if one of the occupants was present and objected. Discussions behind the scenes between Souter and Roberts, who was writing for the dissent-ers, were not easy. In his opinion for the majority, Souter claimed that Roberts's dissenting view marked "a deliberate attempt to devalue the importance of the privacy of a dwelling place," a view that he believed would mean the end of "centuries of special protection for the privacy of the home." Roberts fired back that his position was being mischaracter-ized and that the Souter rhetoric seemed "a bit overwrought." Roberts concluded in his dissent that "the [Souter] majority reminds us, in high tones, that a man's home is his castle, but . . . it is not his castle if he wants to consent to entry, but his co-owner objects."[3]

Roberts wanted to put his personal stamp on Court opinions from the start. His first opinion for the Court, in *Martin v. Franklin Capital Corp.*, involved an award of attorney fees in certain civil cases. He went out of his way to refer to the writings of his mentors, US Appeals Court

Judge Henry Friendly and Chief Justice William Rehnquist.[4] In other early opinions, Roberts quoted the songwriter Bob Dylan, and he even wrote a dissenting opinion in the noir mode of a Raymond Chandler novel: "Officer Sean Devlin, Narcotics Strike Force, was working the morning shift. Undercover surveillance. The neighborhood? Tough as a three-dollar steak." The opinion stirred controversy over whether Roberts was showing off and not taking the defendant's plight seriously.[5]

Roberts appeared relaxed at center stage, in the center chair. When a lightbulb in the courtroom flickered and then popped during oral arguments in his first month, he quipped, "It's a trick they play on new chief justices all the time."[6] At a White House dinner shortly after he became chief justice, former first lady Nancy Reagan asked him if he would speak at the Ronald Reagan Library in Simi Valley, California. Roberts told the audience at the Reagan Library in March 2006 that he had wanted to wait a year before speaking to such a crowd, but that it was futile to explain his "just say no" policy to Mrs. Reagan. "By the time we were finishing the entrees we were just nailing down the date," Roberts said dryly.[7]

Roberts regaled the crowd at the library with stories of his time in the administration. He said he regarded even the routine work of a staff attorney as part of a larger mission. "Many, many mundane tasks go into great enterprises," Roberts said, comparing his work then to laying down one brick after another: "President Reagan never let us forget that what we were doing was building a cathedral."[8]

In his earliest months as chief, Roberts enjoyed good relations with Justice Scalia, who had privately hoped for the chief justice spot but appreciated a fellow wise-cracking conservative next to him on the bench. They often teamed up during oral arguments, firing questions at the lawyers and attempting to one-up each other. When the lightbulb had popped in the courtroom, and Roberts had quipped that it was a trick on a new chief, it was October 31. Scalia jumped in to say, "Happy Halloween," to which Roberts rejoined, "We're even more in the dark now than before."[9]

"I love his questioning," Scalia later remarked in an interview in his chambers. "He's very good in the questioning, gets right to the point. I like to make my remarks punchy. If you're knocking down a point, do it—oomph! He does the same. Why does the argument have to be dull?" Of Roberts's personal dealings with colleagues, Scalia said, comparing him to Rehnquist, "Roberts is much more polished."[10]

"It's a little more relaxed," Justice Ruth Bader Ginsburg said in a separate interview conducted around the same time. She was comparing the new chief to the old one as well. In her view, "Rehnquist did not have a lot of patience." Of Roberts's general approach to the law, she later declared, "He, like Scalia, was born conservative."[11]

At the Court, Roberts occupied a suite of rooms paneled in rich oak and featuring marble fireplaces and glass chandeliers dating to the building's 1930s construction. He adorned his chambers with photos Jane had helped collect and artwork chosen from the Smithsonian galleries. Roberts favored landscapes of Indiana, where he was raised, and Maine, where he vacationed. The view from his windows was of classic brick row houses along Second Street as well as the historic Thomas Jefferson Building of the Library of Congress on East Capitol Street. A sofa in his chambers had come from the Capitol, and Roberts relished telling visitors that John Quincy Adams had died on it. After completing his service as the nation's sixth president, Adams had returned to serve in the House of Representatives; in 1848, he suffered a stroke after casting a vote on the House floor. He had been taken to the Speaker's office to recuperate on the couch, but died two days later.

Adjoining Roberts's chambers is a separate room for private sessions with the justices, known as "the conference," as well as another room where he can eat lunch with law clerks and meet with guests. On the walls of that room are photos from his own clerkship days and time in the Reagan administration.

The conference room has a black marble fireplace, above which hangs a portrait of Chief Justice John Marshall. When the justices gather there, they are alone. No secretaries, law clerks, or other staff are allowed to attend the sessions. The newest associate justice takes notes. In Roberts's early years, that was Samuel Alito.

Alito had a solemn, even glum, presence. "When we first sat down for the interview, he seemed ill at ease," George W. Bush remembered of his interview with Alito when he became a potential nominee to the Court. "I tried the old common-ground icebreaker—in this case, baseball. Sam is a huge Philadelphia Phillies fan. As we talked about the game, his body language changed." Bush had learned from Alito's supporters that he was a rigid conservative. "There was no doubt he would adhere strictly to the Constitution," Bush concluded.[12]

After a contentious Senate Judiciary Committee hearing that focused on his conservative record as an appeals court judge, the Senate had approved Alito 58–42. He had faced a Democratic filibuster attempt, and had trouble putting the scrutiny and criticism behind him. Afterward, Alito told people that he resisted walking in front of the Hart Senate Office Building (about a block from the Court) where the hearings had occurred. "I cross to the other side of the street," he said. "I quicken my step until I'm well past the building."[13]

Once on the Court, Alito did not surprise. He was consistent in his rulings and, if anything, became more conservative the longer he served. Ideology aside, Alito immediately proved himself to be a cunning interrogator during oral arguments, often deploying creative hypotheticals that exposed the flaws in a lawyer's position. In their early years together, Alito readily joined the opinions written by Roberts. The men were of the same generation, both Catholic, both veterans of the US solicitor general's office, and both believers in a strong executive branch. Yet they did differ in important respects. Alito had been an appeals court judge for sixteen years, far longer than Roberts, and he fell into his role on the high court with confidence on issues across the board and without concerns about institutional appearances. Roberts, as chief justice, cared decidedly more about public regard for the Court as an institution.

For Roberts, Justice Anthony Kennedy was an unpredictable character. Before he joined the Supreme Court, Roberts had considered Kennedy as an equivocal, unreliable conservative—which was Kennedy's reputation among Reagan adherents who became disappointed that the president's 1988 appointee had moderate tendencies. Roberts was also aware that with O'Connor retired, Kennedy would have more influence. Kennedy was poised to be the deciding vote in many cases, positioned between the rightward bloc of Roberts, Scalia, Thomas, and Alito and the left-leaning foursome of Stevens, Souter, Ginsburg, and Breyer.

Justices Ginsburg and Breyer had been nominated by Democratic president Bill Clinton in 1993 and 1994, respectively. Both had been law professors and had served as US appeals court judges. Ginsburg's passion was gender equality, dating back to her time as a women's rights advocate. A native of Brooklyn with a serious demeanor and oversized glasses, she came most immediately from the DC Circuit, where she had a reputation for her intense, late-night work habits and a mind that missed nothing. Breyer, on the other hand, presented the air of an absent-minded professor. He once failed to notice when his law clerks, as a stunt, put goldfish in his office's water cooler. The wiry, balding Breyer was fascinated by regulatory systems, having been a congressional aide to Senator Ted Kennedy and in that capacity helped draft legislation to deregulate the airline industry and to standardize criminal sentencing. The San Francisco native had made a home in Cambridge, Massachusetts, teaching at Harvard law school and then serving at the nearby Boston-based First Circuit US Court of Appeals before joining the Supreme Court.[14]

With the exception of Stevens, the Chicagoan known for his bow ties, who had graduated from Northwestern Law School, the associate justices Roberts led had all graduated from Ivy League schools. They had all been US appeals court judges before their appointment. None had held elected office, as had O'Connor, or represented the poor and disenfranchised, as had Thurgood Marshall, who had helped found the NAACP Legal Defense and Educational Fund. The justices differed primarily in their politics and temperaments.

Chief Justice Roberts believed the justices should work toward greater consensus, because more unanimity would foster a more stable impression of the Court and the law. "There are clear benefits to a greater degree of consensus," Roberts said during his first term, in a speech at Georgetown University Law School. He highlighted the clarity that comes from a single opinion rather than a series of competing ones. "The rule of law and the Court as an institution both benefit from broader agreement," he said, advising that the Court would do well to decide legal dilemmas narrowly to lure as many justices as possible to a single opinion. The chief justice also knew that if the justices dug into their two dueling ideological camps, many cases would come down to the changeable Kennedy.[15]

Roberts added in an interview with the legal affairs journalist Jeffrey Rosen that a 5-to-4 Court made it harder for the justices to win the respect of the public. He noted that as chief he spoke first in the private conference sessions, and he told Rosen that he tried to frame the issue at hand to win over as many justices as possible. "In most cases," Roberts said, "I think the narrower the better, because people will be less concerned about it."[16]

Unanimity was a laudable goal at a time when Washington was growing more polarized. Yet Roberts's objective was not easily reconciled with his priorities in the law. He wanted a less divided Court, but certain beliefs—evident in his early years—superseded his desire for consensus. He would engage in an ongoing balancing act between institutional concerns and ideological commitments.

William Rehnquist had understood the competing demands on a chief justice. "If I had wanted to maximize my influence on the work the Court does deciding cases," he had written in a note to retired justice Arthur Goldberg in July 1986, after Reagan nominated him to be chief justice, "I would have had real doubts about accepting the President's nomination; as you and I both know from experience, Associate Justices can devote their full time to the work of the Court, in a way that the Chief Justice simply cannot."[17]

Chief justices naturally wrestle with such questions. Yet Roberts was more concerned than Rehnquist had been with the institutional reputation of the Court that informally bore his name. For all practical purposes, this was Roberts's first real experience in the public eye, too. He may have felt that much was at stake for him personally. Rehnquist, by contrast, had been a prominent public figure since his tenure as an assistant attorney general, when he had regularly testified before Congress about Nixon's anticrime initiatives and received tough scrutiny from reporters.

In Roberts's first term, in the case of *League of United Latin American Citizens v. Perry*, the justices reviewed a 2003 Texas voting-map plan that had been gerrymandered along partisan and racial lines. In particular, the Republican-controlled state legislature had changed the boundaries of a district in southwestern Texas to lessen the number of Mexican American voters within it and help ensure the re-election of a Republican who had fallen out of favor among Latinos. A five-justice Supreme Court majority ruled that the state legislature's new map was aimed at effectively depriving Mexican Americans of a chance to elect a candidate of their choice. The map violated the Voting Rights Act by diluting their votes, the majority held. Roberts dissented. He had made his opposition to racial considerations in election redistricting clear when he had worked in the Reagan and George H.W. Bush administrations. His views had not changed since. His dissenting opinion in the case foreshadowed decisions on voting rights to come.

Justice Kennedy, who joined the four liberal justices, declared for the majority, "In essence the state took away the Latinos' opportunity because Latinos were about to exercise it." Kennedy wrote that Texas's 2003 redistricting plan contravened the Voting Rights Act.[18] In dissent, and joined by Alito, Roberts asserted that the state had compensated for the loss of the Mexican American Laredo area district with another Hispanic-majority district and had, overall, provided a sufficient number of "majority minority" districts. But to Roberts, this was, in a way, beside the point. He emphasized that federal judges should have a minimal role in "rejiggering the district lines." And voicing strong opposition to any kind of racial emphasis, by courts or legislatures, Roberts declared, "It is a sordid business, this divvying us up by race."[19]

As a writer, Roberts could cut down his opponents: with his use of "divvying up," he suggested a certain carelessness or arbitrariness on the part of government officials. In this case, his substantive position did not escape the notice, and criticism, of Democratic senator Ted Kennedy of Massachusetts, who had been one of the more aggressive questioners at Roberts's confirmation hearing about his record on race in the Reagan administration.

When he had testified as a nominee before the senators in 2005, Roberts had tried to distance himself from his work for Reagan, so among Court watchers there was some question about how closely he would now hew to the positions he had taken as a young lawyer. In the Texas voting rights case, Roberts left behind the equivocation he had displayed before the Senate.

"During Roberts's hearing," Senator Kennedy wrote in a 2006 opinion piece for the *Washington Post*, after the Texas redistricting decision was released, "I asked him about his statement that a key part of the Voting Rights Act constitutes one of 'the most intrusive interferences imaginable by federal courts into state and local processes.' In response, he suggested that his words were nothing more than an 'effort to articulate the views of the administration . . . 23 years ago.' Today—too late—it is clear that Roberts's personal view is the same as it was 23 years ago."[20]

Another highly charged case in early 2006, *House v. Bell*, revealed Roberts's mature position on another Reagan-era flashpoint: the finality of prisoners' death sentences. Condemned Tennessee inmate Paul Gregory House had been convicted of murder some twenty years earlier, and based on new DNA evidence he was attempting to gain a hearing to demonstrate his innocence. Two key pieces of evidence had led to House's conviction: semen on the victim's nightgown and the victim's blood on House's jeans. Advanced DNA testing was not common until after House's conviction, however, and when it was used in his case, analysts discovered that the semen was from the victim's husband, not from House. In addition, it turned out, the blood on the jeans was from autopsy samples that had spilled onto the pants when the FBI was handling the evidence and other vials.

Justice Kennedy again joined with the four liberals to rule that House's habeas petition should be heard in federal court. "The central forensic proof connecting House to the crime—the blood and the semen—has been called into question," Justice Kennedy wrote in his opinion, "and House has put forward substantial evidence pointing to a different suspect. Accordingly, and although the issue is close, we conclude that this is the rare case where—had the jury heard all the conflicting testimony—it is more likely than not that no reasonable juror viewing the record as a whole would lack reasonable doubt." The Kennedy majority allowed House a new habeas hearing under a standard that asks whether, in light of new evidence, "it is more likely than not that no reasonable juror would have found petitioner guilty beyond a reasonable doubt."[21]

In his dissenting opinion, Chief Justice Roberts rebuked the majority for overriding a lower court judge who had not been persuaded by the new evidence and who had concluded that the spill onto House's jeans occurred after the FBI crime lab had tested the evidence. "Witnesses do not testify in our courtroom," Roberts wrote, "and it is not our role to make credibility findings and construct theories of the possible ways in which [the victim's] blood could have been spattered and wiped on House's jeans." Roberts acknowledged that "one or even some jurors" might have come to doubt House's guilt based on the new evidence. But he insisted that it was not more likely than not that every juror would have shared such doubts—"and that is the legal standard," he wrote for the dissenters. Roberts also mockingly referred to the defendant's claims that he had received scratches and bruises from construction work and from a cat, not from the victim. "Sometimes, when identity is in question, alibi is key. Here, House came up with one—and it fell apart, [which he] later admitted to be fabricated when his girlfriend would not lie to protect him. Scratches from a cat, indeed."

As his opinion demonstrated, the new chief justice was not afraid to wield sarcasm, and his writerly flair ensured that his dissent would be read. From Roberts's perspective, an overriding question was whether a federal trial judge should be second-guessed, yet he delved deeply into the record and voiced his own skepticism about the defendant's tale. He simply was not inclined to believe him, perhaps reflecting the tough-on-crime attitude that had pervaded the Reagan and George H.W. Bush administrations, or perhaps based on Roberts's own instincts. In the end, the new DNA evidence was substantial enough to convince a US district judge to order House released on bond in 2008, pending a new trial. The following year, prosecutors decided not to retry House, dropping the charges altogether and expressing their own doubts about House's role in the murder.[22]

HOUSE V. BELL WAS ONE OF A NUMBER OF CASES IN ROBERTS'S FIRST term decided by an eight-justice court. Alito did not take over O'Connor's seat until January 2006. The full Roberts Court was in place for the following term, when the five conservatives limited abortion rights and curtailed campaign finance regulation. Long-standing precedents were discarded or reinterpreted in other areas of the law, too, regarding the separation of church and state, student free speech, and workers' equal pay. In the majority for these closely watched cases were Roberts, Scalia, Kennedy, Thomas, and Alito. In dissent were the liberals Stevens, Souter, Ginsburg, and Breyer. On the issues that mattered most, the Court's divisions were glaring.

The newly reconstituted Roberts Court ruled for the first time that the federal government could ban a specific abortion procedure. The five-justice bloc, led by Roberts, revived a 2003 federal ban on a late-term procedure, intact dilation and extraction, that critics called "partial-birth abortion." The decision, in *Gonzales v. Carhart*, a 2007 case, broke from a 2000 ruling, *Stenberg v. Carhart*, in which the Court had struck down a similar prohibition under Nebraska law. When physicians used this procedure, the woman's cervix was dilated and then the fetus was removed intact, rather than first dismembered.[23]

The controversy had been simmering for years. After *Stenberg v. Carhart*, the case from Nebraska, Congress had adopted its own such prohibition, in the Partial-Birth Abortion Ban Act of 2003. That law, which the five-justice conservative majority upheld in *Gonzales v. Carhart*, included no exception for the health of the mother, based on the premise that the procedure was never necessary. The American College of Obstetricians and Gynecologists differed, believing that in some cases it was the best procedure for a pregnant woman in the second trimester. Challenges to the Nebraska statute and then the federal law were led by Dr. Leroy Carhart, who had performed late-term abortions in Nebraska.

The Supreme Court's new position on the matter resulted from Justice Alito succeeding Justice O'Connor, who had been in the majority in the 2000 Nebraska case. The new 2007 majority, including Roberts, argued that sufficient differences existed between the Nebraska statute and the federal measure to make these seemingly contradictory decisions. The Court said, for example, that Congress had made detailed findings that the procedure was never needed.

Equally striking was that the Court's opinion, written by Justice Kennedy, explored the moral dimensions of Congress's effort to stop women from using the procedure. "Respect for human life finds an ultimate expression in the bond of love the mother has for her child," Kennedy wrote. "In a decision so fraught with emotional consequence some doctors may prefer not to disclose precise details of the means that will be used, confining themselves to the required statement of risks the procedure entails. . . . It is, however, precisely this lack of information concerning the way in which the fetus will be killed that is of legitimate concern to the State." Countering medical arguments that the intact dilation and extraction method might be the safest option for some pregnant women, Kennedy's majority opinion noted that "these contentions were contradicted by other doctors who testified in the District Courts and before Congress. They concluded that the alleged health advantages were based on speculation without scientific studies to support them."

Justice Ginsburg, at that point the only woman on the bench, deemed the majority decision paternalistic, arguing that it wrongly shielded women from a choice they might want to make and that might be necessary in a particular situation. "Today's decision is alarming," Ginsburg wrote in her dissent, joined by Stevens, Souter, and Breyer. She declared that the new ruling failed to take the precedent from 2000, or the Supreme Court's 1992 case upholding *Roe v. Wade*, seriously. "It tolerates, indeed applauds, federal intervention to ban nationwide a procedure found necessary and proper in certain cases by the American College of Obstetricians and Gynecologists (ACOG). It blurs the line, firmly drawn in [the 1992] *Casey*, between previability and postviability abortions. And, for the first time since *Roe*, the Court blesses a prohibition with no exception safeguarding a woman's health."

However fierce the abortion debate on the Court was, the cases that resulted in the greatest acrimony among the nine in the spring of 2007 turned on race. These paired cases concerned the efforts of school districts in Seattle and Louisville to counteract the return of school segregation, a phenomenon that was the result of national housing trends and diminished judicial and federal involvement in desegregation efforts. By the early 2000s, a substantial segment of the black student population throughout the country was again attending schools that were nearly 100 percent black.

Public school districts were initiating programs to restore or maintain the integration gains of earlier decades. In the new Supreme Court cases, school administrators had begun taking race into account as they assigned students to schools. Jefferson County, Kentucky, which includes Louisville, aimed to ensure that none of its schools were less than 15 percent or more than 50 percent black. The lawsuit began when a number of students in Jefferson County, including the five-year-old son of Crystal Meredith (the lead plaintiff), were denied transfers to their schools of choice. This case became *Meredith v. Jefferson County Board of Education.*

Seattle's race-diversity policy applied only at the high school level. When more requests for particular schools were received than could be accommodated, a racial tiebreaker was used to keep schools within district goals for overall racial makeup. The lawsuit was brought by a group of mostly white parents (Parents Involved in Community Schools) whose children had not been assigned to the schools they wanted to attend. It became *Parents Involved in Community Schools v. Seattle School District No. 1.*[24]

Federal appeals courts—the Ninth Circuit based in San Francisco and the Sixth Circuit based in Cincinnati—had upheld the Seattle and Louisville programs, respectively. Judges concluded that the programs met their local governments' compelling interest in racial and ethnic diversity. The Ninth Circuit observed that although the Supreme Court had not yet decided a case involving voluntary-integration plans in secondary schools, "its decisions regarding selective admissions to institutions of higher learning demonstrate that one compelling reason for considering race is to achieve the educational benefits of diversity." In the 2003 University of Michigan law school case of *Grutter v. Bollinger,* the Supreme Court justices had cited the advantages of diverse views in an academic setting and the "greater societal legitimacy" a university gained by cultivating diverse future leaders.[25]

Like the Voting Rights Act case from Texas in 2006, the paired school-integration cases from Louisville and Seattle challenged Roberts's "color-blind" ideal. In response, he wrote a sweeping opinion reinterpreting the principles of the 1954 *Brown v. Board of Education*, asserting that it forbade all practices that took account of race, including those that would increase integration. Roberts believed that policies classifying students based on skin color simply had not worked over the years, and, in fact, that they had exacerbated racism.

The two cases divided the justices from the start. They arrived just as O'Connor was stepping down and Alito was taking her place, and in the private conference held to decide whether to take up the disputes, some of the justices argued the time was not right. Three years earlier, when a narrow majority had upheld the University of Michigan Law School affirmative action program in *Grutter v. Bollinger*, Justice O'Connor's majority opinion had suggested that it might take another twenty-five years to solve racial disparities in education and ensure student body diversity. So, in early 2006, when the Seattle and Louisville petitions arrived, some justices wondered whether it was the right time to hear another controversy over educational diversity. For weeks, the justices debated in private about whether to schedule the cases for oral argument and review. By June, five months after Alito had succeeded the retired O'Connor, there was agreement at least among four justices (the minimum number required to take up a petition) to consider the cases. Roberts, for one, believed the *Grutter v. Bollinger* ruling had been misguided, and he did not feel bound by O'Connor's admonition.

The Seattle case was scheduled to get under way first, and Roberts's distinctive view of *Brown v. Board of Education* became evident immediately during oral arguments. His queries suggested he believed that *Brown*'s segregation policies were indistinguishable, for purposes of the Constitution's equality guarantee, from the contemporary integration policies in dispute in the new cases. The Court in *Brown* had attempted to ensure that blacks were not relegated to inferior schools. Seattle was trying to maintain integration and equal educational opportunities. Roberts suggested to Michael Madden, who argued the case for the Seattle school district, that the district's race-based policy, even as a tie-breaker for stu- dent assignment, was a version of the "separate but equal argument" that *Brown v. Board of Education* had struck down. Madden responded that the Seattle schools were not "racially separate," as in *Brown*, and that the city's goal was to maintain the diversity that had emerged after *Brown* and after many integration efforts had already taken place.[26]

Madden stressed that "not all uses of race trigger the same objections" and that "the Court must be mindful of the context." He said that under the city's program, race becomes a factor only after administrators con- sider a family's choice and how close the student lives to the schools he or she might attend. Roberts was unmoved, again reiterating that skin color could not be a factor, for better or worse. He questioned the value of diversity.

Overall, Roberts revealed just how fundamental his objection to race- based policies was. He had long believed that the Constitution's equal protection clause was intended to ensure that people were treated as in- dividuals, rather than as members of a group that could be singled out for certain treatment based on skin color. This reasoning sounded logical enough, but Roberts's view was (and is) belied by reality. What students were experiencing in the Seattle- and Louisville-area schools was com- mon among students in other parts of the country: after court-ordered plans had ended, de facto segregation returned, creating new problems for educators. Undergirding *Brown* had been evidence that black children suffered when confined to all-minority schools and that children placed in integrated schools improved academically.

A large group of social scientists submitted an amicus brief to the Court in the new cases saying that evidence continued to support the finding that members of racial minorities benefited from integrated schools. They told the justices that many school districts had become resegregated when the desegregation orders were lifted and the federal judges stopped monitoring them. The brief, submitted on behalf of 553 social scientists, referred to harmful effects of resegregation in a number of school districts, including in the Charlotte-Mecklenburg system in North Carolina and the school districts in Denver, San Francisco, Oklahoma

City, and Norfolk, Virginia. "Ideally," the group concluded in its brief to the Court, "we will reach a point where race no longer matters in the life opportunities of American children, but until that time comes, race conscious policies such as the ones in Seattle and Jefferson County are critically needed."[27] The assertion was that Roberts's position, if it prevailed, would harm minority students across the country.

After oral arguments, in the justices' private session, Roberts had the votes to strike down the Seattle and Louisville programs. When he opened the discussion, he reiterated his view that the Constitution's guarantee of equal protection prevented schools from considering race even to improve the school experience for minorities. He believed that both school policies were unconstitutional. Voting with him were Scalia, Kennedy, Thomas, and Alito.

But Kennedy disagreed with Roberts's rejection of diversity as a compelling school interest. Kennedy believed diversity could be a compelling goal, but he wanted proof that the racial classifications were the only way to achieve that diversity. The dissenting justices—Stevens, Souter, Ginsburg, and Breyer—argued that the two school districts had made that case.

Roberts decided to write the Court's opinion himself. He had clearly defined ideas about what the Warren Court had intended in *Brown v. Board of Education* and laid them out in a significant portion of his ruling—a portion joined only by Scalia, Thomas, and Alito. "When it comes to using race to assign children to schools, history will be heard," Roberts declared. "In *Brown v. Board of Education*, we held that segregation deprived black children of equal educational opportunities regardless of whether school facilities and other tangible factors were equal, because government classification and separation on grounds of race themselves denoted inferiority. It was not the inequality of the facilities but the fact of legally separating children on the basis of race on which the Court relied to find a constitutional violation in 1954."

Roberts continued, asserting that "before *Brown*, schoolchildren were told where they could and could not go to school based on the color of their skin. The school districts in these cases have not carried the heavy burden of demonstrating that we should allow this once again—even for very different reasons." As he put it, "the plans are directed only to racial balance, pure and simple, an objective this Court has repeatedly condemned as illegitimate." He criticized school officials for failing to say precisely what level of diversity would provide "the purported benefits" to students' educational, social, and cultural development.

Overall, Roberts questioned the value of diversity in the classroom. "Racial balancing," he asserted, "was not transformed from 'patently unconstitutional' to a compelling state interest simply by relabeling it 'racial diversity.' While the school districts use various verbal formulations to describe the interest they seek to promote—racial diversity, avoidance of racial isolation, racial integration—they offer no definition of the interest that suggests it differs from racial balance."

The chief justice predicted dire consequences if the Supreme Court did not reverse the lower court rulings. "Accepting racial balancing as a compelling state interest would justify the imposition of racial proportionality throughout American society," he wrote. He concluded with a line that reflected his bedrock beliefs: "The way to stop discrimination on the basis of race is to stop discriminating on the basis of race."

This was an area in which Roberts would not yield, and he was not willing to temper his view to accommodate Kennedy, which would have meant a five-vote opinion that spoke for the full Court. This was also an area in which Roberts built on bricks he had laid earlier in his career. He referred to the Court's 1992 decision in *Freeman v. Pitts*, which had limited the oversight role of judges handling desegregation cases, and which Roberts had supported when he was a deputy solicitor general in the George H.W. Bush administration. In the case at hand, he noted that Jefferson County in Kentucky, which had earlier been under a court order because of segregation, had argued that it should be able to continue the race-based assignments it had made when under a desegregation decree: "But what was constitutionally required of the district prior to 2000 was the elimination of the vestiges of prior segregation," Roberts wrote, referring to *Freeman v. Pitts*, "not racial proportionality in its own right.

Once those vestiges were eliminated, Jefferson County was on the same footing as any other school district, and its use of race must be justified on other grounds."

The liberal justices were startled by Roberts's rationale likening the pro-integration efforts in Louisville and Seattle to the school segregation of the Jim Crow era. In separate opinions, Justices John Paul Stevens and Stephen Breyer (joined by their liberal colleagues) claimed that Roberts was turning *Brown* on its head. Stevens, the Court's oldest and longest-serving member at the time, called it "cruel" and argued that "the chief justice rewrites the history of one of this Court's most important decisions"; he added, "It is my firm conviction that no member of the Court that I joined in 1975 would have agreed with [the Court's] decision."

The dissenting justices thought Roberts was ignoring the steps the Supreme Court had taken to induce southern officials to open their school doors to black students. They noted that since 1954, the Supreme Court had consistently encouraged local officials to work toward integration, and that the plurality opinion by Roberts marked a significant shift by discouraging those efforts.

Justice Kennedy, whose vote Roberts needed to reject the individual plans from Seattle and Louisville, took the unusual step of separating himself from the chief justice's approach in a statement read aloud from the bench. He referred to Roberts's "all too unyielding insistence that race cannot be a factor" to ensure equal opportunity in schools. "I cannot endorse that," Kennedy said flatly.[28]

Kennedy believed that Roberts was indifferent to school officials' efforts to maintain integration and develop diversity. "Fifty years of experience since *Brown v. Board of Education* should teach us that the problem before us defies so easy a solution," Kennedy wrote. He thought the policies enacted by Seattle and Louisville had fallen short, but he nevertheless argued that public school districts could account for students' race in other ways—for example, by considering the race of their pupils when deciding where to build a new school, or when determining how to allocate resources. "The enduring hope is that race should not matter," Kennedy wrote, but "the reality is that too often it does."

Kennedy also distanced himself from Roberts's caustic response to Justice Breyer, who in dissent asserted that Roberts was undermining the values of *Brown v. Board of Education*. Breyer took the rare step of reading portions of his opinion from the bench. He spoke for more than twenty minutes, arguing that Roberts had disregarded precedent. He said the majority's decision would obstruct efforts by state and local governments to deal effectively with the increasing resegregation of public schools. Breyer maintained that the Court's long-standing interpretations of the equal protection clause distinguished between government policies that excluded or subordinated racial minorities, on the one hand, and government policies that sought to bring people of all races together, on the other.

Breyer recalled the moment a half-century earlier when the governor of Arkansas, Orval Faubus, had ordered the state militia to block school-house doors so that black children could not enter. In response, President Eisenhower had sent the 101st Airborne to Little Rock to enforce the desegregation decree. "Today, almost 50 years later, attitudes towards race in this Nation have changed dramatically," Breyer said. "Indeed, the very school districts that once spurned integration now strive for it. The long history of their efforts reveals the complexity and difficulties they have faced. And in light of those challenges they here ask us not to take from their hands the instruments that they have used to rid their schools of racial segregation, instruments that they believe are still necessary to overcome the problems of cities that are divided by race and poverty."

"What of the hope and promise of *Brown*?" Breyer asked in his written opinion. "For much of this Nation's history, the races remained divided. It was not long ago that people of different races drank from separate fountains, rode on separate buses, and studied in separate schools. In this Court's finest hour, *Brown v. Board of Education* challenged this history and helped change it." Roberts and the justices who joined his opinion had failed to exercise restraint, Breyer insisted, and were in fact usurping local officials. "It is for them to decide," Breyer said, "to quote the plurality's slogan, whether the best 'way to stop discrimination on the basis of race is to stop discriminating on the basis of race.'"[29]

In one of his more controversial moves, Roberts had quoted the 1952 transcript of a *Brown* oral argument. He said it helped prove that his plurality opinion was "more faithful to the heritage of *Brown*" than the interpretation of the other justices. In it, civil rights lawyer Robert L. Carter had contended that "no State has any authority under the equal-protection clause of the Fourteenth Amendment to use race as a factor in affording educational opportunities among its citizens." Roberts then remarked, "There is no ambiguity in that statement."

But when Roberts's decision came down, *New York Times* reporter Adam Liptak reached out to Carter, who was then a senior federal judge in Manhattan. Carter quarreled with Roberts's interpretation. "All that race was used for at that point in time was to deny equal opportunity to black people," Carter said. "It's to stand that argument on its head to use race the way they use it now." Other lawyers who worked on the *Brown* case echoed that sentiment in interviews with Liptak, calling Roberts's interpretation "preposterous" and "dirty pool."[30]

THE 2006–2007 SESSION WAS A DIFFICULT ONE FOR THE NEW Roberts Court. Many cases had broken along 5–4 lines with the conservatives in control. The liberals were profoundly distressed. Ginsburg believed that her instincts about Roberts's conservatism had proven to be accurate. Breyer had been more hopeful about Roberts at the outset. His frustration was evident as he spoke on behalf of dissenters in the school integration cases, saying, "It is not often in the law that so few have so quickly changed so much." That stinging line did not appear in Breyer's written dissenting opinion, and it caught some of his colleagues off guard. The unexpected retort especially angered Scalia, who was known for his own memorable maxims. He did not appreciate one turned on him.[31]

After the decision in the case of *Parents Involved in Community Schools v. Seattle School District No. 1* was announced and the session had ended, Senator Patrick Leahy, the senior Democrat on the Senate Judiciary

Committee, declared that he regretted voting in favor of Roberts during his 2005 confirmation. Leahy compared Roberts's views to the Supreme Court majority's decision in *Plessy v. Ferguson*, which had upheld separate-but-equal laws maintaining segregation in 1896. Leahy asserted, in an interview with *Politico*, that Roberts had "made the court an arm of the Republican Party."[32]

That was exactly the opposite of how Roberts wanted to be perceived. He constantly referred to the impartial, nonpartisan ideal of judging. Yet his opinion had broken from years of Supreme Court precedent, including the 1978 ruling in *Regents of the University of California v. Bakke*, and demonstrated how differently he viewed race from many of his predecessors. After the *Parents Involved* case, the *New York Times* Supreme Court correspondent Linda Greenhouse contrasted Roberts and Justice Harry Blackmun, who had similarly tried to apply the lessons of history to racial dilemmas. In the 1978 *Bakke* decision, Blackmun had famously written, "In order to get beyond racism, we must first take account of race." The notion of a "color-blind" Constitution would keep black students in an inferior place, Blackmun had believed.

"Harry Blackmun was asking the country to confront its tragic racial history in the course of deciding how best to move beyond it," asserted Greenhouse, author of the biography *Becoming Justice Blackmun*. "John Roberts was asking the country to pretend that the history never happened." Roberts stiffened at such criticism. He thought the country had moved past its history of racial strife.[33]

A decade after the *Parents Involved* decision, Roberts was asked for his views on *Brown v. Board of Education*. His questioner was Shirley Ann Jackson, the African American president of the Rensselaer Polytechnic Institute. At a forum at the institute, Jackson, then age seventy, referred to the benefits that she herself had experienced in the wake of *Brown*. "I ended up being able to travel to good public schools right in my own neighborhood," she said, "instead of traveling miles across the city to a segregated school." A native of Washington, DC, Jackson had then attended the Massachusetts Institute of Technology, obtained a PhD, and become a theoretical physicist.[34]

"We've come a long way on the road to equal justice," President Jackson observed, "yet we both would admit that there are tensions around those issues today."

She asked Roberts, "How do strict interpretations of the Constitution . . . allow fair and reasonable decisions?" Roberts first wanted to correct her phrasing. "I think I would first get the vocabulary settled just a little bit," he said. "The old use of the term 'strict construction' is very misleading. . . . Those aren't really terms that are particularly meaningful." He then spoke of the post–Civil War amendments to the Constitution and said they were "open to interpretation" because they embodied certain principles that the drafters could not have envisioned. "It's not self-evident what the right answer is," he said.

Roberts contended that *Brown v. Board of Education* held similar ambiguity. "To this day," he told Jackson, "it's debated: Does *Brown v. Board of Education* prohibit the assignment of students to school on the basis of race? Or, does it prohibit the maintenance of schools identifiable on the basis of race?

"It makes a huge difference," he continued. "If you think the former then you think . . . assigning white students to a particular school to keep it from becoming too black, as people would say, is impermissible. If you think the latter, that it's supposed to prevent the appearance of segregated schools, then that's exactly what you do, to make sure that there are not all whites at one school and all blacks at others. So yes, the principle carries forward, but the job of interpreting it rests with the courts."

Roberts did not mention that he had answered the question about what *Brown* meant in a case decided ten years earlier. He had made plain in his *Parents Involved* opinion that he believed the 1954 decision, the very one that had launched Jackson's remarkable career, and the careers of countless other people of color, forbade assigning students based on race to enhance diversity and the educational experience.

CHAPTER VIII

POLITICS AND MONEY

A FTER DELIVERING THE SUPREME COURT'S DECISION REJECT-
ing public school integration practices in June 2007, John Roberts
flew to Austria to teach a law school seminar and then went to Paris to
meet with European judges. By late July, he was drained and ready to
retreat to Hupper Island off the central coast of Maine. Roberts had
purchased a 1,300-square-foot home on two acres of land from Steve
Thomas, the host of the PBS series *This Old House* from 1989 to 2003.
The one-story structure had been built in 1965 but had been remodeled
since. In time, the Robertses would buy a second house on the island,
adjacent to the first, for a better view of the water and more room for the
family members and friends who joined them each summer.[1]

The residents of the small island, which was dotted with about twenty
homes, valued their privacy. Although the island is not far from Port
Clyde, there was no ferry for public use. For groceries and other supplies,
Roberts used his boat to cross to the village, which had a population
of about 300. The people in Port Clyde left the chief justice alone. He
usually wore a baseball cap and sunglasses anyway. "This is the kind of

town where people are judged not by their position but how reliable they are as friends," said Kevin Lipson, Roberts's former law partner who had invited him to stay at his home on the island and then encouraged him to buy his own.[2]

A few days after Roberts arrived in July 2007, he experienced a seizure and blacked out while on a dock at the island. He was rushed by boat to Port Clyde and then by ambulance to Penobscot Bay Medical Center. The chief justice was fifty-two years old. The Supreme Court's public information office said that he had had a "benign idiopathic seizure," which meant it arose from an unknown cause. It was his second reported seizure. The first had occurred in 1993, when Roberts, who was then thirty-eight, was golfing.[3]

After the 2007 episode, Roberts tried to return to his usual patterns as much as possible. Medical commentators noted that the threshold for being diagnosed with epilepsy was two seizures, and that typically patients took medication to control the disease. The chief justice already had a personal security detail provided by the Court that accompanied him on his travels, so he could keep his driving to a minimum. The Court Public Information Office's statement at the time of the seizure said that a neurological evaluation showed no serious injury. Since then no new seizure episodes have been reported.[4]

BACK IN WASHINGTON, ROBERTS WAS STILL FINDING HIS FOOTING at the Court.

The chief justice had responsibilities beyond presiding over decisions on cases.[5] He sat at the top of the twenty-seven-member Judicial Conference of the United States, which established policy for federal judges and courthouses nationwide. Early in his tenure, Roberts took an interest in the comparatively low pay of federal judges by the standards of other legal careers. He worried that the federal bench was no longer drawing the best candidates, and he believed pay was a leading reason. It concerned him that so many judicial appointees came from government offices, working their way up from magistrate or US attorney positions, rather than the private bar. Federal judges' salaries had not kept pace with law firm or university salaries. Roberts gathered data showing that in 1969 federal district court judges had made 21 percent more than the deans of top law schools and 43 percent more than senior law professors. By 2006, federal district court judges were being paid substantially less—about half as much as deans and senior law professors.[6]

District court judges made $165,200 annually in 2007, when Roberts took up the matter. The annual salary of an appeals court judge was $175,100, while associate Supreme Court justices made $203,000 and the chief justice made $212,100. Congress had blocked certain cost-of-living adjustments, so there was little or no room for raises.

Roberts decided to arrange a private visit with President George W. Bush at the White House to try to win his support for legislation to raise salaries. He communicated through his old boss Fred Fielding, who had been White House counsel in the Reagan years and had returned to serve in the same capacity for the second President Bush. Fielding recounted that when Roberts met with the president, he brought "talking points" for why judges deserved more money. He was ready to present an extensive case.[7]

President Bush quickly agreed to Roberts's request to try to persuade Congress to increase pay for the judiciary. Roberts pressed on nonetheless. "Don't you realize you've made the sale?" Bush interrupted, finally getting Roberts to back down. Fielding later said he admired Roberts for going directly to the president. Roberts had hesitated before initiating the visit, mindful of the separation of powers between the branches. But he decided to make the request in the end because it had nothing to do with a particular case; rather, it arose from his view that the pay situation had reached the level of a "constitutional crisis" threatening the strength and independence of the federal bench.[8]

President Bush sent word to Congress that he favored the pay increase, but his involvement did not ensure passage of the legislation that year. Incremental congressional action and resolution of a judges' lawsuit seeking full cost-of-living adjustments led to higher pay over the years. By

2018, the chief justice was making an annual salary of $267,000, while associate justices received $255,300, appeals court judges $220,600, and district court judges $208,000. Federal judges still made notably less than experienced law professors and far less than partners at major law firms.[9]

Roberts felt the need to defend judges in other situations that were far from clear-cut. Early in his tenure the justices faced a dispute from West Virginia testing when judges should recuse themselves owing to a conflict of interest. The specific question under scrutiny centered on when elected state judges should be disqualified in disputes involving big donors. In 2004, Donald Blankenship, the chief executive officer of the A. T. Massey Coal Company, had contributed $3 million to a political action committee formed to help elect Brent Benjamin to the West Virginia Supreme Court—about 60 percent of Benjamin's total fund-raising. Hanging over Blankenship and Massey Coal at the time was a $50 million jury award in a fraud case. Hugh Caperton and his small independent mining company had sued after Caperton was excluded from a long-term coal contract. Massey was appealing the verdict favoring Caperton, and the case was heading toward the West Virginia Supreme Court.[10]

Three years after Benjamin was seated, he cast the deciding vote in the fraud lawsuit involving Blankenship's Massey Coal. Judge Benjamin ruled for Massey and against Caperton in the 3–2 case. Appealing to the US Supreme Court, Caperton argued that his constitutional due process rights were violated when Judge Benjamin participated in the case.

During oral arguments in *Caperton v. A. T. Massey Coal Co.* in 2009, Justice Kennedy expressed concerns that public confidence in the judiciary suffered when one person could give so much money to help elect a judge, who then turned around and ruled for the donor. Kennedy then cast the deciding vote, with the four liberals, for a majority opinion declaring that West Virginia justice Benjamin should have recused himself from the case based on a "probability of bias."

When Roberts took the lead for the four dissenters, he suggested that the public presumes judges will be fair and honest. "All judges take an oath to uphold the Constitution and apply the law impartially," he wrote, joined by Justices Scalia, Thomas, and Alito, "and we trust that they will live up to this promise." Roberts criticized the majority's rule for offering no elaboration on when recusal would be constitutionally required. "This will inevitably lead to an increase in allegations that judges are biased," Roberts wrote, "however groundless those charges may be. The end result will do far more to erode public confidence in judicial impartiality than an isolated failure to recuse in a particular case."

With his focus on the public's perception, the chief justice seemed more concerned with protecting the judiciary's reputation than with ferreting out actual impartiality. How the public perceived judges mattered to him. Sometimes it seemed this concern was overriding. Six years later, in *Williams-Yulee v. Florida Bar*, as Roberts voted to uphold a Florida ban on the personal solicitation of campaign money by state judicial candidates, he emphasized the importance of "public confidence in judicial integrity."[11]

LIKE MANY OTHER BABY BOOMERS WHO HAD CHILDREN IN THEIR late thirties and forties, Roberts was helping to care for his young children at home and at the same time keeping an eye on his elderly parents. Jack and Rosemary Roberts had retired to Ellicott City, Maryland, about thirty miles west of the Sparrows Point plant that Jack had managed prior to his retirement in 1985 and about forty miles northeast of Washington, DC, and Bethesda. In November 2008, after several years of struggling with Alzheimer's disease, the elder Roberts died, and the memorial service was held in Johnstown, Pennsylvania. The chief justice delivered an emotional eulogy, recounting how he had learned to knot a tie from his father, and saying he still felt his father's arms around his neck each morning as he dressed for work. Jack Roberts was buried at Grandview Cemetery, high on a hill, not far from the old family home on Wonder Street.[12]

That same fall, the nation elected a new president, Barack Obama, a forty-seven-year-old Democrat who had served as US senator from Illinois from 2005 to 2008. Roberts had been keenly aware of how much control the president had over the composition of the federal courts since his early days as a lawyer in Washington. In 1992, when Bill Clinton had won the presidency, defeating White House incumbent George H.W. Bush, Roberts had felt the loss in a personal way, as he was immediately struck from contention for a position on the DC Circuit Court.

Obama and Roberts had both gone to Harvard Law School, where they had served on the *Harvard Law Review*. But their paths after graduation had differed significantly. Obama had earned the top position on the *Review* and had become its first-ever black president. After graduation, he had worked in Chicago as a civil rights lawyer, a community organizer, and a law professor. He had served three terms in the Illinois Senate before his 2004 election to the US Senate. In his run for the White House, he had chosen Joe Biden, the former chairman of the Senate Judiciary Committee who had stalled Roberts's appeals court bid in 1992, as his running mate.

On Inauguration Day, January 20, 2009, the chief justice was set to administer the presidential oath. The inaugural for the nation's first black president occurred the day after the Martin Luther King Jr. national holiday commemorating the birthday of the slain civil rights leader. An estimated two million people crowded the National Mall to watch Obama's swearing-in. Hundreds of millions more watched on television around the world.

Chief Justice Roberts had rehearsed sufficiently that he decided not to use a reference card bearing the words and notes about when to pause. The choice was unusual for a man who usually left nothing to chance. After all, when he had argued before the Supreme Court earlier in his career, he had always brought a legal pad to the lectern with the opening line, "Mr. Chief Justice, and may it please the Court," written on it in case he needed it. The presidential oath was not too long, and Roberts thought he would have no problem remembering it.

At noon on January 20, 2009, the two Harvard law graduates faced each other, and Obama placed his left hand on a Bible that had been used to swear in Abraham Lincoln in 1861. As Roberts began to read the oath, he stumbled over where the word "faithfully" should go. The oath is in the

Constitution: "I," followed by the president's name, "do solemnly swear that I will faithfully execute the Office of the President of the United States, and will to the best of my ability, preserve, protect and defend the Constitution of the United States." But Roberts prompted Obama to say, "that I will execute the Office of the President of the United States faithfully." Obama paused, sensing something was not quite right, yet repeated the chief's words.[13]

As small as that mistake was, it immediately generated speculation about whether Obama had been properly sworn in. The White House asked Roberts to administer the oath again the next day, so that the order of the words would be exact, and he readily obliged. It seemed like the kind of gaffe that could have happened to anyone. Or perhaps it subtly revealed the deeper disconnect between the two men. Obama had, of course, voted against Roberts's confirmation in 2005, and their politics were starkly different. Whatever the reason, Roberts bridled at reports that the mistake was his. He thought more should have been made of an Obama interruption of the chief at the very outset. Obama had immediately begun to repeat Roberts when he heard the prompt of, "I, Barack Hussein Obama," even though Roberts was going right into "do solemnly swear." Obama then repeated the full phrase. That false start likely threw Roberts off.

In early 2009, as President Obama undertook his first big priority—a sweeping health-care overhaul—one justice was going through a profound illness and another through a personal transition. Justice Ruth Bader Ginsburg was diagnosed with pancreatic cancer. A decade earlier she had survived colorectal cancer. Pancreatic was one of the most lethal of all cancers, but because of her first cancer scare, she had been getting regular checks, and the one-centimeter tumor in the center of her pancreas was caught early enough that her physicians offered a good prognosis for recovery. She underwent surgery in early February and began a regime of chemotherapy. Ginsburg never missed an oral argument session and even made sure she attended a joint session of Congress on the evening of February 24 for the new president.

"First, I wanted people to see that the Supreme Court isn't all male," she said in an interview in early 2009. Justice O'Connor had retired in

2006, and Sonia Sotomayor, who would become the third woman appointed to the Court, would not be nominated until later that year. "I also wanted them to see I was alive and well contrary to that senator who said I'd be dead within nine months." Ginsburg was referring to Senator Jim Bunning, a Republican from Kentucky, who had made that prediction in reference to the pancreatic cancer. Bunning later apologized for the comment.[14]

In that same interview, Ginsburg recalled that her male colleagues had often ignored her voice when she had been a young lawyer. "I don't know how many meetings I attended in the '60s and the '70s, where I would say something, and I thought it was a pretty good idea. . . . Then somebody else would say exactly what I said. Then people would become alert to it, respond to it," she said. The same thing, she added, happened on the Court. Even after more than a decade on the bench, she experienced the same phenomenon in the justices' private sessions. "It can happen even in the conferences in the Court," she said. "When I will say something—and I don't think I'm a confused speaker—and it isn't until somebody else says it that everyone will focus on the point." Chief Justice Roberts was surprised when her comments were published. He considered himself fair to all, and he had not realized Ginsburg felt herself at any disadvantage.[15]

A few weeks after Ginsburg's surgery, David Souter announced that he would soon retire. A bookish man with a dry sense of humor, Souter, who was from New Hampshire, embodied a New England austerity. Although he had lived in Washington since 1990, he had not taken to the city's social scene. He kept the lights in his office dim and enjoyed a small cup of yogurt and an apple each day for lunch. He had dissented in the *Bush v. Gore* case of December 2000, and his frustration with the decision, along with the Court's increasing conservatism, stuck in his craw. He had considered stepping down before 2009 but had decided to wait until a Democratic president took office and could appoint his successor.

"He came to the bench with no particular ideology," President Obama said of the sixty-nine-year-old Yankee Republican as he accepted Souter's retirement letter on May 1, 2009. "He never sought to promote a political ideology. And he consistently defied labels and rejected absolutes." A few days later, Souter appeared at a previously scheduled judicial conference in Philadelphia. "For most of us, the very best work that we do sinks into the stream very quickly," he said. "We have to find satisfaction in being part of the great stream."[16]

To replace Souter, President Obama chose Sonia Sotomayor, who was then sitting on the Manhattan-based US Court of Appeals for the Second Circuit. The first Latina to be nominated to the Court, she had grown up in a housing project in the Bronx and made her way through Princeton University and Yale Law School. Sotomayor's life tracked the rise of Latinos in America. She had been born in 1954, the year of *Brown v. Board of Education*, which ended the doctrine of "separate but equal" and opened schools to blacks and Hispanics. That was also the year of *Hernandez v. Texas*, a separate landmark in which the Supreme Court held that the Constitution protected Hispanics from discrimination just as it protected blacks.[17]

Two controversies marked Sotomayor's confirmation hearings in the summer of 2009, which in the end went relatively smoothly. One related to remarks she had made in 2001 at a legal conference at the University of California, Berkeley. "I would hope that a wise Latina woman with the richness of her experiences would more often than not reach a better conclusion than a white male who hasn't lived that life," Sotomayor had said. Some detractors claimed the sentiment was "racist," and that a white person would have never been able to make such a pronouncement, valuing white experience, without ruining his or her chances of confirmation. Former House Speaker Newt Gingrich, a Georgia Republican, complained, "Imagine a judicial nominee said, 'My experience as a white man makes me better than a Latina woman.' Wouldn't they have to withdraw?"[18]

During her hearings, Sotomayor backed away from the comments, telling senators, "I want to state up front and unequivocally and without doubt, I do not believe any ethnic, racial, or gender group has an advantage in sound judging. . . . I regret that I have offended some people. I believe that my life demonstrated that that was not my intent to leave the impression that some have taken from my words." Democrats held a majority in the Senate at the time, and most of the senators were satisfied by her explanation.

The other controversy arose from a case that, coincidentally, was at the Supreme Court in the spring of 2009 when Obama nominated her. New Haven, Connecticut, city officials had thrown out the results of a fire department promotional exam after African Americans had scored disproportionately low. Officials said they feared the test had been flawed, and that, if they did not disqualify it, they would be open to a lawsuit under the 1964 Civil Rights Act from blacks on the grounds of "disparate impact" discrimination. (Such claims arose from the results of written exams, strength tests, and other seemingly neutral criteria that could have a disproportionately harmful effect on women and racial minorities.) The city ended up facing a different kind of lawsuit, one for intentional discrimination, from eighteen other firefighters who had taken the exam, seventeen of them white and one Hispanic. The firefighters claimed that the city's move to discard the tests violated their right to equal protection under the law.[19]

A US district court judge dismissed the firefighters' lawsuit, saying New Haven had sufficient grounds to believe it would be liable for a claim of indirect bias. Sotomayor was on the Second Circuit panel that heard the appeal in *Ricci v. DeStefano*. The panel issued a brief unsigned decision affirming the district court judge's decision and ruling against the white firefighters. A few months later, amid controversy over its summary order, the panel added a single paragraph that read, "We are not unsympathetic to the plaintiffs' expression of frustration. Mr. Ricci, for example, who is dyslexic, made intensive efforts that appear to have resulted in his scoring highly on one of the exams, only to have it invalidated." Critics of the ruling complained not only about the substantive outcome but about the seemingly perfunctory way it was handled. The panel had not crafted its own opinion exploring the legal issues and, rather, tacitly accepted the district court's explanation.

When the Supreme Court ruled in *Ricci v. DeStefano*, the justices divided along ideological lines, with the conservatives prevailing. Justice Souter, in his final days on the bench, characterized the city's dilemma as a "damned if you do, damned if you don't situation." He voted, like Sotomayor had, in favor of the city's efforts. He wanted to uphold the Second Circuit's decision. Chief Justice Roberts, meanwhile, made clear at oral arguments that he was sympathetic to the white firefighters' claims that "they didn't get their jobs because of intentional racial action by the city." Kennedy aligned himself with Roberts and the three other conservative justices. Roberts assigned Kennedy the opinion.

"The city . . . turned a blind eye to evidence that supported the exams' validity," Kennedy wrote for the majority. The fivesome declared that New Haven lacked the required "strong basis in evidence" that it would face lawsuits from those who failed to score high enough for promotion. The dissenting justices, led by Ginsburg, contended that the majority's evidentiary standard wrongly raised the bar for employers who wanted to change a test or other job criteria because they disadvantaged racial minorities. "Firefighting is a profession in which the legacy of racial discrimination casts an especially long shadow," Ginsburg also observed in *Ricci v. DeStefano*.

The Supreme Court handed down the decision on June 29, 2009. Sotomayor's hearings before the Senate Judiciary Committee began on July 13. Senator Lindsey Graham, a South Carolina Republican, set the tone as much as any Democrat could have. "Unless you have a complete meltdown," Graham told Sotomayor, "you're going to get confirmed."[20] Regarding *Ricci*, Sotomayor explained that her appeals court panel had had confidence in the seventy-eight-page decision that had been produced by the district court judge in the case, and she insisted that her panel's decision had been based on Second Circuit precedent. That, of course, was now changed, she acknowledged, because of the high court's late June decision.

The Senate confirmed Sotomayor by a vote of 68–31 on August 6.

By 2009, THE ROBERTS COURT HAD DEVELOPED A REPUTATION FOR being pro-business. It had sided with companies in a series of cases brought by workers and consumers, routinely deciding them by 5–4 votes controlled by the conservative bloc of Roberts, Scalia, Kennedy, Thomas, and Alito. Now, the justices began considering a case that would define the chief justice's early tenure, more than any other, in favor of corporate America: *Citizens United v. Federal Election Commission.*

The case arose from Congress's efforts to regulate monied interests in elections and reduce the likelihood of corruption. Roberts, however, beginning with his first campaign-finance case in the 2006–2007 term, was leading the Court to decisions that diminished government regulations and expanded what was meant by political speech. He was suspicious of government attempts to target the effects of wealth in elections. He did not think money was naturally corrosive, and he felt that government had gone too far in curtailing the ability of corporations to engage in political speech. He did not believe that legislators, or, even worse, judges, should intervene to try to equalize the field. Critics of Roberts's campaign finance jurisprudence contended that he failed to comprehend how money could undermine campaigns and distort the fundamentals of who gained access to elected officials.

The modern era of campaign finance regulation traced to the Watergate scandal in the early 1970s. President Richard Nixon and his campaign team had been accused of widespread fund-raising abuses during his 1972 reelection bid. Confronted with evidence of the same, Congress put new limits on contributions to candidates for federal office and political action committees. It also limited how much a candidate could spend on his or her campaign. There was already a law requiring public reporting of contributions and expenditures.

James Buckley, a Republican senator from New York, and Eugene McCarthy, a Democratic senator from Minnesota, challenged the 1974 revisions as an unconstitutional infringement on the rights of free speech and association. As a practical matter, they worried that the law would disproportionately benefit incumbents, because its regulations could hinder full-throated challenges to entrenched opponents. The Supreme Court accepted some of their constitutional claims but rejected others. The justices emphasized government's interest in preventing corruption as well as the appearance of corruption, and they drew a line between contributions and expenditures. That meant, in the 1976 ruling *Buckley v. Valeo*, federal contribution limits on the amount of money citizens could give to candidates would stand. But the Court rejected as unconstitutional the limits on spending by campaigns, independent entities, and candidates from their personal resources. The Court said the expenditure restrictions impinged on a campaign's free political speech.[21]

The ruling left room for Congress and the states to target the corruptive influence of campaign contributions and the appearance of corruption that could also undermine public confidence. But "corruption" was in the eye of the judicial beholder. A significant test came to the Supreme Court in a 1990 dispute, *Austin v. Michigan Chamber of Commerce*, over a Michigan law that prohibited corporations from using their general treasury funds for independent expenditures to support or oppose a state candidate. The Michigan Chamber of Commerce sought an exemption so that it could use its general funds to buy a newspaper ad to support a candidate for the US House of Representatives. The Chamber argued that it should be exempted because it was a "nonprofit ideological corporation," more like a political association than a business firm. The Chamber won in a lower federal court.

At the Supreme Court, in its 1990 ruling, a six-justice majority upheld the state's requirement that corporations make all independent political expenditures through a separate regulated fund. Justice Thurgood Marshall, writing for the majority, concluded that the Chamber was similar to a business group because of its activities, membership, and connections to corporations. The tone of the opinion reflected the majority's distrust of corporations. Marshall endorsed Michigan's effort aimed at "the corrosive and distorting effects of immense aggregations of wealth that are accumulated with the help of the corporate form." He repeated the state's assertion of "the significant possibility that corporate political expenditures will undermine the integrity of the political process."[22]

Justice Kennedy thought the majority was misguided. He favored a broader interpretation of the First Amendment as he dissented in the case, and he criticized the majority for "failing to disguise its animosity and distrust" of corporate political speech. "Far more than the interest of the Chamber is at stake," Kennedy warned. "We confront here society's interest in free and informed discussion on political issues, a discourse vital to the capacity for self-government."

But government and public opinion was moving against Kennedy's view. Congress was trying to close the loopholes that had appeared after the Watergate reforms, and in 2002 it passed the Bipartisan Campaign Reform Act. The 2002 act was commonly known as "McCain-Feingold" after its Senate sponsors, John McCain, an Arizona Republican, and Russell Feingold, a Wisconsin Democrat. At its core was a ban on unrestricted "soft money" donations made directly to political parties, often by corporations, unions, or wealthy individuals. The McCain-Feingold law also placed limits on the advertising that certain corporations and unions could finance within sixty days of an election.

Advertising was crucial to the dissemination of a candidate's message. But airtime was expensive, and candidates searched for deep-pocket donors. From Watergate in the 1970s to the early 2000s, congressional reformers thought that reliance on the costly advertising increased the potential for corruption. Critics on the other side believed it was unfair to single out the wealthy for restrictions: in their view, the more political speech, the better. Conservatives believed that campaign-finance regulations should target explicit quid pro quo arrangements; liberals focused more broadly on wealth and special access.

After McCain-Feingold passed, Senator Mitch McConnell, a Republican from Kentucky, sued federal campaign regulators. He was joined in the case of *McConnell v. Federal Election Commission* by an array of McCain-Feingold opponents who believed the law impinged on free political speech rights.

With Justice O'Connor still on the bench, a Court majority upheld most of McCain-Feingold in a 5–4 decision. The 2003 opinion was written jointly by Justices Stevens and O'Connor. They endorsed the central ban on unlimited contributions to political parties, known as "soft money," and the limits on advertising broadcast close to an election and paid for by corporations and labor unions. "As the record demonstrates, it is the manner in which parties have sold access to federal candidates and officeholders that has given rise to the appearance of undue influence," the majority declared. "It was not unwarranted for Congress to conclude that the selling of access gives rise to the appearance of corruption." Since the 1907 Tillman Act, corporations had been prevented from directly contributing to political candidates. The law was amended in the 1940s to prohibit direct contributions from labor unions, too.[23]

Chief Justice Rehnquist dissented in *McConnell*, with Justices Scalia, Kennedy, and Thomas joining him. Rehnquist emphasized the constitutional values undergirding citizens' rights to political alliances and donor access, writing, "A close association with others, especially in the realm of political speech, is not a surrogate for corruption; it is one of our most treasured First Amendment rights."

Justice Kennedy, who was still disturbed by the 1990 decision, separately wrote, "The majority compounds the error made in *Austin v. Michigan Chamber of Commerce* and silences political speech central to the civic discourse that sustains and informs our democratic processes." Again, Kennedy deemed the majority's attitude toward potential corporate corruption misguided. "The hostility toward corporations and unions that infuses the majority opinion is inconsistent with the viewpoint neutrality the First Amendment demands of all Government actors, including the members of this Court," he wrote. "Corporations, after all, are the engines of our modern economy."

Two years after the ruling in *McConnell*, Roberts succeeded Rehnquist. He shared his mentor's interest in narrowing the reach of campaign finance regulation and believed that "corruption" should be specifically defined as the exchange of cash for an official political act, a quid pro quo. And Roberts soon had what Rehnquist had lacked, a key fifth vote.

During Roberts's confirmation hearing in 2005, he had assured senators of his commitment to the legal concept of *stare decisis*, "to stand by things decided," that is, to ensure continuity in the law through the principle of following precedent. Yet at the same time, he had said that precedents could be dismantled over time. In an important exchange with Senator Arlen Specter, Roberts had elaborated on what he called the "workability and erosion of precedents" to suggest the Court's latitude to reverse, as he eventually did, decisions that a majority of the justices believed were wrong. He would sound the same themes as he voted to dismantle campaign finance precedents. In time, Senator Specter would become one of Roberts's strongest critics in this area as the Court rolled back more than one hundred years of regulation designed to provide a check on the power of money in elections.[24]

Roberts started out slowly, or, as Justice Scalia described it, with "faux judicial restraint."[25] The first campaign dispute after Roberts and Samuel Alito, his fellow Bush appointee, had joined the Court centered on the radio advertisements of a nonprofit advocacy group called Wisconsin Right to Life. It was supporting a number of President George W. Bush's judicial nominees who were stalled by Senate Democrats. The group aired two radio ads in 2004—"Wedding" and "Waiting"—that urged listeners to contact the state's two Democratic US senators, Russ Feingold and Herb Kohl, who were both participating in filibusters of the president's appointments. The ads compared the senators' delaying tactics with those of a fictitious father of a bride in "Wedding," and with those of a loan officer for a couple awaiting a mortgage loan in "Waiting." Both the father and the loan officer went off on digressions to avoid performing their respective duties.

Wisconsin Right to Life, which took contributions from for-profit corporations, wanted to run the ads through the 2004 election cycle. The McCain-Feingold law, however, prohibited such corporate-financed "electioneering communications," for thirty days before a primary and for sixty days before a general election, if they constituted "express" advocacy intended to urge voters to support or oppose a specific candidate.

Before the McCain-Feingold measure went into effect, corporations and labor unions could spend unlimited sums on advertising that criticized a candidate as long as they avoided certain "magic words" that told viewers whom to vote for. To close a loophole that had allowed a flood of de facto advertising for and against specific candidates, the McCain-Feingold law instituted its ban on *any* labor union or corporate-financed broadcast ads in the lead-up to an election. This provision had been upheld by the Court in the sweeping 2003 *McConnell v. Federal Election Commission* decision.

Roberts was ready to rule for Wisconsin Right to Life, but he wanted to move cautiously. The 2006–2007 session was already a tumultuous one, owing to the abortion and school integration rulings. The chief justice cobbled together a majority to reject enforcement of the law against Wisconsin Right to Life, but based on an open-ended rationale that justices to his right and to his left criticized. In his opinion for *Federal Election Commission v. Wisconsin Right to Life*, Roberts wrote that the Wisconsin ads would be unlawful only if they had "no reasonable interpretation other than as an appeal to vote for or against a specific candidate." Of the core constitutionality of McCain-Feingold's advertising restriction, which had been upheld in 2003, Roberts said, "We have no occasion to revisit that determination today." The occasion would come soon enough.

Roberts was joined in his opinion only by Alito, whose vote signaled that he would not follow his predecessor, O'Connor, when it came to campaign finance. Scalia, Thomas, and Kennedy joined a separate opinion to say they would have simply nullified the McCain-Feingold advertising restrictions. Scalia, writing for the trio, criticized Roberts for adopting an awkward test that was, in its application, at odds with the premises of *McConnell* and *Buckley*. Scalia noted that the four liberal dissenters agreed that the Roberts standard undercut *McConnell*. "Indeed, the [Roberts] opinion's attempt at distinguishing *McConnell* is unpersuasive enough," Scalia wrote, "and the change in the law it works is substantial enough, that seven justices of this Court, having widely divergent views concerning the constitutionality of the restrictions at issue, agree that the opinion effectively overrules *McConnell* without saying so. This faux judicial restraint is judicial obfuscation." Roberts, in only his second year on the Court, may not have wanted to move against precedent rapidly, but the left did not regard him as so cautious.

Liberal dissenters wanted to preserve the broadcast rules and brought even more passion to the case than Scalia, asserting that the Court's judgment undercut Congress's efforts to preserve electoral integrity in the face of large sums of money from corporate and union treasuries. Justice Souter, joined by Stevens, Ginsburg, and Breyer, wrote that the majority had discounted how the demand for large contributors had "produced a cynical electorate." He emphasized that the Court had just four years earlier upheld the electioneering prohibition in *McConnell*.

"The court (and, I think the country) loses when important precedent is overruled without good reason," Souter wrote. Looking back to congressional efforts since the 1907 Tillman Act, he added, "Campaign finance reform has been a series of reactions to documented threats to electoral integrity obvious to any voter, powered by large sums of money from corporate or union treasuries, with no redolence of 'grassroots' about them."

The following year, in *Davis v. Federal Election Commission*, the Court heard a case involving Jack Davis, a wealthy Democratic candidate for the US House of Representatives from New York's 26th Congressional District, who challenged the constitutionality of the so-called Millionaire's Amendment of McCain-Feingold. The provision allowed individuals running against self-financed candidates who spent more than $350,000 to receive contributions from individuals at triple the limit otherwise imposed. Proponents of the legislation argued that it leveled the playing field for people running against wealthy candidates who could tap their personal fortunes.

At issue was whether government could attempt to equalize influence in election campaigns, and the Court, again 5–4, with Roberts in the majority, said no. Roberts assigned the opinion to Alito, who wrote that the Millionaire's Amendment impinged a candidate's First Amendment right to spend his own money for campaign speech.[26]

Up to this point, Roberts had not attempted to reverse the 2003 case of *McConnell v. Federal Election Commission*. He was moving incrementally. The opportunity to confront campaign finance regulations head-on came when the Court agreed to hear the case of *Citizens United v. Federal Election Commission* in 2009. The dispute could have marked just another small step against campaign-finance restrictions, but, in the event, Roberts helped to lead a revolution that cleared the way for unlimited spending on political campaigns by corporations and unions.

The case began during the 2008 presidential campaign, when a conservative advocacy group led by longtime critics of Bill and Hillary Clinton wanted to widely distribute a movie produced for cable TV video-on-demand services. *Hillary: The Movie* attacked Hillary Clinton, a candidate for the Democratic presidential nomination. It featured news footage and denunciations of the former first lady, who was then a US senator from New York. The conflict with the Federal Election Commission turned, at least initially, on whether the McCain-Feingold law prohibiting the airing of campaign ads close to an election applied to a feature-length movie.

Lawyers for the advocacy group, Citizens United, had not argued for a broad ruling. Rather, they simply wanted the movie to be declared exempt from the advertising restriction. They contended that under Chief Justice Roberts's standard in the Wisconsin Right to Life case, the movie was not "the functional equivalent of express advocacy." The Federal Election Commission countered that the movie advanced the clear message that Clinton "lacked both the integrity and the qualifications to be President" and therefore could not "reasonably be interpreted as something other than an appeal to vote against" her.

At the Supreme Court in the spring of 2009, conservative justices worked to show that the government's positions could lead to prohibitions on all manner of media. During the first round of oral arguments, Justice Alito asked deputy US solicitor general Malcolm Stewart, who was defending the McCain-Feingold law, whether books could be covered, and Stewart, apparently caught off guard, said a book could indeed be covered. "That's pretty incredible," Alito said. "You think that if a book was published, a campaign biography that was the functional equivalent of express advocacy, that could be banned?"

"I'm not saying it could be banned. I'm saying that Congress could prohibit the use of corporate treasury funds," Stewart answered. Kennedy and Roberts jumped in with similar questions, and Stewart repeated his answer that if a book contained express advocacy, a corporation would be prevented from using its general treasury funds to support it. The corporation would instead have to finance the communication through a regulated political action committee. "If it's a 500-page book, and at the end it says, 'And so vote for X,' the government could ban that?" Roberts asked incredulously.[27]

After oral arguments, a five-justice majority including Roberts was ready to use the case to fully overturn the 1990 *Austin v. Michigan Chamber of Commerce* holding related to the corruptive dangers of corporations. The Court's conservatives had been heading down this path since Alito had succeeded O'Connor. But the constitutional question of corporate First Amendment rights had not been part of the question briefed and presented to the Court.

As a result, the liberal justices did not believe the conservatives should resolve the constitutional issue. Justice Kennedy, to whom Roberts had assigned the majority opinion, was drafting language that would overturn *Austin* outright, even though the question of its validity had not been fully addressed by Citizens United and the Federal Election Commission. Justices on the left believed that was an unwarranted leap and were infuriated by the turn of events. Souter, who had taken the lead for the dissenters in *Wisconsin Right to Life*, argued passionately about the dangers of big money in politics and policy. Now he was equally fervent that the majority was denying a full and proper airing of the constitutional issues. The question that had been subjected to oral arguments had turned on the specific *Hillary* video in a cable TV context.

Souter angrily set down his concerns in a draft dissenting opinion. Roberts, who wanted to avoid the airing of backstage conflict, agreed that the larger First Amendment question should be reargued before the justices.[28]

The inevitable—new free-speech protections for corporations and labor unions—would simply be delayed for a few more months. On June 29, 2009, the Supreme Court issued an order stating that the case of *Citizens United v. Federal Election Commission* would be reargued and that the justices would specifically decide whether to overrule *Austin v. Michigan Chamber of Commerce* and part of *McConnell v. Federal Elec-*

tion Commission. Arguments were set for September 9, even though the Court traditionally did not return until the first Monday in October. The message was that the Roberts Court was positioned to reverse precedent and would do it quickly, before the 2010 congressional midterm campaigns heated up.

Although the outcome might have been a foregone conclusion, the new hearing did not lack for drama. It was the first case in which the Obama administration's new solicitor general, Elena Kagan, stood at the lectern. Educated at Princeton University and Harvard Law School, Kagan's career path mirrored that of Roberts. Both had been law clerks at the Supreme Court, Kagan to Thurgood Marshall. Roberts had served in the Republican administrations of Ronald Reagan and George H.W. Bush, whereas Kagan had worked for two Democratic presidents, Bill Clinton and Barack Obama. Perhaps because of their respective backgrounds in the executive branch, they both had sensitive political antennae.

Those similarities, in fact, may have caused their initial clashes. As Kagan began to appear regularly before the Court on behalf of the federal government, Roberts sometimes bristled at her direct style. The former star advocate reprimanded her at one point for responding to a question from the bench with a query in return. "Usually we have the questions the other way," the chief justice said. She apologized. The sparring would eventually lead *Newsweek* to run a story with the headline: "Does the Chief Justice Hate Elena Kagan?"[29]

When Kagan stood up to argue the *Citizens United* case, she later said, she was so nervous that she thought she would collapse at the lectern. But like the man who sat directly in front of her in the central chair, Kagan had the ability to suppress her apprehension and concentrate on her argument. She opened by asserting that business corporations supporting a political candidate were more likely to give the appearance of corruption than individual advocacy. She urged the justices to rule narrowly on the facts of the distribution of *Hillary: The Movie* and avoid overturning the 1990 precedent. Trying to allay concerns from the previous set of arguments in the spring, she said flatly that the Federal Election Commission had never tried to regulate the distribution of books.

When the justices retreated to their private conference room on the case, the resulting vote was the same as on the first round in 2009, with the five conservatives in control. The only difference was that Souter was gone; he had been succeeded by Sotomayor, who was now in dissent with the other liberal justices. The majority was ready to clear the way for corporations and unions to spend unlimited amounts on election ads regardless of the timing or specific message.

Roberts assigned the opinion to Kennedy, but he also prepared to write a separate concurring statement that explained his view of when the Court need not follow its precedents, and he hoped this would shape the public response to the case. This was a moment of vindication for Kennedy, who for two decades had been protesting Justice Thurgood Marshall's decision in *Austin v. Michigan Chamber of Commerce*. He would also reverse portions of the 2003 *McConnell v. FEC* decision. Kennedy believed that neither of those rulings was true to the limits imposed by the 1976 *Buckley v. Valeo* decision. "When *Buckley* identified a sufficiently important governmental interest in preventing corruption or the appearance of corruption, that interest was limited to quid pro quo corruption," Kennedy said when he announced the Court's opinion in January 2010.[30]

"The fact that speakers may have influence over or access to elected officials does not mean that these officials are corrupt," Kennedy wrote in his opinion for the *Citizens United* majority, adopting language from his dissenting position in *Austin*. He declared that the 1990 *Austin* ruling interfered with the "open marketplace" of ideas protected by the First Amendment and led to "censorship . . . vast in its reach." Kennedy expressed concern that corporate voices had been squelched. "By suppressing the speech of manifold corporations, both for-profit and nonprofit, the Government prevents their voices and viewpoints from reaching the public and advising voters on which persons or entities are hostile to their interests." Kennedy's bottom line: Let all entities speak freely. Voters will judge what is true or false.

Justice Stevens and the other dissenters insisted that corporations should be treated differently from individuals, because their vast sums of money could distort debates and corrupt candidates. "Although they make enormous contributions to our society," Stevens wrote for the four liberals, "corporations are not actually members of it. They cannot vote or run for office. . . . The financial resources, legal structure, and instrumental orientation of corporations raise legitimate concerns about their role in the electoral process. Our lawmakers have a compelling constitutional basis, if not also a democratic duty, to take measures designed to guard against the potentially deleterious effects of corporate spending in local and national races."

Stevens resisted the majority's characterization of Citizens United as a victim of oppressive regulation. "Citizens United is a wealthy nonprofit corporation that runs a political action committee with millions of dollars in assets," he wrote. "It could have used those assets to televise and promote *Hillary: The Movie* wherever and whenever it wanted to. It also could have spent unrestricted sums to broadcast *Hillary* at any time other than the 30 days before the last primary election. Neither Citizens United's nor any other corporation's speech has been 'banned.'"

It was not simply the substance of the majority's opinion that distressed the dissenters; it was the way the majority arrived at the opinion, by reversing established precedent when a more modest ruling could have been made. Stevens was troubled by the direction Roberts was taking the Court. He liked Roberts personally. In his younger years in the Chicago area, Stevens had had a summer home not far from Long Beach, where Roberts had grown up. He felt like he understood his fellow midwesterner and wanted to give him time to settle in as chief justice. But Stevens believed the Roberts majority was wrongly asserting that certain past cases were poorly reasoned, simply to contrive an argument for reversal.[31]

"In the end," Stevens maintained, "the Court's rejection of *Austin* and *McConnell* comes down to nothing more than its disagreement with their results. Virtually every one of its arguments was rejected in those cases, and the majority opinion is essentially an amalgamation of resuscitated dissents. The only relevant thing that has changed since *Austin* and *McConnell* is the composition of this Court."[32]

Stevens had joined the bench in 1975, just after the oral arguments in *Buckley v. Valeo* had been held, and over time he had seen an ideological shift take place on the Court and in American politics overall. He was once regarded as a moderate, but as more conservative jurists joined the Court, he had found himself moving to the left. On the morning of January 21, 2010, in the rare Thursday sitting arranged specifically for *Citizens United*, Stevens read portions of his ninety-page dissenting opinion aloud. The silver-haired justice, who was in his thirty-fifth year of service and about to turn ninety, stumbled over his words and seemed to lose his place in the pages before him. (He later said, after he announced his retirement three months later, that he took his difficult, halting recitation as a sign that it was time to retire.) Yet Stevens's central message came through: he and the other dissenters believed it was dangerous to put corporations and individual people on equal footing.[33]

Chief Justice Roberts used his concurring statement to defend the Court from criticism that it was recklessly tossing out long-standing precedent. He began with warnings about censorship. The government's theory, Roberts insisted, would empower it "to prohibit newspapers from running editorials or opinion pieces supporting or opposing candidates for office, so long as the newspapers were owned by corporations—as the major ones are." Then Roberts articulated his central point defending the reversal of precedent. "Because the stakes are so high, our standard practice is to refrain from addressing constitutional questions except when necessary to rule on particular claims before us," he said. But, he stressed, "we must balance the importance of having constitutional questions *decided* against the importance of having them *decided right*."[34]

Roberts contended that the conservative-led reversals on campaign finance flowed from purely neutral decision-making. Yet the cases were all decided by 5–4 votes along ideological lines that reinforced the appearance of a nakedly political institution. And the shift in court legal standards over such a short period of time failed to contribute to "the stable and orderly development of the law" that Roberts held up as a Court goal in his concurring opinion for *Citizens United*.

Citizens United v. FEC had immediate repercussions. It led in short order to a DC Circuit decision lifting a federal ceiling on contributions made to independent political action committees that spend money on federal candidates. That prominent lower court decision, on March 26, 2010, in *SpeechNow.org v. Federal Election Commission*, invoked *Citizens United* as grounds for a decision allowing political action committees to raise and spend unlimited amounts on an election as long as the spending is independent of the candidate's spending. In an en banc ruling, the DC Circuit noted that the Federal Election Commission had relied on the Supreme Court's 2003 ruling in *McConnell* to argue that large contributions could lead to preferential access for donors and undue influence over elected officials. "Whatever the merits of those arguments before Citizens United," the DC Circuit said, "they plainly have no merit after Citizens United. In light of the Court's holding as a matter of law that independent expenditures do not corrupt or create the appearance of quid pro quo corruption, contributions that make only independent expenditures also cannot corrupt or create the appearance of corruption."[35]

The following year, Roberts took the lead in another 5–4 campaign finance case, striking down an Arizona law that offered public financing to candidates who agreed to limit the expenditure of private funds, participate in at least one public debate, and honor an overall spending cap. The Roberts majority said the law unfairly penalized privately funded candidates and independent groups that wanted to spend more money in campaigns. "'Leveling the playing field' can sound like a good thing," the chief justice wrote in *Arizona Free Enterprise Club's Freedom Club PAC v. Bennett*. "But in a democracy, campaigning for office is not a game."[36]

Arizona state officials had said the target of their Citizens Clean Elections law was corruption or the appearance of corruption. But during oral arguments, Roberts, who sometimes criticized colleagues for referring to materials outside the record of the case, had pinned down the state's lawyer, saying, "Well, I checked the Citizens Clean Elections commission website this morning and it [said] that this act was passed to, quote, 'level the playing field' when it comes to running for office.

Why isn't that clear evidence that it's unconstitutional?" Roberts said any "equalizing" argument would not be valid under the First Amendment. In his opinion for the Court, he observed that the website had been changed since oral arguments to say, "The Citizens Clean Elections Act was passed by the people of Arizona in 1998 to restore citizen participation and confidence in our political system."

Writing for the four dissenting liberals, Kagan mocked Roberts's supposed "smoking guns" regarding the state's intentions. "The only smoke here is the majority's, and it is the kind that goes with mirrors," Kagan wrote. She faulted Roberts for emphasizing Arizona's pitch to "level the playing field" when the overriding state interest was in fighting corruption and the appearance of corruption.

Later on, in a 2014 dispute, *McCutcheon v. Federal Election Commission*, Roberts further limited options for regulation in an opinion striking down a federal aggregate cap on individual donors. (Donors were forbidden from giving more than $123,000 combined in a single election cycle to federal candidates and parties.) "Money in politics may at times seem repugnant to some, but so too does much of what the First Amendment vigorously protects," Roberts wrote. "If the First Amendment protects flag burning, funeral protests, and Nazi parades—despite the profound offense such spectacles cause—it surely protects political campaign speech despite popular opposition."[37]

Quoting Kennedy's opinion in *Citizens United*, Roberts said, "Ingratiation and access . . . are not corruption." Rather, "they embody a central feature of democracy—that constituents support candidates who share their beliefs and interests, and candidates who are elected can be expected to be responsive to those concerns." He added that when donors can spread an unlimited amount of money among many candidates, the potential for corruption is diluted.

Dissenting, Justice Breyer argued that Roberts's opinion "creates a loophole that will allow a single individual to contribute millions of dollars to a political party or to a candidate's campaign." As Breyer put it, "Taken together with *Citizens United v. Federal Election Commission*, today's decision eviscerates our Nation's campaign finance laws, leaving a remnant incapable of dealing with the grave problems of democratic legitimacy that those laws were intended to resolve. . . . Where enough money calls the tune, the general public will not be heard."

Breyer, joined by fellow liberals Ginsburg, Sotomayor, and Kagan, faulted Roberts for declining to acknowledge that the new decision conflicted with precedent. Justice Thomas, though he signed on to Roberts's judgment striking down the regulations, similarly questioned the chief justice's transparency. "I regret only that [his opinion] does not acknowledge that today's decision, although purporting not to overrule *Buckley*, continues to chip away at its footings. In sum, what remains of *Buckley* is a rule without a rationale."

THE COURT'S CAMPAIGN FINANCE RULINGS HAD SUPPORTERS, INcluding Senate Majority Leader McConnell, who believed corporations had been "deprived of full participation in the political process." The critics were louder, more persistent, and often targeted Roberts. The Brookings Institution's Thomas Mann said *Citizens United* "made a mockery" of Roberts's "pious statements" about judicial modesty during his confirmation hearings.[38]

Perhaps the strongest denunciation came in January 2010, just six days after *Citizens United* was handed down, from President Obama at his first State of the Union Address. Six of the nine justices, including Roberts, were in front-row seats in the House of Representatives chamber.

"Last week, the Supreme Court reversed a century of law," Obama declared, "to open the floodgates for special interests—including foreign corporations—to spend without limit in our elections. . . . I don't think American elections should be bankrolled by America's most powerful interests, and worse, by foreign entities. They should be decided by the American people, and that's why I'm urging Democrats and Republicans to pass a bill that helps to right this wrong."[39]

At that moment, caught on national television, Justice Alito shook his head and mouthed the words, "not true," an apparent reaction to

Obama's contention—in error—that *Citizens United* lifted rules for foreign contributions. The moment went viral, offering a public example of the clash between the Obama administration and the Roberts Court over campaign finance law.[40]

Afterward, Roberts revealed his displeasure at the State of the Union to an audience at the University of Alabama. "The image of having the members of one branch of government standing up, literally surrounding the Supreme Court, cheering and hollering while the Court—according to the requirements of protocol—has to sit there expressionless, I think is very troubling," Roberts said two months after the *Citizens United* ruling. "To the extent it has degenerated into a political pep rally, I'm not sure why we're there."[41] He repeated his admonition that the Court was above politics.

It just so happened that during the negotiations among the justices over the first round of the *Citizens United* case in 2009, Roberts had sat for an extensive interview with C-SPAN. He had tried to lay out the Court's mission and explain how it differs from the work of politics. "All we're doing is interpreting the law," he said. "The decision has been made by Congress and the president and we're just exercising our responsibility to say what the law is. We're not ruling in favor of one side or in favor of another."

Roberts emphasized how distinct the justices were from elected politicians. "The most important thing for the public to understand is that we are not a political branch of government," he said. "They don't elect us. If they don't like what we're doing, it's more or less just too bad."[42]

CHAPTER IX

A SWITCH IN TIME

JOHN ROBERTS ARRIVED AT THE VALLETTA CAMPUS OF THE UNI-versity of Malta on July 3, 2012, to teach a class on Supreme Court history. As he emerged from the back seat of a black sedan, he held his brown leather briefcase in front of him, almost as a shield. He wore a blue blazer, striped button-down shirt, and tan khakis. His clothes looked crisp, though his face was haggard. He was as exhausted and distressed as he had been in years.[1]

Roberts had left behind a storm in Washington over his opinion up-holding President Barack Obama's health-care overhaul in *National Federation of Independent Business v. Sebelius*. Roberts had cast the deciding vote for the constitutionality of the 2010 law known as the Affordable Care Act (ACA). For the first time in his seven years as chief justice, he had sided in a high-profile case with the four liberal justices against all four of his fellow conservatives. Republicans in Congress had fought the Affordable Care Act at every turn, and all the GOP presidential candidates in 2012 had vowed to repeal it. Amid unusually intense public attention, Roberts, a Republican appointee, saved a Democratic initiative.

It was a stunning validation of Obama's signature domestic achievement, and it altered public perceptions of Roberts. But Roberts's moves behind the scenes were something else altogether. He had changed course multiple times. A full account of his actions during the justices' private negotiations has not previously been reported and is detailed here for the first time. It was not publicly known that a majority of the justices first voted to strike down the individual insurance mandate and to uphold an expansion of the Medicaid program. Roberts shifted on both, ultimately to find the core of the law dubbed Obamacare constitutional and to declare the provision requiring the expansion of Medicaid coverage unconstitutional. Two other justices also changed their votes on the latter provision. The final tallies, 5–4 to uphold the individual insurance mandate and 7–2 to curtail the Medicaid plan for people near the poverty line, came after weeks of negotiations and trade-offs among the justices.[2]

The full decision has reverberated in the public arena ever since. Assessments naturally vary. Roberts continues to be perceived as unreliable by many conservatives. For liberals, Roberts's actions at the time appeared to reflect an independent streak. (That liberal approval has evaporated over time as Roberts has remained a reliable conservative in virtually every other area of the law.) Within the Court, the chief justice's various positions on the ACA crystallized a distrust that had been building among his colleagues in his early years on the bench. His most ardent outside supporters, on the other hand, point to the Obamacare case as evidence for his assertion that judging is not partisan—or, at least, that the chief himself is not an ideologue.

The Affordable Care Act, signed by President Obama on March 23, 2010, followed decades of failed attempts in Washington to control spiraling medical costs and provide Americans with higher-quality health care.

The act, which attempted to provide coverage for forty-five million Americans who were without health insurance, created a new marketplace where the uninsured could buy coverage and be protected from insurance-company exclusions based on preexisting conditions such as diabetes, cancer, and other chronic health issues. To support the system and draw in the healthy as well as the sick, the law required that most uninsured people obtain insurance (the "individual mandate") or pay a penalty. That penalty, or fee, would be collected as part of an individual's annual taxes.[3]

A separate provision expanded Medicaid benefits. Since passage of the Social Security Amendments of 1965, the Medicaid program had provided the states with substantial federal funding to offer medical care to poor families. The Medicaid program also set criteria for who would be covered (for example, pregnant women, the elderly, and the disabled) and what services would be provided. ACA provisions required states to provide Medicaid coverage to a wider range of needy individuals, including adults with incomes up to 133 percent of the federal poverty level. States were previously not required to cover childless adults or even all low-income families below the federal poverty level, and as a result, only the most destitute families received coverage. The money for about 90 percent of that expansion would come from the federal government. But it would come with a strict condition: if states did not broaden their programs as dictated by the ACA, they would lose all Medicaid funds.

Congressional Republicans and other critics believed the individual mandate exceeded Congress's powers to regulate commerce in the states. On the Medicaid expansion issue, they said the federal government's threat to withhold funds infringed on states' sovereignty by coercing their compliance.

Many legal analysts took a different view. Although some conservative and libertarian law professors agreed with the critics in Congress, much of legal academia thought the complaints ill founded.[4] As stated in Article I of the Constitution, the commerce clause gives Congress the power "to regulate commerce with foreign nations, and among the several states, and with the Indian tribes." Since the late 1930s, the Supreme Court had interpreted that broadly, granting Congress latitude over anything that could be construed as substantially affecting interstate business activity.

The states and businesses challenging the ACA's insurance require-ment argued that a decision to forgo insurance did not involve commercial activity, but rather "inactivity." The mandate applied to people who were not buying insurance. Some critics argued that if government could force people to buy health insurance, it could compel people to join gyms, pur-chase certain vehicles, or even consume healthy food such as broccoli. The Obama administration countered that opting not to purchase insurance affected commerce because uninsured people inevitably required health care, incurred costs, and burdened the whole system.

The State of Florida, initially joined by twelve other states, filed a law-suit on the same day that President Obama signed the Affordable Care Act. The National Federation of Independent Business, an association of small businesses, filed a lawsuit of its own, as did more states, Liberty University in Virginia, and the Thomas More Law Center in Michigan. As the lawsuits piled up, many legal scholars declared the challenges to be without merit. Harvard law professor Charles Fried, who had been a US solicitor general under President Reagan, said he was confident that the individual mandate was valid. He was so confident, in fact, that he would eat his hat—"bought in Australia . . . made of kangaroo skin"—if the law was struck down.[5]

Public interest in the case swelled. The number of Americans who had been uninsured before passage of the Affordable Care Act—estimated at forty-five million—represented about 16 percent of the population. Meanwhile, the health-care industry constituted one of the largest busi-ness sectors in the nation, representing nearly 20 percent, or approximately $3 trillion, of the gross domestic product. In Washington, the scope of Congress's power to solve the health-care dilemma was a crucial question.

During the initial hearings in lower courts, most of the judges sided with the Obama administration and rejected challenges to the law. But by mid-2011, an important split in opinion had emerged among regional US appeals courts. The Sixth Circuit (based in Cincinnati), the Fourth Circuit (based in Richmond), and the DC Circuit upheld the mandate as a valid exercise of Congress's commerce power, but the Eleventh Cir-cuit (based in Atlanta) ruled that the insurance requirement exceeded

Congress's power. The Eleventh Circuit judges concluded that the requirement to purchase health insurance represented "a wholly novel and potentially unbounded assertion of congressional authority: the ability to compel Americans to purchase an expensive health insurance product they have elected not to buy." The judges also found, however, that the invalid provision could be severed from the remainder of the Affordable Care Act and that most of the ACA could still stand. As a sign of how polarized the American judiciary had become, all of the Democratic-appointed judges (except one) who heard these cases voted to uphold the law, and all of the Republican-appointed judges (except two) who acted in these cases voted to strike it down.[6]

The split in the lower courts over the individual insurance mandate prompted the Supreme Court to consider the case. The justices were inclined to hear challenges to important federal legislation, especially to resolve conflicting interpretations of a law. It should be noted, however, that not one of the lower courts had ruled the Medicaid expansion unconstitutional.

By the time the Court considered the case, a new justice had joined the bench. John Paul Stevens had resigned in 2010, and President Obama had chosen Elena Kagan, whom he had earlier named as US solicitor general, to succeed him. Kagan's hearings had been dominated by senators' complaints over the *Citizens United* decision rejecting federal regulation of corporate campaign spending. Kagan as an administration lawyer had argued that the McCain-Feingold law was constitutional. At her Senate hearings, she defended it based on extensive congressional findings of the corrupting influence of independent expenditures by corporations and unions.

Also controversial was her support, while dean at Harvard Law School, for a ban on military recruiters, because of the federal policy at the time prohibiting openly gay troops. Kagan told the senators that she believed the federal policy was "unjust," but had tried to work out a compromise for recruiting on campus. She had allowed recruitment to proceed through the Harvard Law School Veterans Association, rather than through the university's Office for Career Services. "I'm confident that the military had access to our students and our students had access to the military throughout my entire deanship," she said. Many Republican senators were dubious and continued to oppose her nomination. The Senate confirmed her on a vote of 63–37. Every senator who voted against her confirmation was Republican.

Once Kagan was confirmed, in August 2010, Chief Justice Roberts, who had sometimes been dismissive of her as she had argued before the justices, took steps to welcome her. The minute the Senate reached a decisive fifty votes in her favor on the afternoon of August 5, he was on the phone from Australia, where he was teaching a short course, ready to congratulate her. The call came in to her office as Kagan watched the count on television. Then, before her formal investiture, he gave her a personal tour of the Court's inner rooms that visitors do not see, including the conference room, the robing area, and the justices' dining room. He began in the robing room, where each justice has a tall wooden locker that is identified by a little brass nameplate. When they started the tour, Justice Stevens's name was still on his locker. By the time the tour ended and Roberts ushered Kagan back to the robing room, the chief justice had ensured that Stevens's nameplate was off his locker and Kagan's new one was installed on her locker at the end of the row of nine. She appreciated the touch and spoke warmly of the way Roberts had welcomed her.

With Kagan replacing Stevens, an appointee of Gerald Ford, the Court's ideological divisions now lined up neatly with the justices' political affiliations. The five conservatives, Roberts, Scalia, Kennedy, Thomas, and Alito, had all been named by Republican presidents. The four liberals, Ginsburg, Breyer, Sotomayor, and Kagan, had been named by Democratic presidents. It was becoming more difficult for the public to accept the assertion that the justices were not voting along political lines: in the most closely watched cases, they divided exactly that way.

Donald Verrilli replaced Kagan at the lectern as US solicitor general. Like Roberts, Verrilli had been a Supreme Court law clerk (in his case, to Justice William Brennan), and also like Roberts, he had later become a leading appellate attorney at a large corporate firm. He had argued twelve cases at the Supreme Court before joining the Obama administration, first in the Department of Justice and then in the White House counsel's office. The Senate confirmed him as solicitor general by a 72–16 vote in June 2011, in time to begin writing briefs defending the Affordable Care Act.

Multiple lawyers appeared for each side, but the primary match-up was between Verrilli and Paul Clement, who also came into the case in 2011. He had been chosen after Florida's attorney general, Pam Bondi, taking the lead for the state challengers, had flown to Washington to conduct a "beauty contest," as the process was known among Supreme Court advocates. (Roberts was familiar with the routine of clients seeking an appellate specialist and had often won the competition.) Bondi borrowed a conference room at a downtown law firm to hear pitches from three firms, and Clement, who had been US solicitor general in the George W. Bush administration and had kept up a Republican-tilted portfolio in private practice, easily prevailed. He had come to Washington by way of Harvard Law School, much like Roberts, and had clerked for Scalia. At the time he was hired, he was representing the Bipartisan Legal Advisory Group of Congress in *United States v. Windsor*, the lawsuit challenging Congress's Defense of Marriage Act, the federal law prohibiting recognition of same-sex marriages.[7]

The Supreme Court scheduled multiple hours of arguments over three days in late March in the ACA case, which involved various procedural and substantive questions. A typical case received a single one-hour session on one day.

The dispute over the Affordable Care Act was reminiscent, to some legal observers, of an earlier era's tests of federal power. Coincidentally, that era had also witnessed an unexpected move by a Justice Roberts—Owen Roberts, no relation to the current chief justice—that became known as the "switch in time that saved nine."

In the early 1930s, when Charles Evans Hughes was chief justice, America had been in the throes of the Great Depression. In what became known as the New Deal, President Franklin D. Roosevelt had launched a series of federally financed programs to improve labor conditions, provide jobs and housing for citizens, and safeguard their investments. Businesses had challenged many of the initiatives on the grounds that the federal government was exceeding its constitutional authority. As disputes landed at the Supreme Court, four of the nine justices dug in against FDR's programs: Willis Van Devanter, James C. McReynolds, George Sutherland, and Pierce Butler. They became known as the Four Horsemen and were often joined by Justice Owen Roberts in ruling against the new administration.

For decades before the Depression, the Court had been dominated by conservative justices who were committed to an unregulated economy. The justices had struck down scores of laws designed to protect workers based on a theory of due process that valued economic liberty and enforced a right of contract between employers and employees. The period was known as the Lochner era, taking its name from a 1905 case, *Lochner v. New York*, that voided a New York law limiting the hours that bakery employees could work. The Court had found the restrictions on hours to be an infringement on the freedom to enter into contracts, and *Lochner* ultimately led to the rejection of nearly two hundred worker and social welfare regulations.[8]

The Supreme Court then began gutting Roosevelt's New Deal legislation, including key parts of the National Industrial Recovery Act in 1935. The next year, the Court struck down the Agricultural Adjustment Act and the Bituminous Coal Conservation Act, which required minimum-wage and maximum-hour standards for the coal industry. Implementation of the law was to be financed by a tax on producers, and coal companies sued. The Court sided with the challengers, ruling that coal production was a local activity with no direct bearing on interstate commerce such that Congress could regulate it.[9]

Roosevelt was outraged. Emboldened by his reelection in November 1936, he introduced a plan to add more justices to the bench to increase the chances of his economic relief program surviving judicial scrutiny. The president proposed the appointment of a new justice for every current justice who was more than seventy years old. Six of the nine were then over seventy.[10]

Chief Justice Hughes met privately with Senate leaders to try to sink the legislation, arguing that the Court was working efficiently and effectively with nine members. Public sentiment also tilted against Roosevelt's plan. But it was a shift in the direction of the Court itself that guaranteed an end to the "court packing" proposal. In March 1937, the majority upheld a Washington State minimum-wage law that was similar to a wage law that the Court had previously invalidated.[11] The new majority reversed the Court's earlier view that government could not interfere with employers' rights to contract freely with their workers. A month later, the Court affirmed the Wagner Act, which had created the National Labor Relations Board, thus permitting government to regulate labor-management relations throughout the country.[12]

Justice Owen Roberts's pivotal vote with the majority that spring was the vote that became popularly known as "the switch in time that saved nine," because FDR no longer had reason to push his "court-packing" plan. The majority now interpreted Congress's power over commerce more broadly, repudiating the Court's earlier rulings shielding business enterprises from government regulation. Soon afterward, the "Four Horsemen" began to leave office, and Roosevelt replaced them with justices ready to uphold the New Deal and federal power.

The rulings that followed bolstered Congress's ability to address social problems, and proponents of Obamacare believed they were following in this tradition. Administration lawyers warned the Court in their written filing that if it rejected the ACA it would be striking down a major federal social welfare law for the first time since the Lochner era and the Court's 1937 shift.

AS THE ORAL ARGUMENTS OVER THE AFFORDABLE CARE ACT approached, Washington's powerful, both Republicans and Democrats, beseeched individual justices and other Court officials for one of the courtroom's three hundred spectator seats. Others paid people to stand in line on their behalf for days before the scheduled March 26 start of the arguments, now collected under the title of *National Federation for Independent Business v. Sebelius*. On the first day of the case, among those in attendance were Health and Human Services Secretary Kathleen Sebelius, whose agency was overseeing the new law; US Attorney General Eric Holder, whose lawyers were defending it; and the Florida attorney general, Bondi, who led the state challengers.

The Obama administration offered three main arguments in support of the individual insurance mandate. It contended first that the mandate fell within Congress's power to regulate interstate commerce. The administration also defended the law under Congress's authority in the Constitution to make all laws "necessary and proper" to carry out other specific powers, maintaining that the individual mandate was "necessary" to carry out Congress's comprehensive reforms of the insurance market. Finally, the administration argued that the mandate was valid based on Congress's taxing power. During the debates over the legislation in 2009 and 2010, congressional Democrats and President Obama had tried to avoid the term "tax." But for the legal case, administration lawyers said the individual mandate operated on a practical level as a tax. The penalty for not purchasing insurance was based on a percentage of household income and had to be recorded on annual income tax forms.

Before the arguments began, legal analysts, commentators, and journalists had speculated that the Court would split along political lines. There were some predictions about Justice Kennedy, as the swing vote on the Court, possibly deciding the case. Veteran Court analysts believed that his commitment to limited congressional power, however, would lead him to join the more consistent conservatives. Some thought that Roberts's position was uncertain, because of the political pressures upon him in a presidential election year and his concern for the Court's institutional image.[13]

When the justices took up the individual mandate provision in arguments, Solicitor General Verrilli was the first to stand at the lectern. The fifty-four-year-old native of New York, six foot three with a graying mustache, was the face of the Obama administration at the Court, and as such he often ended up on the defensive during the give-and-take with Roberts and the other conservative justices. Verrilli stressed "the unique nature" of the health-care insurance market, in which people were required to buy a product they would eventually need.[14]

"Yes, but your theory," Roberts interjected, "is that there is a market in which everyone participates because everybody might need a certain range of health care services. And yet, you're requiring people who are never going to need pediatric or maternity services to participate in that market." Verrilli said Congress had the latitude to decide who would be covered and the breadth of services. He stressed the importance of full participation: "This is a market in which you may be healthy one day, and you may be a very unhealthy participant in that market the next day."

Verrilli provoked a strong reaction from Roberts when he referred to the Lochner era. If the Court were to limit congressional powers over health care, Verrilli insisted, "it would be a very substantial departure" from rulings since the 1930s that allowed Congress to regulate economic activity to the benefit of individual citizens.

"It seems to me," Roberts countered, "it's an entirely different question when you ask yourself whether or not there are going to be limits on federal power, as opposed to limits on the states, which was the issue in *Lochner.*" Roberts would not abide a comparison to the Lochner era. Verrilli had remembered that the *Lochner* decision was one of the few that Roberts had denounced during his confirmation hearings in 2005. As a nominee, Roberts had referred to the inherent "immodesty" of the decision and "its reweighing of the legislative determination."

"You can read that opinion today and it's quite clear that they're not interpreting the law," Roberts had told the Senate Judiciary Committee. "They're making the law. The judgment is right there. They say: We don't think it's too much for a baker to work whatever it was, 13 hours a day. We think the legislature made a mistake in saying they should regulate this for their health. We don't think it hurts their health at all. It's right there in the opinion. You can look at that and see that they are substituting their judgment on a policy matter for what the legislature had said." Roberts was correct when he said, during the ACA arguments, that *Lochner v. New York* had overturned a state maximum-hour law for bakers. But its rationale had also supported rejection of a broad swath of state and federal social welfare measures.[15]

When Verrilli pivoted to Congress's authority to levy taxes, and claimed that this authority offered equally strong grounds on which to uphold the mandate's validity, Roberts asked, "Why didn't Congress call it a tax, then? You're telling me they thought of it as a tax, they defended it on the tax power. Why didn't they say it was a tax?" Verrilli acknowledged the unpopularity of anything deemed a "tax," but reminded the Court that the law had amended the Internal Revenue Code and required the penalty to be collected by the IRS every April 15.

At the lectern next was Clement, a forty-five-year-old native of Wisconsin. He argued without notes and fell into an easy conversational manner with the justices. Because he had clerked for Justice Scalia, the two often sparred good-naturedly in the oral argument sessions.

"The mandate represents an unprecedented effort by Congress to compel individuals to enter commerce in order to better regulate commerce," Clement told the justices. "The Commerce Clause gives Congress the power to regulate existing commerce. It does not give Congress the far greater power to compel people to enter commerce." Few of the justices raised the issue of Congress's taxing power, and Clement himself said little to counter Verrilli's contention that that the individual mandate could be grounded in that power. Clement did mention the issue near the end of his time at the lectern, saying, "I would like to say two very brief things about the taxing power, if I could. There are lots of reasons why this isn't a tax. It wasn't denominated a tax. It's not structured as a tax."

In Verrilli's four minutes at the lectern for rebuttal, he circled back to his argument about taxation. "If there's any doubt about [the validity of the individual mandate] under the Commerce Clause," he told the nine justices, "then I urge this Court to uphold the minimum coverage provision as an exercise of the taxing power. The Court . . . has a solemn obligation to respect the judgments of the democratically accountable branches of government, and because this statute can be construed in a manner that allows it to be upheld that way, I respectfully submit that it is this Court's duty to do so."

When Chief Justice Roberts and the eight associate justices gathered in conference on March 30, the discussion focused on the individual insurance mandate and Congress's power to regulate commerce. Roberts went first, as was the custom, laying out his views. He detailed his understanding of the history of the commerce clause and emphasized that he believed it never was intended to cover inactivity, such as the refusal to buy insurance. He acknowledged being torn between his heart and his head, as he put it, and expressed some hesitancy to strike down a law intended to solve the nation's health insurance crisis. After the chief, Justices Scalia, Kennedy, and Thomas offered their views. Like Roberts, they thought Congress's commerce authority did not cover an individual's decision to forgo—rather than obtain—health insurance.[16]

There were thus four immediate votes cast to invalidate the mandate. No one at the table was surprised, based on the questions during oral arguments. The network of law clerks inside the building also had been circulating intelligence about the views from each justice's chambers. That meant the votes of the liberals were known, too. Justice Ginsburg, fifth in seniority, was the first to cast a vote to uphold the individual mandate. She believed Supreme Court precedent demanded the law be found constitutional, particularly the precedent set by the 1942 case *Wickard v. Filburn*, which allowed Congress to regulate agricultural production even if a farmer's yield was not meant for commercial sale. That decision had essentially bolstered the government's regulatory powers.

Justice Ginsburg was followed by Justice Breyer, who agreed with her. Next in seniority was Justice Alito, who cast the fifth and final vote to strike down the law. The eighth and ninth justices at the table, Sotomayor and Kagan, joined Ginsburg and Breyer in voting for the law as part of Congress's power to regulate interstate commerce.

There was no sign at that March 30 private session that any of the nine justices would defy the usual ideological and partisan alignment. That political division bothered Roberts, but he felt just as strongly about boundaries on the commerce-clause power as did the other four in the majority.

Regarding the expansion of Medicaid for poor people, all four liberal justices—Ginsburg, Breyer, Sotomayor, and Kagan—voted to uphold the program. During oral arguments on the expansion, they had effectively punctured Clement's arguments that Congress had exceeded its spending power and its ability to attach conditions to federal funds. Now in the private March 30 conference, Roberts also voted to uphold the Medicaid expansion, yet he expressed some tentativeness on this provision.

Even though the Medicaid provision seemed secondary—at least in terms of constitutional debate and public controversy—to the individual insurance mandate, it was significant. The expansion was intended to bring affordable health insurance to Americans whose health was most at risk. (Before the Supreme Court ruled, the Congressional Budget Office estimated that the Medicaid expansion would provide health insurance for about seventeen million more people.[17])

When the nine walked out of their initial conference, the core of Obamacare was in peril. A clear five-justice majority was prepared to reject the individual mandate on commerce-clause grounds. No vote had been taken related to congressional taxing power. It did not seem to matter, because the individual mandate was not going to survive. The only uncertainty was what would fall with it.

ROBERTS WANTED TO CRAFT A COMPROMISE DECISION THAT COULD validate a portion of the ACA. But his four fellow conservatives believed that if the individual mandate was going down, it would take the whole law with it. Congress had not written in any "severability" clause, which would have allowed an unconstitutional element to be excised, and the justices on the right believed that all the pieces were interlocked.

The chief justice thought the individual mandate was entwined with only two other provisions, those known as the "community rating" and "guaranteed issue." The community-rating section prevented health insurers from charging some individuals higher premiums than others based on health status, and the guaranteed-issue section required insurers to cover people regardless of preexisting conditions.

As was his prerogative as chief justice, Roberts kept the majority opinion for himself. Senior liberal justice Ginsburg was ready to write for the dissenting foursome. Both immediately began drafting their dueling opinions in the case.

When he started working on an opinion, Roberts wrote with a pen on a yellow legal pad. For the health-care case, he began drafting a history of Congress's authority under the commerce clause and relevant cases. He wanted the opinion to show that the framers would not have tried to compel the purchase of any product. Roberts was a disciplined worker with a set schedule, waking around 6:00 each morning and going to bed at 10:00 p.m.

Down the corridor, Ginsburg was in her chambers poring over the same constitutional history as Roberts, yet reaching the opposite conclusion: that Congress had ample latitude to require Americans to buy insurance to support the health-care system. Ginsburg worked best at night and sometimes through the night. Early on in her legal career, when she had been raising her children, she sometimes went for days on only two or three hours of sleep.

Ginsburg was known not only for her unusual work habits but also for her speed. She was usually the first justice in each session to finish an opinion. She spoke in an interview once of a lesson she had learned early on from Sandra Day O'Connor, who had a similar record in producing opinions. In 1993, soon after Ginsburg had become a justice, she had gone to O'Connor for help dealing with then chief justice Rehnquist on her first opinion assignment. Instead of giving her a relatively easy case on which all nine had agreed, Rehnquist had assigned her a complex pension dispute.

"Sandra, how can he do this to me?" Ginsburg asked O'Connor, thinking she might sympathize with her predicament. "Ruth, you just do it, and get your opinion in circulation before he makes the next set of assignments," O'Connor said. Recounting the episode, Ginsburg said, "That is so typical Sandra."[18]

The Court had a ten-day break before its final set of oral arguments for the 2011–2012 term, in late April. Scalia headed to St. John's

University in Queens to teach a class, then flew to Hattiesburg, Mississippi, near one of his favorite places for hunting. Kagan went first to Marquette University Law School in Wisconsin to judge a moot court, and later to Massachusetts for a speech at Harvard. Thomas traveled to the University of Kentucky in early April, around the time Sotomayor was heading to the University of Pennsylvania Law School.

Kennedy stayed in Washington for most of early April, and Roberts took advantage of his presence to try to persuade him to find that the unconstitutional insurance requirement could be severed from the rest of the law. These conversations were not easy. Kennedy offered a number of reasons why the law that Congress wrote could not be broken apart. As he saw it, the various parts were interdependent: without the financing from the individual insurance requirement, the system could not be funded. In fact, many proponents of the law had argued essentially the same thing, saying that the mandate was crucial to avoid a "death spiral" scenario in which the law became unsustainable. Without the mandate, the healthiest people would leave the system, and premiums would rise. The cost of insurance would be too high for the remaining participants, who presumably would tend to be the sickest Americans, and the new system would disintegrate as insurers pulled out of the new health-insurance marketplace.

Kennedy was unusually firm in his position that all the provisions for benefits and financing were interrelated and could not be severed from the entirety of the law. He was puzzled, and then put off, by Roberts's view that the ACA provisions could be severed. From the start of their time together, Roberts and Kennedy had had a symbiotic relationship. Roberts had cultivated Kennedy for his crucial fifth vote. Kennedy, older and with more tenure, was nonetheless junior to the chief justice and depended on him for opinion assignments and other considerations around the Court building.

Here, though, their differences were irreconcilable. The chief justice continued to believe that only two provisions were linked to the individual mandate and expected increase in participation: the one preventing insurers from charging higher premiums based on health status, and the one requiring insurers to cover people regardless of preexisting conditions.

As THE CASE WAS BEING DEBATED INSIDE, OUTSIDE CRITICS WERE already lining up with complaints against the chief justice and his fellow conservatives. *Washington Post* columnist E. J. Dionne warned immediately after oral arguments that the Court was about to demonstrate that it believed its power to be limitless. He especially targeted Roberts, writing, in reference to the chief justice's objection concerning people being required to purchase insurance for situations they would never confront, such as maternity and pediatric services, that he had offered "one of the most astonishing arguments" of the entire case.[19]

"Well, yes," the liberal Dionne wrote, "men pay to cover maternity services while women pay for treating prostate problems. It's called health insurance. Would it be better to segregate the insurance market along gender lines?" Furthermore, he said in his conclusion, "This is what conservative justices will do if they strike down or cripple the health-care law. And a court that gave us *Bush v. Gore* and *Citizens United* will prove conclusively that it sees no limits on its power, no need to defer to those elected to make our laws. A Supreme Court that is supposed to give us justice will instead deliver ideology." The constant references to the 2010 *Citizens United* case irritated Roberts. It also irked him when news accounts focused on corporations. After all, the *Citizens United* ruling had lifted spending rules for labor unions, too.

President Obama weighed in a week later. "Ultimately, I am confident that the Supreme Court will not take what would be an unprecedented, extraordinary step of overturning a law that was passed by a strong majority of a democratically elected Congress," he said at an April 2 news conference. "And I'd just remind conservative commentators that, for years, what we have heard is, the biggest problem on the bench was judicial activism, or a lack of judicial restraint, that an unelected group of people would somehow overturn a duly constituted and passed law. Well, this is a good example, and I'm pretty confident that this court will recognize that and not take that step."[20]

Obama's statements rankled Roberts, and any suggestion that he could be influenced by politics galled him. He was hearing not only from political foes. Legal analyst Jeffrey Rosen, who had earlier written admiringly about the chief justice, declared, "This is John Roberts's moment of truth." In a column for *Politico*, Rosen said, "In addition to deciding what kind of chief justice he wants to be, he has to decide what kind of legal conservatism he wants to embrace. Of course, if the Roberts Court strikes down health care reform by a 5–4 vote, then the chief justice's stated goal of presiding over a less divisive Court will be viewed as an irredeemable failure."[21]

Although Roberts remained firm in his belief that the individual mandate exceeded Congress's commerce power, he did not want the entire law to fall. A pro-business conservative, he understood the importance of the insurance industry to US businesses, and he was genuinely concerned about invalidating an entire law that had been approved through the democratic process to solve the intractable health-care problem. Some justices thought the chief feared that the public would blame the Court for a resulting insurance crisis. He and Kennedy remained at odds.

In mid-April, Roberts moved into new territory. He began exploring whether Congress's taxing power could, as the Obama administration had argued, serve as a pillar of support for the individual mandate if the commerce authority failed to do so. Roberts decided he could make a case for the taxing-power grounds. He continued to try to negotiate with Kennedy, but he now also turned to Breyer and Kagan, the liberal justices most likely to work with him on contentious issues, to find common ground.

The situation put Kennedy in an unusual spot. For years, at least since Justice O'Connor had retired, in January 2006, Kennedy had been the key vote in the middle, the individual who weighed his options and whose legal reasoning could determine the outcome of a dispute. Some of Kennedy's colleagues, particularly Scalia, who saw the world in black and white, were impatient with Kennedy's hesitations, especially on social dilemmas such as abortion rights. But on matters of congressional power, Kennedy had a surer conservative streak. The case of *National Federation of Independent Business v. Sebelius* surfaced his concern about federal encroachment on state prerogatives.

Amid the building drama, the five other justices knew exactly where they each stood. On the far right, Scalia, Thomas, and Alito were not going to alter their positions. They thought the entire law was unconstitutional. On the left, Ginsburg and Sotomayor believed the legislation fell squarely within Congress's authority. As Ginsburg worked on her dissenting opinion, she occasionally heard through the clerk grapevine about Roberts's vacillation. Yet she rightly estimated that however he might change his mind, he would not retreat on his belief that Congress could not require health insurance based on its power to regulate commerce. So she pressed on with her dissent.

By early May, Roberts was crafting an argument that would support the individual mandate based on Congress's taxing authority. At the same time, he began incorporating arguments that would invalidate the Medicaid expansion. This was a strange turn. None of the lower courts that had taken up the Affordable Care Act had rejected the Medicaid expansion. The federal government was paying a substantial percentage of Medicaid funding for the states, and not since the 1930s had the Court rejected a federal measure for exceeding Congress's spending power.

Breyer and Kagan, who were conferring with Roberts, had voted in the justices' private conference to uphold the new Medicaid requirement to help the poor, and their votes had been unequivocal. But they were aware that Roberts was now making a concession on the individual mandate, and they were open to compromising.

During oral arguments on the Medicaid controversy, Clement had insisted that forcing states to accept more poor people into their Medicaid programs would encroach on their sovereignty and interfere with choices on the use of funds. The federal government had agreed to pick up 90 percent of the cost of the expansion; the states would be responsible for the other 10 percent.[22]

Roberts posited in his draft opinion that Congress had in effect held "a gun to the head" of the states by conditioning all Medicaid money on the expanded coverage. He saw the expansion as transforming the Medicaid program, not simply changing it to a degree. Yet he was not prepared to find that the expansion had to be scrapped altogether, only that states could not be forced to join through the leverage of all Medicaid funding.

Breyer and Kagan disagreed with Roberts's new thinking on Medicaid, but they were pragmatists. If there was a chance that Roberts would cast the critical vote to uphold the central plank of the Affordable Care Act—and negotiations in May were such that they still considered that a shaky proposition—they were willing to meet him partway. At this point, law clerks and others working on the case assumed that even without the mandatory expansion requirement, most states would adopt the Medicaid expansion anyway, because the federal government was going to pay for the bulk of the new coverage. That turned out to be a false assumption.[23]

IT IS EXTRAORDINARILY RARE FOR WORD OF INTERNAL NEGOTIATIONS on cases to slip out of the Marble Palace and into the public realm. Clerks take a vow of confidentiality, and the justices themselves rarely reveal anything about the decision-making process. But in the high-stakes health-care controversy, rumors were rampant. Law professors who had helped engineer the arguments against the individual mandate expressed confidence that a majority was ready to strike it down, yet they were also hearing that Roberts had gone "wobbly." Some observers began to think he might be ready to defy his conservative instincts and vote to uphold the Affordable Care Act.

A new round of competing commentary filled the airwaves and the newspapers. Some of the commentary was in response to other commentary. On the Senate floor on May 14, for example, Senator Patrick Leahy, who had been the senior Democrat at Roberts's 2005 Senate Judiciary Committee hearings, provoked responses in the press when he declared, "I trust that he will be a Chief Justice for all of us and that he has a strong institutional sense of the proper role of the Judicial Branch."[24]

In response to Leahy's comment, *Washington Post* columnist Kathleen Parker, who was on the other side of the debate, wrote, a few days later, that "novelist John Grisham could hardly spin a more provocative fiction. The president and his surrogates mount an aggressive campaign to intimidate the chief justice of the United States, implying ruin and ridicule should he fail to vote in a pivotal case according to the ruling political party's wishes. If only it were fiction."[25]

Some associate justices were concerned about the public speculation and thought Roberts might remind law clerks of their obligation to maintain confidentiality. But it turned out that law clerks were not the only ones quietly passing around information about the dissension behind the scenes. The conservatives were feeling blindsided by Roberts's defection, and their anger was rising.

The chief justice was concentrating on revising his opinion in a way that would allow the Supreme Court to uphold the law, and he was lacing it with multiple references to Chief Justice John Marshall, the nation's early, influential chief justice. Perhaps it was a reflection of his belief that he was adhering to institutional principles. Scalia, Kennedy, Thomas, and Alito began working on a separate opinion that would echo Roberts's on the limits of the commerce clause but attack his fallback rationale related to Congress's power to tax. Scalia believed the taxing-power possibility had never received a full airing before the justices. He was drafting an opinion that scoffed at the "fly by night briefing" related to the tax issue. However, the taxing power argument had been fully briefed by the two sides. Still, it had not been put to a vote in the justices' private conference. An element that had previously seemed inconsequential was now making all the difference in the outcome of the case.

Michael Carvin, who had represented the National Federation of Independent Business in its challenge to the Affordable Care Act, heard the rumors of a switched vote by Roberts in May. Carvin had known Roberts for nearly two decades, and he said he put no stock in the chatter. "I refused to believe the Obama administration's relatively naked effort would change the situation," Carvin later said in an interview. "I thought, if anything, it would backfire." He understood Roberts's investment in his own personal integrity. Roberts would never want to be seen as being influenced by outside forces.[26]

When Ginsburg found out about Roberts's new position, her first thought was, "It ain't over 'til it's over." She understood that the process could continue to be fluid, especially in such a monumental case. "People change their minds about what they thought. So, it isn't at all something extraordinary, and that's how it should work. We're in the process of trying to persuade each other and then the public," she said in an interview after the ruling.[27]

At the time, Ginsburg knew that Roberts was not deviating from his view of limited commerce-clause power, and she wanted to make her dissent as persuasive as possible. "I was forcing myself to stay awake and work on the opinion," she said. She also began crafting a fresh response to Roberts's arguments regarding the Medicaid expansion and Congress's spending power. (She and Sotomayor were not going to compromise on that, as Breyer and Kagan had.) Another complication for Ginsburg was that in late spring she had fallen on the marble floor of her bathroom and cracked several ribs. There was nothing to be done except to work through the pain.[28]

The final weeks of any Court session are tense, and this June was especially so. As Ginsburg was in physical agony, Roberts was feeling the mental strain of his fellow conservatives' wrath. The justices circulated multiple draft opinions among themselves, negotiating over the wording of legal rationales and the precedents to be cited and responding to each other's criticism.

ALL WAS REVEALED ON JUNE 28, THE LAST SITTING OF THE 2011–2012 session. At 10:00 a.m. sharp, Marshal Pam Talkin gave the familiar cry of "Oyez! Oyez! Oyez!" As the nine justices entered through the scarlet drapes and took their seats, Roberts smiled slightly in the direction of the section for the justices' special guests, where his wife, Jane, was seated. Also in that section were Maureen Scalia, Mary Kennedy, Virginia Thomas, Joanna Breyer, and Martha-Ann Alito. It was common for spouses to attend the last day of the session.

Directly in front of Roberts, at the table reserved for the government's top appellate lawyer, sat Solicitor General Verrilli. Verrilli had heard rumors about how the case might be resolved but was counting on nothing.

As he began reading his opinion from the bench, Roberts tried to speak steadily and without much emotion, but he was nervous. About thirteen minutes into the twenty-minute announcement, after he had summarized various legal rationales, he misstated the overall judgment. Few noticed the slip because he had already laid out the reasoning.

In his rendition, he had first told spectators that the health-insurance requirement could not be upheld under Congress's power to regulate interstate commerce. He said people cannot be forced into a market. He acknowledged that Congress had expansive authority covering commerce, but said "the distinction between doing something and not doing something would not be lost on the Framers."

Yet that was not the end of the matter, he noted. Roberts went on to explain that the government had asked the Court to interpret the mandate as imposing a tax if it would otherwise violate the Constitution. "Granting the Act the full measure of deference owed to federal statutes," Roberts said, the law could be read that way. "It is estimated that four million people each year will choose to pay the IRS rather than buy insurance," he added, endorsing the government's tax arguments.

Possibly reflecting his nervousness, Roberts then referred to the "taxing power" when he meant the "commerce power." He said (italics mine), "In sum, a majority of the Court holds that the federal government cannot use the *taxing* power to order people to buy health insurance, but a majority also holds that the statute here may be upheld as a *tax* increase on those without health insurance which is within Congress' power to tax."[29]

As Roberts spoke, he occasionally looked out at the spectators. Among them was retired justice John Paul Stevens, who later said he thought the chief had shown integrity. "He had to be thinking he did the right thing," Stevens said, "because he certainly made himself very unpopular" with the conservatives.[30]

Owing to usual Supreme Court decorum, spectators tried to stifle any response. But people were stunned. "Holy crap," said Garrett Epps, a writer for *The Atlantic*, clearly but not loudly. If he was heard beyond the press seats, the usually vigilant courtroom police officers did nothing.

"There are separate writings on this subject, but the majority of this Court agrees that the Commerce Clause cannot sustain the individual mandate," Roberts said. "Separate writings," although the correct terminology, was putting it gently. Justices Scalia, Kennedy, Thomas, and Alito agreed with Roberts's view on the commerce clause limits, but, revealing their anger, had declined to sign the parts of his opinion with which they agreed.

Justice Kennedy was agitated enough to read portions of his dissenting statement from the bench. "The Court regards its strained statutory interpretation as judicial modesty," Kennedy told the rapt spectators of Roberts's opinion. "It is not. It amounts instead to a vast judicial overreaching." Kennedy spoke faster than usual, and his face reddened. His anger was manifest. He said Roberts had essentially rewritten the statute to find it constitutional. Kennedy declared that the act was invalid in its entirety and that the majority "saves a statute that Congress did not write."

Justice Ginsburg had a separate complaint, which she, too, detailed from the bench that morning. She homed in on the majority's view of Congress's commerce power, which she claimed contradicted rulings going back to 1937. She also mocked the oft-made argument that if the Court upheld the individual mandate, people would be forced to eat healthy foods like broccoli. "Health care is not like vegetables," she said flatly.

Turning to the part of the ruling relating to Medicaid, she said that she and Justice Sotomayor "strongly disagree[d]" with the majority's view that Congress had created a wholly new program and coerced the states to accept it under threat of lost funds. As she put it, the 2010 provision simply added more poor people to the Medicaid population. She quarreled with Roberts's view that they were not among the neediest of Americans, observing that to be covered by the expansion people could not make more than $15,000 a year. Ginsburg emphasized that Congress had repeatedly amended the program since its 1965 inception to cover more people and provide greater services.

Outsiders presumed that the justices had become locked into their positions early on, which is typically what happens. But that was not what happened this time. Roberts's evolution aggravated the conservative justices and baffled the liberal justices. Some conservatives believed he was not voting his true sentiment, but trying to shore up his reputation and institutional legacy.

Criticism on the right was swift. The day after the ruling, the *Wall Street Journal* editorial board denounced Roberts's preservation of the individual mandate. "The remarkable decision upholding the Affordable Care Act is shot through with confusion—the mandate that's really a tax, except when it isn't, and the government whose powers are limited and enumerated, except when they aren't," the board declared. "One thing is clear: This was a one-man show, and that man is John Roberts."[31]

Donald Trump, three years from launching his presidential run, went right to Twitter: "Wow, the Supreme Court passed @ObamaCare," he tweeted. "I guess Justice Roberts wanted to be part of Georgetown society more than anyone knew." Trump later added, "John Roberts arrived in Malta yesterday. Maybe we will get lucky and he will stay there."[32]

Roberts had scheduled his Malta course on the Supreme Court months earlier. However, on the evening of June 28, he joked at a judicial conference that a retreat to "an impregnable island fortress" seemed necessary. His humor belied the toll the case had taken on him. Friends said they had never seen him so dispirited before. He tried to turn his attention to the course he was to teach in Malta. A group of four law schools, called the Consortium for Innovative Legal Education, had enlisted him for the event, paying for his travel and lodging in addition to a $20,000 honorarium. In 2011, the same consortium had sought him out for a course in Galway, Ireland, the home county of his wife's family. As they had for such excursions in the past, Roberts's family joined him in Malta. He was sharing the teaching responsibilities with his old law school classmate Richard Lazarus.[33]

As he arrived in Malta, the CBS Supreme Court correspondent Jan Crawford published a story asserting that Roberts had changed his vote on the individual mandate portion of the case and described the anger evident among his fellow conservatives on the Court. "At least one conservative justice tried to get him to explain it, but was unsatisfied with the response," Crawford wrote. She noted that "Roberts pays attention to media coverage. As chief justice, he is keenly aware of his leadership role on the court, and he also is sensitive to how the court is perceived by the public." She intimated that he had been dissuaded from striking down the mandate because of public pressure.[34]

Crawford did not know when the justices' votes had changed or what had happened with the Medicaid portion of the case, but she had learned enough to reveal that Roberts had in fact changed course after his initial assessment of the case. And she had learned it with the help of insiders. Roberts felt betrayed, just as some of his colleagues had felt betrayed by him. A few weeks after the ruling, Scalia said in an interview, "By my standards, things I cared about, it may be the worst term I've ever had."[35]

Criticism of Roberts was not fleeting. Despite seven years of prior opinions that pleased the right, skeptics inside and outside the Court could not shake off the sense that his decisions in the health-care case were a blemish on his integrity and a breach of the law. At the same time, liberal advocates who rejected many of Roberts's other opinions, particularly on race and campaign finance, were thrilled by his move to save the ACA. But few believed he was voting based on legal principles. They viewed it as a move on behalf of the Supreme Court as an institution in an election year and, more pragmatically, one motivated by a desire to keep the Court from being blamed for the problems of the billion-dollar health industry.

The chief justice would not talk for the record about the tensions that the Affordable Care Act case had caused with his colleagues. Friends said that, as much as the criticism had bothered him, he was moving on, even if others were not.

Two of the men Roberts had beaten out for appointment to the Supreme Court in 2005 had contrasting assessments. "I think it was basically a decision of restraint," US Appeals Court Judge J. Harvie Wilkinson III said in an interview years later. He commended Roberts for letting an act of Congress that was crucial to the national economy stand in the middle of a presidential election year. "It took some courage," Wilkinson said.

"No judge worth his or her salt is going to be with you 100 percent of the time. His position should have been respected. I thought the volume level, among some erstwhile friends, was unwarranted."[36]

Michael Luttig, working as Boeing's general counsel after having left the federal bench, thought the Court had erred in not striking down the law as impermissible under commerce *and* tax power. "For the record, he was, of course, wrong," Luttig said in an interview, referring to Roberts. "But he is and will always be my friend."[37]

Luttig could not help mentioning Roberts's decision among the old Reagan White House crowd on a number of occasions. One of these opportunities came as former White House deputy counsel Richard Hauser put together a seventy-fifth birthday video tribute for former White House counsel Fred Fielding. Hauser persuaded the men who had served in the counsel's office to produce short clips that he could then piece together.

Roberts's contribution was whimsical; he feigned ignorance about who exactly Fielding was. The video showed him in his chambers, the fireplace crackling. Wearing a white shirt and red tie, Roberts begins, "I'd like to send special birthday greetings to my good friend Frank Fielding." A voice corrects him: "Cut, Chief, it's actually Fred Fielding." Then Roberts says they worked together at the Department of Justice, and he again is corrected: it was the White House counsel's office. Roberts goes on: "Fred worked for me in the White House counsel's office." No, the voice says, it was the other way around. "Get out of here," Roberts responds. "Are you kidding me? Fred and I both worked for Dick Hauser. I'm sure that's true. . . . Happy Birthday, Fred, and that's a wrap."

Luttig made his video in the cockpit of a plane, pretending to be readying for take-off. In the video, he jokes that Hauser has just telephoned to let him know Fielding has reached a milestone birthday of eighty years, intentionally getting his age wrong. "You're losing altitude," Luttig tells Fielding. "Flying on a . . . descending glidepath." But then Luttig remarks that there is an upside to whatever ailments old age brings. "Thanks to John Roberts, you got Obamacare. So, everything is going to be good for you, and the rest of us are going to be paying for you and taking care of you from here on out."[38]

Perhaps Roberts's move was born of a concern for the business of health care. Perhaps he had worries about his own legitimacy and legacy, intertwined with concerns about the legitimacy and legacy of the Court. Perhaps his change of heart really arose from a sudden new understanding of the congressional taxing power. However the chief would explain it—and he would not explain it beyond what he had already written in his opinion—the case added a new dimension to a man who insisted that he always decided cases based on the law. And although it was sometimes lost in subsequent accounts, at the same time that Roberts saved the individual insurance mandate, he took the lead to undo Congress's counterpart plan to enhance Medicaid coverage for the poor.

Viewed only through a judicial lens, his moves were not consistent and his legal arguments were not entirely coherent. But he brought people and their different interests together. He acted, in short, more like a politician. His moves may have been good for the country at a time of division and real crisis in health care, even as they engendered anger, confusion, and distrust. "In the end, the Chief comes out the winner," wrote Charles Fried, the former Reagan solicitor general who had vowed to eat his hat if the act was struck down. "Not because he made the best arguments or even consistently adhered to his own principles, but because it is evident that in this most fraught, pressured, and political of cases, he tried to do the right thing and was willing to pay the price in the esteem of those with whom he was in closest political, doctrinal, and temperamental agreement."[39]

CHAPTER X

DIVIDED BY RACE

In 2012, the Supreme Court began considering a challenge to the landmark Voting Rights Act that brought John Roberts's work full circle. While in the Reagan administration three decades earlier, he had written a series of memos arguing against federal involvement in the election practices of the states. He had fervently argued that the 1965 Voting Rights Act should be narrowly interpreted, a view that followed from his opposition to measures that protected groups of people based on race or ethnicity. He believed then, and believes to this day, that the focus should be on individuals who have been personally wronged.

Roberts's actions in the 2013 *Shelby County v. Holder* case emerged from his long-held views on the failure of racial remedies in America. Each of his moves in the case, from the way he prefaced it with a 2009 opinion in a related dispute, to his trenchant questioning during oral arguments in *Shelby County*, to the rationale and rhetorical flourishes he used in the final opinion in the case, revealed his priorities on the law and his approach to his colleagues. In the end, his opinion in *Shelby County* marked the first time since the nineteenth century that the Supreme Court struck down a provision of civil rights law protecting people based on race.

During the same months when the justices were entangled in that Voting Rights Act dispute, they were negotiating a separate racial controversy over affirmative action policies at universities. In that case, from the University of Texas, the justices engaged behind the scenes in a fractious debate over whether such programs, dating to the 1960s and 1970s, were still necessary to ensure diversity in higher education. After Justice Sonia Sotomayor, the first Latina on the Court, drafted a caustic statement suggesting that her colleagues were disregarding contemporary racism—while the *Shelby County* case was also being negotiated—a majority of the justices decided to send the University of Texas case back to a lower court for further hearings.[1]

As those racial conflicts boiled inside the colossal marble Court building, the building's facade was covered with a full-size color picture of the front columns. A modillion from the front pediment had fallen onto the plaza in 2005, and the scrim concealed scaffolding and construction as workers repaired the building's marble. The Court had put up protective netting while a survey of the damage could be done, and the repair was intended to prevent further deterioration. The use of a scrim covering, a common practice in European countries, but not in the United States, was a curiosity. If an observer stood back far enough, the Court scrim almost looked like the real thing.

PRESIDENT LYNDON JOHNSON HAD SIGNED THE MILESTONE VOTing Rights Act in August 1965 as civil rights demonstrations and police violence roiled the South. One of the most troubling events that forced passage of the act occurred on March 7, 1965, at the Edmund Pettus Bridge in Selma, Alabama. In what became known as Bloody Sunday, Alabama state troopers wielding clubs and bullwhips had attacked some six hundred activists who were marching slowly and silently through the streets of Selma. Among the fifty-eight people hospitalized for their injuries was John Lewis, whose skull was fractured. Lewis later became a member of Congress from Georgia. The Voting Rights Act recognized the fact that nearly a century after the Fifteenth Amendment to the US Constitution had prohibited states from racial bias in voting, blacks were still being blocked from registering and casting ballots in many states. Ratified in 1870, the Fifteenth Amendment dictated that "the right of the citizens of the United States to vote shall not be denied or abridged by the United States or by any State on account of race, color, or previous condition of servitude." Congress was given the power under the amendment to enforce it with "appropriate legislation." But well into the twentieth century, southern states were using poll taxes, literacy tests, and other practices to systematically deny blacks the franchise. Congress had been moving slowly on legislation to prevent such practices, but after Bloody Sunday, when millions of television viewers witnessed the horror of Alabama state troopers clubbing, whipping, and firing tear gas at people who were marching peacefully across the bridge, it became clear that something more needed to be done. On March 15, President Johnson pressed Congress to pass voting rights legislation.[2]

The Voting Rights Act addressed discrimination in two main ways: by permitting lawsuits against direct government bias in election practices (in Section 2 of the law), and by requiring certain states (and localities within those states) to obtain federal approval before instituting new election procedures (in Section 5). Section 5, according to a so-called Section 4 formula, applied to states that had used a banned test or device in November 1964 and had less than 50 percent voter registration among all voters or less than 50 percent turnout in that year's presidential election.[3]

Localities with a history of bias had to obtain approval for any proposed change in their election procedures from the US attorney general or a panel of three federal trial judges in Washington. The Section 5 oversight was expected to be temporary. But voter discrimination was not easy to eliminate, and Congress continually reauthorized the act and its preclearance rules. In 1982, Congress amended a "bailout" option to the act so that cities and other political subdivisions of covered states could be exempt from the preclearance rules if they had not been found in violation of the act for a decade. Congress's 1982 action had reauthorized Section 5 for twenty-five years.[4]

The Supreme Court had repeatedly upheld the Voting Rights Act over the years, beginning with the 1966 case *South Carolina v. Katzenbach*, in which Chief Justice Earl Warren had written for an 8–1 Court that the act was a valid exercise of Congress's authority to enforce the Fifteenth Amendment. As members of Congress worked on a reauthorization in 2005 and 2006, however, they recognized that the legislation would be tested at the Roberts Court. Lawmakers prepared tens of thousands of pages of documentation related to contemporary discrimination at the polls. They wanted to demonstrate that Alabama and the eight other states still covered, mainly in the South, were continuing to erect barriers for black and Hispanic voters.[5]

The 2006 legislation, which passed by 98–0 in the Senate and 390–33 in the House, extended the preclearance rules for another twenty-five years. It was called the Fannie Lou Hamer, Rosa Parks, and Coretta Scott King Voting Rights Act Reauthorization and Amendments Act. Hamer, from Mississippi, had been a voting rights activist in the 1960s and 1970s; Parks had sparked the Montgomery, Alabama, bus boycott in 1955 when she had refused to give up her seat to a white passenger; and King had been the wife of the Reverend Martin Luther King Jr. and had become a civil rights leader in her own right.[6]

John Roberts was ten years old during the march on Selma and thirteen when riots erupted in nearby Chicago after King's April 4, 1968, assassination. In Long Beach, Indiana, in the shadow of Chicago and not far from Detroit, he and his parents had read daily headlines of racial unrest. His father, as an executive at Bethlehem Steel, knew about the federal government's efforts to end discrimination in the workplace through firsthand experience. Soon after passage of Title VII of the 1964 Civil Rights Act, the Department of Justice had targeted the steel industry. Major companies as well as the United Steelworkers of America had been accused of conspiring to keep blacks in low-level jobs in the mills. Industry and Justice Department officials had worked out court-supervised agreements under which racial minorities were allowed to move into better positions and promotional tracks.

When Roberts was at Harvard in the 1970s, affirmative action was hotly debated. The campus newspaper and classroom discussions often focused on the numbers of minorities and women accepted as students, faculty, and staff. Were they too low? Too high? Were qualifications sacrificed? What was fair? What was constitutional? The case of Allan Bakke, the thirty-five-year-old white man twice rejected for admission to the University of California Medical School at Davis, arguably because of racial quotas, attracted wide attention as it worked its way through federal courts, ultimately reaching the Supreme Court as *Regents of the University of California v. Bakke.*[7]

It would have been difficult for Roberts to escape the churning arguments over the topic and the Supreme Court's 1978 resolution in *Bakke*, which allowed schools to consider race as a factor in admissions, but disallowed quotas. Roberts was in law school at Harvard by the time the case was decided, and the university was put in the spotlight in the Court's ruling because it had created a model for using race as one of many non-quantitative factors in admissions to ensure a diverse student body.

Roberts, both at that time and later, felt that too much attention was being put on the numbers of racial minorities in classes and in hiring. As a law student, he was impressed by Justice John Marshall Harlan's famous dissent in the 1896 case *Plessy v. Ferguson*, and he agreed with Harlan's ideal of a "color-blind" society. Roberts believed that categorizing people by race, even as a remedy for past bias, was counterproductive, in that it only deepened racial tensions. It is hard to know when or how it happened, but his views became entrenched, changing little, if at all, from his time in the Reagan administration to the moment of his elevation as chief justice. "It is a sordid business, this divvying us up by race," Roberts wrote in a 2006 voting rights case, *League of United Latin American Citizens v. Perry*, less than a year after he became chief justice.[8] The next year, when the Court ruled against public school integration practices, Roberts admonished that "the way to stop discrimination on the basis of race is to stop discriminating on the basis of race."[9]

Now, in late 2012, the dispute before the justices revolved around the crucial plank of the Voting Rights Act, the one requiring states with a history of race discrimination to submit any changes in their election rules to federal officials for preclearance. From 1982 to 2006, when Congress reauthorized Section 5, the Department of Justice had blocked more than seven hundred new registration and voting-related rules from taking effect based on the determination that they were discriminatory. The preclearance rule did not apply to all the states—only those with a history of discrimination—and their numbers had shifted through the years. Nine states were still subject to the rule when the *Shelby County* case came before the justices.[10]

SHELBY COUNTY, LOCATED IN THE MIDDLE OF ALABAMA NORTH OF Selma, had witnessed racial violence and conflict since the Civil War. The county had a long record of keeping blacks from the polls and, like every other county in Alabama, was covered by the Voting Rights Act's preclearance provision. Alabama had the distinction of having been successfully sued for discrimination under the act more than any other state but Mississippi. Shelby County had been singled out by federal officials for its at-large, rather than single-member, voting districts, a system that ensured disproportionate power for the white majority on Election Day.[11]

In 2008, when the City of Calera in Shelby County wanted to institute a new voting-district map, it therefore had to obtain Department of Justice approval. City officials had redrawn districts to accommodate a growing population and recent land annexations. But the new map also eliminated the only black-majority district in the city. In their request for preclearance under Section 5, local officials told the Justice Department that the new boundaries would not impact black voters. The Justice Department disagreed and sent Calera a three-page letter voiding the new map. The city's legal team believed it could eventually persuade federal authorities to accept the map and went ahead with previously scheduled city council elections. In those elections, Ernest Montgomery, the only African American on the five-member city council, lost his bid for reelection. His district had been diluted by new white voters, and the Justice Department swiftly blocked certification of the results.[12]

The department's letter to Calera rejecting the redistricting plan had been posted on the department's website, where it caught the attention of Edward Blum, a national opponent of racial remedies who had engineered a number of cases that had progressed to the Supreme Court. Blum had been trolling for test cases to challenge the Voting Rights Act.

A former stockbroker in Houston, Texas, Blum had made an unsuccessful bid for Congress in 1992 in a racially gerrymandered district. Running as a white Republican against a popular African American Democratic incumbent, Blum had been soundly defeated. Yet during his failed effort, he came to the conclusion that the Houston-area district had been drawn by the Texas legislature to consolidate minorities and maximize their voting power. He believed that was unfair, and he set out to do something about it. The creation of "majority minority" districts was not an uncommon practice in the years immediately following the 1990 census, when many legislatures reapportioned districts and tried to meet federal mandates to enhance the rights of racial minorities that had been historically disenfranchised. But, beginning in 1993, the Supreme Court started to reject these racial gerrymanders in cases brought by white voters. Seeing an opportunity in a newly sympathetic Supreme Court, Blum sued Texas officials. He and the five local GOP precinct leaders who joined him eventually prevailed at the high court. In their 1996 case, *Bush v. Vera*, the justices struck down two majority-black districts and one majority-Hispanic district in Texas, declaring that state officials had unconstitutionally used race as the predominant criterion for boundaries.[13]

Blum was invigorated. No longer a political candidate, he was now a legal activist. He founded the Campaign for a Color Blind America, a private nonprofit group seeking to end racial affirmative action. For the next several years, as he moved from Texas to Washington, DC, and eventually to Maine, he raised money from conservative donors for his efforts through a foundation he called the Project on Fair Representation.

He looked for viable plaintiffs and hired lawyers to challenge affirmative action and other race-based policies.

When Blum spotted the Calera letter on the Justice Department's website in 2008, he was already invested in a separate Voting Rights Act challenge bound for the Supreme Court, *Northwest Austin Municipal Utility District No. 1 v. Holder*. In that case, from Texas, he had worked with an Austin lawyer, Gregory Coleman, a former clerk to Justice Clarence Thomas and a former Texas solicitor general, and a small utility district that had wanted to move its polling location without first getting Justice Department permission. Officials for the utility district believed they should be exempted from the Voting Rights Act's preclearance rule, and they were willing to offer their district as a means of striking at the constitutionality of a core section of the act.[14]

This case would constitute the first round in Blum's attack on the preclearance rule. It would mark the first round for Chief Justice Roberts, too.

ROBERTS HAD BEEN CHIEF JUSTICE FOR FOUR YEARS WHEN THE 2009 Northwest Austin controversy came to the Court. The nation's first African American president, Barack Obama, had recently been elected. Gaps in white and black voter registration throughout the South had faded. But the Justice Department, defending Congress's reauthorization of the Voting Rights Act's preclearance rule, pointed to multiple instances of continued intimidation of African Americans at the polls and to the dilution of minority voting strength in district maps in certain states. It also pointed to the sixteen-thousand-page record that Congress had assembled to justify keeping the Sections 4 and 5 preclearance rules intact. In the report, Congress had documented continued race discrimination in the covered jurisdictions as well as the success of Section 5 in blocking discriminatory election practices. Members of Congress collected first-person accounts of alleged discrimination since the 1982 reauthorization. The Senate report noted, for example, that in 1991, Mississippi legislators had rejected proposed redistricting plans that would have given African American voters greater opportunity to elect representatives of their choice, referring to one such alternative on the House floor as the "black plan," and privately calling it "the n-plan."[15]

Blum and his lawyers had filed the Northwest Austin test case just days after President George W. Bush had signed the 2006 reauthorization bill. At the signing ceremony on the South Lawn of the White House on July 27, 2006, Bush referred to "the courage shown on a Selma bridge one Sunday afternoon in March 1965" and to the many pernicious methods that had been used to disenfranchise blacks. "In four decades since the Voting Rights Act was first passed," Bush observed, "we've made progress toward equality, yet the work for a more perfect union is never ending."[16]

Blum and other critics were challenging this basic claim, contending that Congress lacked sufficient evidence of modern-day discrimination to continue to justify the preclearance rule. If members of Congress had dreaded a test of the reauthorization bill before the Roberts Court, Blum, in contrast, could not have been more eager to see one.

When the Northwest Austin utility district case reached the Court in April 2009, Chief Justice Roberts and his fellow conservatives were skeptical that the US government could continue to single out jurisdictions based on past patterns of discrimination. But several factors made Roberts cautious. He was not certain, for example, that the time was right to invalidate a major section of the Voting Rights Act. The 2008–2009 term had already been a bruising one. The justices had held the first round of arguments in the *Citizens United* campaign finance case, and they were bitterly split over how broadly to scale back government regulations intended to curtail money in elections. Justice Souter was especially angered by the conservative effort to ratchet up protections on corporate political speech. He was also getting ready to retire, and Roberts did not want to exacerbate any ill will. At the same time, Justice Ginsburg was recovering from pancreatic cancer, and *Ricci v. DeStefano*, the case brought by white firefighters in New Haven, Connecticut, concerning a promotion test that had been set aside because of poor scores by black test-takers, had split the justices again 5–4 along ideological lines.

For Roberts, there was yet another important dimension to the timing of the *Northwest Austin* voting rights case—the Court's calendar. Oral arguments were in late April, with only two months of the session left. The magnitude of the issue was too great for the justices to tackle it quickly. More personally for Roberts, the early months of 2009 had been proving to be unusually busy. In February, he had spent a couple of days in Tucson, Arizona, speaking to students at the University of Arizona College of Law, where a new Rehnquist Center had been founded. In March he flew to Boise to deliver a lecture at the University of Idaho. In April he did back-to-back events at North Carolina Central University in Durham and the University of Louisville in Kentucky. All of these engagements had been scheduled months in advance, and he had a four-day trip to the University of Cambridge in the United Kingdom coming up in May, where he was to deliver a lecture on Abraham Lincoln and the Supreme Court. Roberts made it through the sessions with his usual pleasant attitude and focus. Yet the trips back and forth across the United States, and then across the Atlantic, as he left his two children, both just eight years old, behind, as well as the justices with their own battles, were wearying.[17]

In the justices' private session for *Northwest Austin*, Roberts's liberal colleagues argued against making any drastic change to the Voting Rights law. Roberts agreed that the better course was to rule narrowly for the utility district, declaring that it qualified for exemption from the act, or what was known as bailout, because of its discrimination-free record. Still, in his eventual opinion for the majority, Roberts laid groundwork for the future. He warned Congress that it should revise the Section 5 scheme to reflect changes in the South. Roberts knew it was unlikely that Congress would amend the law, but he also knew he had the votes to strike down the preclearance rule in the next case to come before the Court.

Because Roberts was not going to invalidate Section 5, which many liberals inside and outside the Court believed the conservative majority was poised to do, he was able to win the Court's liberals to his side. Certainly, Ginsburg, Breyer, Stevens, and Souter did not embrace every part of his opinion, but they signed it after agreeing with the bottom-line judgment favoring the Northwest Austin utility district on bailout. They regarded his broader criticism of the Voting Rights Act as nonbinding observations—"dicta" rather than any hard rule.

As would become clear four years later, in the 2012–2013 session, Roberts saw it differently.

The only justice who did not sign Roberts's 2009 opinion was Clarence Thomas, who believed the Court should fully invalidate Section 5. Thomas, only the second African American to sit on the Court, argued that the federal intrusion on state elections could no longer be justified. He believed that a systematic campaign to deny blacks access to the ballot no longer existed. "The days of grandfather clauses, property qualifications, 'good character' tests . . . are gone," he wrote in a concurring opinion. "There is thus currently no concerted effort in these jurisdictions to engage in the unremitting and ingenious defiance of the Constitution that serves as the constitutional basis for upholding the uncommon exercise of congressional power embodied in Section 5."[18]

Chief Justice Roberts agreed with Thomas in principle, but he wanted to take a more modest approach in a controversy that had been brought, as he wrote in his opinion, by "a small utility district raising a big question—the constitutionality of Section 5 of the Voting Rights Act." In the most straightforward section of the decision, Roberts said the utility district qualified for an exemption. He explained that the Court was deliberately avoiding the larger constitutional question, but then he launched into the reasons why he thought Section 5 was problematic.[19]

"Things have changed in the South," Roberts wrote. "Voter turnout and registration rates now approach parity. Blatantly discriminatory evasions of federal decrees are rare. And minority candidates hold office at unprecedented levels." He laid out evidence to support his views. "Today, the registration gap between white and black voters is in single digits in the covered states; in some of those states, blacks now register and vote at higher rates than whites. Similar dramatic improvements have occurred for other racial minorities."

Roberts acknowledged that these improvements were by themselves insufficient and that there could still be grounds for continuing the preclearance rule. But, as he said in one of the most significant lines of the opinion, "the Act imposes current burdens and must be justified by current needs."

ON JUNE 24, 2009, WHEN ROBERTS DELIVERED THE COURT'S DECI-sion, Edward Blum was sitting in the courtroom. He listened to Roberts attack Section 5 but back away from killing it. "I was waiting for a few key words, and I didn't get them," he said. As disappointed as Blum was in the outcome in *Northwest Austin*, he understood that Roberts had invited further challenges to the Voting Rights Act.[20]

And Blum had the redistricting controversy in the Shelby County locale of Calera waiting in the wings. He hired a new legal team to pick up where *Northwest Austin* had left off. Blum believed that the preclear-ance requirement was an unconstitutional vestige meant to police the Old South, and his objective was a ruling that would invalidate it. There would be no bailout possibility this time. Shelby County had such an in-disputable history of racial bias in elections that it would never qualify for the Voting Rights Act exemption the way the Texas utility district had.

The Shelby County challenge went first to a three-judge court in Washington. In a decision for the court rejecting the challenge, the pre-siding judge, David Tatel, highlighted the "second generation barriers" cited by Congress that still blocked minority voters from fully exercising their voting rights. "Although such methods may be more subtle than the visible methods used in 1965," he wrote, "Congress concluded that their effect and results are the same, namely a diminishing of the mi-nority community's ability to fully participate in the electoral process and to elect their preferred candidates of choice." The court endorsed Congress's conclusion that intentional discrimination remained so seri-ous and widespread in covered jurisdictions that the preclearance mech-anism was justified.[21]

In late 2012, the Supreme Court agreed to hear Shelby County's ap-peal, scheduling arguments for February 2013. Roberts was in his eighth term as chief justice and had just turned fifty-eight. Since the 2009 ruling in *Northwest Austin*, Justices Sotomayor and Kagan had replaced Justices Souter and Stevens. Although this meant that two generally liberal justices had been replaced by two other generally liberal justices, the two women, who were decades younger than their predecessors and more actively engaged during oral arguments, changed the Court's public face and the tone of its public sessions.

Sotomayor, President Obama's first appointee, wore her ethnicity proudly. In 2013, as the Supreme Court prepared to hear *Shelby County v. Holder*, she had just published a memoir, *My Beloved World*, and was on the road promoting the book describing her Bronx background and what she had overcome to reach the pinnacle of the legal profession. It was an inspirational story.

On the bench, Sotomayor shook up oral arguments. She interrupted often, sometimes talking over another justice or cutting off a lawyer as he or she was still answering a question that another justice had posed. She also tended to take up the rebuttal time of a lawyer, a practice that Roberts, a former advocate, loathed. Sotomayor appeared not to care that the chief grew irritated when she dominated the sessions. She had questions to ask, and she was going to ask them.

Justice Kagan, the former solicitor general, could also be a relentless questioner, but she tended to wait until the more senior justices had had sufficient time before she began firing her queries. She also listened to her colleagues and strategically responded to them as well as to the lawyer at the lectern.

During oral arguments in *Shelby County*, the county was represented by Bert Rein, an old Washington hand who had worked with Blum on and off since the 1990s. Rein cited Chief Justice Roberts's earlier ruling. "Almost four years ago, eight justices of the Court agreed the . . . preclearance obligation . . . raised a serious constitutional question," Rein said. "Those Justices recognized that the record before the Congress in 2005 made it unmistakable that the South had changed."[22]

The two newest justices were incredulous that a county in Alabama, with its record of discrimination, would be at the forefront of an attempt to roll back protections for minority voters. "Assuming I accept your premise," Justice Sotomayor began, "and there's some questions about that, that some portions of the South have changed, your county pretty much hasn't." She referred to a number of discriminatory electoral measures that had been blocked by the Department of Justice. "Why would we vote in favor of a county whose record is the epitome of what caused passage of this law to start with?"

Along the same lines, Justice Kagan told Rein, "Think about the state that you're representing. If Congress were to write a formula that looked to the number of successful Section 2 [claims of direct discrimination] suits per million residents, Alabama would the number one state on the list. . . . You're objecting to a formula, but under any formula that Congress could devise, it would capture Alabama."

Rein tried to defend Alabama, and Shelby County in particular, and yet his appeal was broader. He was seeking a nationwide ruling so that no jurisdiction would automatically be covered by Section 5 of the Voting Rights Act. "The Court said in Northwest Austin, 'Current needs have to generate the current burden.' So what happened in 1965 in Alabama, that Alabama itself has said was a disgrace, doesn't justify a current burden," Rein insisted.

Roberts asked no questions of Rein, who was making good use of what Roberts had written in the 2009 case. But when Solicitor General Donald Verrilli stepped to the lectern to defend the Voting Rights Act, Roberts leaned forward in anticipation, his reading glasses down on his nose.

"Everyone acknowledges . . . [including] this Court in *Northwest Austin*," Verrilli said, "that the Voting Rights Act made a huge difference in transforming the culture of blatantly racist vote suppression that characterized parts of this country for a century. Section 5 preclearance was the principal engine of that progress." Verrilli argued that Congress had compiled a sufficient record to demonstrate that the decades-old formula targeted the places with the most serious problems of voting discrimination.

"Do you know which state has the worst ratio of white voter turnout to African American voter turnout?" Roberts interjected.

"I do not," Verrilli responded.

"Massachusetts," Roberts said, then asked, "Do you know where African American turnout actually exceeds white turnout?"

Verrilli said he did not.

"Mississippi," the chief answered. His point was clear. The South had greatly improved its record of shutting out black voters over the years, and the North had its own racial problems.

Roberts continued in that vein. "Which state has the greatest disparity in registration between white and African?"

Again, Verrilli said he did not know. "Massachusetts," Roberts answered with evident satisfaction.

Roberts's line of attack seemed effective in the moment, although he often warned other justices not to bring up information outside the record of the case. Massachusetts state officials and other critics of Roberts's approach later voiced concerns that the data he used was suspect. Citing wide margins of error and inconsistencies in the likely source, the Politifact troubleshooting website wrote, "Even if this data source had been reliable for his purposes, Roberts' decision to hold up Massachusetts as his primary example amounts to cherry picking, since its data diverges significantly from that of its regional neighbors." In fact, black voter turnout in the state was at about 50 percent, generally mirroring the turnout rate of the overall population.[23]

During oral argument, Verrilli's primary message was that Congress had the authority to address voting bias in the manner it chose. "Congress wasn't writing on a blank slate in 2006," Verrilli said. "It faced a choice. And the choice was whether the conditions were such that it could confidently conclude that this deterrence and this constraint was no longer needed."

As the solicitor general closed his argument, Roberts asked him, "Is it the government's submission that the citizens in the South are more racist than citizens in the North?" Verrilli said it was not.

Debo Adegbile, an attorney from the NAACP Legal Defense Fund, was representing Ernest Montgomery, the black councilmember who had lost his seat with the Calera redistricting. When he rose for his allotted time at the lectern, he reminded the justices of modern-day instances of discrimination in Alabama, specifically a 2011 case. "There were [Alabama] legislators that sit today that were caught on tape referring to African American voters as illiterates . . . referring to them as aborigines," Adegbile recounted. "Yes, the South has changed and made progress, but some things remain stubbornly the same, and the trained effort to deny African American voters the franchise is part of Alabama's history to this very day."

"Have there been egregious episodes of the kind you are talking about in states that are not covered?" Roberts asked.

"Absolutely," Adegbile responded. Yet he resisted Roberts's point that the law made unfair distinctions. He urged the Court to step back and consider "our march through history to keep promises that our Constitution says for too long were unmet." During the entire 2012–2013 session, he was the only African American lawyer to appear before the justices, a reflection of the white male domination of the elite Supreme Court bar.[24]

In the justices' private session after arguments on *Shelby County*, the negotiations were quite different from those in the Seattle and Louisville school integration disputes of 2007, when it had taken the justices weeks to decide even to hear the cases, and when Roberts had clashed with Kennedy. Now, in the *Shelby County* case, Roberts had a ready majority for his views. Kennedy, displaying his federalist principles, fully agreed with the chief justice that Congress should not draw lines between the states. "If Alabama . . . wants to acknowledge the wrongs of its past," Kennedy had suggested during oral arguments, it is better off doing it on its own terms as "an independent sovereign" than "under the trusteeship of the United States government."

Justices Ginsburg, Breyer, Sotomayor, and Kagan were in dissent. Ginsburg decided to write the opinion. As she and Roberts retreated to their respective chambers to work on *Shelby County v. Holder*, there were still two more rounds of oral arguments in other cases left that term, in March and April. Furthermore, a separate dispute over campus affirmative action had been pending since an October hearing with no resolution.

THAT CASE, *FISHER V. UNIVERSITY OF TEXAS AT AUSTIN*, HAD ALSO been ushered to the Court by Edward Blum. He had enlisted Abigail Fisher, whose father he had known from the Houston area, to be the lead plaintiff in a claim against the flagship campus of the state's largest university. Fisher had not been admitted to the university and enrolled in Louisiana State University instead. But Blum believed that Fisher, who was white, had been wrongly edged out by a diversity policy that favored black and Hispanic applicants. Texas admissions officers had asserted that their practice was to take a broad range of criteria into consideration when choosing among a field of many qualified applicants. These criteria included race and family socioeconomic background.

Fisher v. University of Texas at Austin was the first college affirmative action dispute to have made it to the Court since the University of Michigan case in 2003, *Grutter v. Bollinger.* In that case, a five-justice majority, in an opinion by Sandra Day O'Connor, had upheld a law school admissions policy that boosted the chances of applicants who were members of racial minority groups. O'Connor had since been succeeded by Samuel Alito, who, like Roberts, had established a record against race as a factor in admissions. During oral arguments, in which Rein, again enlisted by Blum, represented Fisher, it appeared the justices were ready to rule against the University of Texas. And at the ensuing justices' conference, that seemed the likely outcome, at least at the start.

Justice Sotomayor, however, provoked a different outcome, based on arguments from her own experience. She had attended Princeton University and Yale Law School, owing in part to affirmative action programs. She had excelled, graduating Phi Beta Kappa from Princeton and going directly to Yale, where she became an editor on the law journal. "I am the perfect affirmative action baby," she had once declared.[25]

Justice Thomas, the only other person of color on the bench, had had a different experience with affirmative action. He lamented that he could never "escape the stigmatizing effects of racial preference," and said he feared "that it would be used forever after to discount [his] achievements." In a 2007 memoir, Thomas said he believed he had made a mistake going to Yale Law School because of the presumption he faced that he had gotten in because he was black. "I felt as though I'd been tricked, that some of the people who claimed to be helping me were in fact hurting me," he wrote, referring to "big-city whites who offered you a helping hand so long as you were careful to agree with them, but slapped you down if you started acting as if you didn't know your place."[26]

The personal histories of these two justices were well known to advocates on both sides of *Fisher*. But a crucial element of the negotiations between the justices on the case was not known outside of their personal communications until later: Sotomayor had in fact forced a compromise among the nine during the tense 2012–2013 session, ensuring that the University of Texas program survived, at least for the time being.[27]

After the justices had heard oral arguments in the case, five of them sided with Abigail Fisher, and three were opposed. (Justice Kagan, who had earlier been involved in the case as the US solicitor general, had recused herself.) The five conservatives, led by Roberts, were ready to rule against the Texas policy and limit the ability of the University of Texas and other universities to rely on race in admissions, a practice that had been endorsed in the 2003 case *Grutter v. Bollinger* and that dated back to the 1978 case *Regents of the University of California v. Bakke*.[28]

Justice Ginsburg assigned the dissenting opinion to Sotomayor, and Sotomayor began drafting a statement in which she reflected on the disadvantages and slights that people of color continued to face. She defended the University of Texas program and attempted to explain to her brethren in the majority that they did not understand what it was like to be a person of color in America.

As with the health-care case testing the Affordable Care Act a year earlier, an intense behind-the-scenes drama changed the presumed fate of the case. The justices were accustomed to stark differences among them, but Sotomayor's writing was so personal that it put some of them on the defensive. Her draft was kept secret, as is the tradition, but her colleagues later said in interviews that she had addressed the suspicions that people of color constantly sense, a theme that resurfaced in her dissent a year later in a separate case, *Schuette v. Coalition to Defend Affirmative Action*. "Race matters," Sotomayor emphasized in *Schuette*. "And race matters for reasons that really are only skin deep, that cannot be discussed any other way, and that cannot be wished away. . . . Race matters because of the slights, the snickers, the silent judgments that reinforce that most crippling of thoughts: 'I do not belong here.'"[29]

That moved Kennedy. He had dissented in *Grutter v. Bollinger* and was ready for his view to become that of the majority. In *Grutter*, he had demanded empirical evidence from universities to support their claim that affirmative action was the only way to produce campus diversity. After he read Sotomayor's draft opinion, he began to have second thoughts, and he wanted to lower the temperature. Justice Breyer, who had worked closely with O'Connor in the University of Michigan case, urged Kennedy to compromise.

The exceedingly personal flavor of Sotomayor's draft opinion offended Roberts. He never wanted to call attention to his own background and prior experiences, or to suggest that he was making a policy judgment rather than decision on the law. It puzzled him when other justices seemed to drop a veneer of neutrality. More significantly, he was concerned about how the Court might be perceived with the airing of such personal differences—especially on race, the subject of the *Shelby County* case that was shaping up to be the term's blockbuster. So, for many reasons, Roberts was willing to compromise in the University of Texas dispute. Even Justice Scalia, who was similarly against racial remedies, saw a way to take a smaller step. After all, Abigail Fisher's legal team had not asked for *Grutter*, which had upheld affirmative action, to be overturned. The case had been initially presented as a narrow one involving the Texas admissions process. The justices, of course, could have taken it further if they had chosen to do so. But with all the tensions in the air, a majority backed down.

Kennedy revised his opinion. He would hold that Fisher's challenge to the University of Texas's race-based policy should return to lower court judges for another review. Kennedy wrote that the lower court judges who had heard the dispute had been too deferential; they should not have taken the university's word for it that race-neutral approaches had failed to provide sufficient diversity among accepted students. He concluded that the lower court should conduct its own inquiry. He left the central holding of *Grutter v. Bollinger* intact.

In response, Sotomayor dropped her dissenting statement, and she and Breyer signed the new Kennedy opinion. All the conservatives except for Thomas did, too. Again, Thomas wanted the Court to go further, to end a racial remedy.[30] Justice Ginsburg chose not to join the compromise. She did not believe the *Fisher* case should be returned to the appeals court for reconsideration; she wrote that universities "need not be blind to the lingering effects of an overtly discriminatory past, the legacy of centuries of law-sanctioned inequality."

With the *Shelby County v. Holder* case also in front of the Court that session, Ginsburg might have had other reasons to hesitate on the *Fisher* compromise. Perhaps she did not want to sign onto an opinion that could ultimately be used to diminish civil rights, particularly after seeing how the 2009 *Northwest Austin* decision on the Voting Rights Act was being used in the *Shelby County* case.

IN MAY 2013, JUST AS THE NINE JUSTICES WERE EXPERIENCING DI-visions over *Shelby County*, Roberts and Kagan attended the annual meeting of the Seventh Judicial Circuit. The event was held in Indianapolis, in Roberts's home state of Indiana. Kagan had become the "circuit justice," meaning that she handled emergency cases from the upper midwestern three-state Seventh Circuit.

Chief Justice Roberts was the keynote speaker, and Kagan was scheduled to introduce him. In a grand hotel ballroom, as the audience ate grilled filet mignon and seared salmon, Kagan began her public remarks by emphasizing what a tricky task she had. How could she precede Roberts, a speaker par excellence? She said that when she had begun her job as the US solicitor general in 2009, advisers had urged her to listen to the old audiotapes of Roberts arguing in front of the Court. Then, when she was nominated to the Supreme Court in 2010, advisers gave her the tapes from his 2005 confirmation and said to just try to do what he did.[31]

Justice Kagan then revealed for the audience another side of Roberts, recounting his call from Australia the minute the Senate had hit fifty votes for her confirmation. She described how he had then made sure that her nameplate was on her locker in the robing room during the course of a personal tour he had given her at the Court. When Roberts stood up, his remarks were brief. He recalled the summer he had spent at an Indianapolis law firm. He quipped about end-of-session deadlines and general suspicions of the Supreme Court press corps. He also offered a joke about that cloth scrim concealing all the repair work being done on the marble facade, calling it "a great cover up."[32]

The banter was perfect for the audience. Anyone watching would never have suspected that Roberts was at that time finishing up what would be the most disturbing decision of the session for his liberal colleagues. Some of the justices—but not all—could confine their irritation to the privacy of the conference room.

THE COURT'S *SHELBY COUNTY V. HOLDER* DECISION EVISCERATING a key section of the Voting Rights Act was announced on June 25, 2013. "Our country has changed," Roberts wrote for the majority, "and while any racial discrimination in voting is too much, Congress must ensure that the legislation it passes to remedy that problem speaks to current conditions." Using his *Northwest Austin* decision as a basis for explaining why the law was no longer justified, Roberts wrote, "Coverage today is based on decades-old data and eradicated practices. The formula captures states by reference to literacy tests and low voter registration and turnout in the 1960s and early 1970s. But such tests have been banned nationwide for over 40 years. And voter registration and turnout numbers in the covered states have risen dramatically in the years since."[33]

Roberts suggested that problems the Voting Rights Act was designed to correct no longer existed. "In 1965, the States could be divided into two groups: those with a recent history of voting tests and low voter registration and turnout, and those without those characteristics," he wrote.

"Today the Nation is no longer divided along those lines, yet the Voting Rights Act continues to treat it as if it were."

The majority based its opinion on novel constitutional grounds. Roberts invoked a principle of "equal sovereignty," which he had earlier used in his *Northwest Austin* opinion. The covered states, he wrote in *Shelby County*, "must beseech the federal government for permission to implement laws that they would otherwise have the right to enact and execute on their own." With this point he was returning to a theme he had voiced in oral arguments: that uncovered states could have worse records on race than covered states.

The principle that Congress must treat all the states in the same way was at odds with the usual understanding of the Fourteenth Amendment. As scholars pointed out, the same Congress that ratified the Fourteenth Amendment also passed the Reconstruction Act that created military rule over the southern states. In fact, according to Section 3 of the Reconstruction Act, southern states could not be readmitted to the union unless they ratified the Fourteenth Amendment. On race, there were numerous examples of Congress treating states differently.

Roberts drew explicitly on the *Northwest Austin* opinion, emphasizing that in 2009 the Court had been nearly unanimous about its suspicions of Section 5. "We questioned whether the problems that Section 5 meant to address were still concentrated in the jurisdictions singled out for preclearance," he wrote. "Eight Members of the Court subscribed to these views, and the remaining Member would have held the Act unconstitutional."

Ginsburg would say in her dissenting opinion that, yes, they had "questioned" it, but they had not answered the question. She said Roberts was making far more of the language of the 2009 decision than warranted. He was, in her mind, elevating nonbinding observations, or "dicta," to a core principle.

That the case came from Alabama and Shelby County, places with long records of voter discrimination that extended into the current era, did not matter to Roberts and the rest of the majority. Roberts criticized Justice Ginsburg and the other dissenters for referring to the Shelby County record. "The dissent . . . turns to the record to argue that, in light of voting discrimination in Shelby County, the county cannot complain about the provisions that subject it to preclearance," Roberts observed. "But that is like saying that a driver pulled over pursuant to a policy of stopping all redheads cannot complain about that policy, if it turns out his license has expired. Shelby County's claim is that the coverage formula here is unconstitutional in all its applications."

That sounded like a clever argument. But it was specious. In this case, a county with a record of long-standing discrimination against black voters—not some random locality—was opposing a rule that attempted to check precisely those states and counties that had historically engaged in discrimination.

At the end of his opinion, Roberts asserted, "We issue no ruling on Section 5," that is, the preclearance rule. He said the majority was striking down only the formula governing which states are covered. As the dissenting justices noted on the first page of their opinion, the Roberts majority "purports to declare unconstitutional only the coverage formula set out in Section 4(b). But without that formula, Section 5 is immobilized."[34]

Ginsburg's dissent attacked the Roberts majority on two fronts: first, its constitutional argument, and second, the practical consequences for minority voters nationwide. "In today's decision," she wrote, "the Court ratchets up what was pure dictum in *Northwest Austin*, attributing breadth to the equal sovereignty principle in flat contradiction of *Katzenbach*." Here she was referring to the 1966 decision in *South Carolina v. Katzenbach*, which upheld the Voting Rights Act. In *Katzenbach*, the Court had rejected the argument that a principle of "equal sovereignty" could prevent differential treatment of states when it came to race. (The notion of "equal sovereignty" derived from a context involving the admission of new states to the union.) Ginsburg deemed the majority's decision an "unprecedented extension" of the equal sovereignty principle, one that was "capable of much mischief."

Ginsburg acknowledged that conditions in the South had improved, but she insisted that subtle "second-generation barriers" had emerged to reduce the impact of minority votes. These barriers included gerrymandering. Ginsburg ridiculed Roberts for claiming that the evidence of discrimination was stale: "The Court criticizes Congress for failing to recognize that 'history did not end in 1965.' But the Court ignores that 'what's past is prologue.' And 'those who cannot remember the past are condemned to repeat it.'" Roberts, for his part, believed that the dissenters' views would in fact lead to a cycle of repeated racial classifications and more discrimination.

"Throwing out preclearance when it has worked and is continuing to work to stop discriminatory changes," Ginsburg insisted, "is like throwing away your umbrella in a rainstorm because you are not getting wet." She cited several examples of contemporary voter discrimination, including the 2001 cancellation of an election by the mayor and an all-white board of aldermen in Kilmichael, Mississippi, after numerous African American candidates announced they were running for office. Another example concerned a 2004 threat by authorities in Waller County, Texas, to prosecute two black students after they announced their candidacies for office. "The county then attempted to reduce the availability of early voting in that election at polling places near a historically black university," Ginsburg wrote.

Ginsburg highlighted "Alabama's sorry history" of voting rights violations, a record that extended to recent decades even as the state was being subjected to continual federal oversight. "Alabama is home to Selma, site of the 'Bloody Sunday' beatings of civil-rights demonstrators that served as the catalyst for the [Voting Rights Act's] enactment," she wrote. She then quoted Martin Luther King Jr., who, after Selma, had led marchers to Montgomery, Alabama, where he had said, "The arc of the moral universe is long, but it bends toward justice."

As Ginsburg concluded, she noted that "history has proven King right." She added, "The sad irony of today's decision lies in its utter failure to grasp why the Voting Rights Act has proven effective." Ginsburg observed, too, that Roberts had deferred to Congress in the dispute over the Affordable Care Act a year earlier, but not to that same Congress when it had compiled the record on voting rights violations. "One would expect more from an opinion striking at the heart of the Nation's signal piece of civil-rights legislation," she wrote. "Hubris is a fit word for today's demolition of the [Voting Rights Act]."

Edward Blum felt vindicated. After the ruling was announced, he stood before press microphones in front of the Supreme Court Building. The ruling, he declared, signified that "the goal of racial equality in voting has been fulfilled." All fifty states would now be treated equally. "This decision restores an important constitutional order to our system of government," Blum said. "The American South long ago laid down the burden of racial disfranchisement." Roger Clegg, the president of the Center for Equal Opportunity, who had previously worked with Roberts in the Reagan and George H.W. Bush administrations, similarly praised the decision, insisting that the "evidence demonstrates beyond any doubt that 'things have changed dramatically.'"[35]

Not everyone agreed, of course. Sherrilyn Ifill, chief counsel of the NAACP Legal Defense Fund, called the decision "an egregious betrayal of minority voters." Others were even more scathing. "Shelby County is the first decision since Dred Scott to invoke the doctrine of equal sovereignty where the right to vote was involved," wrote James Blacksher and Lani Guinier in the *Harvard Law and Policy Review*. "And, once again, just as the Court did in Dred Scott, the Court in Shelby County held that the 'equal sovereignty' of the State of Alabama takes precedence over Congress's exercise of its explicit constitutional power to enforce the voting rights of the descendants of slaves."[36] (No criticism could go further than a lethal comparison to *Dred Scott*. Chief Justice Roberts would use *Dred Scott* himself two years later, although not in a race case. He would invoke it to denounce the Court majority's decision declaring a right to same-sex marriage.)

Roberts was undeterred by the criticism in *Shelby County*. He remained steadfast in his view that claims of discrimination must be made by individuals in specific circumstances and not by groups. He was convinced that racial policies had backfired. Roberts has not deviated from that belief from the 1980s to the present day.

Shelby County v. Holder had immediate consequences. Texas began enforcing a photo ID requirement for voters, a practice that civil rights advocates claimed made it harder for members of racial minority groups to vote. The North Carolina legislature set to work on similarly restrictive measures, including voter ID requirements and new limits on the number of early voting days. When the North Carolina law on early voting days was challenged, the US Court of Appeals for the Fourth Circuit deemed it was an unconstitutional effort to "target African-Americans with almost surgical precision." The court pointedly observed that North Carolina legislators had pushed for the tougher voter-identification rules one day after the *Shelby County* decision came down.[37]

When North Carolina officials appealed, the Supreme Court declined to intervene. It similarly declined to involve itself in an early stage of litigation over the Texas law. Yet the chief justice took it upon himself in a May 2017 statement to try to assure the public that the Court majority was neither signaling disapproval of the North Carolina law nor endorsing the appeals court's rejection of it. "Given the blizzard of filings over who is and who is not authorized to seek review in this Court under North Carolina law," Roberts wrote, "it is important to recall our frequent admonition that 'the denial of a writ of certiorari imports no expression of opinion upon the merits of the case.'"[38]

CHAPTER XI

A FRACTURED COURT

S OON AFTER CHIEF JUSTICE JOHN ROBERTS OPENED THE MORN-
ing's oral arguments on January 21, 2015, pandemonium struck.
Demonstrators in the audience began shouting, "Money out of politics!"
and "Reverse *Citizens United*!" It was the five-year anniversary of the
Court's ruling in the case of *Citizens United v. Federal Election Commission*, and the activists were protesting the decision that had lifted federal
regulation of corporate and union expenditures in political campaigns.
They were working together, jumping up one by one. As Court police
subdued one demonstrator, another rose. "There!" Chief Justice Roberts
called out and pointed as officers rushed to seize another protester.[1]

Spectators are expected to follow the strictest decorum while in the
courtroom. Before entering, they give up their cellphones and any other
electronic devices. Anyone who begins to chat inside the courtroom is immediately hushed. Once the marshal of the Court chants "Oyez, Oyez!"
to open the session, the only voices heard are those of the justices and the
lawyers who stand at the lectern to present their cases. On this particular
morning, however, shouts mixed with the clatter of chairs knocked to the

floor as security officers muscled seven demonstrators out of the courtroom. The leader of the grassroots group 99Rise—a reference to the so-called 99 percent—said later that the demonstrators had been recruited from across the country. They had spent the previous evening rehearsing their moves, chanting such slogans as "One person, one vote" for maximum effect.[2]

The chief justice was disturbed by the disruption. Once the protest was quelled, he said, barely concealing his anger, "We will now continue with our tradition of having open court in the Supreme Court."

"Citizens United" no longer denoted merely the name of a small conservative advocacy group or a single ruling. To people who opposed the January 2010 decision, it stood for the problem of wealthy interests dominating America's electoral democracy. Hundreds of demonstrators had gathered outside the Court on that same snowy morning in January. That was anticipated. The notion of some of the protesters taking their demonstration into the highly supervised marble courtroom setting had not been expected. The divisions seen that morning inside the Court and on the front plaza reflected the deep divisions between the left and the right across the country.

Citizens United had been decided by a five-justice Republican-appointed majority that was dominating most of the other consequential disputes before the Court. The majority had reduced the opportunity for employee and consumer class-action lawsuits (such as in the 2011 *Wal-Mart, Inc., v. Dukes* and 2013 *Comcast Corp. v. Behrend* cases), diminished voting rights (as in *Shelby County v. Holder* in 2013), and curtailed labor and environmental protections (in 2013's *Vance v. Ball State University* and 2015's *Michigan v. Environmental Protection Agency*). Chief Justice Roberts continued to assert that politics played no role in the Court's decisions, but the way the justices divided along political lines undercut that assertion. And it was not just that they divided according to their ideologies; it was that the majority and dissenting opinions in significant cases represented alternate worldviews.

That was seen when the conservative majority foreclosed an antitrust class action in *American Express Co. v. Italian Colors Restaurant* in 2013.

Justice Kagan opened her dissent for the liberals on a sardonic note: "Here is the nutshell version of this case. . . . The owner of a small restaurant thinks American Express has used its monopoly to force merchants to accept a form contract violating the antitrust laws. The restauranteur wants to challenge the allegedly unlawful provision . . . but the same contract's arbitration clause prevents him from doing so. . . . And here is the nutshell version of today's opinion, admirably flaunted rather than camouflaged: Too darn bad." Justice Scalia, who wrote for the majority in the case, swatted back at Kagan's arguments, saying the decision rejecting class actions was based on precedent, particularly a 2011 case: "Truth to tell," he wrote, "our decision in *AT&T Mobility [LLC v. Concepcion]* all but resolves this case."[3] Meanwhile, the entire country was becoming more polarized. The tensions in the world beyond the Court were increasingly mirrored inside the Court, and vice versa. By 2015, few observers were surprised by the conflicts between the liberal and conservative justices. But animosity and distrust also existed within the conservative bloc, some of which stemmed from the 2012 health-care case.

Roberts was naturally reticent and guarded, which made his colleagues wary of his motives. That wariness extended to the staff in some chambers who derisively referred to Roberts as "King John," because of the control he tried to exert throughout the building. Some justices and staff were annoyed at the way he separated himself from the associate justices at times, particularly for investitures and other ceremonial purposes. Justices traditionally had been numbered sequentially. For example, when Chief Justice William Rehnquist welcomed Ruth Bader Ginsburg to the Court in 1993, she had been declared the 107th justice. There had been a total of 107 justices (associates and chiefs) by that point. Roberts's staff began counting the justices by their titles, separating associate justices from chief justices, so that when Elena Kagan joined in 2010, Roberts welcomed her as the 100th associate justice, and in 2017, Neil Gorsuch was welcomed as the 101st associate justice. It was a small change, but it did not escape notice.

Appearances and reality at the Court were not the same. Roberts was outwardly courteous and pleasant. He excelled at the structured settings of oral arguments, presentations, and speeches. He did not have Scalia's belligerence or Alito's tendency to make revealing faces on the bench. Yet away from the public spotlight, Roberts, too, could lapse into a mocking tone or be dismissive of a colleague's argument. He made no secret to friends that he found individual associate justices annoying, demanding, or arrogant.

Roberts did not conceal his lack of respect for academics, either. "I think it's extraordinary these days—the tremendous disconnect between the legal academy and the legal profession," Roberts had told an interviewer in 2007. "They occupy different universes. What the academy is doing, as far as I can tell, is largely of no use or interest to people who actually practice law." He suggested that legal studies were too theoretical. By way of analogy, Roberts said, "Don't expect, if you're going to be a theoretical mathematician, to have an impact on how people build bridges. And if you want to have an impact on how they build bridges, you need to become more of an engineer."[4]

Within the Court, contrasting personal styles, along with strong and opposing views, could be expected to produce tensions with any nine individuals thrown together. Yet Roberts intensified these personal divisions. He created bureaucratic barriers around him. He was not obviously imperious, as Chief Justice Warren Burger had been. He was subtler. But he nonetheless engaged in a closed-off, top-down style in his running of the Court building's operation that rankled colleagues and top staff beyond his chosen few. Strained personal relations among justices did not appear to affect decisions on the law. Rather, they came into play at the margins, when a justice was considering whether to pick up the phone and talk out a compromise, for example, or deciding whether to join a separate opinion that did not affect the judgment of a case.

It is difficult to say whether the interpersonal rivalries and animosities are now worse than they have been under most chief justices. Some associate justices said relations had deteriorated since the end of Rehnquist's tenure. And many insiders privately put the blame for the tensions at the feet of Roberts and his secretive ways, and, perhaps ironically, on his emphasis on appearances. He wants the public to see a unified, collegial group, even as he derides colleagues and closes off communications with justices and staffers beyond a select few.

IN THE SPRING OF 2014, ABOUT A YEAR BEFORE THE COURTROOM demonstration over *Citizens United* took place, Roberts and Sotomayor found themselves in a disagreement that quickly became personal. The justices were considering a dispute from Michigan that tested whether citizens could amend their state constitution to forbid race as a factor in higher education admissions. Michigan voters had approved such an amendment in 2006, responding to an earlier US Supreme Court ruling, in *Grutter v. Bollinger*, that upheld racial affirmative action at the University of Michigan Law School.[5] That ruling applied nationwide but had generated a particular backlash in the state where the case had originated. Michigan's Proposition 2, as the new law was called, forbade the consideration of race in public policies. Faculty from the flagship campus in Ann Arbor and civil rights advocates filed suit to challenge the measure.

When it reached the Supreme Court, the dispute, known as *Schuette v. Coalition to Defend Affirmative Action*, was not a direct test of the constitutionality of campus affirmative-action policies. Rather, it concerned the relationship between state constitutional amendments and the political process. The challengers argued that by preventing the public from lobbying for race-based admissions—even though people could still lobby for admissions policies related to a student's hometown or legacy status, for example—the state amendment had essentially usurped the political process and foreclosed one area of political participation for its citizens.

State officials countered that Michigan citizens were within their rights to decide that they wanted to foreclose any racial considerations in higher education admissions. Similar bans on racial affirmative action were in place in seven other states at the time: Arizona, California, Florida, Nebraska, New Hampshire, Oklahoma, and Washington.

During oral arguments, Chief Justice Roberts was sympathetic to the state's position that race should not be part of the admissions equation.

As he put it, "You could say that the whole point of . . . the Equal Protection Clause is to take race off the table." He repeated his long-standing view that neither whites nor blacks benefited from such special measures. When Shanta Driver, the lawyer representing the Coalition to Defend Affirmative Action, told the Court that black voters "certainly" believed affirmative action valuable to them, as evidenced by the fact that 90 percent of them had opposed the state amendment in 2006, Roberts suggested that the value of such programs was debatable: "There may be a difference between popularity and benefit."[6]

Six of the justices (Roberts, Scalia, Kennedy, Thomas, Breyer, and Alito) were ready to rule that Michigan citizens had a right to amend their state constitution as they did in this instance. (Those six splintered in their legal rationales.) Kagan, who, as a US solicitor general, had been involved in an earlier stage of the dispute, did not vote in the case. That left only Ginsburg and Sotomayor dissenting. Ginsburg asked Sotomayor to write the opinion for the two of them. As Sotomayor began working on her opinion, she went back to sections of the draft opinion she had been writing a year earlier in the dispute brought by Abigail Fisher against the University of Texas at Austin. Fisher was challenging the university's policy giving a boost in some situations to racial minorities. A Court majority had been ready to rule against the University of Texas, but Sotomayor's provocative draft dissent had caused the justices in the majority to back off and work toward a compromise ruling that returned the case to a lower court. Justice Sotomayor had set aside that opinion after the deal with Justice Kennedy had emerged.[7]

Now, as she was writing a new dissenting opinion for the Michigan case, *Schuette*, Sotomayor again brought her personal experience with affirmative action to bear. She knew that Roberts and other justices believed it was time to put racial questions behind them, but she wanted her colleagues to understand that these sorts of issues were still very much part of daily life: "Race matters in part because of the long history of racial minorities' being denied access to the political process. . . . And race matters for reasons that really are only skin deep, that cannot be discussed any other way, and that cannot be wished away." Sotomayor then offered examples from the point of view of people of color: "Race matters to a young man's view of society when he spends his teenage years watching others tense up as he passes, no matter the neighborhood where he grew up. Race matters to a young woman's sense of self when she states her home-town, and then is pressed, 'No, where are you really from?', regardless of how many generations her family has been in the country." And finally, she declared, perhaps most personally from the justice who had spoken of her own early worries about fitting in at the Court, "Race matters because of the slights, the snickers, the silent judgments that reinforce that most crippling of thoughts: 'I do not belong here.'"[8]

Regarding the constitutional question, Sotomayor argued that the Michigan amendment restructured the political process in a way that put a unique burden on members of minority groups who might wish to persuade admissions officials to consider the benefits of racial diversity. Meanwhile, children of alumni and others who wanted special entrée to the admissions process could still lobby for it. "To know the history of our nation is to understand its long and lamentable record of stymieing the right of racial minorities to participate in the political process," she wrote. For people in "historically marginalized groups," the decision would un-derscore the difficulty of participating in the democratic process.

Sotomayor did not shy away from suggesting that her personal experi-ence informed her position. In this way, she could not have differed more from the chief justice, who even went so far as to say that personal experi-ence decidedly did *not* influence his views. Personal experience aside, her view that race matters had been held by many white justices in the past, including Harry Blackmun in the 1978 *Regents of the University of Califor-nia v. Bakke*, the case that first protected racial affirmative action in higher education. "In order to get beyond racism," Blackmun had written in his concurring opinion, "we must first take account of race. There is no other way. And in order to treat some persons equally, we must treat them differ-ently. We cannot—we dare not—let the Equal Protection Clause perpetu-ate racial supremacy." Justice Kennedy touched on that view when he broke from Roberts in the 2007 *Parents Involved in Community Schools v. Seattle School District No. 1* case on public school integration measures. Roberts

simply did not consider racism to be as prevalent or as intractable a problem as many of his contemporaries did.[9]

In the Michigan case, as Sotomayor stressed the same basic point,
she decided for the first time in her five-year tenure to read excerpts of
her fifty-eight-page opinion from the bench. (Justice Kennedy's opinion
for the majority was eighteen pages.) In her public reading, Sotomayor
emphasized her view that her colleagues in the majority "fundamentally
misunderstand" the consequences of racial bias. She suggested they were
running away from the topic.

"In the end," she continued in the portion of her written opinion that
she read from the bench, "my colleagues believe that we should leave
race out of the constitutional picture entirely and let the voters sort it
out. This reasoning ignores the stark reality, all too apparent in communities throughout the country: that race still matters." Justice Sotomayor
went beyond simply pointing out the perceived flaws in the Michigan
measure to the Court's responsibility for safeguarding the Constitution.
"As members of the judiciary tasked with intervening," she said in the
courtroom, "to carry out the guarantee of equal protection, we ought not
sit back and wish away rather than confront the racial inequality that
exists in our society."

If there was any doubt which justice or justices she might have especially had in mind, Sotomayor swept it away when she turned Roberts's
well-known adage about race discrimination against him: "The right way
to stop discrimination on the basis of race," she said in her bench statement, "is to speak openly and candidly on the subject of race and to apply
the Constitution with eyes open to the unfortunate effects of centuries of
racial discrimination."

Roberts could not abide that sentiment when he saw it in Sotomay-
or's written opinion, drafts of which had circulated among the justices in
the weeks before the opinion would be announced. Roberts had already
joined Kennedy's opinion for the Court but decided to write a rare (for
him) concurring statement to challenge Sotomayor. In a brief two-page
opinion, he made clear that he did not appreciate Justice Sotomayor's assessment. He opened by asserting that Sotomayor was merely giving voice

to her own personal views. "The dissent devotes 11 pages to expounding its own policy preferences in favor of taking race into account in college admissions, while nonetheless concluding that it 'do[es] not mean to suggest that the virtues of adopting race-sensitive admissions policies should inform the legal question before the Court,'" he wrote, suggesting that Sotomayor was oblivious to the irony.

Then Roberts moved on to the part of Sotomayor's opinion that disturbed him the most. "The dissent states that 'the way to stop discrimination on the basis of race is to speak openly and candidly on the subject of race.' And it urges that 'race matters because of the slights, the snickers, the silent judgments that reinforce that most crippling of thoughts: "I do not belong here."' But it is not 'out of touch with reality' to conclude that racial preferences may themselves have the debilitating effect of reinforcing precisely that doubt, and—if so—that the preferences do more harm than good."

Roberts had long maintained that such measures diminished a person, in his or her own eyes and in the eyes of others. That is why he regarded them as "debilitating." They reinforced the notion that a person of color was not up to the task. "To disagree with the dissent's views on the costs and benefits of racial preferences," he pointedly added, "is not to 'wish away, rather than confront' racial inequality. People can disagree in good faith on this issue, but it similarly does more harm than good to question the openness and candor of those on either side of the debate."

As Justices Kennedy and Sotomayor read portions of their opinions in the courtroom, printed copies of the decision were distributed by hand and on the Court's website, as is the practice of the Court's public information office. So before the justices even moved on to other business that morning, Sotomayor's words were quickly being picked up on social media and in news stories. Many liberal commentators were heartened by a prominent Hispanic justice, the only one ever appointed, giving voice to her experiences and attempting to speak to a broader audience beyond the law.

Roberts's how-dare-you response to Sotomayor did not escape notice either. "Now, Chief Justice Roberts has been called many things in his life," *Slate* columnist Dahlia Lithwick wrote archly. "But there is something about being told that he is blind, clueless, and also silencing that affects him viscerally. His entire two-page concurrence in *Schuette* . . . is a rebuke to Sotomayor; not on matters of doctrine, but on good taste and decorum in public discourse over race. It's not just that he doesn't like what she is saying. He doesn't like how she is saying it."[10]

Roberts and Sotomayor were opposed ideologically and stylistically. Her background was foreground. Within months of becoming a Supreme Court justice, she had contracted to write a memoir. On the speaking circuit, she poured out her life in front of audiences. She shared the details of her troubled relationship with her mother, her challenges as a diabetic, her professional setbacks, her strategies for picking herself up, her continued feelings of inadequacy, and more.

Roberts wondered why a judge would want to reveal so much of his or her personal experiences. He strove to be as neutral as his dark suit, starched white shirt, and conventional tie. Yet he, of course, was shaped as much by his background and upbringing as Sotomayor, or anyone else, for that matter. It is not difficult to draw a line from, for example, Roberts's comfortable youth in northern Indiana, through his time in the Reagan administration, to his mature views on the harms of racial classifications to remedy society's ills.

It was rare for Roberts to answer Sotomayor's anger with anger of his own. But he was not accustomed to being lectured. His opinion in this case remains one of the most revealing of his tenure so far. It reflects the passion with which he approaches questions of race as well as his disdain for anything from a justice that could be interpreted as a personal or policy judgment.

That spring, as the justices criticized each other in the Michigan racial dispute, a new controversy over the Affordable Care Act was under way. *Burwell v. Hobby Lobby Stores, Inc.*, forced the Court to confront a clash between religion and reproductive rights. Under Obama administration regulations tied to the ACA, employers were required to provide insurance for contraceptive coverage to their employees. The question for the justices was whether corporations could assert a right of religious freedom to obtain exemptions. Two family-owned entities operating as for-profit corporations brought the challenge: Hobby Lobby, an Oklahoma-based arts and crafts retailer run by evangelical Christians, and Conestoga Wood Specialties, a Pennsylvania-based cabinet manufacturer owned by Mennonites. Both petitioners claimed they believed that life begins at conception and protested the "morning-after pill" and other emergency methods of contraception that prevented fertilization.

The retailers sought an exemption based on a 1993 law, the Religious Freedom Restoration Act, which dictated that the federal government could not substantially burden the exercise of religion unless the action met a compelling interest and was the least restrictive way of serving that interest. Congress enacted the Religious Freedom Restoration Act in response to a 1990 decision, *Employment Division, Department of Human Resources of Oregon v. Smith*. In that case, the justices had rejected an appeal from two members of the Native American Church who had been fired from their state jobs for using peyote, an illegal hallucinogen, in a religious ceremony. Their use of the drug barred them from state unemployment compensation, which they argued violated their First Amendment right to free religious exercise. The Court in the *Smith* case said the state could enforce a neutral, generally applicable law. In response, the Religious Freedom Restoration Act required government to allow a religious exemption unless a compelling reason existed.

In 2015, the central question before the Supreme Court justices was whether a corporation, as opposed to an individual, could be protected by that law. The Obama administration countered the Hobby Lobby arguments for a religious exemption by asserting that once a company had taken the corporate form, it could not "exercise religion" or impose its beliefs on its employees.[11]

The five conservatives, led by Roberts, sided with the companies. Roberts believed "the whole point of" the Religious Freedom Restoration Act was "that Congress wanted to provide exemptions for the religious views of particular . . . proprietors, individuals." He also thought the Court should respect the view that the owners in this case believed they were being forced to pay for contraceptive methods that they likened to abortifacients.[12]

Roberts assigned the opinion to Alito, his fellow appointee from the George W. Bush administration, whom he often tapped for controversial disputes over religion and reproductive rights. The *Hobby Lobby* decision, marking the first time the justices found that secular corporations held religious rights, was announced on the last day of the 2013–2014 session. As usual for the last day, the courtroom was filled with relatives and friends of the justices, including retired justice John Paul Stevens. Alito opened by explaining that David and Barbara Green, Hobby Lobby's founders, had built their family enterprise into a nationwide chain of five hundred stores. The retail empire of Norman and Elizabeth Hahn, Conestoga Wood, had found similar success. It had begun as a modest woodworking project in the family's garage and had grown into a business with one thousand employees.[13]

Alito declared that these corporations plainly fell under the protections of the Religious Freedom Restoration Act. He said Congress had not intended to exclude people who ran their businesses as for-profit entities from the free exercise of religion. He scoffed at those who believed the owners' religious beliefs were "excessively fastidious" and asserted that the Court would not question the grounds for people's beliefs. That was an implicit response to medical groups that had disputed the Hobby Lobby and Conestoga Wood view that some of the contraceptive methods were abortifacients.

The lead dissenter, Ruth Bader Ginsburg, sat next to Alito, as dictated by their seniority at the time. When he finished reading excerpts from his majority opinion, which had taken seventeen minutes, she started reading from her opinion and went nearly as long. Ginsburg deemed the majority's ruling one of "startling breadth" and warned that there may be no "stopping point" to exemptions for corporate employers' religious views. The former women's rights advocate observed that in past rulings, the Supreme Court had asserted that contraceptive coverage was crucial to women's participation in the nation's economic and social life.

As she concluded her statement from the bench, Ginsburg said the Alito majority was effectively allowing religious business owners to impose their views on employees who might not share them. "Our cosmopolitan nation is made up of people of almost every conceivable religious preference," Ginsburg said. "In passing [the Religious Freedom Restoration Act], Congress did not alter a tradition in which one person's right to free exercise of her religion must be kept in harmony with the rights of her fellow citizens, and with the common good." Ginsburg was joined in full only by Justice Sotomayor. Justices Breyer and Kagan agreed that the two companies could not opt out of the contraceptive mandate, but they stopped short of taking on the larger question of corporate religious rights.

During that same session, in *Town of Greece v. Galloway*, the Court was fractured by a dispute over prayers before council meetings in Greece, New York. The challengers, two women who attended the meeting to speak on local issues, argued that prayer at a meeting held to conduct civic business should not include such sectarian themes. The challengers emphasized that the town had traditionally invited only Christian clergy. The five justices on the right rejected the arguments, noting that the Court had historically found that prayer in such a limited context at the start of a legislative session did not breach constitutional standards against the establishment of religion.[14]

This time, Roberts asked Kennedy to write for the majority. As the conservatives were divided in their rationale, only Roberts and Alito signed the full Kennedy opinion, which made the point that prayer at civic functions need not be nonsectarian. "The relevant constraint," Kennedy wrote, "derives from its place at the opening of legislative sessions, where it is meant to lend gravity to the occasion and reflect values long part of the Nation's heritage. Prayer that is solemn and respectful in tone, that invites lawmakers to reflect upon shared ideals and common ends before they embark on the fractious business of governing, serves that legitimate function."

Even though Alito signed the opinion in full, he broke off from Roberts and Kennedy, joined only by Justice Scalia, to make a stronger argument for legislative prayer and to attack the dissenting view of

Kagan, who was joined by fellow liberal justices Ginsburg, Breyer, and Sotomayor. Alito and Kagan traded more sarcasm than usual. "That the [Alito] opinion thinks my objection to [the town's practice] is 'really quite niggling,' says all there is to say about the difference between our respective views," Kagan wrote in the dissent.

Justice Kagan had criticized the town of Greece for failing to reach out to religiously diverse people in choosing who would offer the prayers at council meetings. "In arranging for clergy members to open each meeting, the Town never sought (except briefly when the suit was filed) to involve, accommodate, or in any way reach out to adherents of non-Christian religions," she wrote. Alito suggested that she was being too picky, arguing that a town does not violate the Constitution "simply because its procedure for lining up guest chaplains does not comply . . . with what might be termed a 'best practices' standard." Kagan had posed scenarios in which people seeking local government action would have to first stand and pray in a way that conflicted with their beliefs. Alito called those "highly imaginative hypotheticals" and claimed that the dissenters were on a quest to curb prayer altogether or make it "generic."

Kagan quoted Alito back to him, writing, "It bears repeating. I do not remotely contend that 'prayer is not allowed' . . . nor is that the 'logical thrust' of any argument I made." Kagan contended that the majority had taken a giant leap beyond the ruling in a 1983 case, *Marsh v. Chambers*, that had allowed nonsectarian prayers in the Nebraska legislature. She maintained that the setting of the legislature was quite different from a small town's council meeting, where individuals might attend to seek government assistance. She contrasted "morning in Nebraska" with "evening in Greece." That prompted Alito to refer to the locale of the first Continental Congress in 1774, where Christian prayers were delivered, and to write mockingly, "It is more instructive to consider 'morning in Philadelphia.'"

Their exchange was evidence of how polarized the two sides had become on religious liberty. Like race, this area broke along traditional conservative-liberal lines, with both camps talking past each other. Arguments were ideological, political, and nasty. There was no center left on religion, as had been the situation when Justice Sandra Day O'Connor, who served from 1981 to 2006, brokered narrow compromises and wrote concurring opinions to limit major shifts from the Court's precedent.

NOT ALL OF THE IMPORTANT CASES IN 2014 AND 2015 WERE AS tense as these. In the paired 2014 cases *United States v. Wurie* and *Riley v. California*, Roberts pulled together the entire Court to rule that police generally need a warrant before searching the cellphone, and all its contents, of a person who has been arrested. His unanimous opinion acknowledged Americans' reliance on smartphones in a way that contrasted with his earlier questions at oral argument, when he wondered why anyone would ever carry more than one phone. "What is your authority for the statement that many people have multiple cell phones on their person?" he asked a lawyer at the lectern. "Just observation," the lawyer responded. Roberts, who had suggested that carrying multiple cellphones might be a sign of criminal transactions, soon found out from his colleagues that some of them had two smartphones, one for work and one for personal use.[15]

"Modern cell phones are not just another technological convenience," Roberts ended up writing in his opinion. "With all they contain and all they may reveal, they hold for many Americans 'the privacies of life.' The fact that technology now allows an individual to carry such information in his hand does not make the information any less worthy of the protection for which the founders fought. Our answer to the question of what police must do before searching a cell phone seized incident to an arrest is accordingly simple—get a warrant." The decision offered an important departure from the Court's trend of siding with the government over defendants in search cases. (The year before, for example, the Court had ruled 5–4, in *Maryland v. King*, that police could take DNA samples from people arrested for serious offenses to test whether the sample matched the DNA from unsolved crimes.)[16]

In 2015, the justices took up another case connected to the Affordable Care Act, *King v. Burwell*. This time Roberts was able to lead a majority of six justices without the divisiveness of *National Federation of Independent Business v. Sebelius*, the monumental 2012 case that had left the individual insurance mandate intact. Yet internal discussions in the new dispute were not without some suspense.

King v. Burwell tested when people would be eligible for federal tax credits after buying insurance on federal and state exchanges. The federal tax credits were intended to make insurance more affordable and draw more people into the system. The question for the justices was whether the law was written in a way that allowed tax credits only for those who used state exchanges, or if it also covered those who had used federally facilitated exchanges. This possible distinction mattered, because only fourteen of the fifty states had their own exchanges at the time the dispute came before the Court.[17]

The case had been brought by the libertarian think tank Competitive Enterprise Institute (CEI), which had been determined to eviscerate the ACA from the very start. In 2010, when the law was first passed, Michael Greve, the chairman of the institute, had told a legal conference, referring to the act, "This bastard has to be killed as a matter of political hygiene. I do not care how this is done, whether it's dismembered, whether we drive a stake through its heart, whether we tar and feather it and drive it out of town, whether we strangle it."[18] CEI hired the lawyer Michael Carvin, whose experience dated to the Reagan years, and who had argued against the ACA in the 2012 battle. The institute also enlisted four low-income Virginians who were forced to buy insurance under the subsidies formula to be the face of the lawsuit. The crux of their argument was that the tax-credit subsidies could go only to people who purchased insurance on marketplaces "established by the state," as a section of the law said. Most of the low- and moderate-income people who qualified happened to live in about three dozen states with exchanges run by the federal government and not by the states—meaning they would not be eligible for the credits.

The Obama administration argued in its legal briefs that Congress intended the tax credits to be applied broadly. Its lawyers said the subsidies must accompany the individual insurance requirement because Congress could not "mandate people having something they can't afford." The health insurance exchanges would not survive unless the tax credits were available.

Chief Justice Roberts and Justice Kennedy vacillated in their initial assessments when the nine met after the March 25 oral arguments, mainly because of the discrepancies in the text. But in the end, Roberts was ready to accept the administration's argument, even as he emphasized that the drafting of the ACA was far from perfect. Several provisions could be read to be in conflict with one another or were clumsily drafted. One example, he noted, was that the law had "three separate Section 1563s."[19]

"Anyway we must do our best," Roberts wrote for a six-justice majority that eventually included Kennedy, "bearing in mind the fundamental canon of statutory construction that the words of the statute must be read in their context and with a view to their place in the overall statutory scheme." Although the text was at times ambiguous, its overall intention was not. "Those credits are necessary for the Federal Exchanges to function like their State Exchange counterparts, and to avoid the type of calamitous result that Congress plainly meant to avoid," he added.

Furthermore, he said, "in a democracy, the power to make the law rests with those chosen by the people. Our role is confined—to say what the law is. That is easier in some cases than in others. But in every case we must respect the role of the Legislature, and take care not to undo what it has done. A fair reading of the legislation demands a fair understanding of the legislative plan."

Roberts, who had previously represented health insurers and medical companies in private practice, also noted that "Congress passed the Affordable Care Act to improve health insurance markets, not to destroy them." He referred to a cartoon that Justice Felix Frankfurter had described in 1947. It featured a senator telling his colleagues, "I admit this new bill is too complicated to understand. We'll just have to pass it to find out what it means." When Roberts related the Frankfurter joke in his announcement from the bench, most people laughed. But not Scalia, who for the second time was on the losing side of a major ACA case. He was one of three dissenters, along with Justices Alito and Thomas, in the 2015 *King v. Burwell* decision.

Scalia complained that in 2012, when Roberts had found that Congress's power to regulate interstate commerce did not cover the ACA, the chief justice "rewrote the mandate-cum-penalty as a tax." In the new ruling, Scalia continued, the Court rewrote "the law to make tax credits available everywhere. We should start calling this law SCOTUScare."[20]

Roberts was insulated from Scalia's ire this time, because he had drawn Kennedy's vote. This case may not have been as important as the first major test of the ACA, as it involved a statutory issue, rather than a constitutional question about the power of Congress. Yet, as Roberts noted in his opinion, the health insurance exchanges would have collapsed without the Court's interpretation.

Four days after the *King v. Burwell* health-care case, Roberts lost a tightly fought dispute over the constitutionality of a commission Arizona voters had established to take control of redistricting. Hoping to diminish partisan gerrymandering, state voters in 2000 had passed a measure creating the Arizona Independent Redistricting Commission. The state legislature sued the entity, saying it compromised the legislature's authority and breached the Constitution's election clause, which says election rules "shall be prescribed in each State by the Legislature thereof." The Supreme Court majority, with Kennedy joining the four liberals, upheld the voter-approved commission. Ginsburg asserted for the majority that the elections clause "surely was not adopted to diminish a State's authority to determine its own lawmaking processes . . . in line with the fundamental premise that all political power flows from the people."

Roberts, joined by Scalia, Thomas, and Alito, dissented, invoking what likely was the first use of the term "chumps" in a Supreme Court opinion. "Just over a century ago," Roberts wrote, "Arizona became the second State in the Union to ratify the Seventeenth Amendment." He observed that the Amendment gave the people of each state power to choose their US senators; the power previously had rested with state legislatures. "The Amendment resulted from an arduous, decades-long campaign in which reformers across the country worked hard to garner approval from Congress and three-quarters of the States," Roberts noted.

"What chumps!" he then exclaimed. "Didn't they realize that all they had to do was interpret the constitutional term 'the Legislature' to mean 'the people'? The Court today performs just such a magic trick with the Elections Clause."[21]

JEAN PODRASKY WAS CHIEF JUSTICE ROBERTS'S FIRST COUSIN ON his mother's side. Jean had kept in touch with Roberts's family, partly because his mother, Rosemary Podrasky Roberts, was her godmother. Jean was also close to the grandmother she shared with John Roberts—Josephine Gmucza Podrasky, a woman who had kept her family going when her husband had died young. "Grandma Jo," as she was known, had earned an accounting degree, and she had instilled a sense of drive in her daughter, Rosemary. "She constantly stepped up," Jean said of her aunt, the chief's mother.[22]

Jean followed the goings-on in the Roberts household through Aunt Rosemary and John's sisters—"the girls," as they were collectively known. She recalled her cousin John as "the quiet one." When she graduated from high school in 1982, and John was a young lawyer in the Reagan administration, he arranged a tour for her at the White House.

By 2005, when he was nominated to the Supreme Court, Jean Podrasky had come out as a lesbian. She was not going to make any kind of public revelation during his hearings, and neither was anyone else in the family. Podrasky, who by then was working as an accountant, attended the Senate Judiciary Committee hearings as a supportive relative, sitting near Roberts's parents, Rosemary and Jack, on the opening day.

Podrasky followed her cousin's views on LGBTQ rights leading up to the momentous test in 2015 concerning whether gays and lesbians had a constitutional right to marry. Through the chief justice, Podrasky was able to get a seat in the courtroom for the 2013 dispute, *United States v. Windsor*, that laid the groundwork for the famous 2015 case *Obergefell v. Hodges*. She had been wary about reaching out to the chief justice directly, so she went through one of his sisters. Podrasky was thrilled to be in the spectator seats in the spring of 2013 to hear the justices' questions regarding a 2008 California ban on same-sex marriage known as Proposition 8 as well as a broader question involving the federal Defense of Marriage Act, or DOMA.[23]

DOMA, signed by President Bill Clinton in 1996, defined marriage as a union between a man and a woman and dictated that only opposite-sex couples qualified for federal marriage benefits such as Social Security. Edie Windsor, a New York woman, challenged the law after she was denied federal death benefits when her spouse, a woman, died. She wanted to obtain the Social Security and other death benefits that heterosexual couples typically could get. By a one-vote majority in the case of *United States v. Windsor*, the justices ruled for Windsor, declaring that Congress could not deny married same-sex couples the federal benefits given their opposite-sex counterparts. In an opinion written by Justice Kennedy, the Court struck down a key provision of the DOMA law. Kennedy had taken the lead on the Court's gay rights opinions since 1996. Basing his decision on a robust view of equal liberty embodied in the Fifth Amendment, he was joined in the majority decision by the four liberals. Roberts was among the four dissenters.[24]

New York, where Windsor and her spouse resided, had legalized same-sex marriage, and Kennedy noted that the Defense of Marriage Act essentially forced them to live as married for purposes of state law but as unmarried for purposes of federal law. "By this dynamic DOMA undermines both the public and private significance of state sanctioned same-sex marriages," he wrote, "for it tells those couples and all the world, that their otherwise valid marriages are unworthy of federal recognition. This places same-sex couples in an unstable position of being in a second-tier marriage. . . . The differentiation demeans the couple, whose moral and sexual choices the Constitution protects and whose relationship the State has sought to dignify. And it humiliates tens of thousands of children now being raised by same-sex couples."

Scalia wrote the main dissent, but Roberts added a separate dissenting statement stressing that the majority's decision should not be interpreted to defend same-sex marriage. First, Roberts asserted he believed that Congress had been acting constitutionally in passing the 1996 law, which was a direct response to early action in Hawaii and other states toward legalizing same-sex marriage. "Interests in uniformity and stability," Roberts wrote, "amply justified Congress's decision to retain the definition of marriage that [at the time of the law's passage] had been adopted by every State in our Nation, and every nation in the world." Roberts then made clear that he disagreed with Scalia's warning that Kennedy's constitutional equality rationale could be used ultimately to sanction same-sex marriage. In a part of Scalia's dissent that Roberts did not sign, Scalia had chided, "It takes real cheek for today's majority to assure us, as it is going out the door, that a constitutional requirement to give formal recognition to same-sex marriage is not at issue here—when what has preceded that assurance is a lecture on how superior the majority's moral judgment in favor of same-sex marriage is to the Congress's hateful moral judgment against it. I promise you this: The only thing that will 'confine' the Court's holding is its sense of what it can get away with."

Until the *Windsor* case, legal observers had few clues about Roberts's position on gay rights. During his 2005 confirmation, the White House disclosed that in the mid-1990s, when he was a partner at Hogan and Hartson, he had assisted with a moot court in a gay rights case. Along with other appellate lawyers from the firm, Roberts had undertaken the moot court to help in the Supreme Court preparation of a lawyer who was challenging a Colorado law that barred local governments from protecting gay people. The dispute in the 1996 case of *Romer v. Evans* arose after Colorado voters had approved an initiative that would have allowed employers and landlords to discriminate against gay people. The initiative forbade local anti-bias laws based on sexual orientation. Roberts's participation in that case seemed minimal—he said he had been involved for less than ten hours—and no indication of his sentiment one way or another had since become public.

The chief's cousin was not disheartened by his decision in *United States v. Windsor*. The decision energized gays and lesbians, and Podrasky and her longtime partner began planning a fall 2013 marriage. The case also quickly began to change the national landscape. Within a few months, four more states (New Jersey, Hawaii, Illinois, and New Mexico) took steps to legalize same-sex marriage. Lower federal court judges began invoking the decision to favor same-sex marriage, beginning with a US district court decision in Utah, and then with new decisions against state same-sex marriage bans in Oklahoma, Kentucky, Virginia, Texas, Michigan, and Tennessee.

That momentum led the Supreme Court to take up state appeals just two years after *Windsor*. For the collection of four cases that came to be known as *Obergefell v. Hodges*, Podrasky did not even try to get a seat in the courtroom. She knew the demand for a place would be greater than in 2013, and she instead followed the case from her home in San Francisco. The cases had been brought by couples in the states of Ohio, Michigan, Kentucky, and Tennessee. The key question was whether the bans on same-sex marriage in those states violated Fourteenth Amendment equality rights.

The magnitude of the moment could not have been overstated. The country had undergone an incredibly swift transformation in its cultural attitudes. In 2008, Barack Obama and his Democratic primary challenger, Hillary Clinton, had declined to support same-sex marriage. Obama had switched his position in 2012, and in 2013, Clinton followed suit. By 2015, when the Supreme Court took up the constitutional question, there were scores of prominent public officials, business leaders, and cultural icons pushing for a nationwide change. The first state to allow same-sex marriage had been Massachusetts, in 2004, following an unprecedented decision a year earlier by the Massachusetts Supreme Judicial Court. But by 2015, a total of thirty-seven states and the District of Columbia had legalized same-sex marriage either through legislation or court rulings.[25]

Yet Roberts did not want the Court to rule on the question of same-sex marriage. He had signaled his position in 2013, when he had dissented from the *Windsor* case, and he had urged his colleagues—unsuccessfully—not to take up the constitutional question in 2015. He believed that the national conversation should continue and that it was better for elected officials and those who put them into office to control the trajectory of the debate.

As had happened with the 2012 Obamacare case, would-be spectators began lining up in front of the Supreme Court Building four days before oral arguments were to begin, hoping to secure a seat in the courtroom. They had come from across the country and represented a wide swath of professions and interests, but they were all determined to witness the pivotal case. Many of them camped out in the cold to secure their places, although some well-heeled people hired surrogates—for up to thousands of dollars—to stand in line in their place.[26]

Representing the couples who were challenging state law was Mary Bonauto, a litigator with the Boston-based Gay & Lesbian Advocates & Defenders (GLAD). Bonauto, who was fifty-three years old at the time, had been a leading strategist for gay rights since the 1990s. Former US representative Barney Frank, who was openly gay, had called her "our Thurgood Marshall," and the label had stuck. Bonauto had never argued before the Supreme Court, but she had prevailed in an intense competition—including moot courts—among prominent appellate lawyers who wanted to handle *Obergefell* before the justices.

"Mr. Chief Justice, and may it please the Court," Bonauto began on the morning of April 28, 2015. "The intimate and committed relationships of same-sex couples, just like those of heterosexual couples, provide mutual support and are the foundation of family life in our society. If a legal commitment, responsibility and protection that is marriage is off limits to gay people as a class, the strain of unworthiness that follows on individuals and families contravenes the basic constitutional commitment to equal dignity."[27]

Citing the Fifth Amendment equal liberty principles laid down in the *Windsor* case from two years earlier, Bonauto said, "Here we have a whole class of people who are denied the equal right to be able to join in this very extensive government institution that provides protection for families."

Chief Justice Roberts interrupted Bonauto early in her remarks. "Every definition that I looked up, prior to about a dozen years ago," he told her, "defined marriage as unity between a man and a woman as husband and wife. Obviously, if you succeed, that core definition will no longer be operable."

"What we're really talking about here," Bonauto responded, "is a class of people who are, by state laws, excluded from being able to participate in this institution."

"No," Roberts countered, " . . . you're seeking to change what the institution is. The fundamental core of the institution is the opposite-sex relationship and you want to introduce into it a same-sex relationship." Roberts had not been persuaded that the Defense of Marriage Act was unconstitutional, and now he was not persuaded that same-sex couples should have a right to marry.

Two months later, on June 26, the chief justice entered the packed courtroom with a sheaf of papers in hand. Roberts looked tense, his jaw tight. The papers he carried were a sign that he would read to the courtroom. Could he possibly have the majority opinion in *Obergefell v. Hodges*? In fact, the case marked the occasion of his first dissenting statement from the bench.

Once again it was Justice Kennedy who controlled the majority in a gay rights case. Kennedy was joined by the four liberals, and he would read excerpts of his opinion first. "Since the dawn of history, marriage has transformed strangers into relatives," Kennedy said as he occasionally looked out at the solemn spectators. "This binds families and societies together, and it must be acknowledged that the opposite sex character of marriage, one man, one woman, has long been viewed as essential to its very nature and purpose. And the Court's analysis and the opinion today begins with these millennia of human experience, but it does not end there."[28]

Kennedy cited the revolution in Americans' attitudes concerning gay rights, saying, "Until recent decades few persons had even thought about or considered the concept of same-sex marriage. In part, that is because homosexuality was condemned and criminalized in many states through the mid-20th Century." He noted that in the 2003 case *Lawrence v. Texas* (for which he had written the majority opinion), the Supreme Court had held for the first time that intimate relations between same-sex couples could not be criminalized.

"Yet it does not follow that freedom stops there," Kennedy said. "Outlaw to outcast may be a step forward, but it does not achieve the full promise of liberty." Then Kennedy addressed the law and his understanding of the Constitution's reach. "The nature of injustice is that we do not always see it in our own times," he observed.

Kennedy concluded that the constitutional principles of due process and equal protection must cover same-sex unions in the same way that they cover opposite-sex unions. Although some people might have regarded this change as coming too fast, in fact "substantial deliberation" on the subject had occurred in the states and on the national level and there was no longer any reason to wait.

Chief Justice Roberts then offered the dissenting view. Speaking in his characteristically measured tones, he began by recounting the history of marriage as he saw it. He referred to the long-standing understanding that a marriage is a union between a man and a woman. "That is true for the Kalahari Bushmen and the Han Chinese, for the Carthaginians and the Aztecs, for any civilization at any time at anyplace in the world, and certainly for those who wrote and ratified our Constitution."

Roberts's main complaint centered on the justices' handling of a question that he believed should be decided by elected legislators. He dismissed the majority as "five lawyers" who had done nothing less than reorder society.

"Just who do we think we are?" he asked rhetorically. "This is a court, not a legislature. . . . We have to say what the law is, not what it should be." He likened the majority's approach to the discredited Lochner era, which was "now regarded as one of the most unprincipled in history," as he put it.

There would be consequences to shutting down debate, Roberts warned, as closing debate tends to close minds. Gay rights advocates were losing the opportunity to win acceptance, he said, "just when the winds of change . . . are at their back." Finally, he admonished, "If you are among the many Americans—of whatever sexual orientation—who favor expanding same-sex marriage, by all means celebrate today's decision. Celebrate the achievement of a desired goal. Celebrate the opportunity for a new expression of commitment to a partner. Celebrate the availability of new benefits. But do not celebrate the Constitution. It had nothing to do with it."

In his written opinion, Roberts went further, comparing the ruling to the Court's infamous *Dred Scott* decision of 1857. In that case, the Court had declared that Dred Scott, a black man suing for his freedom from slavery, was not a citizen and had no rights under the Constitution. Led by Chief Justice Roger Taney, the Court ruled that Congress lacked the authority to prohibit slavery in the territories, thus invalidating part of the 1820 Missouri Compromise. Taney's opinion was full of the rhetoric of white supremacy. Leading up to the Constitution's ratification, Taney wrote, slaves had been "regarded as being of an inferior order, and altogether unfit to associate with the white race, either in social or political relations; and so far inferior, that they had no rights which the white man was bound to respect, and that the negro might justly and lawfully be reduced to slavery for his benefit."[29]

Referring to perhaps the most disreputable opinion in Court history, Roberts wrote, "the Court invalidated the Missouri Compromise on the ground that legislation restricting the institution of slavery violated the implied rights of slaveholders. The Court relied on its own conception of liberty and property in doing so." Roberts's suggestion was that the majority in *Obergefell* was imposing its own view of liberty on the American people, in the form of same-sex marriage, just as the Taney Court had imposed his view of slavery. He implied that *Obergefell* was just as egregious. Deriding his colleagues, he quoted the dissenting opinion from *Dred Scott v. Sandford*, which had been written by Justice Benjamin Robbins Curtis. Curtis had said that when the "fixed rules which govern the interpretation of laws [are] abandoned, and the theoretical . . . opinions of individuals are allowed to control [the Constitution's] meaning, we have no longer a Constitution; we are under the government of individual men."

Roberts wanted to make the point that the justices were usurping the political process and undermining the Constitution. He was trying to be less strident than Scalia, whose dissents in gay rights cases—including comparisons between homosexuality and bestiality—had provoked outrage. Roberts did not want to be seen as callous and critical when it came to gay people. But the use of *Dred Scott* and his rebuke not to celebrate the Constitution ("It had nothing to do with it") rang harsh. Critics said that, in resisting the tide of history, Roberts was setting himself up to be regarded as the Roger Taney of his time.

The legal establishment was decidedly with the Kennedy majority. One of the strongest detractors of Roberts and the other dissenters was the Chicago-based US Court of Appeals Judge Richard Posner, a prolific, influential judge whom Ronald Reagan had appointed in the early 1980s. Posner called Roberts's position "heartless" and mocked his view of history. He recounted the persecution of gay people such as Oscar Wilde, Pyotr Ilyich Tchaikovsky, and Alan Turing and noted that American gays and lesbians had long concealed their homosexuality to avoid discrimination.[30]

Some would-be critics gave Roberts a pass because his vote, in the end, did not matter. The majority had sanctioned same-sex marriage. Joining the outpouring of enthusiasm for the ruling was Roberts's cousin Jean Podrasky. "I would have been ecstatic if he had went the other way," she said. "But he was not the fifth vote [that defined the decision]. And I will always love him."[31]

It is difficult to imagine that Roberts was not aware of the historical trajectory of same-sex marriage. Yet he took a stand against it and called attention to that stand by reading his opinion from the bench. This crucial moment in his tenure is often overlooked because of the ultimate outcome favoring same-sex marriage, and because Roberts, unlike Scalia, was never regarded as antagonizing gay men and lesbians. His moves illustrated that over the course of his legal life, at a time when American social attitudes were changing rapidly, John Roberts was not changing. Central to his personality was a constancy, an immovability. His views were fixed.

CHAPTER XII

AN OPEN SEAT

A FTER ANTONIN SCALIA DIED, HIS HIGH-BACK CHAIR ON THE Supreme Court bench was draped in black wool crepe. It was left like that for 30 days, after which the chair was removed, and the remaining eight black leather chairs were situated so that the hole in the Court would not be so obvious. The politicking around Scalia's successor lasted 422 days. Under normal circumstances, the vacancy would have been President Barack Obama's to fill. But Senate Republicans blocked action on Obama's choice for nearly a year. The appointment was made only after Donald Trump had become president.

The period from February 2016 to April 2017, when the high court had just eight members, was one of the most difficult of Chief Justice Roberts's tenure. On February 13, 2016, the night of Scalia's death, Roberts rushed to put out a statement responding to his colleague's passing and to return to Washington, DC. The first hours after the justice's body was found in his room at the Texas hunting resort were highly consequential for the Court and the nation. Senate Majority Leader Mitch McConnell, a Kentucky Republican, had received an early call about Scalia's death.

Leonard Leo, a close friend of Scalia's and executive vice president of the Federalist Society, heard the news that Saturday afternoon from Scalia's family. Scalia's adult children knew how close Leo had been to their father. Some of them also understood that Leo worked with McConnell on judicial nominations. Even while dealing with the shock of their loss, key friends of Scalia were ready to act to continue his conservative legacy. Once Leo learned of the justice's death, he tried McConnell's cellphone number, and when McConnell did not pick up, he called one of the senator's top aides. Leo later said that no words were exchanged about what McConnell would say publicly. There was no need. A tight group of conservative advocates who had been working with McConnell since 2009, when Obama took office, had arrived at an understanding that if a vacancy arose in the last year of his presidency, the Senate Republican leader would try to block it.

The group had in fact been involved in a concerted effort since the very first month of Obama's tenure to minimize his opportunity for court appointments. On January 22, 2009, two days after Obama's first inauguration, a small group of former Republican administration lawyers who had been active in judicial selections for decades, including Leonard Leo and Edwin Meese III, Reagan's attorney general from 1985 to 1988, had written to McConnell and other Senate leaders, urging them to be on guard for Obama judicial nominees. They told them to examine possible nominees "with an unprecedented level of Senate scrutiny." Two months later, the full Senate Republican Conference sent Obama a letter. It said, "We hope your Administration will consult with us as it considers possible nominations to the federal courts from our states. Regretfully, if we are not consulted on, and approve of, a nominee from our states, the Republican Conference will be unable to support moving forward on that nominee."[1]

McConnell saw the federal bench as a crucial battleground. A lawyer by training, he had studied the nomination process since he was a Senate aide in the 1970s, and as a senator he had experienced firsthand how judges affected policy. McConnell had sued to fight federal campaign finance regulations. He had lost a 2003 contest against the McCain-Feingold law, *McConnell v. Federal Election Commission*, but had backed Citizens United's successful case lifting regulations on corporate and union expenditures in 2010. From the start of Obama's presidency, McConnell had put up hurdles to Obama's lower court nominations, ensuring, for instance, that not a single appointment was confirmed to the DC Circuit in Obama's first term.

There was no question among key conservative insiders that an Obama nomination had to be blocked. McConnell needed to be told only that Scalia was dead. Soon after Chief Justice Roberts formally announced Scalia's death at 5:35 p.m. Eastern Time, McConnell was ready to express condolences regarding Scalia—and to issue a warning to the president about filling his seat.

"The American people should have a voice in the selection of their next Supreme Court Justice," McConnell said in his statement. "Therefore, this vacancy should not be filled until we have a new President." McConnell had not conferred with other Senate Republican leaders, some of whom were thrown off by his decision and the immediacy of it. Initial speculation in the media was that it would backfire. Wasn't such a declaration premature?[2]

But the top Senate Democrat, Harry Reid of Nevada, who had dealt with McConnell for three decades, knew McConnell's statement could spell trouble. Reid quickly put out his own statement, saying it would be unprecedented for the Supreme Court to go for nearly a year with a vacant seat. Reid urged the president to nominate a justice immediately. President Obama had been golfing in California when he received word of Scalia's death. Later that night, he announced that he would nominate a successor "in due time."

Coincidentally, that same Saturday evening, the candidates for the 2016 Republican presidential nomination were about to begin a previously scheduled debate in Greenville, South Carolina. The candidates weighed in, all of them agreeing that Scalia's successor should be named by the next president. Former Ohio governor John Kasich, at least, lamented the situation: "I just wish we hadn't run so fast into politics." Donald Trump, meanwhile, emphatically reinforced McConnell's message: "Delay. Delay. Delay."[3]

WHEN SCALIA WAS MEMORIALIZED THE FOLLOWING WEEKEND AT the Basilica of the National Shrine of the Immaculate Conception in Washington, DC, Chief Justice Roberts attended along with the seven associate justices and retired justice John Paul Stevens. Also gathered for the ceremony were Vice President Joe Biden, former vice president Dick Cheney, and many other government officials and lawyers who had known Scalia over the years, including former US solicitor general Ted Olson, who had first met Scalia during the Reagan years; former solicitor general Paul Clement, who had clerked for Scalia; and the current solicitor general, Donald Verrilli.

Scalia's son Paul, a priest, delivered the homily. Leonard Leo and Clarence Thomas offered readings from the Bible. Many of Scalia's colleagues had considered him a close friend. Justice Thomas felt the loss deeply. After Thomas's difficult confirmation in 1991, Justice Scalia had taken the lead for a celebratory black-tie dinner on his behalf. "It is hard to imagine the Court without my friend," Thomas said in a statement, describing him as "a man who loved his wife and family . . . a towering intellect."[4]

Justice Ruth Bader Ginsburg, another close friend of Scalia's, who had served with him first on the DC Circuit before joining the high court, was also shaken by his death. But her experiences with death from an early age, beginning with that of a sister who had died of meningitis before Ruth was two years old, and then her mother, had steeled her to face it with fortitude. She had lost her husband in 2010, and Scalia had been a great comfort to her at the time. Ginsburg and Scalia had traveled widely together for many years, and they shared a passion for opera. With their spouses, they had celebrated New Year's Eve in each other's company for decades. Ginsburg was three years older than Scalia, and she said she could not help but think, when she heard the news, that "I was supposed to go first."[5]

Scalia was one of the most vibrant of the nine justices, and he was loved and loathed in equal measure. He had grown up in a first-generation Sicilian American home. Born in Trenton, New Jersey, and reared in Queens in New York, he was an only child and the only offspring of his generation in a large and devout Roman Catholic family. (His mother was one of seven children, and his father one of two. None of the aunts and uncles had children of their own.)[6] He had attended Georgetown University and then Harvard Law School. After working in private practice and completing an early stint as a law professor at the University of Virginia, he had worked in the Nixon and Ford administrations, serving as an assistant attorney general from 1974 to 1977. From 1977 to 1982, he had been a law professor at the University of Chicago. While there, he had become a faculty adviser to the newly created Federalist Society. Scalia had enjoyed the pace and policy debates of the nation's capital and returned eagerly to Washington when President Reagan selected him for a judgeship on the DC Circuit in 1982. Four years later, Scalia became the first Italian American justice to serve on the Supreme Court, having been approved by the Senate in a 98–0 vote.

Scalia's death at a Texas hunting resort indicated his passion for the sport. Perhaps his most memorable majority opinion, the 2008 *District of Columbia v. Heller*, had involved the right to bear arms. Of hunting, he said in an interview, "It gets me outside of the Beltway, gets me into the woods, far away from all this." Scalia became excited when describing turkey hunting, where the hunter induces the bird to come closer and closer. "You have to take your shot, or else you've lost him," he said. "You get one shot. If you miss, the whole day's ruined."[7] He knew how to maximize his shot on the Court, too. He had transformed the debate over the US Constitution with his "originalist" view that the document should be interpreted in its eighteenth-century context, rather than adapted to the needs of modern society. When he had declared there was an individual right to bear arms, in the *Heller* case, he had drawn on an originalist understanding of the text of the Second Amendment.

Scalia was fervently conservative on social issues, opposing abortion rights, same-sex marriage, and race-based policies intended to give minorities a boost. His criticism of his liberal colleagues was scathing, but he directed the sharpest barbs at Republican appointees such as Justice Anthony Kennedy, who he thought had betrayed the cause. "Nino, in my view, sometimes does go overboard," Justice Ginsburg once said in an interview, referring to Scalia by his nickname. "It would be better if he dropped things like: 'This opinion is not to be taken seriously.' He might have been more influential if he did that."[8]

ON THE BENCH, ROBERTS AND SCALIA HAD BEEN MORE IN SYNC than they often appeared to be, given the chief's restraint and Scalia's flamboyance. Both had been raised in Roman Catholic households, both had attended Harvard Law School, and both had served in Republican administrations. They shared a caustic sense of humor, although Roberts kept his in check. They shared political commitments and judicial ideologies as well, although Scalia typically was further to the right.

Just a few months earlier, before Scalia's death, when the justices had heard arguments in the second round of *Fisher v. University of Texas at Austin*, Scalia and Roberts had both expressed skepticism about the value of the affirmative action policy that was in dispute. Roberts homed in on the diversity rationale, asking dubiously, of a lawyer for the University of Texas, "What unique perspective does a minority student bring to a physics class?"[9]

"Your Honor," responded lawyer Gregory Garre, representing the university, "we can talk about different classes, but this Court has accepted in *Bakke* and *Grutter*, and I think it accepted again in *Fisher I* [in 2013], that student body diversity is a compelling interest."

Scalia interjected, saying, "I'm not sure we said it's class by class." He continued, offering a view that Roberts had not been planning to advance: "There are those who contend that it does not benefit African-Americans to get them into the University of Texas where they do not do well, as opposed to having them go to a less-advanced school, a slower-track school where they do well. One of the briefs pointed out that most of the black scientists in this country don't come from schools like the University of Texas. . . . They come from lesser schools where they do not feel that they're being pushed ahead . . . in classes that are too fast for them."

Garre responded firmly, "This Court heard and rejected that argument, with respect, Justice Scalia, in the *Grutter* case, a case that our opponents haven't asked this Court to overrule. If you look at the academic performance of holistic minority admits versus the top 10 percent admits over time, they fare better.

"And, frankly, I don't think the solution to the problems with student body diversity can be to set up a system in which not only are minorities going to separate schools, they're going to inferior schools," Garre added. "I think what experience shows, at Texas, California, and Michigan, is that now is not the time and this is not the case to roll back student body diversity in America."

To Roberts, however, the time was past due. "This is consideration of race," he said later in the session. "It's a serious matter."

SCALIA'S DEATH AFFECTED JOHN ROBERTS'S WORK AT THE COURT in two principal ways. It meant, in the first place, that a handful of cases could not be decided. The justices—four conservatives and four liberals— were often deadlocked, and a deadlock meant that a lower court ruling would stand, with no national precedent set. One of the most notable 4–4 stalemates came in a dispute over the power of organized labor, in *Friedrichs v. California Teachers Association*. The justices had heard an appeal of a lower court ruling that had allowed California to compel non-union workers to pay fees in lieu of dues for collective bargaining and other activities. A group of California public school teachers was challenging the so-called "fair share" fees as a violation of constitutional free-speech rights. If the justices had ruled for the teachers, it could have cost organized labor millions of dollars in California and spurred similar challenges nationwide. When that case was argued in January, Scalia had still been on the bench, with the Court heading for a 5–4 vote. Now locked 4–4, they were going to have to let the lower court ruling stand, without any opinion.

Scalia's absence also put the Court in the middle of the national political scene, to Roberts's consternation. A week before Scalia's death, Roberts happened to tell a university audience in Boston that he was worried about how the increasingly polarized judicial confirmation process could taint the judiciary. He noted that—unlike in past decades—votes on judicial candidates were routinely falling along party lines. In 1993, for example, the Senate had approved Ginsburg by a 96–3 vote; the following year, Breyer had won confirmation by an 87–9 vote.[10]

As McConnell and Senate Judiciary Committee chairman Chuck Grassley, a Republican from Iowa, were fighting off pressure from Democratic senators to act on the Court's new vacancy, Grassley warned Roberts and other judges not to get involved. Grassley even criticized Roberts for his early February complaints about the politics of the confirmation process. "The chief justice has it exactly backwards," Grassley said. "The confirmation process doesn't make the justices appear political. The confirmation process has gotten political precisely because the court has drifted from the constitutional text and rendered decisions based instead on policy preferences." Grassley added, "Physician, heal thyself."[11]

Grassley's complaint was odd, especially in its suggestion that Roberts was somehow engaged in the political drama surrounding the Scalia vacancy, when Roberts had in fact been silent. Throughout the entire ordeal, he refrained from saying anything publicly about the empty seat and the Senate's refusal to act. Senate Minority Leader Harry Reid, a Nevada Democrat, deemed Grassley's criticism of Roberts "an epic display of buck-passing."[12]

On March 16, in a Rose Garden ceremony, President Obama put forward a moderate liberal nominee, veteran appeals court judge Merrick Garland, whom, under any other circumstances, Republicans would have backed. Obama noted that he had sought advice across the political spectrum, characterizing Garland as "someone who brings to his work a spirit of decency, modesty, integrity, even-handedness, and excellence." Garland, the chief judge on the US Court of Appeals for the District of Columbia, was a former prosecutor who had never shown himself to be an activist during his two decades on the bench. At sixty-three, he was also on the older side for a nominee, which meant his tenure would likely be shorter than that of most justices.[13]

Chief Justice Roberts liked Garland, who also happened to be a grad-uate of Harvard Law School. Garland, like Roberts, had clerked for US Appeals Court Judge Henry Friendly as well. Roberts knew that Gar-land was about as close to a moderate as anyone a Democratic president would appoint. Obama's supporters on the left were not enamored of the choice, but they vowed to try to help push him over the barrier that McConnell and Grassley were erecting. Judge Garland visited dozens of Senate offices on so-called "courtesy" visits. Everyone was indeed courte-ous. But no confirmation hearing was scheduled. McConnell was hold-ing his caucus together in opposition to any hearings for Garland.

Meanwhile, without the fifth conservative justice, the Court continued to deadlock on key cases or tipped to the liberal side. The Court was split over the Obama administration's attempt to revive a policy—blocked by a lower court judge—that would have let unauthorized immigrants who were parents of citizens or lawful permanent residents stay and work in the United States. The justices, 4–4, affirmed the injunction with no opinion. Justice Kennedy made the difference when he joined with the liberals for two of the most closely watched cases, a battle over a restrictive Texas abortion law, in *Whole Woman's Health v. Hellerstedt*, and a reprise of the 2013 University of Texas racial admissions fight, in *Fisher v. University of Texas at Austin*.

Few subjects were as weighty or as controversial as abortion rights, and it had been nearly a decade since the Court had taken up a test of government abortion regulations. The Texas law in question required physicians who performed abortions to possess "admitting privileges" at a local hospital in case surgery was needed; separately, it also required abortion clinics to convert themselves to costly, hospital-grade facilities. When the Republican-controlled Texas legislature had passed the law in 2013, lawmakers had said the regulations were necessary to protect ma-ternal health. Abortion providers sued state officials, saying the law was intended to block women from obtaining abortions, and in fact several clinics had closed because of the new requirements.

During oral arguments in *Whole Woman's Health v. Hellerstedt*, Roberts challenged the abortion providers' assertion that the state law had caused the immediate closure of nearly a dozen clinics. He also questioned whether the legislature's motive—arguably to try to impede abortions—even mattered if the regulations could be found to be reasonable for health care. Roberts grew testy throughout the oral arguments over repeated interruptions by Justices Sotomayor, Kagan, and Ginsburg, who plainly found the challengers' arguments meritorious. Roberts was without Scalia, of course, who had been one of the Court's strongest opponents of abortion rights.[14]

Separating himself from the chief justice, Kennedy joined with the four liberal justices and agreed that the law went too far in placing a substantial burden in the path of women seeking to end their pregnancies. That majority, in an opinion by Breyer, concluded that neither of the abortion regulations offered enough medical benefit to justify the burden they put on access to abortion. Roberts and the other dissenters believed the Court should have rejected the case out of hand, because the Whole Woman's Health clinic and its physicians had brought an earlier, related case. (The majority had said that the previous litigation, which had been lodged immediately after the law was enacted, did not concern specific allegations arising from the law's enforcement, including that it had caused the closure of some clinics.) The chief assigned the dissenting opinion to Alito, who contended that the challengers should not have won a victory "on the very claim that they unsuccessfully pressed in the earlier case." He said the justices could have avoided delving into the contentious dispute over the constitutionality of abortion regulations.[15]

In *Fisher II*, the justices heard the second round of the lawsuit brought by white applicant Abigail Fisher, who had asserted that the University of Texas's affirmative action program had led to the rejection of her application back in 2008. In *Fisher I* in 2013, the justices had sidestepped a constitutional question on the validity of the university's policy of using race as a factor in selecting students, returning the case to the US Court of Appeals for the Fifth Circuit for further review. The Fifth Circuit again ruled the program constitutional, saying that the university had sufficiently considered other options before deciding to use race to ensure campus diversity.[16]

With Roberts in dissent, Kennedy voted to uphold the University of Texas admissions policy giving some preference to black and Hispanic applicants. Kennedy had done just the opposite thirteen years earlier, in the milestone University of Michigan case *Grutter v. Bollinger*, and was headed in that same direction when the justices first heard the Fisher case in the 2012–2013 session. But in 2016, he wrote that a university had "considerable deference" to ensure student diversity. "It remains an enduring challenge to our nation's education system," as Kennedy put it, "to reconcile the pursuit of diversity with the constitutional promise of equal treatment and dignity." This second iteration of *Fisher v. University of Texas at Austin* marked the first time Kennedy had voted to endorse a university's race-conscious admissions policy, and it may have reflected a new realization about the country's intractable racial divisions on his part. Much had happened between 2013 and 2016 to bring about a change of attitude. Among other developments, the new Black Lives Matter movement had come into being, forcing the nation to reckon with questions of racism, particularly in policing, after Michael Brown, an eighteen-year-old unarmed black man, had been killed by police in 2014 in Ferguson, Missouri.[17]

Once again, Roberts assigned Alito the opinion for the dissenters. Writing for himself, Roberts, and Thomas, Alito declared that "something strange has happened since our prior decision in this case." Alito noted that Kennedy's majority opinion in *Fisher I* had put a burden on the university to prove that its affirmative action policy was needed. As Alito also knew, when the justices had heard the case three years earlier, Kennedy had initially been ready to reject the Texas program. Sotomayor's scathing draft opinion had prompted him to back down and work out a compromise with the liberal justices.

When the justices had returned the case to a lower court for further hearings, Alito argued, the University of Texas had failed to sufficiently justify its affirmative action program. "The University has still not identified with any degree of specificity the interests that its use of race and ethnicity is supposed to serve," Alito wrote in dissent. He then quoted Roberts's earlier views from the 2007 *Parents Involved* case, which had forbidden the Seattle and Louisville school integration efforts: "Classifying and assigning students according to race," he said, "'requires more than . . . an amorphous end to justify it,'" and "racial balancing is not transformed from 'patently unconstitutional' to a compelling state interest simply by relabeling it 'racial diversity.'"

IN THE SUMMER OF 2016, AS THE PRESIDENTIAL ELECTION CAM-
paign intensified and Donald Trump became the Republican nominee,
Justice Ginsburg joined in the criticism of the blustery nonconventional
candidate. "He is a faker," she said in an interview. "He has no consistency about him. He says whatever comes into his head at the moment.
He really has an ego." Ginsburg, then eighty-three, said she expected
Clinton to win the White House, adding, "She is bound to have a few
appointments [to the Supreme Court] in her term."[18] Trump fired back
on Twitter that Ginsburg's mind "was shot," and in response, there was
enough of an uproar that Ginsburg then said she had been wrong to make
public remarks about a political campaign.[19]

Still, liberal advocates who had been fighting the trends of the Roberts
Court were already planning for a whole new bench. Given the ages of
some of the justices, it looked like the new president would have as many
as three appointments in his or her first term. Lawyers on the left began
strategizing about litigation to reverse recent conservative patterns that
Roberts had spearheaded.

The chief justice had faced relatively few bumps in his professional
life, but now he appeared to be facing a challenge like no other. He would
become the first chief justice in more than half a century to preside over
a Court with a majority of justices who held a different ideology. Some of
his friends speculated that his life tenure would come to seem more like
a life sentence.[20]

During the period when the Court had only eight justices, Roberts
tried harder to build consensus, conferring regularly with Justices Kennedy, Breyer, and Kagan. Kagan characterized the pattern as the "silver
lining" of being shorthanded and gave due credit to Roberts. "We didn't
want to look as though we couldn't do our job," she told an audience at the
Aspen Institute in the summer of 2017 as she recalled the fourteen-month
period. "Across the board, people said, every 4–4 decision where we just
throw up our hands, and say we just affirm the decision below, every 4–4
decision is a failure on the part of this court. And so we worked very, very
hard to reach consensus and to find ways to agree that might not have
been very obvious." She acknowledged that "sometimes that led to a kind

of silliness. Sometimes the thing we found to agree on, was something that really nobody cared about. But often I thought the process was very good in terms of finding ways to massage issues, modify issues, in such a way that all of a sudden we could see the prospect of a broader consensus than might have appeared on first glance."[21] She explained that Roberts had wanted the public to know that the justices were working together more often, that they were not as polarized as the rest of the country.

Roberts himself revealed little of his thinking on the state of the Court. He wrote the fewest opinions of any of the justices during the period, even as his conservative colleagues Alito and Thomas issued bitter warnings, in opinions, about where the Court was headed, notably on religion and gun control, without Scalia and a conservative majority.[22]

TRUMP WON THE PRESIDENCY ON NOVEMBER 8, 2016, PUSHING TO a victory in the electoral college by slim margins in Pennsylvania, Michigan, and Wisconsin. Ten days after his January 20 inauguration, he announced his selection of Neil Gorsuch, a judge on the Denver-based US Court of Appeals for the Tenth Circuit, for the Scalia seat.

The announcement came amid controversy over one of Trump's first moves as president. Within two weeks of taking the oath of office, Trump signed an executive order barring refugees and other foreigners from majority-Muslim nations from entering the country. The order spurred a raft of litigation. Over his eight years as president, Barack Obama had initiated numerous policies that had been challenged in federal courts, including on immigration, health care, and environmental regulation. But none had prompted such an immediate response or mass protests. Demonstrators flooded the nation's airports and public squares. Trump asserted that the refugee restrictions would improve national security and protect the country from terrorists. Congressional leaders from both parties, along with immigration experts and legal analysts, condemned the policy, saying that it was both counterproductive to security interests and unlawful.

In the selection process that led him to Gorsuch, Trump said he was looking for a justice who would generally side with his policies. By his campaign statements, he suggested he wanted a reversal of *Roe v. Wade* and opposition to the Affordable Care Act. Trump signaled that he wanted judges who would diminish the force of the federal government in people's lives. Newly installed White House counsel Donald McGahn later reinforced that message by asserting that Trump would favor appointees who shared his vision of trimming government regulations across the board. Overall, according to McGahn, Trump wanted solid conservatives who, once seated on the bench, would not "turn into someone else," as David Souter had. That fear, of another justice like Souter who would move to the left after joining the Court, had been in the minds of President George W. Bush and his advisers when they had vetted Roberts in 2005. The conservatives advising Trump had the same concern.[23]

McGahn worked closely with the Federalist Society's Leonard Leo in the vetting of candidates for the Scalia seat. Leo had also helped expand Trump's original May 2016 list of possible candidates, so that it included Gorsuch. When the time came to name the Scalia successor, Trump interviewed three finalists and "clicked" especially with Gorsuch. (The other two were Judges Thomas Hardiman of the Third Circuit and William Pryor of the Eleventh Circuit.) The new president was especially impressed with Gorsuch's Harvard law degree and time at Oxford as a Marshall Scholar. Gorsuch had also been a law clerk to Justice Anthony Kennedy. At a youthful age forty-nine, tall with prematurely gray hair, Gorsuch was right from central casting, which also appealed to Trump.

When announcing Gorsuch as his nominee in a televised address, Trump's manner suggested the atmosphere of the beauty pageants he had once hosted. "So was that a surprise? Was it?" Trump asked under the bright lights of the cameras in the East Room after he called Gorsuch up to the stage.[24]

When Gorsuch was presented in the prime-time TV rollout, the judge struck themes that recalled Roberts's debut as a nominee under President George W. Bush in 2005. Gorsuch, who was then living in Boulder,

Colorado, invoked the vastness of the American West, just as Roberts had referred to the open fields of his home state of Indiana. Gorsuch, like Roberts earlier, also tried to speak humbly and with wit. When Gorsuch referred to the late Supreme Court Justice Byron White, a scholar and football legend, for whom Gorsuch also clerked, he called him "the only justice to lead the NFL in rushing."

Both Roberts and Gorsuch had been born in relative privilege and had attended prep schools before eventually reaching Harvard Law School. Gorsuch had served in George W. Bush's Justice Department as a principal deputy associate attorney general, just as Roberts had worked in the Reagan Justice Department and the White House counsel's office. Before becoming an appeals court judge, each had worked at a prestigious Washington law firm, though Roberts had had a much longer tenure as an appellate advocate. Gorsuch had spent ten years as an appeals court judge, compared to Roberts's two years. In his running of the policy-making Judicial Conference, Roberts had worked with Gorsuch and selected him to chair a prominent committee on appellate rules.

When he testified before the Senate Judiciary Committee, Gorsuch referred to the "modest station" of judges and their limited role in society. He employed folksy expressions and chose to sit at a plain wooden desk rather than the customary draped table. "There is no such thing as a Republican judge or a Democratic judge," he asserted. "We just have judges in this country." Roberts, of course, had used the metaphor of the judge as umpire throughout his confirmation.[25]

Two opinions from Gorsuch's tenure on the Tenth Circuit attracted Senate scrutiny and particular Democratic criticism. Gorsuch had ruled against a truck driver whose trailer had broken down in subzero temperatures after the brakes had frozen. The driver had unhitched the rig and driven away to warm up. His employer had fired him for leaving the trailer. The Tenth Circuit had ruled for the trucker, who claimed that under the circumstances, he should have been protected by federal worker-safety law. Gorsuch had dissented, stressing that the truck company had told the driver to wait for help and that leaving the scene, even temporarily, violated the rules. Gorsuch insisted that the driver's refusal to follow his boss's order meant he was no longer covered by the usual labor law protections and therefore could not get his job back. Democratic senator Al Franken of Minnesota called the reasoning of Gorsuch's position "absurd." When he asked Gorsuch what he would have done under the circumstances, the judge said, "Senator, I don't know. I wasn't in the man's shoes."

In another case the Democrats in the Senate highlighted, Judge Gorsuch had minimally construed the coverage of a federal law that required equal opportunity for children with disabilities in school instruction and services. Gorsuch said the law dictated that schools provide benefits "merely . . . more than de minimis," that is, with some educational benefit, no matter how small. It was coincidental that a related case was resolved by the Supreme Court as Gorsuch was testifying. In that case, *Endrew F. v. Douglas County School District RE-1*, the Court soundly rejected Gorsuch's reasoning. In a unanimous decision, Chief Justice Roberts said the standard of the Individuals with Disabilities Education Act is "markedly more demanding" than the one Gorsuch had adopted. "When all is said and done," Roberts wrote in the decision made public as Gorsuch was testifying, "a student offered an educational program providing 'merely more than de minimis' progress from year to year can hardly be said to have been offered an education at all." When Gorsuch was then asked about the ruling, he told the senators that he had adhered to Tenth Circuit precedent as it stood before the justices had ruled. "If anyone is suggesting that I like a result where an autistic child has to lose," he said, "that's a heartbreaking accusation."[26]

Throughout the hearings, Gorsuch hewed to the notion with which he had opened the hearing: "Putting on a robe reminds us," he said, "that it's time to lose our egos and open our minds. . . . Ours is a judiciary of honest black polyester."

Democrats worried about Gorsuch's conservatism, not only because of his past rulings, but because of whatever he might have implicitly promised to Trump and the advocates from the Federalist Society and the Heritage Foundation involved in screening candidates for Trump. Trump, after all, had vowed to appoint judges who would overturn *Roe v. Wade*. Asked what he would have done if Trump had asked for such a promise, however, Gorsuch told the Senate Judiciary Committee, "I would have walked out." Gorsuch was not convincing, at least to the Democratic senators, who were dismayed by his conservative decisions and evasive answers and were still feeling the sting of the Republicans' refusal to act on Obama's nomination of Merrick Garland.

The Democratic senators filibustered the Gorsuch nomination, which, under usual circumstances, would have meant that Republicans would need 60 votes to cut off debate for a vote on the merits of the nomination. The Republicans, who were not going to muster the 60 but controlled the majority, changed the rules instead, so they could approve Gorsuch's nomination by a simple majority vote. In 2013, the Democratically controlled Senate had eliminated such filibusters for lower court nominees as many of President Obama's choices were stalled. Gorsuch was approved on April 7 on a nearly complete party-line vote, 54–45. Three Democrats joined the Republicans, who voted unanimously for Gorsuch. The new Supreme Court justice began hearing cases in mid-April 2017.

In the six months of the 2016–2017 term that had already passed, the shorthanded Court had deliberately avoided major cases. But they had not been able to avoid all of them. One of the cases they heard was on race, and Kennedy had again cast the key vote. *Peña-Rodriguez v. Colorado* concerned racial bias in jury deliberations. Miguel Peña-Rodriguez had been accused of sexually harassing two teenage girls in the bathroom of a Colorado racetrack and attempting to assault them. During the jury deliberations in state trial court, a juror known in the record only as "H.C." had allegedly said, "I think he did it because he's Mexican and Mexican men take whatever they want." After Peña-Rodriguez was convicted of sexual harassment, two of the jurors in the case had told defense lawyers about H.C. The Colorado Supreme Court had denied a new hearing, ruling that H.C.'s comments, no matter how "ideologically loathsome," did not justify an exception to the traditional secrecy of jury deliberations.

In his opinion reversing the Colorado court's decision, Justice Kennedy carved out an exception for possible racial bias in a jury. He described the jury as "a central foundation of our justice system and our democracy . . . a tangible implementation of the principle that the law comes from the people." Roberts, Alito, and Thomas dissented, warning that if an exception was made this time, exceptions could soon be granted for religious and sex discrimination. During oral arguments, Roberts had questioned why the bias against the Colorado defendant would be considered more "odious" than any other kind of discrimination—for example, discrimination based on religious stereotypes about Muslims, Catholics, or Jews. He suggested that once an exception for racial bias was made, others would have to follow.[27]

Alito wrote for the three dissenters that "the real thrust of the majority opinion is that the Constitution is less tolerant of racial bias than other forms of juror misconduct." Alito added, however, that it was "hard to square this argument with the nature of the Sixth Amendment right . . . to an 'impartial jury.' Nothing in the text or history of the Amendment or in the inherent nature of the jury trial right suggests that the extent of the protection provided by the Amendment depends on the nature of a jury's partiality or bias."[28]

In a separate dispute over race early that session, *Buck v. Davis*, a six-justice majority that included Roberts sided with an African American Texas inmate, Duane Buck, in his long-running death-row appeal for a new sentencing hearing. His initial sentence had relied on a psychologist's testimony that Buck, who had been convicted of the 1995 murder of his former girlfriend and a friend, was more dangerous and more likely to commit violent acts than a white defendant would have been. Buck's lawyer had hired the psychologist who offered the damning testimony, and Buck contended that as a result he had been denied effective assistance of counsel. Writing the opinion for the Court, Roberts emphasized that it is patently unconstitutional for a state to argue that a defendant is liable to be a future danger because of his race. "Our law punishes people for what they do," Roberts wrote, keeping the 6–2 opinion for himself to draft, "not who they are." Only Thomas and Alito dissented. Another case of blatant racism, *Foster v. Chatman*, came to the Court a few months earlier. This case involved prosecutors in Georgia who had deliberately kept blacks off a jury, putting "B" next to the name of each potential juror to be struck. The vote was 7–1, and again Roberts chose to write the majority opinion.[29]

After Gorsuch joined the Court, one of the most important cases the justices addressed was *Trinity Lutheran Church of Columbia, Inc., v. Comer*, which tested the line between church and state and had been pending since before Scalia's death. Trinity Lutheran's Child Learning Center, a preschool and daycare facility in Boone County, Missouri, which had wanted to replace pea gravel on its playground with a rubber surface, had applied for a grant from a state scrap tire program in 2012. The state's Department of Natural Resources had created the program to reduce the number of tires in landfills and dumps. It offered grants to reimburse non-profit groups for purchasing playground surfaces made from recycled tires.

Missouri's state constitution dictated that "no money shall ever be taken from the public treasury, directly or indirectly in aid of any church, sect or denomination of religion." So when the center applied for a grant, the state said it was disqualified from receiving one. Trinity Lutheran sued, accusing the state of violating the free-exercise clause of the First Amendment.

The dispute brought another case back into the foreground, *Hosanna-Tabor Evangelical Lutheran Church and School v. Equal Employment Opportunity Commission* from 2012, which had similarly explored the tension between the establishment and free-exercise clauses. In that ruling, Roberts had led a unanimous Court to carve out special protection for religious institutions in a case involving an elementary school teacher, Cheryl Perich. She had been pushed out of her job at Hosanna-Tabor, a member of the Lutheran Church–Missouri Synod, the second-largest Lutheran denomination in America. Perich had been let go after she was diagnosed with narcolepsy and took a short leave of absence.

Hosanna-Tabor had argued that Perich had violated the Synod's belief that Christians should resolve their differences among themselves, not in the courts. In his opinion siding with the church, which all of his colleagues signed, Roberts wrote that the Constitution gives "special solicitude" to religious organizations for a "ministerial exception." Roberts cast the decision as a narrow one related to the church's internal employment decision.[30]

When the justices took up Trinity Lutheran's claim in 2017, Roberts guided the Court toward another fact-specific ruling. Yet the Court nonetheless declared for the first time that the Constitution's guarantee of the free exercise of religion required public funding of a religious entity. With only Justices Ginsburg and Sotomayor dissenting, the Court held that the Missouri state policy preventing funding for the church-school playground violated Trinity Lutheran's free-exercise rights. "Here there is no question that Trinity Lutheran was denied a grant simply because of what it is—a church," Roberts wrote in his opinion for the majority.[31]

Echoing his sentiment from *Hosanna-Tabor*, Roberts wrote that the free-exercise clause "compels" government to respect religious beliefs, and that the establishment clause "permits" the state to extend public benefits to all citizens regardless of their religion. He tried to suggest that the decision was narrower than the dissenting justices had asserted in their opinion. "This case involves express discrimination based on religious identity with respect to playground resurfacing," he wrote. "We do not address religious uses of funding or other forms of discrimination." Roberts included a footnote in his opinion that said it applied only to the playground resurfacing program.

That caveat won the vote of Justice Kagan. But the language also prompted an objection from Justices Thomas and Gorsuch, who wanted a broader rule favoring religious entities. In a short concurring statement, Gorsuch, joined by Thomas, said he worried that the footnote would lead some to believe that the Court's ruling applied only to cases involving playgrounds, children's safety and health, "or perhaps some other social good we find sufficiently worthy."[32]

Dissenting, Justice Sotomayor asserted that Roberts had engaged in a "judicial brush aside" of past Court principles and for the first time required government to provide funds to religious entities. A key principle of the separation of church and state, Sotomayor argued, joined by Ginsburg, is that government cannot tax citizens and then give the money to houses of worship. "The Court today blinds itself to the outcome this history requires and leads us instead to a place where separation of church and state is a constitutional slogan, not a constitutional commitment."

IN JUNE 2017, AS ROBERTS WAS FINISHING THE *TRINITY LUTHERAN* decision, he was participating in two significant ceremonial events, one personal, one at the Court. On June 3, his son Jack graduated from ninth grade at the Cardigan Mountain School, a boys' boarding school in New Hampshire. After working on the text of his speech for weeks and enlisting Jane, his wife, for ideas, Roberts delivered a commencement address that went viral. It showed a more compassionate side of the chief justice.

"From time to time in the years to come," Roberts told the schoolboys, "I hope you will be treated unfairly, so you will know the value of justice. I hope that you will suffer betrayal, because that will teach you the importance of loyalty. . . . And when you lose, as you will from time to time, I hope every now and then your opponent will gloat over your failure. It is a way for you to understand the importance of sportsmanship. I hope you will be ignored, so you know the importance of listening to others. And I hope you will have just enough pain to learn compassion."[33]

Two weeks later, the chief presided over the Court's traditional, brief, but highly staged investiture for its newest justice. Gorsuch had taken his judicial oath earlier, in a small private ceremony in April. But this was the event that made use of a special chair that had belonged to Chief Justice John Marshall during the early nineteenth century. The chair had been brought out for investitures of new justices since 1972. President Trump and First Lady Melania were among the dignitaries attending, as was retired justice John Paul Stevens. Roberts acknowledged those three guests at the outset of the ceremony, saying to Stevens, "Welcome back."

It was Gorsuch's moment, and yet the audience was filled with men who had begun their service in the Reagan administration, and who had been in Roberts's orbit for most of his time in Washington. They had inspired him, groomed him, chosen him. They included Ken Starr, who had given Roberts his first job in the Reagan administration; Fred Fielding, the former White House counsel and longtime Roberts mentor; Alberto Gonzales, the Bush attorney general who had first interviewed Roberts in the Supreme Court selection process; and Senator Mitch McConnell, who had ensured that the Scalia seat remained open for a Republican appointee, guaranteeing that Roberts kept a conservative majority.

They were all part of the process that had, twelve years earlier, helped Roberts to his position in the center chair. Now the conservative, Federalist Society–fueled movement was even more influential in Washington than it had been when he was appointed, and it had delivered Gorsuch.

During the official swearing-in ceremony, which lasted a mere six minutes, Roberts welcomed Gorsuch as the 101st associate justice. Gorsuch was actually the 113th justice of the Supreme Court, but, of course, Roberts and his top aides had begun separately enumerating the associate justices and the chief justices. It was likely that few of the people in the room marked any significance in the number. But for some colleagues, it was a reminder that the chief justice wanted to separate himself from them, or, as he had put it as a young boy, that he "wanted to stay ahead of the crowd."

CHAPTER XIII

THE ROBERTS COURT IN THE TRUMP ERA

I N HIS FIRST YEARS AS PRESIDENT, DONALD TRUMP DISRUPTED the nation's constitutional norms. He revealed disdain for due process of law, proclaimed criminal suspects guilty before trial, and urged police to rough up those they had arrested. He belittled federal judges, and he extended his first presidential pardon to former Arizona sheriff Joe Arpaio, who had been convicted of criminal contempt after targeting Latinos for traffic stops and detention. He instituted extreme measures to stop immigrants from crossing the southern border and seeking asylum, including separating families and placing traumatized children in holding centers. All the while, Trump and several of his associates were under scrutiny by a Department of Justice special counsel investigating Russia's interference in America's 2016 presidential campaign. President Trump repeatedly called the investigation "a witch hunt."[1]

Chief Justice Roberts at first said nothing publicly about any of these episodes, or about Trump's attempts to undermine the legitimacy of the nation's judges. Roberts tried to separate the man from the office of the presidency. His decision to take that approach became clear in the spring of 2018 when the Supreme Court heard a challenge to a travel ban that Trump had instituted against certain Muslim-majority countries. The refugee groups and states that had brought the lawsuit claimed that the immigration restrictions were based on unlawful bias, pointing to Trump's anti-Muslim rhetoric during the presidential campaign to bolster their arguments. (On his campaign website, Trump had called for "a total and complete shutdown of Muslims entering the United States until our country's representatives can figure out what is going on.") During the Court's oral arguments, a dubious Roberts asked whether campaign statements could be used against a president "for the rest of the administration" or could be subject to "a statute of limitations." He suggested, through his remarks at oral arguments, that President Trump could validly claim he was addressing a terrorist threat.[2]

Presiding over a deeply divided bench, Roberts, who by then was sixty-three years old, appeared determined to treat Trump as he would any other president. This was so even as Trump's words and actions compromised the notion of judicial impartiality that has been at the center of Roberts's worldview and self-image for decades. An overriding question, as the Supreme Court finished its first full term with all nine members since Scalia's death, was whether the Court or its chief justice would present a challenge to Trump in any way as the president shattered legal norms.

Roberts was in his thirteenth term as chief justice, which meant he had already served longer than half of his sixteen predecessors in the federal judiciary's top position. The seasons of his home life were moving swiftly. His daughter, Josie, was in her senior year of high school and ready for college. His son, Jack, had moved to a new boarding school and had another two years of high school to go. The chief justice's mother, Rosemary Roberts, was nearing ninety and in declining health. On multiple fronts, the chief justice was taking stock. He had agreed to offer the commencement address at Josie's all-girls' Catholic prep school, Stone Ridge School of the Sacred Heart in Bethesda, Maryland. A year earlier, he had appeared at Jack's ninth-grade graduation from the Cardigan Mountain School in New Hampshire. He had spoken compellingly about how life's setbacks offered lessons, and the speech had drawn more than four hundred thousand views on YouTube. That speech would be hard to top, or even equal, and he knew it. Roberts was working on new themes for Josie's school related to the downside of technology and the rapid pace of a modern life that leaves little time for reflection.[3]

On the bench, Roberts had demonstrated two overriding—and often conflicting—priorities. One was institutional. He wanted high public regard for the Court as an independent branch separate from the other two and cordoned off from politics. The other derived from his interest in changing the Court's role in racial, religious, and other social dilemmas. Roberts's dissenting opinion from the Court's 2015 decision to uphold same-sex marriage still reverberated: "Just who do we think we are?" he had said in protest of the majority's view that the Court should ensure equal treatment of gay men and lesbians who want to marry.[4]

Roberts's long-standing conservatism, especially on race, aligned with the Trump administration's. Soon after Trump had taken office, his lawyers had reversed the federal government's opposition to a Texas voter-identification law—a statute for which Roberts himself had shown support. The administration also sided with Edward Blum and other conservative advocates challenging Harvard's race-based affirmative action policies in admissions. It was Blum who had arranged for the plaintiffs and the legal funding for the Supreme Court case against the Voting Rights Act in *Shelby County v. Holder*, and for the case against the University of Texas's racial-diversity admissions practice in *Fisher v. University of Texas at Austin*.[5]

Perhaps because of the atmosphere of Trump upheaval, or the shifting relations caused by the newest justice, Gorsuch, or Roberts's continued inability to win the personal confidence of his colleagues, conflicts among the justices intensified. Roberts could engage in sly insults in their private sessions, but he usually kept them in check while presiding on the bench. In February 2018, however, Roberts uncharacteristically lashed out in the very public setting of oral arguments. The incident occurred not in a case over a combustible subject like race, but in a relatively minor one that had drawn few journalists to the press section that day, and it was Justice Breyer who drew his ire. It occurred at a time when the justices were stalled on several cases and ensnarled in back-room discussions over immigration, abortion, and other fractious issues.[6]

The case, *City of Hays, Kansas, v. Vogt*, concerned a former police officer's Fifth Amendment right against self-incrimination. Officer Matthew Vogt, working at the time for the City of Hays, had applied for a job with a different police department. That process required Vogt to divulge to the City of Hays an incident involving his possession of a knife, and the city subsequently turned the information over to state criminal investigators. Vogt received a job offer from the new department, but it was then withdrawn because of the criminal investigation. Vogt ended up without a job in either department. He sued the City of Hays for damages, saying compelled statements had been used against him, violating his Fifth Amendment rights. A US district court judge said the Fifth Amendment only applied to a criminal trial, not a preliminary hearing. The US Court of Appeals for the Tenth Circuit reversed, finding that the Fifth Amendment protects beyond trial proceedings. The legal question for the Supreme Court was important because, as Justice Ginsburg observed during oral arguments, the great majority of criminal cases are resolved without a trial. Under the city's contention, Ginsburg told the City of Hays lawyer, "you are shrinking to almost a vanishing point the possibility of using the Fifth Amendment. . . . [Y]ou're shrinking the privilege to nothing because there aren't many trials nowadays; upwards of 95 percent of cases are disposed by plea bargaining."[7]

The conflict between Roberts and Breyer was sparked by Breyer's attempt to find out what information had been used against Vogt. As Breyer began asking Vogt's lawyer about the particulars of the officer's testimony at a preliminary investigative hearing, Breyer acknowledged that what he wanted to know "may not be in the record."

"But that's an important point, isn't it?" Roberts interjected as he urged Breyer not to go beyond the record of the case. Breyer said he was trying to figure out if the justices had grounds to take up the case, given the uncertainty over the "compelled statements."

"Well, before we start having an extended exchange about material and something that's not in the record," Roberts continued, "I would just like to point out that it's not in the record." The chief justice warned that facts not in the record could be of questionable reliability. Roberts also suggested by his questions that the Court had sufficient information to reverse the lower appeals court's interpretation of the Fifth Amendment without confirming exactly what had happened to Officer Vogt.

"It's not just a passing comment that it's not in the record," Roberts added, implying that Breyer was not taking him sufficiently seriously.

"Nor is actually mine a passing comment," Breyer rejoined, refusing to back down, "because Article III of the Constitution says we are to take real cases and controversies." The lawyer representing Vogt tried to speak, but she was barely able to add a "But . . . " or "Yeah . . . " as Roberts and Breyer challenged each other. Breyer expressed concern that the justices were being asked to decide a major Fifth Amendment dispute that might lack a self-incriminating piece of evidence. But Roberts would not let it go. "As far as I'm concerned, coming in and saying I want to know about this thing that's not in the record is no different from somebody else coming off the street and saying: Hey, wait a minute, I know what happened in this case."

It was jarring to hear the chief justice liken a colleague to someone "coming off the street." Roberts capped off his comments by saying: "I will discount the answers [to Justice Breyer] because it's not something that's in the record."

In the end, it appeared that Breyer's concerns may have been valid. Three months after it was heard, the Court dismissed the case as improvidently granted. The order left in place the Tenth Circuit decision reviving Vogt's civil suit and more broadly interpreting the protections of the Fifth Amendment.[8]

It was an unusually difficult session, as many cases were decided by a single vote, with conservatives in the majority and liberals protesting vociferously. Kennedy aligned with the conservatives throughout the term and would not once cast his vote with the four liberals to give them a majority. At the time that Roberts had erupted at Breyer on the bench, Breyer in fact had been writing a caustic dissenting opinion to a five-justice majority in a case involving immigrants seeking asylum in the United States. The question in *Jennings v. Rodriguez* was whether people held in immigrant detention centers were entitled to periodic review for possible bail. Roberts and the four other conservatives in the majority said such hearings were not required under federal law. The ruling, reversing a decision by the US Court of Appeals for the Ninth Circuit, marked the first time the Court had interpreted a statute to allow indefinite detention for someone accused, but not convicted, of wrongdoing. Roberts assigned the opinion to Alito, who wrote that the language of the statute simply did not require bail hearings after an initial review. When Alito finished detailing that position on the morning of February 27, 2018, Breyer read a lengthy excerpt of the dissent, insisting that permitting no periodical bail review for asylum seekers and other individuals who are not serving criminal sentences necessarily violated constitutional due process, a question the majority had not taken on, as it confined the decision to the validity of the statute. "The Fifth Amendment says that '[n]o person shall be . . . deprived of life, liberty, or property without due process of law,'" Breyer observed, "An alien is a 'person.' To hold him without bail is to deprive him of bodily 'liberty.' And, where there is no bail proceeding, there has been no bail-related 'process' at all."[9]

Privately, the justices expressed regret that the collegiality that had developed when they were at just eight justices was fading. Roberts became concerned at reports of rivalrics, particularly involving the newest justice, Gorsuch, who tangled in particular with Ginsburg, both on the bench and in opinions. Gorsuch was subject to an unusual amount of academic and media scrutiny. Law professors poked fun at his lofty, sometimes exaggerated tone under the Twitter hashtag #GorsuchStyle. *New York Times* Supreme Court correspondent Adam Liptak observed that Gorsuch "arrived at the Supreme Court last year with a reputation as a fine writer. He promptly lost it."[10]

During a partisan gerrymandering case from Wisconsin, *Gill v. Whitford*, Gorsuch was apparently frustrated with the line of questioning from his colleagues and said, perhaps ironically, "Maybe we can just for a second talk about the arcane matter, the Constitution. Where exactly do we get authority to revise state legislative lines?" Ginsburg was not going to let Gorsuch's comment pass. "Where did one-person, one-vote come from?" she said, less as a question than as an obvious reference to landmark rulings in the 1960s that permitted the Court to intervene in state redistricting based on the Fourteenth Amendment's guarantee of equal protection. The lawyer at the lectern who was protesting the partisan gerrymander immediately cited voting rights precedents.[11]

With the Court moving rightward, Ginsburg, then eighty-five, ramped up her provocative dissents. This came as she was observing her twenty-fifth anniversary on the court and reveling in the attention from fans, who had adopted an Internet meme of "Notorious RBG." The play on the late rapper Notorious B.I.G. had been generated after her 2013 dissent in *Shelby County v. Holder*, when Ginsburg had condemned the majority for rolling back voting-rights protections. Her dissenting opinions in the five years since had elevated the former women's rights advocate to icon status, particularly for liberals and young women.

When the nine justices divided again along ideological lines in a contest over a provision of the Fair Labor Standards Act, Ginsburg went so far as to declare that the New Deal was under attack. The case, *Encino Motorcars, LLC v. Navarro*, could easily have escaped notice because of the obscure question before the Court. The provision at issue specifically exempted certain employees from overtime pay, including "any salesman, partsman, or mechanic primarily engaged in selling or servicing automobiles, trucks, or farm implements." The question was whether service advisers who consulted with customers were similarly exempt or not. Automobile service advisers at a California Mercedes-Benz dealership had brought the case, and the San Francisco–based Ninth Circuit had ruled that the advisers could claim overtime.

The Supreme Court's conservatives produced a majority to rule the opposite, narrowly interpreting fair labor standards and rejecting a 2011 Labor Department regulation that allowed the overtime. The Trump administration, which had newly reversed that 2011 regulation, argued before the Supreme Court on the side of the automobile industry against the overtime. Joined by the usual three liberal justices, Ginsburg wrote that the conservative majority was undermining worker protections from the 1930s "without even acknowledging that it unsettled more than a half century of our precedent."[12]

The next month, the majority again ruled against workers, but in a more substantial wage dispute, *Epic Systems Corp. v. Lewis*, in which Ginsburg produced an even fiercer dissent. "Nothing compels the destructive result the Court reaches today," she said from the bench, adding, in her written opinion, that the majority was "egregiously wrong" in turning its back on eighty years of labor law.[13]

The majority had determined that employees who had been forced to sign arbitration contracts as a condition of their hiring could not band together to initiate a class-action complaint against employers who underpaid them. The employees had sued under the Fair Labor Standards Act. Roberts assigned the majority opinion to the new justice, Gorsuch, who asserted that the straightforward text of another law, the Federal Arbitration Act, required individualized proceedings, rather than collective class actions.

Ginsburg insisted that federal law protected aggrieved workers from such "isolation" and declared that the Court was inviting a new era of "yellow dog" contracts, that is, contracts in which employers require workers to agree not to join unions as a condition of employment. Gorsuch fired back in his opinion, "Like most apocalyptic warnings, this one proves a false alarm. . . . Those [union] rights stand every bit as strong today as they did yesterday."[14]

Their differences were fundamental, beginning with their contrasting views of how much choice an employee even had regarding how workplace disputes would be resolved. Gorsuch opened his opinion by asking, "Should employees and employers be allowed to agree that any disputes between them will be resolved through one-on-one arbitration?" Ginsburg believed no choice, no real "agreement," was possible because employers unilaterally dictated the terms. The choice, she suggested, was to accept the employer's terms or to lose the job.[15]

AGAINST THE BACKDROP OF THE TRUMP ADMINISTRATION'S VISION of the law and the evolution of democratic norms, two of the 5–4 rulings with perhaps the greatest salience involved voting rights. The first, from Ohio, tested when a state could purge citizens from the voting rolls. In this case, *Husted v. A. Philip Randolph Institute*, residents had been dropped from the voting rolls in a process triggered by the fact that they had not voted for two years. Because of historical efforts in some states to kick voters off the rolls if they moved or failed to cast a ballot, federal law since 1993 had specifically barred removing voters because of a failure to vote. Chief Justice Roberts, along with the four other conservative justices, believed the Ohio law was valid because it did not use the failure to vote as the sole criterion for removing a person from the rolls.[16]

Under the Ohio law, once the process of removing a citizen from the voter rolls was triggered, a postcard was sent to the citizen, who was thus given the opportunity to respond and alert officials that he or she had not moved. If the postcard was not returned and the citizen failed to vote for four more years, he or she was removed from the rolls and forced to reregister before again casting a ballot. The Obama administration had joined the challenge to the law as it headed to the Supreme Court, but when Trump won the White House, the federal government switched positions and sided with Ohio in defense of the voter-purge law.

Endorsing Ohio, the majority declared that a citizen's failure to return the postcard, combined with absence from the polls, constituted sufficient evidence of a move and legitimate grounds for removal from voter rolls.

Liberal dissenters invoked the nation's history of racial discrimination, poll taxes, literacy tests, and other electoral practices that kept blacks and the members of other racial minority groups from voting. Justice Sotomayor then penned a separate dissent to underscore such concerns. The Court's only Hispanic referred to a "backdrop of substantial efforts by States to disenfranchise low-income and minority voters."

Justice Alito, who had written for the majority and had seen drafts of Sotomayor's dissent as the opinions circulated before decision day, addressed her views in his opinion for the majority. "Justice Sotomayor's dissent says nothing about what is relevant in this case," he said, "namely, the language of the [National Voter Registration Act of 1993]—but instead accuses us of 'ignoring the history of voter suppression' in this country and of 'upholding a program that appears to further the . . . disenfranchisement of minority and low-income voters.' Those charges are misconceived."

Those themes, with Alito again for the majority and Sotomayor again in dissent, were repeated later in June 2018 as the Court upheld Texas congressional and legislative districts that a lower court had declared to be discriminatory against Latinos. The majority swept aside concerns about racial discrimination and reinforced the familiar message that Roberts had espoused: that states must be free to determine their own voting maps and election practices. The Court's action happened to come on the exact five-year anniversary of *Shelby County v. Holder*, when the justices had rolled back a provision of the 1965 Voting Rights Act that had required states with a history of racial bias to clear any redistricting or other electoral change with the Justice Department or a federal court.

The Texas case, *Abbott v. Perez*, began after the 2010 census as the state drew new legislative maps. The dispute involved districts that a lower court had determined denied Latinos an equal opportunity to elect candidates of their choice. The Supreme Court majority emphasized the many federal requirements Texas had faced through the years and the protracted litigation the state had endured. Alito wrote that the record failed to prove that the state legislature, when it redrew districts, had acted in bad faith or intentionally discriminated. To get to that conclusion, the high court majority undertook a fresh review of the evidence which the dissenters said usurped lower court judges.[17]

Justice Sotomayor, joined by Ginsburg, Breyer, and Kagan, said the majority was ignoring the factual record. Sotomayor observed that the lower court had found that political processes were "not equally open to Hispanics" in Texas because of its "history of official discrimination," touching on the right of Hispanics to register, vote, and otherwise participate in the democratic process. She repeated her admonition from the Ohio voter-purge case: "Our democracy rests on the ability of all individuals, regardless of race, income, or status, to exercise their right to vote."

Sotomayor also focused on Roberts's vision of racial harmony and his opinion that, as he had written in *Shelby County v. Holder*, "things [had] changed dramatically" since 1965 when Congress passed the act ensuring that blacks and Hispanics could exercise their constitutional right to vote. She threw another line from his *Shelby County* opinion back at him: "Voting discrimination still exists; no one doubts that."

The two sides plainly differed in their perceptions of discrimination in America and the Court's role when state governments perpetuated that discrimination. And when it came to the right to vote, conservatives were more apt to raise concerns about voter fraud; liberals, about voter suppression.

Regard for precedent is the cornerstone of America's legal system. When the law is stable, people understand their rights and responsibilities. That is why the topic of precedent has played such a central role in the questioning during Senate Judiciary Committee hearings for Supreme Court nominees, and why the high court's final decision of the 2017–2018 session provided such a jolt. In *Janus v. American Federation of State, County, and Municipal Employees, Council 31*, the narrow conservative majority reversed a four-decade-old precedent, undercutting the authority of labor unions and firmly siding with the Trump administration. The high court's 1977 ruling in *Abood v. Detroit Board of Education* said states could permit public-sector labor unions to collect from non-members the share of union dues that go toward collective bargaining. Big businesses and other anti-union forces had long argued that these fees impinged on the free-speech rights of non-members. The unions (and twenty-two states that had laws authorizing the "fair share" fees) believed the funds vital to unions that necessarily represented all employees in a workforce. The fees could go only to collective bargaining for wage, hours, and other working conditions, not to support union political activities. States said it was more efficient to bargain with a single union than to have to negotiate with a number of entities or individual workers.

Mark Janus, a child support specialist in the Illinois Department of Healthcare and Family Services, sued over a union requirement that he pay union fees even though he was not a member. Under a collective bargaining deal detailed in the Court's opinion, Janus was required to pay agency fees of about $535 a year.

The union had prevailed in the lower court based on the justices' 1977 precedent, and during oral arguments at the Supreme Court, the union's lawyer told the justices that if they reversed the 1977 *Abood*, they would be spelling the demise of unions: "What we know is that tangibly, when these kinds of obligations of financial support become voluntary, union membership goes down, union density rates go down, union resources go down," he said. "We've seen it again and again. . . . We also know that, intangibly, there are plenty of studies that show that when unions are deprived of agency fees, they tend to become more militant, more confrontational, they go out in search of short-term gains that they can bring back to their members and say stick with us."[18]

"Well," interjected Roberts, "the argument on the other side, of course, is that the need to attract voluntary payments will make the unions more efficient, more effective, more attractive to a broader group of their employees."

Roberts and the other four conservative justices decided the time was right to reverse precedent, and the four liberals dissented. On the basic First Amendment question, Alito, writing for the majority, said the state's extraction of agency fees from non-members essentially forced them to endorse ideas they found objectionable. He justified reversal of *Abood*, saying the case had been "poorly reasoned" and "inconsistent with other First Amendment cases."

Justice Kagan, who spoke for the four liberal dissenters, accused the majority of overruling *Abood* "for no exceptional or special reason, but because it never liked the decision. It overruled *Abood* because it wanted to." She insisted that having a single union in the workplace was more efficient for management. "The majority overthrows a decision entrenched in this Nation's law—and its economic life—for over 40 years," she wrote. "As a result, it prevents the American people, acting through their state and local officials, from making important choices about workplace governance. And it does so by weaponizing the First Amendment, in a way that unleashes judges, now and in the future, to intervene in economic and regulatory policy."

Roberts did not write separately to counter that assertion. As he had done so many times on contentious cases, he left it to Alito. But it just so happened that a week before the *Janus* decision, Roberts had addressed the importance of precedent when dissenting from a decision overturning a 1992 case that had prevented states from taxing out-of-state businesses that sold merchandise to in-state residents. "This Court does not overturn its precedents lightly," Roberts wrote. He noted that the Court had previously been asked twice to allow states to force sellers with no physical presence within their borders to collect tax on sales to residents, and twice had declined the request. "Whatever salience the adage 'third time's a charm' has in daily life," he wrote, "it is a poor guide to Supreme Court decisionmaking."[19]

ROBERTS DID TAKE THE LEAD FOR THE MAJORITY IN THE EQUALLY divisive dispute of *Trump v. Hawaii*, the most anticipated case of the first full session with President Trump's first appointee, Gorsuch. The question was whether President Trump's effort to restrict immigration from certain Muslim-majority countries violated federal immigration law and First Amendment protections based on religious freedom.[20]

During oral arguments, Roberts employed a hypothetical line of questioning related to a president's ability to address national security concerns. Speaking to lawyer Neal Katyal, who represented refugee organizations and states that had sued the government, Roberts said, "Let's suppose that the intelligence agencies go to the President and say, we have 100 percent solid information that, on a particular day, 20 nationals from Syria are going to enter the United States with chemical and biological weapons. . . . [C]ould the President ban the entry of Syrian nationals on that one day?" Katyal resisted the hypothetical, responding that the president would be able to involve Congress. But Roberts persisted. He wanted Katyal to assess the possibility of a president's unilateral action. "We understand the President will have residual authority to keep the country safe," Katyal insisted.

But Roberts was not persuaded, and in the last week of June he announced the Court's decision upholding Trump's order restricting people from designated Muslim-majority countries. Joined by Kennedy, Thomas, Alito, and Gorsuch, Roberts maintained the Court must look past what Trump had said and consider the executive's power over immigration. "This is an act that could have been taken by any other president," he wrote.[21]

He referred to prior presidents' orders suspending the entry of certain foreigners, including a 1986 proclamation involving Cuban nationals by President Ronald Reagan. Trump's twelve-page order contained more details of agency evaluations than prior presidential orders, Roberts said, suggesting that enhanced its legitimacy. By the time the Court ruled, the Trump ban covered the Muslim-majority countries of Iran, Libya, Somalia, Syria, and Yemen as well as North Korea and Venezuela. Roberts noted that those challenging the travel ban believed that Trump's anti-Muslim statements violated America's commitment to tolerance, as well as federal immigration law and the Constitution's protection for religious liberty. "But," he wrote, "the issue before us is not whether to denounce the statements. We must consider not only the statements of a particular president, but the authority of the presidency itself."

In dissent, Sotomayor, joined by Justice Ginsburg, acknowledged that Roberts's opinion recounted some of Trump's inflammatory statements. But, she declared, that "does not tell even half of the story." In one of the more captivating courtroom moments, Sotomayor paused after reading Trump's insults against Muslims aloud, including "Islam hates us," and, "We're having trouble with Muslims coming into the country." "Take a brief moment," she said, "and let the gravity of those statements sink in." She emphasized that such hostility had not been expressed by just anyone. It was the man who had become president of the United States. "Our Constitution demands, and our country deserves," Sotomayor wrote in her opinion, "a judiciary willing to hold the coordinate branches to account when they defy our most sacred legal commitments."[22]

Justices Breyer and Kagan also dissented, separately and less critically, noting that the executive branch usually enjoyed expansive authority over immigration rules. Kennedy also wrote a separate statement in the case. In a two-page opinion concurring with the Roberts majority view, he declared that Trump's statements, while not legally determinative, could still matter. "An anxious world must know that our Government remains committed always to the liberties the Constitution seeks to preserve and protect," Kennedy wrote, "so that freedom extends outward, and lasts."

Yet Kennedy's bottom-line vote went to Trump. For all of Roberts's concern about the appearance of partisanship, the Court could not avoid a decision that pit the five Republican appointees against the four Democratic ones.

DESPITE THE CONTENTIOUS CASES, A VENEER OF COOPERATION emerged in some areas. They may have represented the last of Kennedy's centrist conservatism as he deferred more to Roberts in the spring of 2018, perhaps in a sign of the transition Kennedy was about to make.

Three years after the justices had declared a constitutional right to same-sex marriage, over Roberts's dissent, the justices took up a new case at the intersection of gay rights and religious interests. Wanting a special cake to celebrate their marriage, Charlie Craig and David Mullins had met with Jack Phillips, the owner of Masterpiece Cakeshop, at his shop in Lakewood, Colorado, to discuss ordering a cake. Once Phillips realized what the occasion was, he said baking a cake for them would violate the principles of his Christian religion. Craig and Mullins filed an administrative grievance with the Colorado Civil Rights Commission, which barred discrimination based on sexual orientation. The couple prevailed, and state courts upheld the Civil Rights Commission's order. Phillips turned to federal court, arguing that being forced to provide a wedding cake to a gay couple violated his federal constitutional right to freedom of speech and the free exercise of religion.

When the case came to the Supreme Court, in *Masterpiece Cakeshop v. Colorado Civil Rights Commission*, Chief Justice Roberts, during oral arguments, expressed sympathy for Phillips and fears that a Catholic legal group could lose its state license if it did not provide services in connection with same-sex marriage. Roberts also brushed aside an argument likening states' long-held ability to protect against race discrimination to the effort to protect against bias based on sexual orientation. "The racial analogy obviously is very compelling," Roberts said, but "when the Court upheld same-sex marriage in *Obergefell*, it went out of its way to talk about the decent and honorable people who may have opposing views. And to immediately lump them in the same group as people who are opposed to equality in relations with respect to race, I'm not sure that takes full account of that concept in the *Obergefell* decision."[23]

Justice Kennedy voiced similar concerns. "Tolerance is essential in a free society," he said. "And tolerance is most meaningful when it's mutual. It seems to me that the state in its position here has been neither tolerant nor respectful of Mr. Phillips's religious beliefs." Kennedy homed in on comments made at the commission hearing that appeared to denigrate Phillips's Christianity. Roberts reinforced that view, observing that a single biased member of any panel can affect the decision of all members.[24]

In the end, unlike in the 2015 *Obergefell* decision declaring a right to same-sex marriage, in *Masterpiece Cakeshop* Roberts and Kennedy were on the same side. Kennedy was interested in a narrow ruling this time, and in finding that Phillips's religious rights had been violated, he stressed that the Colorado Civil Rights Commission had revealed "a clear and impermissible hostility toward the sincere religious beliefs that motivated his objection" to creating the cake. Kennedy noted that during a hearing on the issue, a commissioner had disparaged Phillips by asserting that religion had been used to justify slavery and the Holocaust. "This sentiment is inappropriate for a Commission charged with the solemn responsibility of fair and neutral enforcement of Colorado's anti-discrimination law," Kennedy wrote, "—a law that protects against discrimination on the basis of religion as well as sexual orientation." In addition to the chief justice, Kennedy was joined by Breyer, Alito, Kagan, and Gorsuch. Thomas concurred in the judgment, and Ginsburg and Sotomayor dissented.[25]

It was striking how little Kennedy chose to rely on the *Obergefell* landmark. The few references he made to his opinion related to the need to protect religion. "As this Court observed in *Obergefell v. Hodges*," he wrote in *Masterpiece Cakeshop*, "'the First Amendment ensures that religious organizations and persons are given proper protection as they seek to teach

the principles that are so fulfilling and so central to their lives and faiths.'"
Justice Thomas, concurring, injected Roberts's sentiment from his 2015
dissent: "'It is one thing . . . to conclude that the Constitution protects a
right to same-sex marriage; it is something else to portray everyone who
does not share [that view] as bigoted' and unentitled to express a different
view," Thomas wrote. He added, "This Court is not an authority on matters of conscience, and its decisions can (and often should) be criticized.
The First Amendment gives individuals the right to disagree about the
correctness of *Obergefell* and the morality of same-sex marriage."

The two dissenting justices, Ginsburg and Sotomayor, had been increasingly alone on the left. They said that statements from the Colorado
Civil Rights Commission meeting should not have influenced the Court.
"What matters," Ginsburg wrote, "is that Phillips would not provide a
good or service to a same-sex couple that he would provide to a heterosexual couple."

Another Court compromise—this time with Roberts in even greater
control—emerged from the case testing partisan gerrymandering in Wisconsin, *Gill v. Whitford*. Again, it was in an area of the law that Kennedy's
vote and middle-ground view had dictated the outcome of in the past,
and, again, the terms were set by Roberts rather than by Kennedy.

The Wisconsin gerrymandering dispute arose from the decennial practice that occurs across the country as state legislatures draw new political
districts after each census, apportioning members of a state senate and
house based on population numbers. With the use of modern software and
sophisticated data collection, it was becoming a fact of American politics
that whichever party controlled a legislature at the time of redistricting
could entrench itself in power for an entire decade. The Wisconsin case
began after the 2010 elections, as Republicans had taken full control of
the state's house and senate as well as the governor's office. Legislators had
enacted a redistricting plan that maximized Republican votes throughout
the state and diluted the power of Democratic voters. The method was
called "packing and cracking," a reference to how the voters of one party
were consolidated ("packed") into districts where their candidates were
likely to prevail by a great majority, which effectively wasted votes, while

in other regions of the state they were divided ("cracked") among multiple districts, so they would have little chance of victory in these districts.

Democratic Party leaders from Wisconsin contended that the state's partisan gerrymander was so extreme that it violated the Fourteenth Amendment equality guarantee and First Amendment rights related to party affiliation. State Republican officials and the Trump administration argued that there was no role for judges in the politically charged map-drawing process. Wisconsin's GOP leaders also insisted that they had abided by traditional redistricting principles in drawing the state maps. A federal trial court sided with the Democrats challenging the gerrymander. "Whatever gray may span the area between acceptable and excessive," the lower court panel wrote in *Whitford v. Gill*, "an intent to entrench a political party in power signals an excessive injection of politics into the redistricting process that impinges on the representational rights of those associated with the party out of power."[26]

The lower court thus found that the map produced by packing and cracking "reduced markedly the possibility" that Democrats could regain control of the statehouse even if they had a majority of the statewide vote. When the Wisconsin appeal came before Supreme Court justices, the crucial question was whether the Court could even wade into the matter. Three decades earlier, in the 1986 case *Davis v. Bandemer*, the Court had ruled that such disputes could be reviewed—but the justices had never set a standard or found a political gerrymander so extreme as to be invalid. In 2004, the Court's decision in another case, *Vieth v. Jubelirer*, again kept the door open to such claims but without any standard for assessing whether a gerrymander went too far. In *Vieth*, Kennedy had suggested that First Amendment grounds were at stake. "After all," he wrote then, "these allegations involve the First Amendment interest of not burdening or penalizing citizens because of their participation in the electoral process, their voting history, their association with a political party, or their expression of political views."[27]

During oral arguments in *Gill v. Whitford*, the Wisconsin case, Roberts expressed concern for what people would think if the judges continually weighed in on redistricting disputes. "If you're the intelligent man on the street," Roberts said, "and the Court issues a decision, and let's say the Democrats win. . . . That person will say, 'Well, why did the Democrats win?' . . . The intelligent man on the street is going to say . . . it must be because the Supreme Court preferred the Democrats over the Republicans. . . . And that is going to cause very serious harm to the status and integrity of the decisions of this Court in the eyes of the country."

Representing the Wisconsin challengers, lawyer Paul Smith said the risk to democracy would be greater if the Court stayed out of the dispute. "And it may be that you can protect the Court from seeming political, but the country is going to lose faith in democracy big time because voters are going to be like[,] . . . 'It really doesn't matter whether I vote.'"

In the end, Roberts had an easy way to avoid the question. All nine justices concluded that the challengers had not demonstrated legal "standing" to sue because they had not shown individual harm within their legislative districts. The justices therefore declined to answer the more significant question of whether federal judges could ever take up constitutional claims to the partisan gerrymanders proliferating across a polarized America. "This Court," Roberts wrote, "is not responsible for vindicating generalized partisan preferences. The Court's constitutionally prescribed role is to vindicate the individual rights of people appearing before it." As he returned the case to the lower court in Wisconsin, Roberts said the plaintiffs must prove "concrete and particularized" injury to their individual votes.[28]

The justices then divided sharply in their vision for future cases over partisan gerrymanders. Justice Elena Kagan, writing for the four liberal justices and warning of the "evils of gerrymandering" for democracy, tried to offer a road map for future plaintiffs to prove injury on multiple constitutional grounds. She laid out ways that individuals could prove standing based on their constitutional right to equal protection and their right to free association. Roberts responded that her opinion did not matter and should not be followed in future cases. "The reasoning of this Court with respect to the disposition of this case is set forth in this opinion and none other," he said, referring to his own opinion.

For her concurring statement, Kagan had drawn on prior opinions by Kennedy. But he declined to join her effort to advance the notion that a partisan gerrymander claim could be based on a First Amendment right of free association. He wrote nothing.

THROUGHOUT THE SESSION, KENNEDY HAD PULLED BACK. FOR THE previous two years, since 2016 when he turned eighty, speculation about his possible retirement had been constant among Supreme Court lawyers, politicians in Washington, and the news media. His single vote had preserved abortion rights and university affirmative action and established a right to same-sex marriage. He was often the decisive vote in criminal procedure and death penalty disputes. The timing of his retirement would significantly affect the nation.

Kennedy kept his own counsel. Once he made the decision in the late spring of 2018, he told so few people that most of his colleagues were surprised when he broke the news to them on the last day of the session. He said he wanted to spend more time with his wife, Mary. They had known each other since their shared childhood in Sacramento, and both had increasingly suffered from health problems.

Public attention turned immediately to Trump's choice of a possible successor, US Appeals Court Judge Brett Kavanaugh, and how much more conservative the bench would become. Roberts and Kavanaugh had trod similar paths through preparatory schools and Ivy League campuses, and then in their professional lives. They had been friendly since working together in the George H.W. Bush administration's Office of Solicitor General. Both served on the DC Circuit and at times played poker with a tight group of judges and lawyers.

Roberts would now be the member of the conservative bloc closest to the center. But he would be no "swing vote" like Kennedy, whose flexible approach meant the four liberals had a chance to attract his vote.

New influence for Roberts brought a new predicament: With the majority pointed firmly in one direction, how could the chief justice still insist that judging had nothing to do with politics? The Court's reputation could depend on him—and how he cast his vote and steered all nine.

EPILOGUE

A s the Supreme Court was finishing the most difficult cases of its annual session in June 2018, I went to see Chief Justice John Roberts in his chambers. It was near the end of the first full term with nine justices following the death of Antonin Scalia and the lengthy interval of only eight. The fault lines on the Court had shifted with the 2017 appointment of Neil Gorsuch by President Trump. Negotiations were tense as the justices faced end-of-term deadlines, and they were dividing narrowly on their rulings. It was also a poignant time for Roberts at home. The day before our visit, he had delivered the commencement address at his daughter's private Catholic high school. Josie would be headed to Harvard, just as, forty-five years earlier, Roberts had after graduating from La Lumiere. He had left a Catholic prep school and his home in northern Indiana for a path that had ultimately led to the highest echelon of the law.

As the chief justice led me to the sitting area in his office suite where we normally talked, he cut through the Supreme Court's private conference room. That was unusual. Roberts's standard practice was to take me down a side hall and through a separate entrance to the sitting room. He considered the conference room, where the justices privately discuss and vote on cases, off limits, a nearly sacred place. The high-ceilinged, oak-paneled room felt bigger than what I had seen in photos. The rectangular table at which the nine sat seemed larger. Around it were the black leather chairs with each justice's nameplate on the back. It would not be until a few days later that I would discover what cases had been most recently resolved around that table and the many ways in which Roberts had prevailed. The Court had decided to give states more leeway to control elections and voting rights; to diminish the power of labor unions; and to endorse President Trump's actions to limit immigration.

There is an innate mystery to America's highest court. Cases are decided and written in nine cloistered chambers. Sometimes a decision—which is determined not only by bottom-line votes but by legal reasoning—goes through draft after draft, teetering from one side to the other until the very end of the process. Once a decision is issued, the public sees only the final compromise ruling, and people never know exactly how the nine got there. Were votes switched? Did the language get heated? What menacing statements might have been made as the justices circulated draft opinions, only to be excised when cooler heads prevailed?

Chief Justice Roberts is his own enigma. "The notion that John plays his cards close to his vest is a dramatic understatement," said a lawyer who has known him since his Reagan days. Even Roberts's wife, Jane, acknowledged his reserve in our conversations. Those further outside his circle are never quite sure what motivates him.

I have known Roberts for more than twenty years, having covered him as a journalist through his work as a Department of Justice lawyer in the early 1990s, as a star appellate advocate appearing before the justices, and as a lower court judge in Washington, DC. For this book, Roberts allowed me several sessions of interviews in his chambers, totaling more than twenty hours. But, as he would be the first to make clear, he cannot be described as a willing participant. He believes that any biographical endeavor would be best undertaken when he is long gone from the Court. He kept most of his remarks off the record.

Through our conversations, however, I was able to better understand the person beneath the flawless veneer and to comprehend the gap in perceptions among people around him. In large matters related to judging as well as in lesser concerns of personality, differences exist between appearance and reality. David Leebron, Roberts's *Harvard Law Review* colleague who is now president of Rice University, seemed to have it right when he said that Roberts is an introvert who has learned to act like an extrovert. Roberts's longtime friend Dean Colson, with whom he was in Florida on the day that Justice Scalia died, said that Roberts, who today is such an eloquent speaker, had become physically ill when he was supposed to speak to a gathering of law clerks to Justice William Rehnquist back in the 1980s. Even as an experienced advocate, before his appointment to the Court, Roberts's hands would be shaking before he stepped to the lectern. Some co-counsel wondered how that could be happening: this was John Roberts. In the privacy of the justices' chambers, some associates do not trust Roberts and think his diffidence is strategic, that he is not always acting in good faith, that he is not an honest broker. Yet in June 2018 Roberts told a conference of judges, "I feel some obligation to be something of an honest broker among my colleagues and won't necessarily . . . go out of my way to pick fights." He observed that because of his chief justice role, he would "sublimate" his views at times.[1]

Colleagues portray him as strategizing more than sublimating, always with an eye toward what he wants in the ultimate ruling and how he will appear. Even as a young lawyer in the Reagan administration, he demonstrated an awareness of the importance of messaging. He has always shown a keen interest in how he is portrayed in the media.

Other consistent themes mark Roberts's life: the intelligence, drive, and focus evident since he was barely thirteen. He seems most comfortable in small groups reminiscent of life at La Lumiere School. More significantly, the patterns of his opinions have lined up with positions he took early on in the service of the Reagan administration. He has successfully steered the law in America, reversing multiple liberal precedents. Roberts has maintained from the start that he has no political agenda on the bench—and that, for the most part, neither do his black-robed colleagues.

Yet he was part of Republican presidents' efforts to choose judges who would further their respective administrations' policy agendas. Roberts knows well the politics of the bench, and his opinions show that, despite the "umpire" assertion, he did not entirely shed his partisan thinking once he donned the black robe.

Like many people in America, Roberts watched as the Brett Kavanaugh hearings in late September 2018 further refuted the chief justice's assertion that judges operate without regard to politics. Kavanaugh, a federal appellate judge who previously helped investigate President Bill Clinton in the 1990s and then served President George W. Bush, attributed the sudden sexual assault allegations against him to a "calculated and orchestrated political hit, fueled with apparent pent-up anger about President Trump and the 2016 election, fear that has been unfairly stoked about my judicial record, revenge on behalf of the Clintons, and millions of dollars in money from outside left-wing opposition groups." Retired Justice John Paul Stevens was among the prominent legal figures to say Kavanaugh appeared biased and unfit for the Court. Kavanaugh later said he may have gone too far and been too emotional.[2]

Roberts expressed concern about public regard for the judiciary after Kavanaugh's hearings and as President Trump continued to politicize the federal bench. In a speech a few weeks after Kavanaugh's confirmation, the chief justice referred to "the contentious events in Washington" and stressed judges' independence from the executive and legislative branches. A month later, after Trump derided a judge who had ruled against the administration as an "Obama judge," Roberts issued an unprecedented statement publicly rebuking Trump: "We do not have Obama judges or Trump judges, Bush judges or Clinton judges. What we have is an extraordinary group of dedicated judges doing their level best to do equal right to those appearing before them. That independent judiciary is something we should all be thankful for." Roberts was responding to President Trump, to be sure, yet also more broadly trying to shield judges' stature in the American eye. The Kavanaugh appointment reinforced the 5-4 political split at the Supreme Court itself.[3]

It is difficult in any assessment of Roberts not to return to the Obamacare dispute of 2012, when he provoked visceral criticism from conservatives and enduring puzzlement from liberals. That ruling, and another in 2015 again upholding the law, indelibly defined him in the public mind as more moderate. Perhaps the cases reveal the John Roberts who will emerge in an America increasingly influenced by Donald Trump. In some areas, likely not involving race or religion, Roberts may hold in check his usual ideological instincts. He may find his way, as he did in 2012, to something resembling a middle ground.

Or Roberts might choose to retreat to the patterns seen in 2018, when he appeared resistant to compromise. The man who is only the seventeenth chief justice of the United States is likely still in the early chapters of his tenure. When Justice Anthony Kennedy retired in 2018, Roberts gained greater control, no longer yoked to a centrist conservative pulling to the left. Kennedy's successor, Kavanaugh, will bring a different dimension to the Court. He was mentored by some of the same Republicans who had inspired Roberts. The chief justice is leading a Court increasingly in his own image. He is positioned at the center in every way, and the law will likely be what he says it is.

Acknowledgments

I was fortunate to begin this book in Southern California while on a visiting professorship at the law school of the University of California, Irvine. That opportunity brought me into a world of inquisitive students and thought-provoking professors, including Henry Weinstein, a former *Los Angeles Times* legal affairs writer who offered wise counsel throughout the early months of this project. My UCI researcher Hannah McMeans (Class of 2018) was invaluable, and librarian Dianna Sahhar enthusiastically helped me in my pursuit of documents. Yet my deepest appreciation goes to Dean Erwin Chemerinsky, now at the University of California, Berkeley, who proposed the one-year professorship, and whose generosity is infinite.

In my home city of Washington, DC, many friends and colleagues provided guidance for approaching my enigmatic subject and early suggestions on draft chapters. I am indebted to Fred Barbash, Dick Carelli, Pam Fessler, Liz Halloran, Liz Hayes, Toni Locy, Phyllis Richman, and Elder Witt. Three writers who have published their own works on the Supreme Court generously read portions of the manuscript: Marcia Coyle, Linda Greenhouse, and Stephen Vladeck. My longtime friends in the Supreme Court press corps sustained me with ideas about my subject as well as their own reporting on the Court: Bob Barnes,

Jess Bravin, Jan Crawford, Garrett Epps, Chris Geidner, Amy Howe, Lawrence Hurley, Brent Kendall, Adam Liptak, Dahlia Lithwick, Tony Mauro, David Savage, Mark Sherman, Greg Stohr, Nina Totenberg, Mark Walsh, Jesse Wegman, Pete Williams, and Richard Wolf. Friends with special expertise in the law read drafts and offered suggestions, including Joel Gershowitz, Richard Hasen, Jared Roberts, and Ronald Weich. Julie Rovner, who has written extensively on health-care policy, offered guidance on the Obamacare chapter. My interest in the chief justice developed during my years at Reuters, and three colleagues from that time continued to provide advice and camaraderie, always over food and drink: Jack Shafer, John Shiffman, and Howard Goller, who again lent his sharp editing eye.

Now at CNN, I am especially grateful to Jeff Zucker, the original Supreme Court junkie, who brought me to the network first as a contributor and then as a full-time legal analyst. My thanks on that score also go to Rebecca Kutler, overseeing contributors, and to executive vice president Amy Entelis, whose intelligent vision for bringing the law to life is inspiring. I rely on superb editors, Rachel Smolkin, Dan Berman, and Brooke Brower. I thank them, along with the leadership of Sam Feist and Virginia Moseley in Washington, and of Meredith Artley in Atlanta. I am grateful to Rick Davis and Drew Shenkman for keeping us all within legal lines and standards. Justice correspondents and other colleagues in the CNN Washington bureau welcomed me with such warmth that they will always be on my list: Dana Bash, Gloria Borger, David Chalian, Ariane de Vogue (my first-rate partner at the Supreme Court), Nia-Malika Henderson, Steven Holmes, Laura Jarrett, Aaron Kessler, Tammy Kupperman, Elise Labott, Adam Levine, Mary Kay Mallonee, Evan Perez, Mark Preston, Shimon Prokupecz, Jessica Schneider, David Shortell, Ryan Struyk, Jeffrey Toobin (CNN's chief legal analyst), and Jeff Zeleny.

For this project, I cast a large net, talking to people who knew John Roberts as a young boy and who today work closely with him as chief justice. I am grateful to the chief justice for his time and to the relatives, friends, and colleagues who offered insights. I am also deeply appreciative to Supreme Court Public Information Officer Kathy Arberg, her deputy Patricia McCabe Estrada, and their well-organized team that serves the Court press corps. Two individuals who have been enduringly helpful in my hunt for documents related to the justices are Jeff Flannery, head of reference in the Manuscript Division at the Library of Congress, and John Jacob, archivist at the Lewis F. Powell Jr. Archives housed at the Washington and Lee University School of Law. Teams overseeing the Henry J. Friendly Papers at Harvard Law School and the William H. Rehnquist Papers at the Hoover Institution provided assistance throughout my research. In Johnstown, the home of John Roberts's parents, Joyce Homan at the Cambria County Library helped me find materials on the ethnic and economic development of the region.

The single most important person to the progress of this book was Dan Gerstle, senior editor at Basic Books, brilliant and steady throughout. I know how difficult it was to work with a writer who, for the last year and a half of this project, faced the demands of covering the judiciary in the Trump era. But Dan remained patient, and this book is immeasurably better for his meticulous editing. I am also indebted to my agents Gail Ross and Howard Yoon for connecting me to Dan and the superior team led by publisher Lara Heimert. In the final months of production, freelance copyeditor Katherine Streckfus and senior project editors Collin Tracy, Sandra Beris, and Michelle Welsh-Horst at Perseus Books infinitely improved the text.

Finally, I am supported by many siblings, in-laws, nieces and nephews, step-children, and their children. For decades, my late mother and father subscribed to the publications where I worked (no matter that the newspapers arrived days late by mail) and saved copies of my stories. When they died, I ended up with an attic clip file that covers most of John Roberts's career. (I began writing full time about the Court in early 1989, just as Roberts made his first argument before the justices.) Of course, all my newspaper and magazine articles are now online, but I could not bear to throw out the neatly clipped stories, chronologically arranged in dated envelopes, all organized by their hands. While working on this book, I turned to those clippings numerous times.

Nothing I could say would sufficiently convey my appreciation to the two people who matter the most in life: my husband, Clay, and our daughter, Elizabeth. Through book after book—and particularly with this Roberts biography—they have been there for me. The easiest page to write is always the dedication.

Selected Bibliography

ARCHIVES

George H.W. Bush Presidential Library
George W. Bush Presidential Library
Ronald Reagan Presidential Library
Harry A. Blackmun Papers, Library of Congress
William H. Rehnquist Papers, Hoover Institution
Lewis F. Powell Jr. Archives, Washington and Lee University
Henry Jacob Friendly Papers, Harvard University
Cambria County Library, Johnstown, Pennsylvania
La Porte County Historical Society Museum, La Porte, Indiana
Senate Judiciary Committee collections of questionnaires, transcripts, and other materials on Supreme Court nominees John G. Roberts Jr. in 2005, Samuel Alito in 2006, Sonia Sotomayor in 2009, Elena Kagan in 2010, Neil M. Gorsuch in 2017, and on nominee Roberts to the US Court of Appeals for the District of Columbia Circuit in 2003

NEWSPAPERS, MAGAZINES, PRESS AGENCIES, AND NEWS WEBSITES

Associated Press, *Atlantic*, Bloomberg, Buzzfeed, *Chicago Tribune*, CNN, *Congressional Quarterly Weekly Report*, *Harvard Crimson*, *Los Angeles Times*, *The Nation*, *National Journal*, *National Review*, *New Republic*, *Newsweek*, *The New Yorker*, *New York Review of Books*, *New York Times*, NPR, *Politico*, Reuters, *Salon*, *Slate*, *Time*, *USA Today*, *Wall Street Journal*, *Washington Post*

AUDIO ARCHIVE

Oyez, sponsored by Cornell's Legal Information Institute, Chicago-Kent College of Law, and Justia.com, https://www.oyez.org

BOOKS

Axelrod, David. *Believer: My Forty Years in Politics.* New York: Penguin, 2015.

Baker, Peter. *Days of Fire: Bush and Cheney in the White House.* New York: Doubleday, 2013.

Biskupic, Joan. *American Original: The Life and Constitution of Supreme Court Justice Antonin Scalia.* New York: Sarah Crichton Books / Farrar, Straus and Giroux, 2009.

———. *Breaking In: The Rise of Sonia Sotomayor and the Politics of Justice.* New York: Sarah Crichton Books / Farrar, Straus and Giroux, 2014.

———. *Sandra Day O'Connor: How the First Woman on the Supreme Court Became Its Most Influential Justice.* New York: Ecco / HarperCollins, 2005.

Blackman, Josh. *Unprecedented: The Constitutional Challenge to Obamacare.* New York: PublicAffairs, 2013.

Breyer, Stephen G. *Active Liberty: Interpreting Our Democratic Constitution.* New York: Alfred A. Knopf, 2005.

Bush, George W. *Decision Points.* New York: Broadway Books, 2010.

Coyle, Marcia. *The Roberts Court: The Struggle for the Constitution.* New York: Simon and Schuster, 2013.

Dorsen, David M. *Henry Friendly: Greatest Judge of His Era.* Cambridge: Belknap Press of Harvard University Press, 2012.

Epstein, Lee, William M. Landes, and Richard A. Posner. *The Behavior of Federal Judges: A Theoretical and Empirical Study of Rational Choice.* Cambridge: Harvard University Press, 2013.

Frederick, David C. *Supreme Court and Appellate Advocacy.* St. Paul: Thomson West, 2003.

Gillespie, Ed. *Winning Right: Campaign Politics and Conservative Policies.* New York: Threshold Editions, 2006.

Ginsburg, Ruth Bader, with Mary Hartnett and Wendy W. Williams. *In My Own Words.* New York: Simon and Schuster, 2016.

Gonzales, Alberto R. *True Faith and Allegiance: A Story of Service and Sacrifice in War and Peace.* Nashville: Nelson Books, 2016.

Graetz, Michael J., and Linda Greenhouse. *The Burger Court and the Rise of the Judicial Right.* New York: Simon and Schuster, 2016.

Greenburg, Jan Crawford. *Supreme Conflict: The Inside Struggle for Control of the United States Supreme Court*. New York: Penguin, 2007.

Greenhouse, Linda. *Becoming Justice Blackmun: Harry Blackmun's Supreme Court Journey*. New York: Times Books, 2005.

Hasen, Richard L. *Plutocrats United: Campaign Money, the Supreme Court, and the Distortion of American Elections*. New Haven, CT: Yale University Press, 2016.

Hoerr, John P. *And the Wolf Finally Came: The Decline of the American Steel Industry*. Pittsburgh: University of Pittsburgh Press, 1988.

Klarman, Michael J. *From Jim Crow to Civil Rights: The Supreme Court and the Struggle for Racial Equality*. New York: Oxford University Press, 2004.

Kluger, Richard. *Simple Justice*. New York: Vintage, 1975.

Martin, Edmund F., and David J. Morrison. *Bethlehem Steelmaker: My Ninety Years in Life's Loop*. Bethlehem, PA: BMS Press, 1992.

McCague, James. *The Second Rebellion: The Story of the New York City Draft Riots of 1863*. New York: Dial Press, 1968.

McCullough, David. *The Johnstown Flood*. New York: Simon and Schuster, 1968.

Miller, Donald L., and Richard E. Sharpless. *The Kingdom of Coal: Work, Enterprise, and Ethnic Communities in the Mine Fields*. Philadelphia: University of Pennsylvania Press, 1985.

Morawska, Ewa. *For Bread with Butter: The Life-Worlds of East Central Europeans in Johnstown, Pennsylvania, 1890–1940*. New York: Cambridge University Press, 1985.

Newton, Jim. *Justice for All: Earl Warren and the Nation He Made*. New York: Riverhead Books, 2006.

O'Connor, Sandra Day. *Out of Order: Stories from the History of the Supreme Court*. New York: Random House, 2013.

Persily, Nathaniel, Gillian E. Metzger, and Trevor W. Morrison, eds. *The Health Care Case: The Supreme Court's Decision and Its Implications*. New York: Oxford University Press, 2013.

Posner, Richard A. *The Federal Judiciary: Strengths and Weaknesses*. Cambridge: Harvard University Press, 2017.

Smith, William French. *Law and Justice in the Reagan Administration: Memoirs of an Attorney General*. Stanford: Hoover Institution Press, 1991.

Sotomayor, Sonia. *My Beloved World*. New York: Alfred A. Knopf, 2013.

Stevens, John Paul. *Five Chiefs: A Supreme Court Memoir*. New York: Little, Brown, 2011.

Strohmeyer, John. *Crisis in Bethlehem: Big Steel's Struggle to Survive*. Pittsburgh: University of Pittsburgh Press, 1994.

Thomas, Clarence. *My Grandfather's Son: A Memoir*. New York: Harper, 2007.

Toobin, Jeffrey. *The Oath: The Obama White House and the Supreme Court*. New York: Doubleday, 2012.

———. *Too Close to Call: The Thirty-Six-Day Battle to Decide the 2000 Election*. New York: Random House, 2001.

Tribe, Laurence, and Joshua Matz. *Uncertain Justice: The Roberts Court and the Constitution*. New York: Henry Holt, 2014.

Warren, Kenneth. *Bethlehem Steel: Builder and Arsenal of America*. Pittsburgh: University of Pittsburgh Press, 2008.

Whittle, Randy. *Johnstown Pennsylvania: A History*, Part One, *1895–1936*. Charleston, SC: History Press, 2005.

Woodward, Bob, and Carl Bernstein. *The Final Days*. New York: Simon and Schuster, 1976.

Notes

PROLOGUE

1. Roberts had received early glowing reviews from senators. President Bush believed he would be a smooth, uncomplicated choice as he faced the Hurricane Katrina crisis.

2. Janet Malcolm "The Art of Testifying," *New Yorker*, March 13, 2006.

3. Donald J. Trump (@realDonaldTrump), "Supreme Court rules in favor of non-union workers . . . ," Twitter, June 27, 2018, 7:11 a.m., https://twitter.com /realdonaldtrump/status/1011975204778729474.

4. Author interviews with Dean Colson, September 17, 2016, and May 9, 2018.

5. Kennedy recounted the Scalia comment at a Ninth Circuit conference in Big Sky, Montana. "Supreme Court Justice Anthony Kennedy Perspective," C-SPAN, July 11, 2016, https://www.c-span.org/video/?412371-1/supreme-court-justice -anthony-kennedy-perspective.

6. Author interview with Dean Colson, September 17, 2016.

7. The appointment count extends through Elena Kagan in 2010 and does not include Neil Gorsuch, who joined the Court in 2017 after the election.

8. "I just wish we hadn't run so fast into politics," said the Republican governor of Ohio, John Kasich, at the Republican debate on February 13, 2016.

9. Appearing at the debate were Jeb Bush, Ben Carson, Ted Cruz, John Kasich, Marco Rubio, and Donald Trump.

10. In the event of such a tie, a lower court ruling stands but no national precedent is set.

11. Author interview with Ruth Bader Ginsburg, July 11, 2016. By Inauguration Day 2017, Ginsburg would be age eighty-three and Justices Kennedy and Breyer eighty and seventy-eight, respectively.

12. Author interview with Michael Luttig, December 16, 2016.

13. The "Chief Justice of the United States" is a loftier title than the original ("Chief Justice of the Supreme Court") used by John Marshall and other chiefs in the nation's first century. Salmon Chase, who became the sixth chief justice in 1864, appointed by his rival, President Abraham Lincoln, imposed the elevated title. As retired justice John Paul Stevens noted in his memoir about chief justices, "Perhaps motivated by the hope that he would one day be elected president, Chase assumed the more imposing title of 'Chief Justice of the United States,' a title that Congress began to use in subsequent legislation and that has been used by all of Chase's successors." John Paul Stevens, *Five Chiefs: A Supreme Court Memoir*, 20. The size of the Supreme Court itself has fluctuated since the judiciary was established in 1789, from a low of five seats to a high of ten; Congress set it at the current nine positions in 1869. "About the Supreme Court," United States Courts, n.d., www.uscourts.gov/about-federal-courts/educational-resources/about-educational-outreach/activity-resources/about; "The Court as an Institution," Supreme Court of the United States, n.d., https://www.supremecourt.gov/about/institution.aspx.

14. Citizens United v. Federal Election Commission, 558 U.S. 310 (2010); Shelby County v. Holder, 570 U.S. 2 (2013). Roberts worked to limit the reach of the 1965 Voting Rights Act beginning with his work in the Reagan administration during the 1980s. He continued the effort as a deputy US solicitor general for the George H.W. Bush administration in the 1990s.

15. Roberts appeared at the New England School of Law in Boston. "Inside the Supreme Court," C-SPAN, February 3, 2016, https://www.c-span.org/video/?404131-1/discussion-chief-justice-john-roberts.

16. Roberts appeared at the University of Alabama in Tuscaloosa, "Chief Justice John Roberts Remarks," C-SPAN, March 9, 2010, https://www.c-span.org/video/?292439-1/chief-justice-john-roberts-remarks. *Marbury v. Madison*, 1 Cr. 137 (1803), *Scott v. Sandford*, 19 How. 393 (1857).

17. Parents Involved in Community Schools v. Seattle School District No. 1, 551 U.S. 701 (2007).

18. Roberts appeared at Rensselaer Polytechnic Institute with Rensselaer president Shirley Ann Jackson. "A Conversation with Chief Justice John G. Roberts, Jr.," April 11, 2017, YouTube, posted April 12, 2017, https://www.youtube.com/watch?v=TuZEKlRgDEg&t=1363s.

CHAPTER I: FROM LANCASHIRE TO WONDER STREET

1. John Roberts to James Moore, December 22, 1968, copy obtained from La Lumiere School.

2. Author interview with Andrew McKenna, December 16, 2016.

3. Research materials obtained from the Family History Library of the Church of Jesus Christ of Latter-day Saints, Salt Lake City, Utah, April 27, 2017.

4. Lincoln announced the Proclamation in September 1862; it took effect on January 1, 1863.

5. James McCague, *The Second Rebellion: The Story of the New York City Draft Riots of 1863*, 9.

6. The Glovers were in Pennsylvania by 1864 when a fourth daughter was born, according to census records.

7. See, for example, Donald L. Miller and Richard E. Sharpless, *The Kingdom of Coal: Work, Enterprise, and Ethnic Communities in the Mine Fields*, 182: "The Slavs brought with them from the Old World the villager's suspicion of strangers and outsiders and a village clannishness. Unable to speak English, they seemed unusually dour and stiff. They were not at all outgoing and talkative like the Irish. But they did drink like the Irish. . . . In the popular press Slavs were widely described as lawless, slovenly, fatalistic, and stupid." Randy Whittle, *Johnstown, Pennsylvania: A History*, Part One, *1895–1936*, 40, documents the scorn for these new immigrants who crammed into boardinghouses at the end of the nineteenth century. "The first purchase made by a Slovak or Polack when he comes here is a revolver, by an Italian or Sicilian, a stiletto," according to a *Johnstown Tribune* characterization Whittle reprinted. "If the Slovak or Polack is particularly thrifty, he postpones purchasing the revolver for several months, and carries in one pocket a round hard stone, large enough to crush a man's skull, and in another a piece of iron filched from the colliery scrap heap."

8. David McCullough, *The Johnstown Flood*, 30–31.

9. Ibid., 126.

10. Whittle, *Johnstown, Pennsylvania*, 10; Kenneth Warren, *Bethlehem Steel: Builder and Arsenal of America*, 100.

11. Johnstown High School yearbook, 1946.

12. According to the 1930 census, the family paid $20 a month for the property at 752 Park Avenue. A Cambria City field report of 1918 lists Bench and Gmucza at 402 Chestnut, near a church.

13. Johnstown Central Catholic yearbook, 1947. Albert died on April 15, 1948. "The death of her father greatly impacted her," said Jane Roberts, "in that she went to work to support the family." Jean Podrasky, a niece and goddaughter,

added, "She resented that she did not go to college. She was so smart. But they didn't have a lot of money. That was the story. They just ran out of money." Author interview with Jane Roberts, September 26, 2017; author interviews with Jean Podrasky, August 20, 2016, and March 30, 2018.

14. Author interviews with Jean Podrasky, August 20, 2016, and March 30, 2018.

15. Two of Rosemary's aunts in the same Gmucza family had become nuns.

16. Author interview with Jean Podrasky, August 20, 2016 (regarding Rosemary encouraging Jack to improve his golf game); author interview with Jane Roberts, September 26, 2017 (regarding Rosemary clipping newspapers for Jack); author interview with Richard Lazarus, November 4, 2017 (noting that mother seemed more ambitious than father).

17. Brown v. Board of Education of Topeka, 347 U.S. 483 (1954); Brown v. Board of Education of Topeka, 349 U.S. 294 (1955).

18. Warren included a footnote citing social science research on the harms of school segregation on the psychological development and personalities of black children. Brown v. Board of Education of Topeka, 347 U.S. 483 (1954), footnote 11.

19. Chief Justice Warren, for example, regarded *Baker v. Carr*, which declared for the first time that judges could resolve disputes over reapportionment and drawing of voting districts, as the most important case of his tenure. It came to the Court when legislative districts in rural areas held a disproportionate number of seats compared to what they would have held based on population alone. The opinion was written by Justice William Brennan in Baker v. Carr, 369 U.S. 186 (1962).

20. Alabama governor George Wallace, Inaugural Address, January 14, 1963.

21. Author interviews with Bernice Roberts, February 24, 2017, and May 23, 2017.

22. Author interview with Jane Roberts, September 26, 2017.

23. Author interview with Bernice Roberts, February 24, 2017. Mrs. Roberts previously recounted a tale of her husband giving "Jackie" dollar bills for *A*s in a letter to the editor of the *Sun and Erie County Independent*, Hamburg, New York, August 11, 2005.

24. Edmund F. Martin, with David J. Morrison, *Bethlehem Steelmaker: My Ninety Years in Life's Loop*, 68–79; Warren, *Bethlehem Steel*, 176–177.

25. Martin, *Bethlehem Steelmaker*, 140–141.

26. Ibid., 71.

27. La Porte County Historical Society Museum, Long Beach collection.

28. Shelly v. Kraemer, 334 U.S. 1 (1948). The Fair Housing Act of 1968 further prohibited race discrimination.

29. Author interview with Andrew McKenna, December 16, 2016.

30. School officials said they lacked information related to the early 1970s tuition. Andrew McKenna, a La Lumiere founder, estimated it at $6,000 annually, which conformed to the memories of former students interviewed. Author correspondence with Andrew McKenna, September 21, 2018.

31. *The Torch* school paper, recounted in news reports in 2005, e.g., "Roberts Started on Path to Success at Young Age," *Washington Times*, August 16, 2005.

32. La Lumiere yearbook, 1973; author interview with Dave Kirkby, December 15, 2016.

33. Author interview with Chris Balawender, August 25, 2016.

34. Author interview with Dave Kirkby, December 15, 2016; author interview with Allen Filipic, October 25, 2016; author interview with Robert MacLeverty, October 5, 2016.

35. Author interview with Jane Roberts, September 26, 2017.

36. Author interview with Allen Filipic, October 25, 2016.

37. Author interview with Dave Kirkby, December 15, 2016.

38. Roberts told the Senate Judiciary Committee in his 2005 questionnaire for his nomination that for his birth year of 1955, the lottery was held on March 20, 1974; the number for his January 27 birthdate was 323. The questionnaire is included in "Confirmation Hearing on the Nomination of John G. Roberts, Jr. to Be Chief Justice of the United States, Hearing Before the Committee on the Judiciary, United States Senate," 109th Cong., 1st sess., September 12–15, 2005, available at https://www.judiciary.senate.gov/imo/media/doc /GPO-CHRG-ROBERTS.pdf.

39. Author interview with Allen Filipic, December 8, 2017. When Roberts looked back later, in a 2006 appearance at the University of Miami, he said he was put off by antiwar demonstrations. A transcript of the interview, which was conducted by Jan Crawford Greenburg, is online at "Interview with Chief Justice Roberts," ABC News, November 28, 2006, https://abcnews.go.com /Nightline/story?id=2661589.

40. Paul Brownfield, "Laying Down His Own Law," *Los Angeles Times*, January 31, 1999; Dave McNary, "Paris Barclay: DGA Is 'Continuing to Heat Up on Diversity on Studios and Producers,'" *Variety*, February 4, 2016. Barclay, who became the first African American and first openly gay president of the Directors Guild of America, declined requests to speak about Roberts for this book.

41. Roberts's remarks at La Lumiere Commencement, May 24, 2013, available at "La Lumiere Commencement 2013—Chief Justice John Roberts,"

YouTube, posted May 31, 2013, https://www.youtube.com/watch?v=KeEof JsH82w&t=926s; "La Lumiere Commencement 2013—Chief Justice John Roberts," YouTube, posted May 31, 2013, https://www.youtube.com/watch?v =KeEofJsH82w&t=11s.

42. President Lyndon B. Johnson, "Commencement Address at Howard University: 'To Fulfill These Rights,'" June 4, 1965, posted at John Woolley and Gerhard Peters, American Presidency Project, hosted by University of California, Santa Barbara, www.presidency.ucsb.edu/ws/?pid=27021. The speech was three months before the signing of Executive Order 11246.

43. John P. Hoerr, *And the Wolf Finally Came: The Decline of the American Steel Industry*, 174.

44. United States v. Bethlehem Steel Corp., 312 F. Supp. 977 (1970).

45. United States v. Bethlehem Steel Corp., 446 F.2d 652 (2nd Cir. 1971).

46. Philip Shabecoff, "Bethlehem Steel Required to Bar Racial Inequities," *New York Times*, January 17, 1973. According to the Equal Employment Opportunity Commission, its lawsuit, joined by the Department of Labor and the Department of Justice, was against the country's nine largest steel producers for discriminatory hiring, promotion, assignment, and wage policies directed against women and minorities. "Milestones: 1974," Equal Employment Opportunity Commission, n.d., https://www.eeoc.gov/eeoc/history/35th/milestones /1974.html.

47. Warren, *Bethlehem Steel*, 194. See also John Strohmeyer, *Crisis in Bethlehem: Big Steel's Struggle to Survive*, 101–104, noting the evident danger signs, for example, that steel had begun to flow in from Europe and Japan in the 1960s, and emissions and environmental standards impinged on US companies.

48. Author interview with Jane Roberts, September 26, 2017.

49. Lydia Chavez, "Bethlehem Steel to Cut 7,300 Jobs at Upstate Plant," *New York Times*, December 28, 1982: "The American steel industry, operating at under 50 percent of capacity, has had one of its worst years since the end of World War II and steel shipments are expected to reach only 62 million tons for 1982, compared with 87 million last year. Nearly half of the nation's 450,000 steelworkers have been laid off, and half of those on layoff are not expected to work in the industry again. Bethlehem has a workforce of 82,000, with 30,000 of these employees currently laid off before yesterday's announcement."

50. Warren Brown, "Bethlehem Steel to Modernize Two Plants," *Washington Post*, December 5, 1983.

51. Frederick Rasmussen, "John G. Roberts, Sr., Father of U.S. chief justice, *Baltimore Sun*, November 19, 2008, http://articles.baltimoresun.com/2008 -11-19/news/0811180063_1_bethlehem-steel-sparrows-roberts.

CHAPTER II: THE EDUCATION OF JOHN ROBERTS

1. Bob Woodward and Carl Bernstein, *The Final Days*.

2. Roe v. Wade, 410 U.S. 113 (1973); Linda Greenhouse and Reva B. Siegel, "Backlash to the Future? From *Roe* to *Perry*," *UCLA Law Review* 60, no. 240 (2013).

3. Ruth Bader Ginsburg, *In My Own Words*, with Mary Hartnett and Wendy W. Williams, 113–117.

4. Swann v. Charlotte-Mecklenburg Board of Education, 402 U.S. 1 (1971); Morgan v. Hennigan, 379 F. Supp. 410 (D. Mass. 1974).

5. "Interview with Chief Justice Roberts," conducted at the University of Miami on November 28, 2006, by Jan Crawford Greenburg, then of ABC News, transcript at https://abcnews.go.com/Nightline/story?id=2661589.

6. The résumé of John Glover Roberts Jr. on file at the George H.W. Bush Library notes that he entered Harvard in 1973 with sophomore standing. Roberts stated on the résumé that he had graduated from La Lumiere School first in his class, had participated in varsity football and wrestling, and had received the National Council of Teachers of English Award and a National Merit Scholarship in 1973. He advised attendance at church in a May 24, 2013, commencement speech at La Lumiere, as seen at "La Lumiere Commencement 2013—Chief Justice John Roberts," YouTube, posted May 31, 2013, https://www.youtube.com/watch?v=KeEofJsH82w&t=926s.

7. Daniel H. Maccoby, "Republican Club Attracts Freshmen in Record Numbers," *Harvard Crimson*, September 28, 1973.

8. Janny Scott, "Roberts's Harvard Roots: A Movement Was Stirring," *New York Times*, August 21, 2005.

9. Carroll Kilpatrick, "Nixon Forces Firing of Cox; Richardson, Ruckelshaus Quit," *Washington Post*, October 21, 1974.

10. Nicholas Lemann, "Elliot Richardson Will Be Speaker at Commencement," *Harvard Crimson*, May 7, 1974. The story notes that he was the senior class's fourth choice for the speaker, behind the novelist Aleksandr Solzhenitsyn, the journalist I. F. Stone, and the comedian Woody Allen.

11. Yo-Yo Ma, the child prodigy cellist, had already studied at Juilliard. Like Roberts, he had been born in 1955, attended Harvard, and graduated with the class of 1976.

12. Roberts cited these awards on various applications for federal positions, including his Senate Judiciary Committee questionnaire in 2005 for his Supreme Court nomination. The questionnaire is included in "Confirmation Hearing on the Nomination of John G. Roberts, Jr. to Be Chief Justice of the United States,

Hearing Before the Committee on the Judiciary, United States Senate," 109th Cong., 1st sess., September 12–15, 2005, available at https://www.judiciary.senate .gov/imo/media/doc/GPO-CHRG-ROBERTS.pdf.

13. Adam M. Guren, "Alum Tapped for High Court," *Harvard Crimson*, July 2005.

14. John Glover Roberts Jr., "The Utopian Conservative: A Study of Continuity and Change in the Thought of Daniel Webster," submitted for the Bowdoin Prize, 1976.

15. Dartmouth College v. Woodward, 4 Wheat. 519 (1819).

16. "Chicago Tribune Calls on Nixon to Quit for Well-Being of Nation," *New York Times*, May 9, 1974.

17. United States v. Nixon, 418 U.S. 683 (1974).

18. Griswold v. Connecticut, 381 U.S. 479 (1965).

19. Joseph Dalton, "Ex-Governor Carter Predicts Win in '76 Presidential Derby," *Harvard Crimson*, December 10, 1975.

20. Robert Ullmann, "Twelve Student Groups Form Affirmative Action Coalition," *Harvard Crimson*, December 9, 1975; enrollment numbers also appear at Nicholas Lemann, "A Gloomy Outlook for Affirmative Action, at Harvard and Elsewhere," *Harvard Crimson*, June 12, 1975, www.thecrimson.com /article/1975/6/12/a-gloomy-outlook-for-affirmative-action.

21. Mark T. Whitaker, "Sacks to Name Investigator in Racism Charge," *Harvard Crimson*, April 12, 1976; Joan Biskupic, *Breaking In: The Rise of Sonia Sotomayor and the Politics of Justice*, 48–49. Sotomayor complained to Yale and ensured that the firm was barred from recruiting on campus for a year.

22. Regents of the University of California v. Bakke, 438 U.S. 265 (1978).

23. John Roberts suggested in a 2014 case that programs singling out blacks, Hispanics, and members of other racial minority groups for a boost might actually have a "debilitating effect" by specially classifying members of minorities by their race. He expressed little patience for debates that recalled the 1960s and 1970s and insisted it "does more harm than good to question the openness and candor of those on either side of the debate." Schuette v. Coalition to Defend Affirmative Action, 572 U.S. 291 (2014).

24. Author interview with Wayne Strasbaugh, June 15, 2017.

25. More than a third of those who received history doctorates nationally in the 1970s could not find jobs in colleges and universities teaching history. The gap between PhDs and available jobs occurred as undergraduate students moved away from the humanities into business, engineering, and other professional fields. Robert B. Townsend, "Precedents: The Job Crisis of the 1970s," *Perspectives on History*, April 1997.

26. Steven Prye, "More Women, Fewer Blacks in Class of '79, Stats Show" *Harvard Law Record* 63, no. 8 (December 3, 1976): 2.

27. Author interview with Richard Lazarus, November 4, 2016.

28. Author interviews with David Leebron, November 8, 2016, and December 6, 2016.

29. Author interview with David Leebron, November 8, 2016.

30. Honors listed on John Glover Roberts Jr.'s résumé on file at the George H.W. Bush archive. The account of his exhaustion was first printed in Daniel Klaidman, "How Chief Justice John Roberts Will Handle Obamacare," *Newsweek*, September 10, 2012.

31. Author interview with Jane Roberts, March 23, 2018. She said her husband regretted that he did not travel more to Boston.

32. Richard Reeves, "The Court's Door Is Open," November 1979 copy of syndicated column, Lewis F. Powell Jr. Archives.

33. Henry Friendly and other judges to Abe Rosenthal, December 17, 1979, Henry Jacob Friendly Papers.

34. Lewis Powell, confidential memo to his file, October 4, 1977 (addressed to Warren Burger, but not sent, according to a personal notation on the memo); Warren Burger to Lewis Powell, October 23, 1978, Lewis F. Powell Jr. Archives.

35. David M. Dorsen, *Henry Friendly: Greatest Judge of His Era*, 139–140. The full quotation is: "In today's parlance he would be a moderate or centrist on most constitutional issues, identified with John Marshall Harlan, Lewis Powell, Sandra Day O'Connor, and Anthony Kennedy, rather than William Rehnquist, John G. Roberts Jr, Antonin Scalia and Clarence Thomas."

36. Author interview with Richard Posner, March 7, 2017; Dorsen, *Henry Friendly*, 58, 107.

37. Henry Friendly to Jack Weinstein, September 21, 1979, Henry Jacob Friendly Papers.

38. Henry Friendly to Lewis Powell, July 1, 1978, Lewis F. Powell, Jr. Archives; Erwin Griswold to Henry Friendly, September 24, 1979, Henry Jacob Friendly Papers.

39. William Rehnquist to Henry Friendly, September 2, 1981, William H. Rehnquist Papers; author interview with Robert Knauss, October 26, 2017.

40. Author interview with Robert Knauss, October 26, 2017.

41. University of Wisconsin law professor Brad Snyder, who traced the judicial genealogy of Roberts and his mentors, concluded that Roberts "was more of a political animal than Friendly and thrived in the [Supreme] Court's highly politicized atmosphere. Roberts enjoyed Friendly's intense and monastic process of crafting an opinion but also appreciated Rehnquist's more ideological

approach." Like other observers, Snyder expressed interest in Roberts's great efforts to adopt the mantle of Friendly, questioning "why Roberts has gone to great lengths—with friends and law clerks, in his D.C. Circuit opinions, and most prominently during his Supreme Court nominations hearings—to portray himself as a Friendly disciple." Brad Snyder, "The Judicial Genealogy (and Mythology) of John Roberts: Clerkships from Gray to Brandeis to Friendly to Roberts," *Ohio State Law Journal* 71, no. 1149 (2010).

42. Linda Greenhouse, "Justice Rehnquist: Firm Ways, Witty Means," *New York Times*, July 12, 1981; "Role of the Chief Justice," C-SPAN, February 4, 2009, https://www.c-span.org/video/?283847-1/role-chief-justice.

43. Before John Roberts's 2005 appointment, only four other justices had previously served as Supreme Court law clerks—William Rehnquist, John Paul Stevens, Byron White, and Stephen Breyer.

44. Nixon tapes, No. 12-15. The author recounted the history of the Rehnquist nomination in *Sandra Day O'Connor: How the First Woman on the Supreme Court Became Its Most Influential Justice*, 37–50. Rehnquist succeeded Justice John Marshall Harlan, who was suffering from terminal cancer.

45. "Rehnquist Refutes Dems on Harassing Voters," United Press International, November 21, 1971; Ben Cole, "Views Changed on Rights Law, Rehnquist Says," *Arizona Republic*, November 4, 1971; "Supreme Court Memo from Rehnquist," *Newsweek*, December 13, 1971.

46. Richard Kluger, *Simple Justice*, 607–615; Leon Friedman, "He Was a Very Elusive Target," *New York Times*, December 12, 1971.

47. The vote was 5–2; Powell and Stevens did not participate.

48. United Steelworkers of America v. Weber, 443 U.S. 193 (1979).

49. Ibid., Rehnquist dissenting, internal quotations omitted.

50. John Roberts to Fred Fielding (and others), December 18, 1982, Ronald Reagan Library.

51. John Roberts's comment on Rehnquist at University of Arizona, at "Role of the Chief Justice," C-SPAN, February 4, 2009, https://www.c-span.org /video/?283847-1/role-chief-justice.

52. Author interviews with Dean Colson, September 16, 2016, and May 9, 2018.

53. John Roberts to Henry Friendly, November 1, 1980, Henry Jacob Friendly Papers.

54. Since its inception in the 1970s, close observers have criticized the "cert pool" process. Some have said it encourages a least-common-denominator approach. Young clerks have tended to play it safe by recommending against taking

up cases. In late 2018, only Justices Alito and Gorsuch were not in the pool and instead had their own clerks review all petitions.

55. From United States v. Morrison, No. 79-395, Preliminary Memorandum, dated for the February 20, 1981, conference.

56. Author interview with Robert Knauss, October 26, 2017.

57. Letter from John Roberts to Henry Friendly, November 1, 1980, Henry Jacob Friendly Papers.

58. H.L. v. Matheson, 450 U.S. 398. Burger wrote the opinion, which said, "A pregnant minor's right of privacy is not violated by a Utah law requiring a doctor to notify her parents before providing her with an abortion. The law does not give parents a veto, but does require that they be notified."

59. Rehnquist dissenting in Coleman v. Balkcom, 451 U.S. 949 (1981).

60. Ibid., Stevens concurring.

61. Rostker v. Goldberg, 453 U.S. 57 (1981).

62. White was joined by Brennan; Marshall wrote a separate dissent, joined by Brennan.

63. Dames & Moore v. Regan, 453 U.S. 654 (1981).

64. One example: "I share the same admiration, expressed by others, of your fine opinion and of the remarkable way in which you produced it on such short notice," Powell wrote to Rehnquist. "We all are much indebted to you." From letter to Rehnquist from Lewis Powell, June 29, 1981, Lewis F. Powell Jr. Archives.

65. Author interview with Michael McConnell, May 22, 2017.

66. John Roberts to Henry Friendly, November 1, 1980, Henry Jacob Friendly Papers.

CHAPTER III: HEARING THE CALL

1. Ronald Reagan's speech to the Religious Roundtable's National Affairs Briefing. News stories that have recounted the speech include "Ronald Reagan's Ascent to Official Paralleled Rise of Religious Right," *Baptist Global News*, June 7, 2004, https://baptistnews.com/article/ronald-reagans-ascent-to -office-paralleled-rise-of-religious-right/#.WypmwFVKiUk. Reagan won 56 percent of the white vote, Jimmy Carter won 36 percent, and John Anderson won 8 percent, according to the Roper Center. See "How Groups Voted in 1980," Roper Center for Public Opinion Research, Cornell University, n.d., https://ropercenter.cornell.edu/polls/us-elections/how-groups-voted/how -groups-voted-1980.

2. William Schneider, "The New Shape of American Politics," *Atlantic Monthly*, January 1987; Helen Dewar, "New Conservatives Saddle Up," *Washington Post*, December 1, 1980.

3. For John Roberts's speech at the Ronald Reagan Library, see "Reagan Lecture," C-SPAN, March 8, 2006, https://www.c-span.org/video/?191523-1/reagan-lecture.

4. Author interviews with Ken Starr, September 24, 2016, and April 14, 2017. For Rehnquist influence, see, for example, Charles R. Babcock, "The Rehnquist Trend: Court Watchers See His Dissents Becoming Administration Policy," *Washington Post*, February 17, 1982.

5. John Roberts, "Personal Qualifications Statement," April 30, 1982, Ronald Reagan Library; author interviews with Ken Starr, September 24, 2016, and April 14, 2017.

6. Among the examples are Byron White, who served as deputy attorney general in the Kennedy Justice Department; William Rehnquist, who served as an assistant attorney general for Nixon; Antonin Scalia, who served Ford in the same role; and, years later, Elena Kagan, who worked as a political appointee in both the Clinton and Obama administrations. John Paul Stevens never served in the executive branch but benefited from his connections to Attorney General Edward Levi. Sam Alito and Neil Gorsuch have also served in the executive branch.

7. Joan Biskupic, *Sandra Day O'Connor: How the First Woman on the Supreme Court Became Its Most Influential Justice*. O'Connor biographical facts throughout this chapter are drawn from this work.

8. Biskupic, *Sandra Day O'Connor*, 85.

9. John Roberts to Ken Starr, September 17, 1981, Ronald Reagan Library.

10. Fred Barbash, "Abortion Vote Called Mistake by O'Connor," *Washington Post*, September 10, 1981.

11. Roberts pointed to congressional testimony from an undersecretary at the Department of Labor that conflicted with the Department of Justice policy of maintaining "color-blindness and sex-blindness in employment decisions." John Roberts to William French Smith, October 13, 1981, Ronald Reagan Library.

12. For the continuation of his racial views, see Roberts's opinion for the plurality in Parents Involved in Community Schools v. Seattle School District No. 1, 551 U.S. 701 (2007).

13. William French Smith, *Law and Justice in the Reagan Administration: Memoirs of an Attorney General*, 25, 29. Smith wrote that after Reagan's 1980 election, Smith believed that Reagan's policies "had the imprimatur of public mandate."

14. Regarding an expectation of privacy, author interview with Fred Fielding, July 13, 2016; John Roberts to Michael Horowitz, August 29, 1985, Ronald Reagan Library. See also David G. Savage and Henry Weinstein, "Files from Roberts' Reagan Years Are Released," *Los Angeles Times*, August 16, 2005.

15. September 9, 1985, memo cited in Todd S. Purdum and John M. Broder, "Nominee's Early Files Show Many Cautions for Top Officials Including Reagan," *New York Times*, August 19, 2005.

16. Author interview with Michael McConnell, May 22, 2017.

17. Author interview with Roger Clegg, December 21, 2016.

18. John Roberts to Henry Friendly, November 4, 1981, Henry Jacob Friendly Papers.

19. Smith, *Law and Justice*, 97–98.

20. City of Mobile v. Bolden, 446 U.S. 55 (1980). The mayor and three-commissioner system had been in place since 1911, according to the ruling.

21. *City of Mobile v. Bolden* was decided by a 6–3 vote. Stewart wrote the majority opinion, joined by Burger, Powell, and Rehnquist. Blackmun and Stevens concurred, and Marshall, Brennan, and White dissented.

22. Smith, *Law and Justice*, 97–100.

23. John Roberts to William French Smith, January 26, 1982, Ronald Reagan Library.

24. Ibid.

25. John Roberts to William French Smith, December 21, 1981, Ronald Reagan Library.

26. John Roberts to Brad Reynolds, February 8, 1982, Ronald Reagan Library.

27. Bob Jones University v. United States, 461 U.S. 574 (1983).

28. Steven V. Roberts, "Senate Panel Is Told Reagan Supports Voting Rights," *New York Times*, January 26, 1982. Roberts told senators in 2005 that he did not participate in the dispute over Bob Jones University at the Supreme Court.

29. Charlie Savage, "Roberts Showed Way to Shift the Debate: Nominee Advised Using Broad Terms," *Boston Globe*, July 27, 2005.

30. Steven V. Roberts, "Voting Rights Act Renewed in Senate by Margin of 85–8," *New York Times*, June 19, 1982.

31. Plyler v. Doe, 457 U.S. 202 (1982).

32. Carolyn B. Kuhl and John Roberts to William French Smith, June 15, 1982, Ronald Reagan Library.

33. John Roberts to William French Smith, June 16, 1982, Ronald Reagan Library.

34. For an account of Brennan and Powell's private negotiations in *Plyler v. Doe* during O'Connor's first term, see Biskupic, *Sandra Day O'Connor*, 122–124. See also Linda Greenhouse, "What Would Justice Powell Do? The 'Alien Children' Case and the Meaning of Equal Protection," *Constitutional Commentary* 25, no. 101 (2008).

35. David Binder, "Rex Lee, Former Solicitor General, Dies at 61," *New York Times*, March 13, 1996.

36. Author interviews with J. Harvie Wilkinson III, May 22, 2017, and May 24, 2017.

37. Ibid.

38. Author interview with Ken Starr, April 14, 2017. Roberts's undated memo, on file at the Ronald Reagan Library, is titled "Proposals to Divest the Supreme Court of Appellate Jurisdiction: An Analysis in Light of Recent Developments." It notes that, based on the assignment from Starr, "this memo is prepared from a standpoint of advocacy of congressional power over the Supreme Court's appellate jurisdiction; it does not purport to be an objective review of the issue, and should therefore not be viewed as such."

39. David E. Rosenbaum, "Files from 80's Lay Out Stances of Bush Nominee," *New York Times*, July 27, 2005.

40. Charlie Savage, "Roberts Showed Way to Shift the Debate: Nominee Advised Using Broad Terms," *Boston Globe*, July 27, 2005; Tom Brune, "Early On, Roberts Leaned to the Right," *Newsday*, July 27, 2005.

41. Mary Thornton, "Reagan, Aide Differ on Hiring Policy," *Washington Post*, December 18, 1981. The *Wall Street Journal* also reported that Reagan "sees nothing wrong with voluntary affirmative action plans set up with companies and unions." Assistant Attorney General Reynolds, meanwhile, had been saying he wanted to see the 1979 Weber ruling overturned. "Reagan Backs Affirmative Action Plans Set Up Voluntarily by Firms and Unions," *Wall Street Journal*, December 18, 1981.

42. John Roberts to Fred Fielding, December 18, 1982, Ronald Reagan Library.

43. R. Jeffrey Smith, Jo Becker, Amy Goldstein, "Documents Show Roberts Influence in Reagan Era," *Washington Post*, July 27, 2005. Roberts had been responding to a memo written by Assistant Attorney General Theodore Olson that said opposition to Republican legislation to strip the Supreme Court of jurisdiction over such issues as abortion would be "perceived as a courageous and highly principled position, especially in the press." Roberts wrote "NO!" in the margins of Olson's April 12, 1982, note to Smith. Rachel Anne Bradbury, "A Conversation on Leadership, Chief Justice John G. Roberts, Jr.," *La Lumiere Magazine*, Fall 2008.

44. Author interviews with J. Harvie Wilkinson III, May 22, 2017, and May 24, 2017. Wilkinson referred to early Reagan choices for influential appeals courts: Richard Posner, to the Chicago-based Seventh Circuit; Robert Bork, the former solicitor general at the center of Watergate, to the DC Circuit; and Antonin Scalia, a former law professor, also to the DC Circuit.

45. "Reagan Lecture," C-SPAN, March 8, 2006, https://www.c-span.org/video/?191523-1/reagan-lecture. The platform language has been widely cited through the years; see, for example, Robert G. Kaiser, "Republican Right Molds Platform in Reagan's Image," *Washington Post*, July 11, 1980, https://www.washingtonpost.com/archive/politics/1980/07/11/republican-right-molds-platform-in-reagans-image/f6651807-1e31-4e19-891c-a9a4f981ffe8/?utm_term=.5790a48e84d2.

46. Author interview with Richard Lazarus, November 4, 2017.

47. Ken Starr to John Roberts, December 2, 1982, Ronald Reagan Library.

48. "Reagan Lecture," C-SPAN, March 8, 2006, https://www.c-span.org/video/?191523-1/reagan-lecture.

49. David F. Pike, "John G. Roberts," *Los Angeles Daily Journal*, August 14, 1995.

50. Peter Rusthoven to Fred Fielding, June 16, 1983, Ronald Reagan Library; Fred Fielding to Richard Darman, June 16, 1983, Ronald Reagan Library.

51. Author interviews with Fred Fielding, July 13, 2016, and July 15, 2016.

52. Author interview with Richard Hauser, October 12, 2016.

53. Author interview with Michael Luttig, December 16, 2016.

54. John Roberts to Fred Fielding, January 4, 1984, Ronald Reagan Library.

55. John Roberts to Fred Fielding, February 20, 1984, Ronald Reagan Library.

56. John Roberts to Fred Fielding, November 18, 1983, Ronald Reagan Library.

57. John Roberts to Henry Friendly, October 11, 1983, Ronald Reagan Library.

58. John Roberts to Fred Fielding, November 18, 1983, Ronald Reagan Library.

59. Author interview with Richard Lazarus, November 4, 2017.

60. Ibid.

61. John Roberts to Ronald Reagan, April 10, 1986, Ronald Reagan Library.

62. Ronald Reagan to John Roberts, April 15, 1986, Ronald Reagan Library.

CHAPTER IV: "MAY IT PLEASE THE COURT"

1. Rehnquist drew support especially from the Reagan appointees Sandra Day O'Connor in 1981, Antonin Scalia in 1986, and Anthony Kennedy in 1988.

Richmond v. Croson, 488 U.S. 469 (1989); Martin v. Wilks, 490 U.S. 755 (1989); Wards Cove Packing Co. v. Atonio, 490 U.S. 642 (1989); Patterson v. McLean Credit Union, 491 U.S. 164 (1989).

2. Supreme Court order, October 17, 1988.

3. Roberts brief on behalf of the respondent in United States v. Halper, 490 U.S. 435 (1989).

4. All quotations from United States v. Halper, oral arguments, January 17, 1989, Oyez, https://www.oyez.org/cases/1988/87-1383.

5. Roberts told C-SPAN's Susan Swain in a June 19, 2009, interview: "I was very nervous. . . . I think if you are a lawyer appearing before the Supreme Court and you're not very nervous, you don't really understand what's going on." "Supreme Court Chief Justice Roberts," C-SPAN, June 19, 2009, https://www.c-span.org/video/?286078-1/supreme-court-chief-justice-roberts&start=1077.

6. Linda Himelstein, "High Court Ruling Boosts Double-Jeopardy Defense," *Legal Times*, June 5, 1989.

7. The author has chronicled the rise of appellate advocates over many years. See, for example, Joan Biskupic, "Legal Elite Vie for Court Time in Pursuit of Supreme Challenge," *Washington Post*, December 2, 1996; Joan Biskupic, Janet Roberts, and John Shiffman, "Special Report: Echo Chamber," Reuters, December 8, 2014, https://www.reuters.com/investigates/special-report/scotus.

8. Prettyman was a law clerk to Justices Robert Jackson, Felix Frankfurter, and John Marshall Harlan. He may have been the only person to clerk for three justices in succession. Matt Schudel, "E. Barrett Prettyman Jr., Lawyer at Center of Celebrated Cases, Dies at 91," *Washington Post*, November 9, 2016.

9. Maralee Schwartz and Al Kamen, "Starr's 'Political' Deputy," *Washington Post*, September 22, 1989.

10. Author interview with Ken Starr, April 14, 2017.

11. John Roberts's salary information appears on his application form, archived at the George H.W. Bush Library.

12. Author interview with Ken Starr, April 14, 2017.

13. Author interviews with Richard Hauser, October 12, 2016, and December 14, 2016.

14. O'Connor's opinion in Richmond v. Croson, 488 U.S. 469 (1989).

15. Roberts asserted that the FCC program could be upheld only if it fulfilled a "compelling governmental interest." Solicitor general's brief, Metro Broadcasting v. Federal Communications Commission, 497 U.S. 547 (1990).

16. Alfred Sikes to Dick Thornburgh, January 12, 1990, posted by Georgetown University law professor Marty Lederman, September 8, 2005, at https://

balkin.blogspot.com/2005/09/john-roberts-and-sgs-refusal-to-defend.html. Lederman wrote that when Roberts attacked the FCC's policies, "there were more-than-reasonable grounds for defending them," including that the policies did not implicate the president's constitutional powers, that the president had not voiced any constitutional objection to them, and that he in fact had signed a relevant law and appointed three new FCC commissioners who supported the diversity preferences at their confirmation hearings before the Senate. Lederman was deputy assistant attorney general in the Department of Justice's Office of Legal Counsel in 2009–2010; he had been an attorney advisor in OLC 1994–2002.

17. Author interview with Thomas Merrill, July 30, 2017.

18. Neal Devins, "Metro Broadcasting, Inc., v. Federal Communications Commission: Requiem for a Heavyweight," William & Mary Law School Scholarship Repository, Faculty Publications, Paper 422.

19. Metro Broadcasting v. Federal Communications Commission, 497 U.S. 547 (1990).

20. Fay v. Noia, 372 U.S. 391 (1963).

21. Philip Shenon, "Appeals Judge Chosen by Bush to Be Solicitor," *New York Times*, February 2, 1989.

22. Jan Crawford Greenburg, *Supreme Conflict: The Inside Struggle for Control of the United States Supreme Court*, 91: "Thornburgh had been troubled by Starr's disputes with his closest advisers, [William] Barr and [Michael] Luttig, who were adamant in their opposition. Barr and Luttig thought Starr was too malleable, and they clashed with him in style and substance."

23. David J. Garrow, "Justice Souter Emerges," *New York Times*, September 25, 1994, https://www.nytimes.com/1994/09/25/magazine/justice-souter-emerges.html.

24. Brief on behalf of the US Department of Justice submitted in Board of Education of Oklahoma City Public Schools v. Dowell, No. 89-1080, June 1, 1990.

25. Thurgood Marshall dissenting, Board of Education of Oklahoma City Public Schools v. Dowell, 498 U.S. 237 (1991).

26. Brief on behalf of the US Department of Justice submitted in Freeman v. Pitts, No. 89-1290, May 3, 1991, Freeman v. Pitts, 503 U.S. 467 (1992).

27. See, for example, Whole Woman's Health v. Hellerstedt, 579 U.S. __ 2016.

28. Laura Sessions and Ann Devroy, "Bush Cites Abortion 'Tragedy' in Call to 67,000 Protestors," *Washington Post*, January 24, 1989.

29. Brief on behalf of US Justice Department, Rust v. Sullivan, Nos. 89-1391 and 89-1392.

30. Rust v. Sullivan, 500 U.S. 173 (1991).

31. "John Roberts, August 7, 1991," appearance on *MacNeil/Lehrer NewsHour*, YouTube, posted May 2, 2015, https://www.youtube.com/watch?v=wVeeuecssmo.

32. "U.S. Backs Wichita Abortion Protesters," Associated Press, August 7, 1991.

33. Isabel Wilkerson, "Drive Against Abortion Finds a Symbol: Wichita," *New York Times*, August 4, 1991.

34. "Bray v. Alexandria Women's Health Clinic: Oral Reargument—October 6, 1992," No. 90-985, Oyez, https://apps.oyez.org/player/#/rehnquist6/oral _argument_audio/20366.

35. Bray v. Alexandria Women's Health Clinic, 506 U.S. 263 (1993).

36. The two senators from New York, Daniel Patrick Moynihan and Alfonse D'Amato, had a deal for sharing trial court recommendations, irrespective of which party controlled the White House. Traditionally, only senators of the same party as the president can influence his choice of judges, but the New York senators agreed between themselves that they would share recommendations whether the Democrats or the Republicans controlled the White House.

37. Sonia Sotomayor to Joseph Gale, March 1, 1991; Joseph Gale notes from Sotomayor meeting with Justice Department officials, titled "Debriefing After Justice Interviews," April 15, 1991, Moynihan Papers, Library of Congress; Joan Biskupic, *Breaking In: The Rise of Sonia Sotomayor and the Politics of Justice*, 63–67.

38. Joseph Gale to Daniel Patrick Moynihan, June 7, 1991, Moynihan Papers, Library of Congress.

39. The details in this biographical sketch of Clarence Thomas are drawn from the author's coverage of the 1991 confirmation and Thomas's memoir, *My Grandfather's Son: A Memoir*.

40. David S. Broder, "Thomas: Dilemma for Democrats," *Washington Post*, July 7, 1991, citing Thomas's earlier comments to the *Wall Street Journal*.

41. "Nomination of Judge Clarence Thomas to Be Associate Justice of the Supreme Court of the United States, Hearings Before the Committee on the Judiciary, United States Senate," 102nd Cong., 1st sess. October 11–13, 1991, available at https://www.loc.gov/law/find/nominations/thomas/hearing-pt4.pdf.

42. Dan Coats to President George H.W. Bush, October 21, 1991, and Sherrie P. Marshall to Andrew H. Card Jr., September 3, 1991, George H.W Bush Library.

43. Biskupic, *Breaking In*, 107.

44. John Roberts to Barbara Drake and John Mackey, undated list of cases, George H.W. Bush Library.

45. John Mackey to John Roberts, January 24, 1992, George H.W. Bush Library.

46. Author interviews with Ken Starr, September 26, 2016, and April 14, 2014.

47. Author interview with Fred Fielding, July 13, 2016.

48. Author interview with Richard Lazarus, July 5, 2017.

49. Sandra Day O'Connor, *Out of Order: Stories from the History of the Supreme Court*, 97–98.

50. Special House of Representatives Republican crime panel in August of 1993 video: "Republican Anti-Crime Initiatives," C-SPAN, August 23, 1993, https://www.c-span.org/video/?49213-1/republican-anti-crime-initiatives. Also referenced in Senate questionnaire, included in "Confirmation Hearing on the Nomination of John G. Roberts, Jr. to Be Chief Justice of the United States, Hearing Before the Committee on the Judiciary, United States Senate," 109th Cong., 1st sess., September 12–15, 2005, available at https://www.judiciary.senate.gov/imo/media/doc/GPO-CHRG-ROBERTS.pdf.

51. Ibid.

52. Adarand Constructors v. Pena, 515 U.S. 200 (1995).

53. *MacNeil/Lehrer NewsHour*, June 12, 1995.

54. David F. Pike, "John G. Roberts," *Los Angeles Daily Journal*, August 14, 1995.

55. Author interview with Michael Carvin, December 19, 2016.

56. Prettyman, who died on November 4, 2016, sat for a videotaped interview at the Jackson Center in 2012. See "E. Barrett Prettyman, Jr. (2012) on Chief Justice John G. Roberts, Jr.," YouTube, posted May 16, 2012, https://www.youtube.com/watch?v=rnaAocJ7GVg&t=17s.

57. Jane Roberts detailed her family background in a commencement address at New England Law Boston, May 27, 2011 (printed in the *New England Law Review* 46, no. 1 (2011).

58. Author interviews with Jane Roberts, September 26, 2017, and March 23, 2018.

CHAPTER V: THE STANDOUT

1. See, for example, Jeffrey Rosen, "The Next Court," *New York Times Magazine*, October 22, 2000.

2. Jim Yardley, "Execution Approaches in Most Rare Murder Case," *New York Times*, August 10, 2001.

3. Author interview with retired justice John Paul Stevens, June 7, 2016. Of Roberts, Stevens said, "I first saw him as an advocate, and I always admired him. He was one of the lawyers you could count on to not try to give you some sort of phony answer. He is very articulate."

4. Interview of John Roberts conducted by Bryan Garner, March 2007, published by LawProse, www.lawprose.org/bryan-garner/garners-interviews /supreme-court-interviews; Joan Biskupic, "Lawyers Emerge as Supreme Court Specialists," *USA Today*, May 16, 2003.

5. Ibid.

6. David F. Pike, "John G. Roberts," *Los Angeles Daily Journal*, August 14, 1995.

7. Garner interview of John Roberts, LawProse.

8. Biskupic, "Lawyers Emerge."

9. Author interview with Jane Roberts, March 23, 2018.

10. John Roberts's financial disclosure form filed with the Senate Judiciary Committee, included in "Confirmation Hearing on the Nomination of John G. Roberts, Jr. to Be Chief Justice of the United States, Hearing Before the Committee on the Judiciary, United States Senate," 109th Cong., 1st sess., September 12–15, 2005, available at https://www.judiciary.senate.gov/imo/media/doc /GPO-CHRG-ROBERTS.pdf, 496–497.

11. Author interview with Jane Roberts, September 26, 2017. For more insight into their personal life, see "Statement of Henrietta Wright," in "Confirmation Hearing on the Nomination of John G. Roberts, Jr. to Be Chief Justice of the United States, Hearing Before the Committee on the Judiciary, United States Senate," 109th Cong., 1st sess., September 12–15, 2005, available at https://www.judiciary.senate.gov/imo/media/doc/GPO-CHRG-ROBERTS .pdf.

12. In an interview with the author, September 26, 2017, Jane Roberts said, "We signed up for Jack very early on, when this young woman was about two months pregnant, and we were waiting for him to be born in December."

13. Author interviews with Jane Roberts, September 26, 2017, and March 30, 2018.

14. "Eastern Associated Coal Corp. v. United Mine Workers of America, District 17: Oral Argument—October 02, 2000," No. 99-1038, Oyez, https:// apps.oyez.org/player/#/rehnquist10/oral_argument_audio/22251.

15. Transcript of *Today* show, NBC News, November 9, 2000.

16. Author interview with Michael Carvin, December 19, 2016, and December 14, 2017.

17. Ibid.

18. "TrafFix Devices Inc. v. Marketing Displays Inc.: Oral Argument—November 29, 2000," No. 99-1571, Oyez, https://apps.oyez.org/player/#/rehnquist10/oral_argument_audio/22458; Roberts won the case.

19. Bush v. Gore, 531 U.S. 98 (2000).

20. For years after *Bush v. Gore*, as Scalia appeared at law schools and other public forums, he responded to criticism about the case by declaring, "Get over it." The admonition, however, was like tossing kindling on still-burning fires. Joan Biskupic, *American Original: The Life and Constitution of Supreme Court Justice Antonin Scalia*, 231.

21. Author interviews with Jane Roberts, September 26, 2017, and March 23, 2018.

22. Author interview with Kevin Lipson, July 16, 2017.

23. Jane Roberts, commencement address at New England Law Boston, May 27, 2011 (printed in the *New England Law Review* 46, no. 1, 2011).

24. Charles Lane, "Roberts Listed in Federalist Society '97–98 Directory," *Washington Post*, July 25, 2005.

25. Ibid.

26. Author interview with Michael Carvin, December 19, 2016.

27. Author interview with Jane Roberts, September 26, 2017.

28. Senate Judiciary Committee report on the nomination of John G. Roberts Jr. for the District of Columbia Circuit, Serial No. J-108-1, January 29, 2003.

29. Ibid.

30. Ibid.

31. Rancho Viejo, LLC, v. Norton, 334 F.3d 1158 (D.C. Cir. 2003).

32. Jung v. Mundy, Holt & Mance, P.C., 372 F.3d 429 (D.C. Cir. 2004).

33. Laura Krugman Ray, "The Style of a Skeptic: The Opinions of Chief Justice Roberts," *Indiana Law Journal* 83, no. 3 (Summer 2008): 999, 1015, 1001.

34. U.S. v. Jackson, 415 F.3d 88 (D.C. Cir. 2005).

35. Hedgepeth v. Washington Metropolitan Area Transit Authority, 386 F.3d 1148 (D.C. Cir. 2004).

36. Author interview with Alberto Gonzales, May 12, 2017.

37. Ruth Bader Ginsburg to William Rehnquist, William H. Rehnquist Papers.

38. Clarence Thomas to William Rehnquist, October 26, 1994, William H. Rehnquist Papers.

39. William Rehnquist to John Raugh, September 1, 1981, William H. Rehnquist Papers.

40. Three had been elevated while on the Court: Rehnquist, White, and Stone. Two had become chief after having left the bench: Rutledge and Hughes.

41. James Carney and Matthew Cooper, "Justice Scalia: The Charm Offensive," *Time,* January 23, 2005.

42. John Paul Stevens to William Rehnquist, November 3, 2004, William H. Rehnquist Papers.

43. George W. Bush, *Decision Points*, 99.

CHAPTER VI: THE RIGHT PLACE

1. John Roberts's interview dates are drawn from his Senate Judiciary Committee questionnaire, included in "Confirmation Hearing on the Nomination of John G. Roberts, Jr. to Be Chief Justice of the United States, Hearing Before the Committee on the Judiciary, United States Senate," 109th Cong., 1st sess., September 12–15, 2005, available at https://www.judiciary.senate.gov/imo/media /doc/GPO-CHRG-ROBERTS.pdf; author interview with Alberto Gonzales, May 12, 2017. Additional information from Alberto R. Gonzales, *True Faith and Allegiance: A Story of Service and Sacrifice in War and Peace*, 341–365, and Alberto R. Gonzales, "In Search of Justice: An Examination of the Appointment of John G. Roberts and Samuel A. Alito to the U.S. Supreme Court and Their Impact on American Jurisprudence," *William & Mary Bill of Rights Journal* 22, no. 647 (2014).

2. Author interview with Samuel Alito, March 20, 2009.

3. Author interview with Alberto Gonzales, May 12, 2017.

4. George W. Bush, *Decision Points*, 96.

5. Author interview with Alberto Gonzales, May 12, 2017.

6. Charles Babington and Shailagh Murray, "A Last-Minute Deal on Judicial Nominees," *Washington Post*, May 24, 2005, www.washingtonpost.com /wp-dyn/content/article/2005/05/23/AR2005052301970.html.

7. Gonzales also recounted, in the essay "In Search of Justice," "After his appointment to the DC Circuit, Judge Roberts's performance confirmed that he deserved to be on our short list of candidates."

8. Some of the men involved in that process had had a hand in creating administration policy after the September 11 terrorist attacks. Chief among them was Vice President Cheney, a former defense secretary to President George H.W. Bush. Cheney served as a driving force behind the George W. Bush attack on the Taliban in Afghanistan, the subsequent war in Iraq, and the vigorous detention and interrogation of terrorism suspects housed at the Guantanamo Bay Naval Base and elsewhere.

9. Cheney v. United States District Court, No. 03-475, March 18, 2004. In his memorandum, Scalia recalled the history of administration-judicial friendships, including that Justice Byron White had skied in Colorado with Attorney General Robert Kennedy, and declared, "The question, simply put, is whether someone who thought I could decide this case impartially despite my friendship with the Vice President would reasonably believe that I cannot decide it impartially because I went hunting with that friend and accepted an invitation to fly there with him on a Government plane. If it is reasonable to think that a Supreme Court Justice can be bought so cheap, the Nation is in deeper trouble than I had imagined."

10. Author interview with Alberto Gonzales, May 12, 2017. Additional details about the selection process were obtained from several of the participants in "on background" interviews.

11. Sandra Day O'Connor to William Rehnquist, February 1, 2005, William H. Rehnquist Papers.

12. Senate Judiciary Committee questionnaire and financial disclosure documents, included in "Confirmation Hearing on the Nomination of John G. Roberts, Jr. to Be Chief Justice of the United States, Hearing Before the Committee on the Judiciary, United States Senate," 109th Cong., 1st sess., September 12–15, 2005, available at https://www.judiciary.senate.gov/imo/media/doc/GPO-CHRG-ROBERTS.pdf; Kathy Kiely and Joan Biskupic, "Documents Reveal Roberts' Wealth, Philosophy," *USA Today*, August 3, 2005.

13. McCreary County v. American Civil Liberties Union, 545 U.S. 844 (2005), and Van Orden v. Perry, 545 U.S. 677 (2005).

14. George W. Bush, *Decision Points*.

15. The chronology of the selection process was developed from the author's news coverage at the time, published works, including by Bush and Gonzales, and "on background" interviews with individuals involved in the selection of Roberts.

16. Author interview with Clarence Thomas, recounted in Joan Biskupic, *Sandra Day O'Connor: How the First Woman on the Supreme Court Became Its Most Influential Justice*, 333–334.

17. Spencer S. Hsu, "One Judge and the Shaping of Abortion Law," *Washington Post*, July 2, 1998; Staff Report, "Possible Nominees to the Supreme Court," *Washington Post*, July 1, 2005.

18. Author interview with Alberto Gonzales, May 12, 2017.

19. Democrats had essentially forty-five votes at the time (forty-four from the party and one independent). For a filibuster, they would need only forty-one votes, so going into the Supreme Court selection sweepstakes, Democrats had

some leverage. See "Filibuster Derails Supreme Court Appointment," United States Senate, October 1, 1968, https://www.senate.gov/artandhistory/history /minute/Filibuster_Derails_Supreme_Court_Appointment.htm.

20. Memo from Ronald Weich to Senator Harry Reid, July 9, 2005, copy obtained by author from Weich.

21. Ibid. But by this point, Garza, nearing age sixty and with no strong advocates in the White House, was no longer under serious consideration.

22. Hamdan v. Rumsfeld, No. 04-5393, decided July 15, 2005.

23. Bush, *Decision Points*, 98.

24. Author interview with Michael Luttig, December 16, 2016.

25. Bush, *Decision Points*, 98.

26. Ibid.

27. Ibid., 98.

28. Author interview with Michael Luttig, December 16, 2016.

29. Ed Gillespie, *Winning Right: Campaign Politics and Conservative Policies*, 189.

30. Author interview with Alberto Gonzales, May 12, 2017; author interview with Fred Fielding, July 15, 2016.

31. Gillespie, *Winning Right*, 195.

32. Bush, *Decision Points*, 99.

33. "Reagan Lecture," C-SPAN, March 8, 2006, https://www.c-span.org /video/?191523-1/reagan-lecture; "Judge Robert's Son Dancing," YouTube, posted October 17, 2005, https://www.youtube.com/watch?v=-xM0HusfotY.

34. Ibid.

35. Gillespie, *Winning Right*, 191.

36. Kurt Andersen, "The Golden-Boy Nominee," *New York Magazine*, n.d., http://nymag.com/nymetro/news/columns/imperialcity/12547.

37. Author interview with Antonin Scalia, August 26, 2008.

38. "A Service in Celebration and Commitment to God of the Life of William Hubbs Rehnquist, Chief Justice of the United States," program, September 7, 2005; Biskupic, *Sandra Day O'Connor*, 338.

39. Quotations from the hearings are from "Confirmation Hearing on the Nomination of John G. Roberts, Jr. to Be Chief Justice of the United States," Senate Judiciary Committee, September 12–15, 2005, available at https://www .judiciary.senate.gov/imo/media/doc/GPO-CHRG-ROBERTS.pdf.

40. Roberts spoke at Rice University in Houston, Texas. "Remarks from Chief Justice John Roberts," C-SPAN, October 17, 2012, https://www.c-span .org/video/?308879-1/remarks-chief-justice-john-roberts.

41. Stephen Gillers, David Luban, and Steven Lubet, "Improper Advances: Talking Dream Jobs with the Judge Out of Court," *Slate*, August 17, 2005,

www.slate.com/articles/news_and_politics/jurisprudence/2005/08/improper _advances.html. Stevens was writing in *Liljeberg v. Health Services Acquisitions Corp.* in 1988. Title 28 of the U.S. Code, Section 455, requires judges to disqualify themselves when their impartiality might reasonably be questioned.

42. Barack Obama, "Confirmation of Judge John Roberts," September 22, 2005, Best Speeches of Barack Obama Through His 2009 Inauguration, http://obamaspeeches.com/031-Confirmation-of-Judge-John-Roberts-Obama -Speech.htm; Charles Babington and Peter Baker, "Roberts Confirmed as 17th Chief Justice," *Washington Post*, September 30, 2005, www.washingtonpost .com/wp-dyn/content/article/2005/09/29/AR2005092900859.html. For the final vote, see "Supreme Court Nominations: Present–1789," US Senate, https:// www.senate.gov/pagelayout/reference/nominations/Nominations.htm.

43. See, for example, Bork interview at "Robert Bork on Harriet Miers' High Court Bid," National Public Radio, October 11, 2005, https://www.npr .org/templates/story/story.php?storyId=4954108.

44. Bush, *Decision Points*, 99.

45. Ibid, 99.

46. Author interview with Michael Luttig, December 16, 2016.

CHAPTER VII: BLACKS, WHITES, AND *BROWN*

1. Jane Roberts's comments in interview with Kathleen S. Carr, "Off-Campus: Catching Up with Crusaders on the Move and in the News," *Holy Cross Magazine* 40, no. 2 (Spring 2006), https://www.holycross.edu/departments /publicaffairs/hcm/spring06/GAA/gaa5.html; Joan Biskupic, "Roberts Plays Dual Roles: Chief Justice and Father," *USA Today*, June 26, 2006.

2. Author interview with Antonin Scalia, August 26, 2008.

3. Georgia v. Randolph, 547 U.S. 103 (2006).

4. Martin v. Franklin, 546 U.S. 132 (2005).

5. Roberts's dissent from denial in Pennsylvania v. Dunlap, No. 07-1486, October 14, 2008. "I want to raise one note of dissent from the praise," wrote University of Texas law professor Stephen Vladeck. "It's not that I don't think it's clever and fun to read—like most of the Chief Justice's writing, it is clear and to the point. It's that I think the opinion, especially the opening stanza, is to some degree contemptuous of both the defendant and the state courts." Doug Kendall, of the liberal-leaning Constitutional Accountability Center, added: "While we've long been fans of the Chief's writing flair, Roberts' opinion is entirely predictable. . . . Roberts is using rhetorical flourish to make the conservative goals of limiting constitutional protections and court access seem 'cool.' Count

us as unmoved." Comments posted by Doug Kendall, October 15, 2008, 2:22:34 p.m., in response to Steve Vladeck, "A Dissenting Opinion on the Chief Justice's 'Noir' Moment," Prawfs Blog, October 14, 2008, http://prawfsblawg.blogs.com /prawfsblawg/2008/10/a-dissenting-op.html, from http://theusconstitution.org /blog.history/?p=433.

6. Roberts's remark during oral arguments in Central Virginia Community College v. Katz, No. 04-885, October 31, 2005, https://www.supremecourt.gov /oral_arguments/argument_transcripts/2005/04-885.pdf.

7. "Reagan Lecture," C-SPAN, March 8, 2006, https://www.c-span.org /video/?191523-1/reagan-lecture.

8. Ibid.

9. Joan Biskupic, "Roberts, Scalia Strike Similar Chords on Court," *USA Today*, April 10, 2007.

10. Author interview with Antonin Scalia, February 9, 2009.

11. Author interviews with Ruth Bader Ginsburg, March 29, 2007, and July 11, 2016.

12. George W. Bush, *Decision Points*, 101–102. Bush prefaced his account regarding Alito with regret over Miers and the criticism she faced from those within his own party, "so-called friends." "If I had to do it over again," Bush wrote, "I would not have thrown Harriet to the wolves of Washington."

13. Alito remarks at Federalist Society annual dinner, Washington, DC, November 16, 2006.

14. Joan Biskupic, "Breyer Pragmatic Lawyer and Judge," *Washington Post*, June 27, 1994.

15. "Chief Justice Says His Goal Is More Consensus on Court," Associated Press account in *New York Times*, May 22, 2006, https://www.nytimes .com/2006/05/22/washington/22justice.html.

16. Jeffrey Rosen, "Roberts's Rules," *The Atlantic*, January/February 2007, https://www.theatlantic.com/magazine/archive/2007/01/robertss-rules/305559.

17. William Rehnquist to Arthur J. Goldberg, July 28, 1986, William H. Rehnquist Papers.

18. League of United Latin American Citizens v. Perry, 548 U.S. 399 (2006).

19. Ibid.

20. Edward M. Kennedy, "Roberts and Alito Misled Us," *Washington Post*, July 30, 2006.

21. House v. Bell, 547 U.S. 518 (2006).

22. "Jamie Satterfield, "Prosecutor Drops Charges; House's Family 'on Cloud Nine,'" *Knoxville News Sentinel*, May 12, 2009.

23. Gonzales v. Carhart, 550 U.S. 124 (2007); Stenberg v. Carhart, 530 U.S. 914 (2000).

24. Facts drawn from briefs for Parents Involved in Community Schools v. Seattle School District No. 1, No. 05-908; Meredith v. Jefferson Country Board of Education, No. 05-915; Marcia Coyle, *The Roberts Court: The Struggle for the Constitution*, 28–47. The final opinion in the consolidated cases is at 551 U.S. 701 (2007).

25. Grutter v. Bollinger, 539 U.S. 306 (2003).

26. Parents Involved in Community Schools v. Seattle School District No. 1, No. 05-908, oral arguments, December 4, 2006, Supreme Court of the United States, https://www.supremecourt.gov/oral_arguments/argument _transcripts/2006/05-908.pdf.

27. Brief of 553 Social Scientists as Amici Curiae, Nos. 05-908 and 05-915, Parents Involved in Community Schools v. Seattle School District No. 1, Meredith v. Jefferson County Board of Education. Cases consolidated for decision as Parents Involved in Community Schools v. Seattle School District No. 1, 551 U.S. 701 (2007).

28. "Parents Involved in Community Schools v. Seattle School District No. 1: Opinion Announcement—June 28, 2007," No. 95-908, Oyez, https://apps .oyez.org/player/#/roberts2/opinion_announcement_audio/21532.

29. Breyer observed in a footnote to his opinion that Roberts had drawn that line from US Appeals Court Judge Bea, who had been the voice of dissent as the Ninth Circuit majority had upheld the decision: See also Parents Involved VII, 426 F. 3d, at 1222 (Bea, J., dissenting). ("The way to end racial discrimination is to stop discriminating by race.")

30. Adam Liptak, "The Same Words, but Differing Views," *New York Times*, June 29, 2007.

31. Linda Greenhouse, "In Steps Big and Small, Supreme Court Moved Right, *New York Times*, July 1, 2007, https://www.nytimes.com/2007/07/01 /washington/01scotus.html.

32. Roger Simon, "Leahy Attacks Bush, Roberts," *Politico*, August 1, 2007, https://www.politico.com/story/2007/08/leahy-attacks-bush-roberts-005219.

33. Linda Greenhouse, "A Tale of Two Justices," *Green Bag* 11, no. 1 (Autumn 2007): 37–49.

34. Roberts appeared at Rensselaer Polytechnic Institute with Rensselaer president Shirley Ann Jackson. "A Conversation with Chief Justice John G. Roberts, Jr.," April 11, 2017, YouTube, posted April 12, 2017, https://www .youtube.com/watch?v=TuZEKlRgDEg&t=1363s.

CHAPTER VIII: POLITICS AND MONEY

1. Information regarding Roberts's house purchase was included in a roundup of legal news by Tony Mauro, "High Court Veteran Makes Mistake Every Lawyer Dreads," *The Recorder*, September 19, 2006. The chief justice's travel was detailed in Financial Disclosure Report for Calendar Year 2007, May 15, 2008, for the reporting period January 1, 2007, to December 31, 2007. Activities on the island are from author interview with Jane Roberts, March 23, 2018.

2. Author interviews with Kevin Lipson, July 14, 2017, and July 16, 2017.

3. Senator Arlen Specter, the Pennsylvania Republican who had presided over Roberts's 2005 confirmation hearings, said senators had been told privately about the earlier seizure. That 1993 incident had occurred when Roberts was golfing. *Newsweek* reported on that seizure during its 2005 and 2012 coverage of Roberts and quoted a friend saying, "It was stunning and out of the blue and inexplicable." Debra Rosenberg, "Seeking the 'Real' Roberts," *Newsweek*, August 14, 2005, https://www.newsweek.com/seeking-real-roberts -117957; Daniel Klaidman, "How Chief Justice John Roberts Will Handle Obamacare," *Newsweek*, September 10, 2012, https://www.newsweek.com/how -chief-justice-john-roberts-will-handle-obamacare-64631.

4. Denise Grady and Lawrence K. Altman, "Roberts Facing Medical Option on 2nd Seizure," *New York Times*, August 1, 2007; Linda Greenhouse, "Chief Justice Is Hospitalized After Seizure," *New York Times*, July 31, 2007. The Court's press release described the incident as a "benign idiopathic seizure," similar to one he had suffered fourteen years earlier.

5. Roberts told an interviewer, "The chief justice is the head of the Judicial Conference, which sets policy for the federal judiciary throughout the country, and that also is a very important responsibility. And then the chief justice has very odd responsibilities that don't seem to have anything to do with being chief justice. I'm automatically chancellor of the Smithsonian, for example. So over the past couple of years I've been learning a good bit about museums and research institutions." "Supreme Court Chief Justice Roberts," C-SPAN, June 19, 2009, https://www.c-span.org/video/?286078-1/supreme -court-chief-justice-roberts&start=1077.

6. "2006 Year-End Report on the Federal Judiciary," Supreme Court Public Information Office, January 1, 2007, https://www.supremecourt.gov/publicinfo /year-end/2006year-endreport.pdf.

7. Author interviews with Fred Fielding, July 13, 2016, and July 15, 2016.

8. "2006 Year-End Report."

9. "Judicial Compensation," United States Courts, n.d., www.uscourts.gov /judges-judgeships/judicial-compensation.

10. Caperton v. A. T. Massey Coal Co., 556 U.S. 868 (2009).

11. Williams-Yulee v. Florida Bar, 575 U.S. __ (2015).

12. Author interview with Richard Lazarus, July 5, 2017.

13. Jeff Mason, "Obama Takes Oath Again After Inauguration Mistake," Reuters, January 21, 2009, https://www.reuters.com/article/us-obama-oath /obama-takes-oath-again-after-inauguration-mistake-idUSTRE50L09A20090122.

14. Joan Biskupic, "A Feisty Ginsburg Defies Disease. Interview: Goals Keep Her Focused in Cancer Battle," *USA Today*, March 6, 2009.

15. Joan Biskupic, "Ginsburg: The Court Needs Another Woman; Panel's Lack of Diversity Wears on Female Justice," *USA Today*, May 6, 2009.

16. Jesse Lee, "The President's Remarks on Justice Souter," White House, President Barack Obama, May 1, 2009, https://obamawhitehouse.archives.gov /blog/2009/05/01/presidents-remarks-justice-souter; Joan Biskupic, "Souter Emotional, Wry in 'a Sort of Farewell,'" *USA Today*, May 6, 2009.

17. Sotomayor biography drawn from Joan Biskupic, *Breaking In: The Rise of Sonia Sotomayor and the Politics of Justice*. President Obama's statement on Sotomayor nomination at "The President's Nominee: Judge Sonia Sotomayor," White House, President Barack Obama, May 26, 2009, https://obamawhitehouse .archives.gov/blog/2009/05/26/presidentrsquos-nominee-judge-sonia-sotomayor.

18. Biskupic, *Breaking In*, 122.

19. Ricci v. DeStefano, 530 F.3d 88 (Second Circuit order, 2008); Ricci v. DeStefano, 557 U.S. 557 (2009).

20. "Confirmation Hearing on the Nomination of Hon. Sonia Sotomayor, to Be an Associate Justice of the Supreme Court of the United States, Hearing Before the Committee on the Judiciary, United States Senate," 111th Cong., 1st sess., July 13–16, 2009, available at https://www.govinfo.gov/content/pkg /GPO-CHRG-SOTOMAYOR/pdf/GPO-CHRG-SOTOMAYOR.pdf.

21. Buckley v. Valeo, 424 U.S. 1 (1976).

22. Austin v. Michigan Chamber of Commerce, 494 U.S. 652 (1990).

23. McConnell v. Federal Election Commission, 540 U.S. 93 (2003).

24. "Confirmation Hearing on the Nomination of John G. Roberts, Jr. to Be Chief Justice of the United States," Senate Judiciary Committee, September 12–15, 2005, available at https://www.judiciary.senate.gov/imo/media/doc /GPO-CHRG-ROBERTS.pdf.

25. Federal Election Commission v. Wisconsin Right to Life, 551 U.S. 449 (2007).

26. Davis v. Federal Election Commission, 554 U.S. 724 (2008).

27. Citizens United v. Federal Election Commission, No. 08-205, first set of oral arguments, March 24, 2009, Supreme Court of the United States, https://www.supremecourt.gov/oral_arguments/argument_transcripts /2008/08-205.pdf. As Solicitor General Kagan would make clear in subsequent arguments, Congress could not ban a book in the context of campaign finance regulation.

28. See, for example, Marcia Coyle, *The Roberts Court: The Struggle for the Constitution*, 199–278, for a thorough chronology of *Citizens United* and other campaign finance cases.

29. Dahlia Lithwick, "Does the Chief Justice Hate Elena Kagan?," *Newsweek*, July 29, 2010, www.newsweek.com/does-chief-justice-hate-elena-kagan -74245.

30. Citizens United v. Federal Election Commission, 558 U.S. 310 (2010).

31. Author interview with retired justice John Paul Stevens, June 7, 2016, repeating the sentiment: "I profoundly disagree with *Citizens United*."

32. Citizens United v. Federal Election Commission, 558 U.S. 310 (2010).

33. Ibid.; "Citizens United v. Federal Election Commission: Opinion Announcement—January 21, 2010," No. 08-205, Oyez, https://apps.oyez.org /player/#/roberts4/opinion_announcement_audio/23476.

34. Citizens United v. Federal Election Commission, 558 U.S. 310 (2010).

35. SpeechNow.org v. Federal Election Commission, D.C. Circuit Nos. 08-5223, 09-5342, March 26, 2010.

36. Arizona Free Enterprise Club's Freedom Club PAC v. Bennett, 564 U.S. 721 (2011).

37. McCutcheon v. Federal Election Commission, 572 U.S. 185 (2014).

38. "Pols Weigh in on Citizens United Decision," *Politico*, January 21, 2010, https://www.politico.com/story/2010/01/pols-weigh-in-on-citizens-united -decision-031798; Thomas E. Mann, "Citizens United vs. Federal Election Commission Is an Egregious Exercise of Judicial Activism," Brookings Institution, January 26, 2010, https://www.brookings.edu/opinions/citizens-united -vs-federal-election-commission-is-an-egregious-exercise-of-judicial-activism.

39. John H. Cushman Jr., David D. Kirkpatrick, and Eric Schmitt, "Taking a Closer Look at Assertions on Domestic and Foreign Policy," *New York Times*, January 28, 2010, https://www.nytimes.com/2010/01/28/us/politics/28check .html.

40. Louis Jacobson, "Why Alito Shook His Head: Obama Exaggerates Impact of Supreme Court Ruling on Foreign Companies," *Politifact*, January 27, 2010, https://www.politifact.com/truth-o-meter/statements/2010/jan/27 /barack-obama/obama-says-supreme-court-ruling-allows-foreign-com.

41. Roberts appeared at the University of Alabama in Tuscaloosa. "Chief Justice John Roberts Remarks," C-SPAN, March 9, 2010, https://www.c-span .org/video/?292439-1/chief-justice-john-roberts-remarks.

42. "Supreme Court Chief Justice Roberts," C-SPAN, June 19, 2009, https://www.c-span.org/video/?286078-1/supreme-court-chief-justice-roberts &start=1077.

CHAPTER IX: A SWITCH IN TIME

1. The Associated Press was among those news organizations that captured Roberts's arrival in photographs.

2. The author interviewed a majority of the justices soon after the *National Federation of Independent Business v. Sebelius* ruling and followed up with the justices in subsequent interviews for this book.

3. The individual mandate was meant to rely on existing health insurance companies to provide most coverage.

4. Two Washington attorneys, David Rivkin and Lee Casey, published pieces in the *Washington Post* and the *Wall Street Journal*, in August and September 2009, arguing against the individual mandate. Rivkin and Casey, who had worked in the Ronald Reagan and George H.W. Bush administrations, said the new mandate went beyond the bounds of federal authority. They cited constitutional limits on Congress's regulatory and taxing power. David B. Rivkin Jr. and Lee A. Casey, "Constitutionality of Health Insurance Mandate Questioned," *Washington Post*, August 22, 2009, www.washingtonpost.com/wp-dyn/content /article/2009/08/21/AR2009082103033.html; David B. Rivkin Jr. and Lee A. Casey, "Mandatory Insurance Is Unconstitutional," *Wall Street Journal*, September 17, 2009, https://www.wsj.com/articles/SB10001424052970204518504574 4416623109362480. A few months later, Georgetown University law professor Randy Barnett, who became one of the most vocal opponents of the individual mandate, entered the debate with a scholarly essay for the Heritage Foundation. Along with two coauthors, Barnett asserted that the individual mandate would not be regulation of interstate commerce because it "regulates no action." Todd Gaziano, Randy Barnett, and Nathaniel Stewart, "Why the Personal Mandate to Buy Health Insurance Is Unprecedented and Unconstitutional," Heritage Foundation, December 9, 2009, https://www.heritage.org/health-care -reform/report/why-the-personal-mandate-buy-health-insurance-unprecedented -and.

5. Facts drawn from ruling in *National Federation of Independent Business v. Sebelius*, 567 U.S. 519 (2012).

6. Florida v. U.S. Department of Health and Human Services, 648 F.3d 1235 (11th Cir. 2011); Judge Frank Hall, a Democratic appointee on the Eleventh Circuit, ruled against the law; Judge Jeff Sutton, on the Sixth Circuit, and Judge Laurence Silberman, on the DC Circuit, both Republican appointees, ruled to uphold it.

7. Joan Biskupic, "Behind the Healthcare Case: The Challengers' Tale," Reuters, March 13, 2012, https://www.reuters.com/article/us-usa-healthcare -court/insight-behind-the-healthcare-law-case-the-challengers-tale-idUSBRE 82C19J20120313.

8. Lochner v. New York, 198 U.S. 45 (1905).

9. Carter v. Carter Coal Co., 298 U.S. 238 (1936); United States v. Butler, 297 U.S. 1, (1936); Schechter Poultry Corp. v. United States, 295 U.S. 495 (1935).

10. Roosevelt declared in a March 9, 1937, radio address, "We have . . . reached the point as a nation where we must take action to save the Constitution from the Court and the Court from itself." He proposed the appointment of a new justice for every current justice over age seventy, and six of the nine were then over seventy. His plan was widely denounced, yet within weeks the Court reversed a stance it had taken against New York's minimum-wage law by upholding a Washington State requirement of minimum wages for women and children. The Court began adopting a broader view of "interstate commerce" to enhance congressional authority, thus ending the era of special protection for property rights and the favoring of business.

11. West Coast Hotel Co. v. Parrish, 300 U.S. 379 (1937).

12. Of the challenge to the board brought by Jones & Laughlin Steel, Chief Justice Hughes wrote: "When industries organize themselves on a national scale, making their relation to interstate commerce the dominant factor in their activities, how can it be maintained that their industrial labor relations constitute a forbidden field into which Congress may not enter when it is necessary to protect interstate commerce from the paralyzing consequences of industrial war?" National Labor Relations Board v. Reliance Fuel Oil Corp., 371 U.S. 224, 225 n.2 (1963). The decision was essentially a reversal from the *Carter Coal* decision a year earlier that found that coal production was a local activity with no direct bearing on interstate commerce. It also began a modern era of labor relations and unionization.

13. See, for example, Joan Biskupic, "Analysis: Why U.S. High Court May Uphold Healthcare Law," Reuters, March 22, 2012, https://www.reuters.com /article/us-usa-healthcare-court/analysis-why-u-s-high-court-may-uphold -healthcare-law-idUSBRE82L1CJ20120322.

14. National Federation of Independent Business v. Sebelius, individual mandate arguments, March 27, 2012, Supreme Court of the United States,

https://www.supremecourt.gov/oral_arguments/argument_transcripts/2011 /11-398-Tuesday.pdf.

15. "Confirmation Hearing on the Nomination of John G. Roberts, Jr. to Be Chief Justice of the United States, Hearing Before the Committee on the Judiciary, United States Senate," 109th Cong., 1st sess., September 12–15, 2005, available at https://www.judiciary.senate.gov/imo/media/doc/GPO-CHRG -ROBERTS.pdf.

16. To understand the conference deliberations and to reconstruct the chronology of shifting votes, the author interviewed a majority of the justices. Law clerks and others involved in the case added to the sequence of events.

17. "CBO's Analysis of the Major Health Care Legislation Enacted in March 2010 Before the Subcommittee on Health, Committee on Energy and Commerce, U.S. House of Representatives," statement of Douglas W. Elmendorf, director, March 30, 2011, www.cbo.gov/sites/default/files/03-30-health carelegislation.pdf.

18. Joan Biskupic, *Sandra Day O'Connor: How the First Woman on the Supreme Court Became Its Most Influential Justice*, 261.

19. E. J. Dionne Jr., "In the Supreme Court, Activist Justices Take on Health Care," *Washington Post*, March 28, 2012, https://www.washingtonpost .com/opinions/activist-judges-on-trial/2012/03/28/gIQAKdE2gS_story html?utm_term=.e217661a877e.

20. Mark Landler, "President Confident Health Law Will Stand," *New York Times*, April 2, 2012, https://www.nytimes.com/2012/04/03/us/politics /obama-says-hes-confident-health-care-law-will-stand.html.

21. Jeff Rosen, "Moment of Truth for Justice Roberts," *Politico*, March 28, 2012, https://www.politico.com/story/2012/03/moment-of-truth-for-justice -roberts-074605.

22. National Federation of Independent Business v. Sebelius, Medicaid expansion arguments, March 28, 2012, Supreme Court of the United States, https:// www.supremecourt.gov/oral_arguments/argument_transcripts/2011/11-400 .pdf. (For the first years of the expansion, the federal government would pay 100 percent of the costs.)

23. The Medicaid expansion covering more low-income adults took effect on January 1, 2014, but initially about half of the states did not adopt the expansion. There was no deadline to join, and by September 2018, thirty-four states had adopted the expanded program, according to the Henry J. Kaiser Family Foundation, which tracked state developments. See "Status of State Action on the Medicaid Expansion Decision, as of September 11, 2018," Kaiser Family Foundation, accessed September 26, 2018, https://www.kff.org/health

-reform/state-indicator/state-activity-around-expanding-medicaid-under-the
-affordable-care-act.

24. "On Senate Floor, Leahy Shares Observations About SCOTUS Arguments on Affordable Care Act: Statement of Senator Patrick Leahy (D–Vt), Chairman, Senate Judiciary Committee, on the Supreme Court's Review of the Affordable Care Act," Patrick Leahy website, May 14, 2012, https://www.leahy.senate.gov/press/on-senate-floor-leahy-shares-observations-about-scotus-arguments-on-affordable-care-act.

25. Kathleen Parker, "Democrats Put John Roberts on Trial," *Washington Post*, May 22, 2012, https://www.washingtonpost.com/opinions/democrats-put-john-roberts-on-trial/2012/05/22/gIQAijq8iU_story.html?utm_term=.d9fb39e5c3cf.

26. Author interview with Michael Carvin, December 19, 2016.

27. Author interview with Ruth Bader Ginsburg, August 7, 2012.

28. Ibid. Ginsburg cracked her ribs on June 4, 2012, as she was still working on the dissenting opinion.

29. The author was in the courtroom but then checked the Oyez website to hear the bench announcement. See "The Affordable Care Act Cases: Opinion Announcement—June 28, 2012 (Part 1)," No. 11-393, Oyez, https://apps.oyez.org/player/#/roberts6/opinion_announcement_audio/22323.

30. Author interview with retired Justice John Paul Stevens, June 7, 2016.

31. "The Roberts Rules," *Wall Street Journal*, June 29, 2012.

32. Donald J. Trump (@realDonaldTrump), "Wow, the Supreme Court passed @ObamaCare . . . ," Twitter, June 28, 2012, 9:23 a.m., https://twitter.com/realdonaldtrump/status/218379090493849601; Donald J. Trump (@realDonaldTrump), "John Roberts arrived in Malta yesterday . . . ," Twitter, July 5, 2012, 1:42 p.m., https://twitter.com/realdonaldtrump/status/220981019753451521.

33. Author interviews with Fred Fielding, who attended the event, July 13, 2016, and July 15, 2016; Financial Disclosure Report for Calendar Year 2012, May 15, 2013, for the reporting period January 1, 2012, to December 31, 2012. For other examples of his overseas teaching and traveling, see Financial Disclosure Report for Calendar Year 2011, May 11, 2015, for the reporting period January 1, 2011, to December 31, 2011 (including an entry for Florence, Italy); Financial Disclosure Report for Calendar Year 2010, May 15, 2011, for the reporting period January 1, 2010, to December 31, 2010 (with a July 19–23 course on the US Supreme Court in Melbourne, Australia); and Financial Disclosure Report for Calendar Year 2009, May 14, 2010, for the reporting period January 1, 2009, to December 31, 2009 (including the Galway, Ireland, trip, July 13–23, 2009).

34. Jan Crawford, "Roberts Switched Views to Uphold Health Care Law," CBS News, July 2, 2012.

35. Author interview with Antonin Scalia, August 1, 2012.

36. Author interview with Judge J. Harvie Wilkinson III, May 22, 2017.

37. Author interview with Michael Luttig, December 16, 2016.

38. Video from Fielding's seventy-fifth birthday greetings, coordinated by Richard Hauser and provided to the author by Fred Fielding.

39. Charles Fried, "The June Surprises: Balls, Strikes, and the Fog of War," in Nathaniel Persily, Gillian E. Metzger, and Trevor W. Morrison, eds., *The Health Care Case: The Supreme Court's Decision and Its Implications*, 51.

CHAPTER X: DIVIDED BY RACE

1. Shelby County v. Holder, 570 U.S. 2 (2013); Fisher v. University of Texas at Austin, 570 U.S. 297 (2013).

2. President Lyndon Johnson statement, August 6, 1965, National Archives; President Lyndon B. Johnson, "Remarks in the Capitol Rotunda at the Signing of the Voting Rights Act," August 6, 1965, posted at John Woolley and Gerhard Peters, American Presidency Project, hosted by University of California, Santa Barbara, www.presidency.ucsb.edu/ws/?pid=27140.

3. Voting Rights Act of 1965, transcript from National Archives and Department of Justice, https://www.archives.gov/legislative/features/voting-rights -1965/vra.html.

4. The Department of Justice's explanation of the 1965 Voting Rights Act and its subsequent amendments notes: "In 1982, Congress extended Section 5 for 25 years, but no new Section 5 coverage formula was adopted. Congress did, however, modify the procedure for a jurisdiction to end coverage under the special provisions. In 2006, Congress extended the requirements of Section 5 for an additional 25 years." See "History of Federal Voting Rights Laws," US Department of Justice, https://www.justice.gov/crt/history-federal-voting -rights-laws.

5. South Carolina v. Katzenbach, 383 U.S. 301 (1966).

6. "H.R. 9—Fannie Lou Hamer, Rosa Parks, and Coretta Scott King Voting Rights Act Reauthorization and Amendments Act of 2006," 109th Cong. (2005–2006), US Congress, https://www.congress.gov/bill/109th-congress /house-bill/9.

7. Regents of the University of California v. Bakke, 438 U.S. 265 (1978).

8. League of United Latin American Citizens v. Perry, 548 U.S. 399 (2006).

9. Parents Involved in Community Schools v. Seattle School District No. 1, 551 U.S. 701 (2007).

10. Ginsburg dissenting in Shelby County v. Holder, citing House of Representatives Report 109-478. See "H. Rept. 109-478—Fannie Lou Hamer, Rosa Parks, and Coretta Scott King Voting Rights Act Reauthorization and Amendments Act of 2006," 109th Cong. (2005–2006), US Cong., https://www.congress.gov/congressional-report/109th-congress/house-report/478/1.

11. Ginsburg dissenting in Shelby County v. Holder: "Between 1982 and 2005, Alabama had one of the highest rates of successful Section 2 suits, second only to its [Voting Rights Act]–covered neighbor Mississippi."

12. Joan Biskupic, "From Alabama, an Epic Challenge to Voting Rights," Reuters, June 4, 2012.

13. Joan Biskupic, "Behind U.S. Race Cases, a Little-Known Recruiter," Reuters, December 4, 2012.

14. Northwest Austin Municipal Utility District No. 1 v. Holder, 557 U.S. 193 (2009).

15. U.S. Senate Report 109-295, "Fannie Lou Hamer, Rosa Parks, Coretta Scott King, and Cesar E. Chavez Voting Rights Act Reauthorization and Amendments Act of 2006," US Senate, 109th Cong., 2nd sess., transcript at https://www.gpo.gov/fdsys/pkg/CRPT-109srpt295/html/CRPT-109srpt295.htm.

16. "President Bush Signs Voting Rights Act Reauthorization and Amendments Act of 2006," White House, Office of the Press Secretary, news release, July 27, 2006, https://georgewbush-whitehouse.archives.gov/news/releases/2006/07/20060727.html.

17. Financial Disclosure Report for Calendar Year 2009, May 14, 2010, for the reporting period January 1, 2009, to December 31, 2009.

18. Thomas, dissenting opinion, Northwest Austin Municipal Utility District No. 1 v. Holder, 557 U.S. 193 (2009).

19. Northwest Austin Municipal Utility District No. 1 v. Holder, 557 U.S. 193 (2009).

20. Author interview with Edward Blum, May 2, 2012.

21. Shelby County v. Holder, DC Circuit decision, No. 11-5256, May 18, 2012 (Judge Tatel opinion, internal quotations omitted).

22. Shelby County v. Holder, No. 12-96, oral arguments, February 27, 2013, Supreme Court of the United States, https://www.supremecourt.gov/oral_arguments/argument_transcripts/2012/12-96_7648.pdf.

23. Louis Jacobson, "Was Chief Justice John Roberts Right About Voting Rates in Massachusetts, Mississippi?," *Politifact*, March 5, 2013, www.politifact

.com/truth-o-meter/statements/2013/mar/05/john-roberts/was-chief-justice-john-roberts-right-about-voting-.

24. Mark Sherman, "In Entire Court Term, Justices See 1 Black Lawyer," Associated Press, in *San Diego Union Tribune*, May 12, 2013, www.sandiego uniontribune.com/sdut-in-entire-court-term-justices-see-1-black-lawyer-2013 may12-story.html.

25. Joan Biskupic, *Breaking In: The Rise of Sonia Sotomayor and the Politics of Justice*, 35–57.

26. Clarence Thomas, *My Grandfather's Son: A Memoir*, 75–76.

27. Fisher v. University of Texas at Austin, 570 U.S. 297 (2013). This account of the Fisher case was first revealed in the author's 2014 book *Breaking In*, following interviews with a majority of the justices involved in the compromise.

28. Grutter v. Bollinger, 539 U.S. 306 (2003); Regents of the University of California v. Bakke, 438 U.S. 265 (1978).

29. Sotomayor dissenting, Schuette v. Coalition to Defend Affirmative Action, 572 U.S. 291 (2014).

30. Scalia, concurring opinion, noting he would have reconsidered *Grutter* but was deterred because Abigail Fisher did not request it. Thomas, concurring opinion, declaring *Grutter* should be overturned and all uses of race in higher education prohibited. Fisher v. University of Texas at Austin, 570 U.S. 297 (2013).

31. The author attended the Seventh Circuit conference event, May 6, 2013, Indianapolis.

32. Roberts noted that the Court would be changing the time for the release of public documents, partly in response to news reporters' requests. By tradition, the opinions and orders list were both released at 10:00 a.m. Reporters asked whether the orders list could come at 9:30 a.m. so they could get a jump on them and be finished for the 10:00 a.m. release of opinions. He joked that he had "thought long and hard about why not to do it—because it was the press corps."

33. Shelby County v. Holder, 570 U.S. 2 (2013).

34. Thomas, concurring, wrote that "by leaving the inevitable conclusion unstated," the Roberts opinion prolonged uncertainty about the fate of Section 5. Shelby County v. Holder, 570 U.S. 2 (2013).

35. Edward Blum appears on video at "Project on Fair Representation on Voting Rights Act Decision," C-SPAN, June 25, 2013, https://www.c-span.org/video/?313571-2/project-fair-representation-voting-rights-act-decision; Roger Clegg, "This Isn't 1965," *USA Today*, June 25, 2013, https://www.usatoday.com/story/opinion/2013/06/25/voting-rights-act-center-for-equal-opportunity-editorials-debates/2457037.

36. James Blacksher and Lani Guinier, "Free at Last: Rejecting Equal Sovereignty and Restoring the Constitutional Right to Vote," *Harvard Law and Policy Review* 8, no. 39 (Winter 2014).

37. North Carolina State Conference of the NAACP v. McCrory, No. 16-1468, July 29, 2016, US Court of Appeals for the Fourth Circuit, www.ca4.uscourts.gov/opinions/published/161468.p.pdf.

38. North Carolina v. North Carolina State Conference of the NAACP, No. 16-833, May 15, 2017, Supreme Court of the United States, https://www.supremecourt.gov/opinions/16pdf/16-833_7l48.pdf.

CHAPTER XI: A FRACTURED COURT

1. The Court was hearing oral arguments in Texas Department of Housing and Community Affairs v. Inclusive Communities Project, Inc., No. 13-1371. The author was in the courtroom.

2. Author interview with 99Rise spokesman Timothy Brown, January 21, 2015. A secret video taken of the protest showed up on YouTube a month later. See "Supreme Court Caught on Video," n.d., YouTube, posted February 26, 2014, https://www.youtube.com/watch?v=2K-8FJ114kU.

3. American Express Co. v. Italian Colors Restaurant, 570 U.S. 228 (2013); AT&T Mobility LLC v. Concepcion, 563 U.S. 333 (2011).

4. Interview of John Roberts conducted by Bryan Garner, March 2007, published by LawProse, www.lawprose.org/bryan-garner/garners-interviews/supreme-court-interviews.

5. The decision in *Grutter v. Bollinger*, written by Justice O'Connor and crafted with a bare five-justice majority, reinforced the values of educational diversity from the 1978 *Bakke* ruling that traced to Roberts's law school days.

6. Joan Biskupic, "In U.S. Top Court Race Case, John Roberts Is Chief Phrasemaker," Reuters, October 15, 2013; Schuette v. Coalition to Defend Affirmative Action, No. 12-682, October 15, 2013, Supreme Court of the United States, https://www.supremecourt.gov/oral_arguments/argument_transcripts/2013/12-682_8n6a.pdf.

7. Schuette v. Coalition to Defend Affirmative Action, 572 U.S. 291 (2014). Kennedy wrote the plurality opinion, joined by Roberts and Alito; Scalia, joined by Thomas, filed an opinion concurring in the judgment; Breyer wrote separately to concur in the judgment. Fisher v. University of Texas at Austin, 570 U.S. (2013).

8. Sotomayor, bench announcement in Schuette v. Coalition to Defend Affirmative Action, April 22, 2014. See "Opinion Announcement—April

22, 2014 (Part 2)," Oyez, https://apps.oyez.org/player/#/roberts6/opinion
_announcement_audio/23219.

9. Regents of the University of California v. Bakke, 438 U.S. 265 (1978),
Blackmun concurring.

10. Dahlia Lithwick, "What We Talk About When We Talk About Talking
About Race," *Slate*, April 24, 2014.

11. Congress adopted the 1993 Religious Freedom Restoration Act after the
Supreme Court's Employment Division, Department of Human Resources of
Oregon v. Smith, 494 U.S. 872 (1990).

12. Oral arguments in Burwell v. Hobby Lobby, March 25, 2014 (formerly
known as Sebelius v. Hobby Lobby).

13. Burwell v. Hobby Lobby Stores, 573 U.S. 682 (2014). Ginsburg was
joined in full only by Justice Sotomayor. Justices Breyer and Kagan agreed that
the two companies could not opt out of the contraceptive mandate, but they
stopped short of taking on the broader question of corporate religious rights. For
the bench announcements of Alito and Ginsburg, see "Burwell v. Hobby Lobby
Stores," Oyez, https://www.oyez.org/cases/2013/13-354.

14. Town of Greece v. Galloway, 572 U.S. 565 (2014).

15. U.S. v. Wurie, No. 13-212, and Riley v. California, oral arguments, April
29, 2014, Supreme Court of the United States, https://www.supremecourt.gov
/oral_arguments/argument_transcripts/2013/13-212_d1o2.pdf.

16. Riley v. California, 573 U.S. 373 (2014).

17. King v. Burwell, 576 U.S. __ (2015). (The full citation is not yet available
for cases decided in more recent years.)

18. Jeffrey Toobin, "Hard Cases," *New Yorker*, March 9, 2015, https://www
.newyorker.com/magazine/2015/03/09/hard-cases-jeffrey-toobin.

19. King v. Burwell, 576 U.S. __ (2015).

20. Scalia dissenting and playing off of the six-letter acronym for the Supreme Court of the United States.

21. Arizona State Legislature v. Arizona Independent Redistricting Commission, 576 U.S. __ (2015).

22. Author interviews with Jean Podrasky, August 20, 2016, and March 30,
2018. Chris Geidner, legal editor for BuzzFeed, argued that Roberts's moves to
dissuade the justices from taking up the same-sex marriage controversy in 2014
likely helped the case in 2015 because several more states had adopted marriage
equality laws in the intervening months. Chris Geidner, "Cert. Denied, Stays
Denied, Marriage Equality Advanced," *Ohio State Law Journal* 76 (2015): 161,
http://moritzlaw.osu.edu/students/groups/oslj/files/2015/11/Vol.-76-161-172
-Geidner-SCR-Essay.pdf.

23. Windsor v. United States, 570 U.S. 744 (2013); Hollingsworth v. Perry, 570 U.S. __ (2013). In June 2013, when the *Windsor* case was handed down, the justices did not address the merits of a Proposition 8 case, *Hollingsworth v. Perry*; in an opinion by Roberts, the Court said the Christian groups defending Proposition 8 lacked legal standing to bring the case on appeal. California officials were not defending the law. The justices dismissed a challenge to a lower court ruling that threw out Proposition 8.

24. Windsor v. United States, 570 U.S. 744 (2013).

25. Goodridge v. Department of Public Health, 798 N.E. 2d 941 (Mass. 2003). Marriage licenses were issued beginning in 2004. On state laws in 2015 prior to the ruling, see "State Same-Sex Marriage State Laws Map," *Governing*, n.d., www.governing.com/gov-data/same-sex-marriage-civil-unions-doma -laws-by-state.html.

26. Dahlia Lithwick and Mark Joseph Stern, "Not All Must Rise," *Slate*, April 27, 2015, www.slate.com/articles/news_and_politics/jurisprudence/2015 /04/standing_in_line_for_supreme_court_gay_marriage_arguments_draw_crowd _days.html.

27. Obergefell v. Hodges, No. 14-556, oral arguments, April 28, 2015, Supreme Court of the United States, https://www.supremecourt.gov/oral _arguments/argument_transcripts/2014/14-556q1_l5gm.pdf.

28. Obergefell v. Hodges, 576 U.S. __ (2015); bench announcements available at "Obergefell v. Hodges," Oyez, https://www.oyez.org/cases/2014 /14-556.

29. Roberts dissenting in Obergefell v. Hodges; Scott v. Sandford, 19 How. 393 (1857).

30. Richard A. Posner, "The Chief Justice's Dissent Is Heartless," *Slate*, June 27, 2015, www.slate.com/articles/news_and_politics/the_breakfast_table /features/2015/scotus_roundup/supreme_court_gay_marriage_john_roberts _dissent_in_obergefell_is_heartless.html. In a subsequent interview with the author, March 7, 2017, Posner asserted, "These justices might be superficially civil, but I think there are a lot of differences. . . . I don't think he's honest intellectually. You talk about him being a historian. He's such a phony."

31. Author interview with Jean Podrasky, March 30, 2018.

CHAPTER XII: AN OPEN SEAT

1. "Letter to the President on Judges," March 2, 2009, Senate Republican Conference, https://www.republican.senate.gov/public/index.cfm/2009/3/letter tothepresidentonjudges.

2. Senator Mitch McConnell, press statement, February 13, 2016, posted on Facebook, https://www.facebook.com/mitchmcconnell/posts/washington-dc -us-senate-majority-leader-mitch-mcconnell-made-the-following-state /1021148581257166.

3. Team Fix, "The CBS News Republican Debate Transcript, Annotated," *Washington Post*, February 13, 2016, https://www.washingtonpost.com/news /the-fix/wp/2016/02/13/the-cbs-republican-debate-transcript-annotated/?utm _term=.da75c18bd2e9.

4. Supreme Court Public Information Office statements on the death of Scalia, February 13–14, 2016, quoted at "Read the Statements of Supreme Court Justices on Antonin Scalia's Death," *Washington Post*, February 14, 2016, https:// www.washingtonpost.com/news/post-nation/wp/2016/02/14/read-the -statements-of-supreme-court-justices-on-antonin-scalias-death/?utm_term =.5eb907f439a7.

5. Author interview with Ruth Bader Ginsburg, July 11, 2016.

6. Biographical details on Scalia are drawn from Joan Biskupic, *American Original: The Life and Constitution of Supreme Court Justice Antonin Scalia.*

7. Joan Biskupic, "'You Get One Shot': How Justice Antonin Scalia Viewed the World," Reuters, February 16, 2016, https://www.reuters.com/article/usa -court-idUSL2N15V0TN.

8. Author interviews with Ruth Bader Ginsburg, March 29, 2007, and March 10, 2009.

9. Fisher v. University of Texas at Austin, No. 14-981, oral arguments, December 9, 2015, Supreme Court of the United States, https://www.supremecourt .gov/oral_arguments/argument_transcripts/2015/14-981_onjq.pdf.

10. Roberts appeared at the New England School of Law in Boston. See "Inside the Supreme Court," C-SPAN, February 3, 2016, https://www.c-span .org/video/?404131-1/discussion-chief-justice-john-roberts.

11. Adam Liptak, "When a Senator Passes Judgment on a Chief Justice," *New York Times*, April 18, 2016, https://www.nytimes.com/2016/04/19/us /politics/supreme-court-charles-grassley-john-roberts.html.

12. Mike Zapler, "Grassley Calls Out John Roberts on Senate Floor," *Politico*, April 5, 2016, https://www.politico.com/story/2016/04/grassley-calls-out -john-roberts-on-senate-floor-221607.

13. "Remarks by the President Announcing Judge Merrick Garland as His Nominee to the Supreme Court," White House, Office of the Press Secretary, March 16, 2016, https://obamawhitehouse.archives.gov/the-press-office /2016/03/16/remarks-president-announcing-judge-merrick-garland-his-nominee -supreme. Republican presidents tended to nominate younger jurists who could

serve longer. Roberts was fifty when he was nominated, and Alito was fifty-five. A decade earlier, Thomas was forty-three when he was elevated.

14. Whole Woman's Health v. Hellerstedt, No. 15-274, oral arguments, March 2, 2016, Supreme Court of the United States, https://www.supreme court.gov/oral_arguments/argument_transcripts/2015/15-274_d18e.pdf.

15. Whole Woman's Health v. Hellerstedt, 579 U.S. __ (2016).

16. Abigail Noel Fisher v. University of Texas at Austin, No. 09-50822, July 15, 2014.

17. Fisher v. University of Texas at Austin, 579 U.S. __ (2016).

18. Author interview with Ruth Bader Ginsburg, July 11, 2016.

19. Joan Biskupic, "Justice Ruth Bader Ginsburg Calls Trump a 'Faker,' He Says She Should Resign," CNN, July 12, 2016, https://www.cnn.com/2016 /07/12/politics/justice-ruth-bader-ginsburg-donald-trump-faker/index.html.

20. Author interview with David Leitch, September 7, 2016.

21. "Sandra Day O'Connor Conversation Series: Associate Justice Elena Kagan," Aspen Institute, n.d., https://www.aspeninstitute.org/events/oconnor _kagan.

22. Joan Biskupic, "Chief Justice John Roberts' Game of Chess," CNN, July 10, 2016.

23. In an interview at the Conservative Political Action Conference (CPAC) meeting in February 2018, Don McGahn said President Trump was looking for candidates "who he can relate to." He added, "The president really looks for folks who, not surprisingly, have demonstrated the ability to stand strong, as he has his whole life." Joan Biskupic, "How Donald Trump Is Remaking the Law in His Own Image," CNN, March 6, 2018.

24. "Full Transcript and Video: Trump Picks Neil Gorsuch for Supreme Court," *New York Times*, January 31, 2017, https://www.nytimes.com/2017/01 /31/us/politics/full-transcript-video-trump-neil-gorsuch-supreme-court.html.

25. "Nomination of the Honorable Neil M. Gorsuch to Be an Associate Justice of the Supreme Court of the United States," Senate Judiciary Committee, March 20–23, 2017, video and transcripts available at https://www .judiciary.senate.gov/meetings/nomination-of-the-honorable-neil-m-gor. See also Joan Biskupic, "Inscrutable Gorsuch Raises Democrats' Ire," CNN, March 28, 2017, https://www.cnn.com/2017/03/28/politics/neil-gorsuch -supreme-court-testimony/index.html.

26. Endrew F. v. Douglas County School District RE-1, 580 U.S. __, decided March 22, 2017, as Gorsuch was testifying. See Supreme Court of the United States, https://www.supremecourt.gov/opinions/16pdf/15 827_0pm1.pdf.

27. Peña-Rodriguez v. Colorado, No. 15-606, oral arguments, October 11, 2016, Supreme Court of the United States, https://www.supremecourt.gov/oral_arguments/argument_transcripts/2016/15-606_5iel.pdf.

28. Peña-Rodriguez v. Colorado, 580 U.S. __ (2017).

29. Buck v. Davis, 580 U.S. __ (2016); Foster v. Chatman, 578 U.S. __ (2016).

30. Hosanna-Tabor Evangelical Lutheran Church and School v. Equal Employment Opportunity Commission, 565 U.S. 171 (2012).

31. Trinity Lutheran Church of Columbia v. Comer, 582 U.S. __ (2017).

32. Trinity Lutheran Church of Columbia v. Comer, 582 U.S. __ (2017). A second liberal, Stephen Breyer, joined Roberts's conclusion allowing playground resurfacing, but he declined to sign the opinion. Of the liberals, only Elena Kagan joined his opinion in full, with no caveat.

33. "Cardigan's Commencement Address by Chief Justice John G. Roberts, Jr.," June 3, 2017, YouTube, posted June 6, 2017, https://www.youtube.com/watch?v=Gzu9S5FL-Ug&t=25s.

CHAPTER XIII: THE ROBERTS COURT IN THE TRUMP ERA

1. Joan Biskupic, "Trump's Sustained Attacks on American Rights," CNN, May 26, 2018, https://www.cnn.com/2018/05/26/politics/trump-rights-due-process-curiel/index.html, describes episodes in which President Trump scorned judges, derided the American court system, and trampled on all manner of constitutional principles. Trump especially ridiculed due process of law, the bedrock against government's arbitrary denial of a person's life, liberty, or property. At that point, Trump was suggesting that immigrants at the border could be summarily deported without any hearing to determine whether they deserved asylum or were US citizens wrongly apprehended. Earlier episodes included his references to "so-called judges" and his support, even if in jest, for police brutality in a Long Island speech to law enforcement officers. "Please don't be too nice," Trump told police at a Suffolk County Community College event, encouraging officers not to protect suspects' heads as they were putting them into squad cars. "You can take the hand away, OK?"

2. The ban the justices took up in April 2017 covered the Muslim-majority countries of Iran, Libya, Somalia, Syria, and Yemen; it also covered North Korea and Venezuela. Trump v. Hawaii, No. 17-965, oral arguments, April 25, 2018, Supreme Court of the United States, https://www.supremecourt.gov/oral_arguments/argument_transcripts/2017/17-965_15gm.pdf.

3. "Cardigan's Commencement Address by Chief Justice John G. Roberts, Jr.," June 3, 2017, YouTube, posted June 6, 2017, https://www.youtube.com /watch?v=Gzu9S5FL-Ug&t=25s.

4. Obergefell v. Hodges, 576 U.S. __ (2015).

5. Joan Biskupic, "How Donald Trump Is Remaking the Law in His Own Image," CNN, March 6, 2018, detailing the administration's reversals of the US government's legal position on voting rights and election law, the arbitration of workplace disputes, labor union power, and protections for gay and transgender people.

6. City of Hays, Kansas, v. Vogt, No. 16-1495. The conflict between Roberts and Breyer was first recounted by Mark Walsh at SCOTUSblog.com, in "A 'View' from the Courtroom: An Anniversary, and Later a Tense Exchange," February 20, 2018, www.scotusblog.com/2018/02/view-courtroom -anniversary-later-tense-exchange.

7. City of Hays, Kansas, v. Vogt, No. 16-1495, oral arguments, February 20, 2018, Supreme Court of the United States, https://www.supremecourt.gov /oral_arguments/argument_transcripts/2017/16-1495_4814.pdf.

8. City of Hays, Kansas, v. Vogt, No. 16-1495, opinion, May 29, 2018, Supreme Court of the United States, https://www.supremecourt.gov/opinions /17pdf/16-1495_e1pf.pdf.

9. Jennings v. Rodriguez, No. 15-1204, opinion, February 27, 2018, Supreme Court of the United States, https://www.supremecourt.gov/opinions /17pdf/15-1204_f29g.pdf.

10. Adam Liptak, "#GorsuchStyle Garners a Gusher of Groans. But Is His Writing Really That Bad?" *New York Times*, April 30, 2018.

11. Gill v. Whitford, No. 16-1161, oral arguments, October 3, 2017, Supreme Court of the United States, https://www.supremecourt.gov/oral_arguments /argument_transcripts/2017/16-1161_bpm1.pdf.

12. Encino Motorcars, LLC, v. Navarro, No. 16-1362, April 2, 2018.

13. Epic Systems Corp. v. Lewis, No. 16-285, bench statement, May 21, 2018. See Joan Biskupic, "Ruth Bader Ginsburg Takes Off the Gloves," CNN, May 22, 2018.

14. Epic Systems Corp. v. Lewis, No. 16-285, May 21, 2018.

15. Ibid.

16. Husted v. A. Philip Randolph Institute, No. 16-980, June 11, 2018.

17. Abbott v. Perez, No. 17-586, June 25, 2018. Joan Biskupic, "How the Supreme Court Is Changing the Rules of Voting," CNN, June 26, 2018.

18. Janus v. American Federation of State, County, and Municipal Employees, Council 31, No. 16-1466, oral arguments, February 26, 2018, Supreme

Court of the United States, https://www.supremecourt.gov/oral_arguments/argument_transcripts/2017/16-1466_bocf.pdf.

19. South Dakota v. Wayfair, No. 17-494, June 21, 2018.

20. Trump v. Hawaii, No. 17-965, oral arguments, April 25, 2018, Supreme Court of the United States, https://www.supremecourt.gov/oral_arguments/argument_transcripts/2017/17-965_l5gm.pdf.

21. Trump v. Hawaii, No. 17-965, June 26, 2018, Supreme Court of the United States, https://www.supremecourt.gov/opinions/17pdf/17-965_h315.pdf.

22. Joan Biskupic, "Roberts Treats Trump Like a Normal President; Sotomayor Says No Way," June 27, 2018, https://www.cnn.com/2018/06/27/politics/sotomayor-roberts-trump-president-normal/index.html.

23. Masterpiece Cakeshop v. Colorado Civil Rights Commission, No. 16-111, oral arguments, December 5, 2017, Supreme Court of the United States, https://www.supremecourt.gov/oral_arguments/argument_transcripts/2017/16-111_f29g.pdf.

24. Ibid.

25. Masterpiece Cakeshop v. Colorado Civil Rights Commission, No. 16-111, June 4, 2018.

26. Whitford v. Gill, US District Court for the Western District of Wisconsin, filed November 21, 2016, SCOTUSblog, www.scotusblog.com/wp-content/uploads/2017/04/16-1161-op-bel-dist-ct-wisc.pdf. See also https://www.brennancenter.org/sites/default/files/legal-work/Whitford-Opinion112116.pdf.

27. Vieth v. Jubelirer, 541 U.S. 267 (2004).

28. Gill v. Whitford, No. 16-1161, June 18, 2018.

EPILOGUE

1. "Supreme Court Chief Justice John Roberts on 2017–18 Term," C-SPAN, June 29, 2018, https://www.c-span.org/video/?447323-1/interview-supreme-court-chief-justice-john-roberts.

2. "Kavanaugh Hearing: Transcript," *Washington Post*, courtesy of Bloomberg Government, September 27, 2018, https://www.washingtonpost.com/news/national/wp/2018/09/27/kavanaugh-hearing-transcript/?utm_term=.b676a09a77d9; Adam Liptak, "Retired Justice John Paul Stevens Says Kavanaugh Is Not Fit for Supreme Court," *New York Times*, October 4, 2018; Joan Biskupic, "Partisan Questions Threaten to Shadow Kavanaugh on the Court," CNN, October 5, 2018.

3. Chief Justice John Roberts's statement issued by the Supreme Court Public Information Office, November 21, 2018, after Trump disparagingly referred to an "Obama judge" following US District Court Judge Jon Tigar's order temporarily blocking an administration asylum policy; Joan Biskupic, "Why Chief Justice John Roberts Spoke Out," November 21, 2018, CNN. https://www.cnn.com/2018/11/21/politics/trump-roberts-judges-judiciary /index.html.

Index

JOAN BISKUPIC is a legal analyst at CNN. Previously, she served as an editor-in-charge for legal affairs at Reuters and as the Supreme Court correspondent for the *Washington Post* and *USA Today*. A Pulitzer Prize finalist and author of books on Sandra Day O'Connor, Antonin Scalia, and Sonia Sotomayor, Biskupic holds a law degree from Georgetown University. She lives in Washington, DC, with her husband and daughter.